Beyond Central Paris & Day Trips

Parc Astérix

Pontoise

Seine

Meaux

Jardin d'Acclimatation

Parc de la Villette

PARIS

Disneyland® Paris

Château de Versailles

Pontault-Combault

Orsay

Brie-Comte-Robert

Rambouillet

Evry

ILE-DE-FRANCE

Provins

Etampes

0 km 20

0 miles 20

D1012536

Sightseeing Key

ILE DE LA CITÉ & ILE ST-LOUIS
Conciergerie (pp70–71)
Notre-Dame (pp64–65)

BEAUBOURG & THE MARAIS
Centre Pompidou (pp80–81)
Musée des Arts et Métiers (pp86–87)
Place des Vosges (pp92–93)

TUILERIES, OPÉRA & MONTMARTRE
Musée Grevin (pp116–117)
Sacré-Coeur (pp122–123)
The Louvre (pp104–107)

CHAMPS-ELYSÉES & TROCADÉRO
Arc de Triomphe (pp134–135)
Palais de Chaillot (pp144–145)

EIFFEL TOWER & LES INVALIDES
Eiffel Tower (pp154–155)
Les Invalides (pp160–161)

ST-GERMAIN & THE LATIN QUARTER
Musée de Cluny (pp176–177)
Musée d'Orsay (pp170–171)

LUXEMBOURG & MONPARNASSE
Jardin du Luxembourg (pp190–191)
Panthéon (pp188–189)

BEYOND CENTRAL PARIS & DAY TRIPS
Château de Versailles (pp220–223)
Disneyland® Paris (pp230–233)
Fontainebleau (pp236–237)
Jardin d'Acclimatation (pp210–211)
Parc Astérix (pp226–227)
Parc de la Villette (pp202–203)

Musée des Arts et Métiers

Centre Pompidou

BEAUBOURG & THE MARAIS

Place des Vosges

ILE DE LA CITÉ & ILE ST-LOUIS

Notre-Dame

ST-GERMAIN & THE LATIN QUARTER

La Seine

EYEWITNESS TRAVEL
FAMILY GUIDE
PARIS

EYEWITNESS TRAVEL

FAMILY GUIDE

PARIS

MANAGING EDITOR
Aruna Ghose

SENIOR EDITORIAL MANAGER
Savitha Kumar

SENIOR DESIGN MANAGER
Priyanka Thakur

EDITORS
Beverly Smart, Bidisha Srivastava

PROJECT DESIGNER
Stuti Tiwari Bhatia

DESIGNER
Kaberi Hazarika

PICTURE RESEARCH
Sumita Khatwani

SENIOR DTP DESIGNER
Azeem Siddiqui

SENIOR CARTOGRAPHIC MANAGER
Uma Bhattacharya

SENIOR CARTOGRAPHER
Mohammad Hassan

MAIN CONTRIBUTOR
Rosie Whitehouse

PHOTOGRAPHY
Jules Selmes, Valerio Vincenzo

CARTOONS
Roland Ungoed-Thomas

OTHER ILLUSTRATIONS
Arun Pottirayil, Stephen Conlin,
Stephen Gyapay, Maltings
Partnership

DESIGN CONCEPT Keith Hagan at
www.greenwich-design.co.uk

Printed and bound in China

First published in the United States in
2012 by Dorling Kindersley Publishing,
Inc., 345 Hudson Street, New York 10014.
A Penguin Random House Company

15 16 17 18 10 9 8 7 6 5 4 3 2 1

Reprinted with revisions 2014, 2016

**Copyright 2012, 2016 © Dorling
Kindersley Limited, London**

ISBN 978-1-4654-4044-0

Contents

*One of the many aircraft on display at
the Musée de l'Air et de l'Espace*

How to Use this Guide

This guide is designed to help families to get the most from a visit to Paris, providing expert recommendations for sightseeing with kids along with detailed practical information.

The guide's opening section contains an introduction to Paris and its highlights, as well as all the essentials required in order to plan a family holiday (including how to get there, getting around, health, insurance, money and communications), a guide to family-friendly festivals and a brief historical overview of the city. The main sightseeing section is divided into areas. A "best of" feature is followed by the key sights and other attractions in the area, as well as options for where to eat, drink and play and have more fun.

At the back of the book are detailed maps of Paris, and a language section listing essential words and phrases for family travel.

INTRODUCING THE AREA

Each area chapter is opened by a double-page spread setting it in context, with a short introduction, locator map and a selection of highlights.

Locator map locates the region.

Brief highlights give a flavour of what to see in the area.

THE BEST OF...

A planner to show at a glance the best things for families to see and do in each area, with themed suggestions ranging from history, art and culture to gardens and games.

Themed suggestions for the best things to see and do with kids.

WHERE TO STAY

Our expert authors have compiled a wide range of recommendations for places to stay with families, from hotels and B&Bs that welcome children to self-catering apartments.

Easy-to-use symbols show the key family-friendly features of places to stay.

Price Guide box gives details of the price categories for a family of four.

SIGHTSEEING IN PARIS

Each area features a number of "hub" sights (see below): pragmatic and enjoyable plans for a morning, afternoon or day's visit. These give adults and children a real insight into the destination, focusing on the key sights and what makes them interesting to kids. The sights are balanced by places to let off steam, "take cover" options for rainy days, suggestions for where to eat, drink and shop with kids, ideas for where to continue sightseeing, and all the practicalities, including transport.

Introductory text focuses on the practical aspects of the area, from the best time of day to visit to how to get around using public transport.

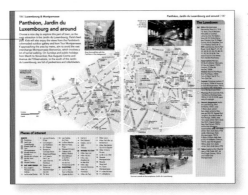

The hub map identifies the sights featured in the chapter, as well as restaurants, shops, places to stay, transport, and the nearest playgrounds, supermarkets and pharmacies.

The Lowdown gives all the practical information you need to visit the area.

The hub sights are the best places to visit in each area, and use lively and informative text to engage and entertain both adults and children.

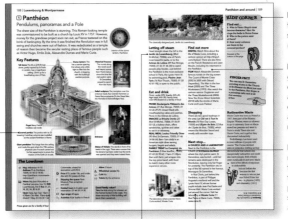

Kids' Corner is featured on all sightseeing pages (see below).

Key Features uses illustrated artworks to show the most interesting features of each sight, highlighting elements likely to appeal to children.

Find out more... gives suggestions for downloads, games, apps or films to enthuse children about a place and help them to learn more about it.

Eat and drink lists recommendations for family-friendly places to eat and drink, from picnic options and snacks to proper meals and gourmet dining.

The Lowdown provides comprehensive practical information, including transport, opening times, costs, activities, age range suitability and how long to allow for a visit.

Letting off steam suggests a place to take children to play freely following a cultural visit.

Next stop... suggests other places to visit, either near the key sight, thematically linked to the sight or a complete change of pace for the rest of the day.

Further sights around each hub, selected to appeal to both adults and children, are given on the following pages.

Places of interest are recommended, with an emphasis on the aspects most likely to attract children, and incorporating quirky stories and unusual facts. Each one includes a suggestion for letting off steam or taking cover.

The Lowdown provides the usual comprehensive practical and transport information for each sight.

Kids' Corners are designed to involve children with the sight, with things to look out for, games to play, cartoons and fun facts. Answers to quizzes are given at the bottom of the panel.

Main entrance to the Louvre in Cour Napoléon

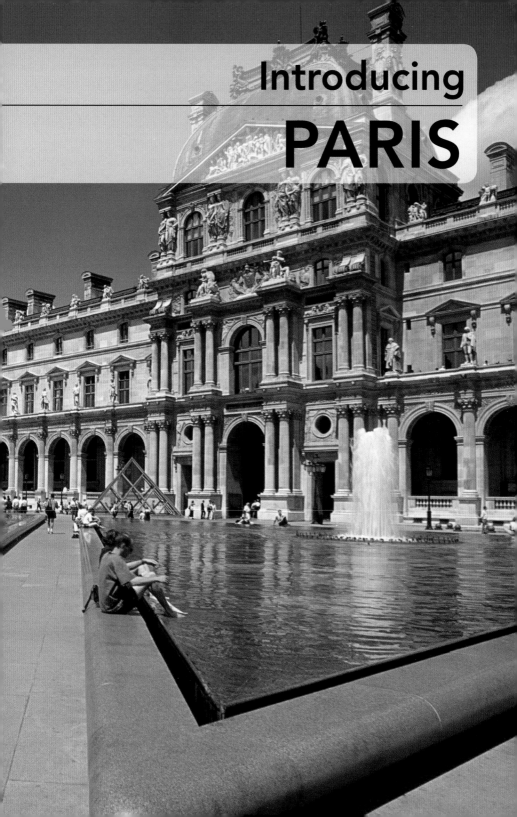

Introducing
PARIS

The Best of Paris

Families are spoilt for choice in Paris. The city is bursting with history and culture, from ancient monuments to modern art, but is also full of fantastic cake shops and cafés, carousels and marionettes. "Paris in the spring" is a time-honoured saying, but actually this is a city for all seasons as far as families are concerned, with events and activities to delight and entertain young and old at any time of the year.

Paris in a weekend

The best and easiest introduction to the sights on the first day is a tour on an open-top bus (see p22). Afterwards, take a stroll around **Notre-Dame** (see pp64–5) and watch the street entertainers before an early dinner – you have a busy time ahead of you.

Start Saturday with a cruise along the Seine. Buy goodies for a picnic lunch on **Ile St-Louis** (see p68), and eat in the garden of the **Square du Vert-Galant** (see p72) which juts out into the river.

Walk across to the **Louvre** (see p104) to meet the mummies and Mona Lisa. Then watch the sun set from the top of the **Arc de Triomphe** (see pp134–5) before dinner at the **Drugstore Publicis** (see p135), a Paris institution. On Sunday, be just like a real Parisian family and unwind in

Right Interior of the Galerie d'Apollon, Louvre
Below View of the Arc de Triomphe from Avenue Marceau

Above *Formal gardens at the Château de Versailles*

the **Jardin du Luxembourg** (see pp190–91) while the kids ride its magical carousel. Buy picnic supplies from **Eric Kayser** (see p191) before enjoying an afternoon of breathtaking art in the **Musée d'Orsay** (see pp170–71).

Finally comes the highlight of the tour – a trip up the **Eiffel Tower** (see pp154–5). Saving it for last on the agenda means the kids will have great fun spotting all the places they have been.

Paris in a week

Get your bearings on arrival with a tour of the sights on an open-top bus. Another perfect way to get a feel of the city is on a cruise along the Seine, especially at twilight, perhaps at the end of your first day.

Allow a good half-day for exploring Ile de la Cité and its star attraction, **Notre-Dame**. At lunchtime you can graze your way along the main street of **Ile St-Louis**. Another district not to be missed is Montmartre, with its artists, its own vineyard and the stunning **Sacré-Coeur** (see pp122–3). You could easily spend an entire

afternoon in the **Louvre**, the world's biggest museum. Decide in advance what and where your "must-sees" are, and focus on them. Do not miss the Impressionist masterpieces of **Musée d'Orsay**, perhaps combined with some fresh air in the nearby **Jardin du Luxembourg**. Allow half a day for one of the world's best military museums, including a visit to Napoleon's tomb, in **Les Invalides** (see pp160–61), and take a day trip out to the splendid **Château de Versailles** (see pp220–23) built by Louis XIV.

On a Sunday, stroll through the streets of the Marais, one of Paris's most historic districts.

If you need a break from cultural sightseeing, visit the cutting-edge aquarium, **Cinéaqua** (see p144), or the old-fashioned amusement park of **Jardin d'Acclimatation** (see pp210–11).

And no family trip to Paris should end without heading to the top of the **Eiffel Tower**.

Paris season-by-season

Paris is lovely in the spring. Kids will adore the funfair in the **Bois de Vincennes** (see p204) and the shops are full of chocolate fish for April Fool's Day and spectacular Easter eggs.

In summer, the Seine's Right Bank turns into a beach, with sand, deck chairs and open-air events. On 14 July, there is a big military parade along the **Champs-Elysées** (see pp134–5), a fly-past and fabulous late-night fireworks.

It is still warm enough to eat lunch outside, and easier to tour the museums and art galleries as there are fewer tourists about.

At Christmas there are ice-skating rinks and decorations. Many hotels have special events for families, where Père Noël might drop in.

Left *Strolling through the cobbled Place du Tertre, with Sacré-Coeur in the background*

Paris on a budget

There are plenty of ways to enjoy the city on a budget. Start by exploring the heart of ancient Paris, the **Ile de la Cité** and **Ile St-Louis**. **Notre-Dame** is free to visit and it is a quintessential Paris pleasure just to stroll along the quaysides soaking up the atmosphere.

If you only visit one museum in Paris, it should be the **Louvre**. Children under 18 are admitted free, and, on the first Sunday of the month from November to March, there is no charge for adults. This is the case all year round for most public museums. The Paris Museum Pass cuts costs too, and can be used as many times as you wish, in more than 55 museums including the **Louvre, Musée d'Orsay**, **Centre Pompidou** (see pp80–81) and parts of the **Château de Versailles**, without queuing. It is ideal for families as it makes short visits to museums cost-effective.

There are plenty of places where kids can let off steam, including the beautiful **Jardin des Tuileries** (see p108), where the playground is free. They are also perfect places for a picnic. Paris is full of inexpensive bakeries and street markets that sell top-class food at reasonable prices, so eating well on a budget will never be a problem.

To keep accommodation costs down, consider renting an apartment, or opt for one of the family-friendly **Accor Group Hotels** such as Hotel Baltimore (see p241).

Culture vultures

Nearly all museums in Paris have children's workshops and activities. The city's museums and galleries are all on the "school trip circuit" and so are used to accommodating kids as young as three years old. Children's museums include the **Musée en Herbe** (see p113) which introduces kids to the art world, and the **Cité des Enfants**, part of the cutting-edge science museum **Cité des Sciences et de l'Industrie** at **Parc de La Villette** (see pp202–203).

For art lovers, the big draw is the Impressionist paintings in the **Musée d'Orsay**, but the city is also full of smaller galleries. Some studios where now-famous artists lived and worked are open as museums and are great to visit with kids.

History buffs will be in paradise. Paris has some excellent Roman remains and the **Louvre** has one of the best Egyptology collections in the world. Visiting the places where the key events in the French Revolution happened brings history to life, and marching determinedly like Napoleon through **Les Invalides** must be a boy's idea of heaven.

For mini ballerinas a trip to **Opéra Garnier** (see p119) is a must, at least for a twirl down the staircase, but, if the budget allows, do see a show as well. There is plenty, too, for musical and theatrical kids, with concerts and opera, puppet shows and children's theatre.

The great outdoors

Paris is a wonderful city for walking and is full of great parks. The way to feel like a real Parisian is to watch the kids sailing a wooden boat in the **Jardin des Tuileries** or **Jardin du Luxembourg**, or riding on the city's merry-go-rounds.

For adults, there is nothing to beat strolling around the **Ile de la Cité** and **Ile St-Louis** in the moonlight, or as the sun sets on a summer evening, and there is little more romantic than picnicking on the **Pont des Arts** (see p73).

Below left Cycling in the Jardin du Luxembourg
Below Carousel and Ferris wheel, Jardin des Tuileries

Above *Terrace of Fauchon, one of the grand food shops in Place de la Madeleine*

For children, there is more fun to be had on a boat cruise along the Seine. Or, in high summer, splashing, building sandcastles and playing *boules* at Paris Plages *(see p68)*, cycling in the **Bois de Boulogne** *(see pp210–11)* or meeting farm animals in the **Bois de Vincennes**.

A day trip to the **Château de Versailles** need not be all about sumptuous interiors and great historical events – the gardens are magnificent. Pack a picnic and escape from the city, Marie Antoinette-style.

A wilder alternative lies just to the south of Paris, where the vast forest of **Fontainebleau** *(see pp236–7)* is a rock-climber's paradise and surrounded by lovely countryside.

Paris from on high

Nothing beats gazing down on what is one of the most beautiful cities in the world. The most obvious place from which to do this is the **Eiffel Tower**. The view is at its best in the early morning, on a clear day, when you will see not just the stunning Parisian skyline but up to 72 km (45 miles) around. Closer to the ground, but no less of an adventure, is the tethered hot-air balloon in the **Parc André Citroën** *(see p212)*.

Children will enjoy climbing up the towers of **Notre-Dame** and pretending to be Quasimodo, as well as the funicular ride up to Montmartre's **Sacré-Coeur**, the highest point in Paris.

The best place from which to watch the sun set is **Tour Montparnasse** *(see p192)*, the tallest building in the city. You can see the planes taking off at Orly airport and then the lights of Paris start to twinkle like magic. But a sunset view from the top of the **Arc de Triomphe** has a magic all of its own.

Gourmet treats

Paris's colourful street markets are an appetizing education for all the family. Among the best are classy Rue Cler and bohemian Rue Mouffetard. Sunday mornings are a good time to visit. Everything is in perfect condition, from *pâtisserie* and pâtés to speciality cheeses. Choose whatever takes your fancy, grab a baguette, and head for the city's picnic spots.

Paris is perfect if you have a sweet tooth (and what kid doesn't?). Indulge in multicoloured macaroons at **Ladurée** *(see p135)* or try a mouthwatering Victor-Hugo at **Béchu** *(see p147)*. **Aki Boulangerie** *(see p113)*, in the Little Japan district of Paris, serves scrumptious snacks with a Japanese twist. But above all else, treat the kids to an ice cream from the legendary **Berthillon** *(see p68)* on **Ile St-Louis**.

Place de la Madeleine *(see p139)* is a foodie mecca, with **Fauchon** *(see p139)* and **Hédiard** *(see p139)*, two gourmet grocers, and specialist shops for mustard, caviar and truffles – both the chocolate kind and the real thing.

The city's luxury hotels are keen to welcome young gourmets. The former French president Nicolas Sarkozy dines with his teenage son at **114 Faubourg** *(see p138)* at **Le Bristol** *(see p241)* just up the road from the **Palais de l'Elysée** *(see p138)*. **The Shangri-La** *(see p242)* has two Michelin-starred restaurants – one French and the other Chinese – either of which are a treat. The brunch at the **Trianon Palace** *(see p222)* is packed with local families as well, and the fabulous spread of food is something to be seen. The **Plaza Athénée** *(see p241)* has a fairytale restaurant, run by Alain Ducasse. It is great for a special-occasion tea, with its gorgeous range of children's cakes.

Paris Through the Year

Paris is a delight in the springtime, when blossom covers the trees, but it can get very busy at this time of year. The autumn colours are equally beautiful and the sun is usually still warm enough for lunch outdoors. Big events such as Bastille Day, Paris Plages and the end of the Tour de France fill the summer, though the city is at its quietest in August, when Parisian families take their holidays. Restaurants and shops in some areas close, but there are hotel bargains to be had. Finally, winter is a sparkling affair in the "City of Light".

Spring

This is an excellent time to visit Paris with children, as the spring flowers, the cherry blossom and the lengthening days bring the city's parks back to life. It is a good time to explore on foot; sunny spells and breezy days are the perfect weather for city sightseeing before the warmer summer days to come. Bring an umbrella, as the chance of an April shower is high; the air can be chilly, too, so pack clothes that can be layered. Spring is the most popular season for visiting the city, so book well in advance.

MARCH

A big draw for children in the period up to Easter is the mouthwatering array of chocolate creations on display. Paris boasts some of the best chocolatiers in the world,

and this time of the year gives them the chance to show off their skills. The shops are full of chocolate bells, Easter eggs and April Fool's Day fish. No bells are rung on Good Friday or Easter Saturday. Legend has it that all the church bells fall silent on Good Friday and fly off to Rome, only to return on Easter Sunday. On Saturday night, children place nests on their balconies and in their gardens. They wake to find them full of chocolate eggs that are said to have been brought from Rome by the bells.

Hunt for Easter eggs in **Galeries Lafayette** (see p117) or in the grounds of the lovely **Château de Vaux-le-Vicomte** (see p234) just outside Paris, which has lots of special Easter events for children. On Good Friday, the Archbishop of Paris walks from the bottom of

Montmartre up to the cathedral of **Sacré-Coeur** (see pp122–3) as he performs the Stations of the Cross. Bear in mind, most shops and many restaurants will be closed on Easter Sunday and Monday, although not usually Good Friday.

The big family attraction this month is the opening of the giant funfair, the **Foire du Trône**, in the **Bois de Vincennes** (see p204), which begins at the end of March and continues until late May. It has its origins in a festival over 1,000 years old. There are plenty of rides, candy floss and fairground fun.

APRIL

A victim of **April Fool's Day**, on 1 April, is known as a *Poisson d'Avril* (April Fish) in France. Kids make paper fish and try to stick them on the backs of as many people

Below left The colourful Foire du Trône, Bois de Vincennes
Below right Bastille Day Parade, Champs-Elysées

as possible without being caught. And shop windows glitter with shoals of silver-foil-wrapped chocolate sardines.

The **Paris International Marathon**, raced from **Place de la Concorde** *(see p138)* to Avenue Foch, takes in many of the city's major sights so, wherever you are in Paris, you are likely to see fancy-dressed charity runners and toned elite competitors pounding out the course. Bring a picnic to a course of a different kind at **Dimanches au Galop** (Sundays at the Races). There are pony rides and behind-the-scenes tours, as well as the thrill of the horse races, at the hippodromes d'Auteuil and Longchamp, and admission is free.

MAY

For culture vultures, the museums stay open late during **La Nuit des Musées** one Saturday in mid-May. For sports fans, the **French Open**, at **Stade Roland Garros** *(see p211)* is an unmissable, star-studded Grand Slam tennis tournament. There is a lot of family fun at the **Fête du Pain** bread-making festival, during which a giant oven is set up in front of **Notre-Dame** *(see pp64–5)*. This is the busiest tourist month of the year but also the one when the city lives up to all its loveliest movie clichés.

Summer

Summer months are full of festivities but, just as the season reaches its peak, the city empties out while the locals take their holidays. It is a good time to visit with kids as the streets are at their quietest, although some restaurants and shops close during August, especially in residential districts.

The big attraction for kids is **Paris Plages** *(see p68)* – spots along the Right Bank of the Seine are transformed into sandy beaches, where it is possible to build a sand-castle with a view of Notre-Dame.

The city can feel like a huge, open-air museum, but there is a rare tranquility away from the tourist hot spots. July and August can get very hot, so be sure to reserve a hotel room with air-conditioning, but August is also the wettest month of the year, due to occasional short, sharp thunderstorms.

JUNE

On 21 June, Paris celebrates the summer solstice with the **Fête de la Musique**, when music is played in the streets, in cafés and in bars. **Les Pestacles**, meanwhile, is a music fest just for kids, held from June to September on Wednesdays in the Parc Floral of the Bois de Vincennes. A huge draw for kids is the annual

funfair, the **Fête des Tuileries**, which runs from end-June to end-August in the **Jardin des Tuileries** *(see p108)*. It offers a giant Ferris wheel and fairground rides. There is more fun to be had at **l'Eté du Canal**, along the **Canal de l'Ourcq** *(see p203)* and at the **Bassin de la Villette** from July to August. There are shows, boat trips, exhibitions and games for families.

JULY

It is party time from now until mid-August, at **Paris Plages** along the Seine and by the **Canal de l'Ourcq**, when fine sand, deck chairs, parasols, "beach" cafés and street theatre replace the traffic.

On 14 July – **Bastille Day**, as France's **Fête Nationale** is usually known – Paris celebrates the French Revolution with a huge military parade down the Champs-Elysées, a fly-past, street fairs and late-night fireworks. Make sure to get a place on the route in good time. Later in the month it is the turn of bikes to whizz down the Champs-Elysées, at the finish of the gruelling **Tour de France** race. At a slightly slower pace, waiters bearing trays of bottles and glasses race off from the **Hôtel de Ville** *(see p69)* for the 8-km (5-mile) **Course des Garçons de Café** in late June or early July.

Below left Carousel at the annual Fête des Tuileries next to the Musée du Louvre
Below right Approaching the finish of the Tour de France, on the Champs-Elysées

AUGUST

This is the ideal time to cruise along the river or picnic in a park. It is also a good time to take day trips out of the city, as many commuters are on holiday so public transport and roads are less crowded.

At the end of the month, the **Fête au Bois de Boulogne** offers more family fairground fun, and during **Le Cinéma en Plein Air**, **Parc de la Villette** (see pp202–203) becomes a free open-air cinema showing everything from cartoons to classics. Bring a picnic, and a blanket in case the evening turns cool.

Autumn

Festivals and events abound now, as Parisians return home with a burst of renewed energy and prepare for *La Rentrée*, as the "Back to School" season is known. It is a great time to visit with kids as the sun is still warm and one can comfortably eat outside at lunchtime. In October the city is a riot of autumn colours, perfect for strolling along the banks of the Seine and in the city's parks.

On weekdays in autumn, the city's hotels get very booked up with trade and fashion shows, but there are bargains to be had at the weekend, especially in September. Queues at museums and other

sights are much shorter and there are plenty of activities for kids during October school holidays.

SEPTEMBER

On the **Journées du Patrimoine** (European Heritage Days) all sorts of normally inaccessible buildings are open to the public, including the **Palais de l'Elysée** (see p138), the official home of the French president. The other main cultural event this month is the **Festival d'Automne**, a celebration of modern music, theatre, ballet, cinema and art. In complete contrast, **Famillathlon** is a lively family sports day, staged in the **Champ-de-Mars** (see p156) one Sunday towards the end of the month.

OCTOBER

During the **Fête des Vendanges**, the wine harvest is celebrated in the tiny vineyard of Montmartre, while honey takes centre stage at the **Fête du Miel** in the **Jardin du Luxembourg** (see pp190–91).

On **La Nuit Blanche**, in the last week of September or the first week of October, museums, monuments, cinemas, parks and even swimming pools stay open all night. **Mon Premier Festival**, a children's film festival, has showings in all Paris cinemas, while, for budding

scientists, there is the **Fête de la Science**, which takes place at a different institution every year.

NOVEMBER

On 11 November 1918, the guns of World War I fell silent. To mark the date, blue cornflowers are worn and the president lays a wreath at the **Arc de Triomphe** (see pp134–5).

Now's a good time to explore the city's museums but, if out and about in the cold, kids can warm up with a cup of rich hot chocolate, while the grown-ups might enjoy a glass of **Beaujolais Nouveau**, launched on the third Thursday of the month.

Winter

The skies may be grey but there is plenty of tinsel in town. There are skating rinks, Nativity cribs, fairy lights, Christmas trees, magical window displays and an array of seasonal food, such as *bûches de Noël* (chocolate logs).

It is a fun time to visit **Disneyland® Paris** (see pp230–33), which has lots of special events, but be sure to wrap up warm. Many restaurants close on Christmas Day, so opt for self-catering or a hotel with its own restaurant. The French enjoy their blow-out meal late on Christmas Eve, feasting on oysters and *foie gras*.

Below left *The Fête des Vendanges, Montmartre Vineyard*
Below right *Movies for children being screened at the Mon Premier Festival*

DECEMBER

Get into the festive spirit by taking to the ice. Paris's two most thrilling outdoor rinks are at the **Hôtel de Ville**, especially when it is lit up at night, and on the enchanted terrace on the first level of the **Eiffel Tower** (see pp154–5), with wonderful views of the city 57 m (187 ft) below.

The 11pm Christmas Eve carol service at **Notre-Dame** is a magical event. On **New Year's Eve**, make merry with the crowds along the Champs-Elysées.

JANUARY

In the run-up to the **Fête des Rois** (Epiphany) on 6 January, *pâtisseries* sell a sweet puff pastry pie, a *galette des rois*, with a tiny porcelain figure inside. Whoever gets it in their slice wins the right to wear a gold crown (sold with the cake) for the day, and be king or queen. For **Chinese New Year**, in late January or early February, parades, dragons and firecrackers fill the streets of the 13th *arrondissement*.

FEBRUARY

The **Carnaval de Paris** has been brightening up the late winter since the Middle Ages with music, dancing and lots of fun. The parade departs from Place Gambetta at 3pm for the Hôtel de Ville.

The Lowdown

Spring

Dimanches au Galop
www.dimanchesaugalop.com
Fête du Pain www.lafetedupain.com
Foire du Trône www.foiredutrone.com
French Open www.rolandgarros.com
La Nuit des Musées
www.nuitdesmusees.culture.fr
Paris International Marathon
www.parismarathon.com

Summer

Le Cinema en Plein Air
www.villette.com
Course des Garçons de Café
www.waitersrace.com
L'Eté du Canal, L'Ourcq en Fête
www.tourisme93.com
Fête au Bois de Boulogne
www.quefaire.paris.fr
Fête de la Musique
www.fetedelamusique.culture.fr
Fête des Tuileries
www.quefaire.paris.fr
Fête Nationale www.parisinfo.com
Les Pestacles www.lespestacles.fr
Tour de France www.letour.fr

Autumn

Famillathlon www.famillathlon.org
Festival d'Automne
www.festival-automne.com
Fête du Miel www.la-sca.net
Fête de la Science
www.fetedelascience.fr
Fête des Vendanges
www.fetedesvendangesdemontmartre.com

Journées du Patrimoine
www.journeesdupatrimoine.culture.fr
Mon Premier Festival
www.monpremierfestival.org
La Nuit Blanche www.paris.fr

Winter

Carnaval de Paris
www.carnaval-paris.org

Events in Paris

For a full list of events, visit:
Paris Convention and Visitors Bureau
www.parisinfo.com

French school holidays

Though staggered, holidays are always two weeks in Feb; two weeks in Apr; all of Jul–Aug; two weeks in Oct/early Nov; and two weeks over Christmas. During school holidays, few museums have extended opening hours. Some museums and galleries host activities on Wednesdays, when primary school kids have time off.

Public holidays

New Year's Day (1 Jan)
Easter Monday (late Mar/Apr)
Labour Day (1 May)
VE Day (8 May)
Ascension Day (6th Thu after Easter)
Pentecost (2nd Mon after Ascension)
Bastille Day (14 Jul)
Assumption (15 Aug)
All Saints' Day (1 Nov)
Remembrance Day (11 Nov)
Christmas Day (25 Dec)

Below left Chalkboard announcing the arrival of the new Beaujolais, Café de l'Industrie
Below right Colourful parade during the Carnaval de Paris

Getting to Paris

Paris is an important air hub, and direct flights from around the world serve its two main international airports. Paris is also a major hub of Europe's high-speed rail network, including Eurostar from London, Thalys from Brussels, Amsterdam and Cologne, and high-speed TGVs from Geneva and Frankfurt and most larger French cities. Many major motorways converge here from neighbouring countries including, via the Channel Tunnel, the United Kingdom.

Arriving by air

Air France is the main French airline. From the UK, **British Airways**, **Flybe**, **easyJet** and **Jet2** fly regularly to Paris. **Ryanair** flies to Beauvais-Tillé airport, from Scotland, England and Ireland.

From the USA there are regular direct flights on **American Airlines**, **United** and **Delta**; and there are flights on **Air Canada** and **Qantas** from Australia and New Zealand.

Flight times to Paris average an hour from London and 90 minutes from Dublin. Montreal is 7.5 hours, New York is 8 hours, Los Angeles is 12 hours and Sydney is 23 hours.

Airports

Paris airports have good facilities for families, including free play areas, Playstations, baby-changing areas and buggy loan.

ROISSY CHARLES-DE-GAULLE (CDG)

Most international flights arrive at **Roissy Charles-de-Gaulle**, 30 km (19 miles) northeast of Paris. It has three terminals, two of which – T1 and T2 – are linked by a driverless train. The best option for travelling into the city will depend on which part of Paris is your destination.

The **RER** line B is the fastest route into the centre, about 40 minutes, stopping at Gare du Nord, Châtelet–Les Halles, St-Michel–Notre-Dame and Luxembourg. Trains run every 15 minutes from 4:58am to 11:58pm. The RER station is within walking distance of T3.

Air France buses run daily every 15 minutes from 6am to 11pm from both terminals with links to Métro Etoile (40 minutes); and from 6am to 10:30pm to Gare de Lyon and Gare Montparnasse (50 minutes). The **RATP Roissybus** runs daily every 15–20 minutes from 5:45am to 11pm to Opera Garnier, and is the easiest option if you are travelling to the Grands Boulevards area.

A taxi from CDG to central Paris takes between 30 minutes and an hour, and costs over €60, with a mini-bus for a large family up to €100. The **VEA** bus, which can be booked online, is a frequent and direct shuttle to Disneyland® Paris.

ORLY (ORY)

Domestic and international flights arrive at the airport's two terminals 18 km (11 miles) south of the city. Air France buses leave from both terminals every 30 minutes from 6am to 11:40pm and stop at Invalides and Montparnasse. The **Orlybus** runs to Denfert-Rochereau (about 30 minutes) every 15–20 minutes from 6am to 11:50pm Mon–Fri, and until 12:50am on weekends. **Orlyval**

Below left Travellers waiting in the departure lounge, Roissy Charles-de-Gaulle Airport
Below right The Orlyval train connects Orly Airport to the Métro system

is an automatic metro link from both terminals, and connects with RER line B at Métro Anthony. Taxis take about 45 minutes – expect to pay €40 or more. The VEA bus links direct to Disneyland® Paris.

BEAUVAIS-TILLÉ
Beauvais, 70 km (44 miles) north of Paris, is used by charter flights and some budget carriers like Ryanair. Buses depart for Porte Maillot 15–30 minutes after each arrival, and leave Porte Maillot for the airport 3 hours and 15 minutes prior to departure. There is also a VEA bus service to Disneyland® Paris.

Arriving by rail

The easiest way to get to Paris from within France and from Belgium, Holland, western Germany and southern Britain is by train. There are even special family carriages on **Eurostar** trains, which also has a direct service to Disneyland® Paris.

Via the vast network of **TGV** and **SNCF** routes, **Gare d'Austerlitz** serves central and southwest France and Spain; Gare de Bercy connects with Italy and eastern Spain, and also Burgundy. Gare de l'Est links to eastern France, Germany, Switzerland and Luxembourg, and Gare de Lyon has connections to southeastern

France, Languedoc-Roussillon, Rhône-Alpes, the Riviera and Geneva. Trains for Brittany, western and southwestern France leave from Gare Montparnasse, and for Normandy from Gare St-Lazare. Gare du Nord has Eurostar connections to London St Pancras, the Channel ports and northeast France. There are also high-speed **Thalys** connections to Germany, Belgium and Holland.

Arriving by car

If you are driving to Paris, factor in the cost of motorway tolls, and bring your driving licence and the car's registration and insurance papers. Major motorways link Paris to all Europe's neighbouring cities, with no border controls. The Périphérique ring road runs around the city; the exits lead to *portes*, or gates, which open into the city.

If driving from the UK, the best option may be **Eurotunnel**, as it can cut the journey time and is not affected by bad sea conditions. **P&O** sail to Calais, and **Irish Ferries** from Rosslare to Cherbourg and Roscoff.

There is plenty of parking in central Paris, but it is still advisable to reserve a parking space through **Parkings de Paris**.

Below left Ice-cream stand at the Eurostar terminal, Gare du Nord
Below right Vehicles on the Périphérique ring road

Arriving by coach

The main coach operator to Paris is **Eurolines**. International coach services arrive at **Gare Routière Internationale de Paris-Gallieni** at Porte de Bagnolet in eastern Paris. From here, take Métro line 3 to change to the line you need.

The Lowdown

Arriving by air
Aer Lingus *www.aerlingus.com*
Air Canada *www.aircanada.ca*
Air France *www.airfrance.fr*
American Airlines *www.aa.com*
British Airways *www.british airways.com*
Delta *www.delta.com*
easyJet *www.easyjet.com*
Flybe *www.flybe.com*
Jet2 *www.jet2.com*
Qantas *www.qantas.com*
Ryanair *www.ryanair.com*
United *www.united.com*

Airports
39 50 (within France); +33 (0) 1 70 36 39 50 (from outside France); *www.aeroportsdeparis.fr*
Orlyval *www.orlyval.com*
Air France buses 08 92 35 08 20; *www.lescarsairfrance.com*
RER trains 32 46 (within France); *www.ratp.fr*
RATP Roissy/Orly bus 32 46 (within France); 08 92 68 41 14; *www.ratp.fr*
VEA *www.vea.fr*

Arriving by rail
Eurostar *www.eurostar.com*
TGV & SNCF 36 35; *www.sncf.com*
Thalys *www.thalys.com*

Arriving by car
Eurotunnel *www.eurotunnel.com*
Irish Ferries *www.irishferries.com*
P&O *www.poferries.com*

Parking
Parkings de Paris *www.parkingsde paris.com*

Arriving by coach
Eurolines 08 92 89 90 91 (within France); 08705 143219 (from the UK); *www.eurolines.com*
Gare Routière Internationale de Paris-Gallieni 28 Ave du Général de Gaulle, 93170 Bagnolet; 08 92 89 90 91

Getting around Paris

Paris has an excellent public transport system. The Métro is fast, efficient and extensive, although, for a family, buses are by far the easiest way to get about and offer great views of major sights into the bargain. Paris is a compact city that is a pleasure to explore on foot, just so long as a buggy is available when little ones get tired. Driving in the city centre is not recommended, and even far-flung sights can be reached by RER or SNCF rail services.

Buses and trams

Buses run from 6:30am to 8:30pm, with some routes running until 12:30am. A few routes have a night service. There are limited services on Sundays and public holidays. Some routes are very scenic, notably the 29, 69, 95 and 96. On boarding, tickets must be time stamped in the box next to the driver. There are nine tram lines in Ile de France, three of which serve Paris. A bus map is available online and in Métro stations. The **RATP** public transport company website is a useful resource for journey planning.

Métro and RER

Métro trains run from 5:30am to 1am the next day, and till 2:15am on Fridays and Saturdays. The 16 individual lines are numbered, and signposted for the terminus in each direction. Métro stations are easily identified by their logo, a large, circled "M", and some of them have charming Art Nouveau entrances.

The suburban rail service, the **RER**, also runs from 5:30–1am through Paris and into the suburbs. The lines are named by letters of the alphabet. Each line has branches, and each branch is numbered (C1, C2, etc). Within the city, the RER is faster than the Métro, but stations are further apart. The RER really excels for trips out of town, especially to the **Château de Versailles** (see pp220–23) and **Disneyland® Paris** (see pp230–33), and for airport connections. RER stations all display a blue "RER" logo on a white background in a blue circle.

Suburban destinations are also served by the national rail network **SNCF**. When using the SNCF service you must punch your ticket in the yellow *composteur* machine on the platform before you board.

Both Métro and RER lines are identified by colour, but on maps the RER lines are bolder. Maps can be found inside all stations. Signs on all platforms indicate the direction by naming the final destination of the line, and display the number of the Métro line or the letter of the RER. Within Paris, RER line C links the **Eiffel Tower** (see pp154–5) with **Notre-Dame** (see pp64–5).

Double, side-by-side buggies are impossible to use on Parisian public transport. Quick-folding buggies will make life considerably easier on the Métro, which has entrance gates that are difficult to negotiate with small children, and lots of steps. If you have two small children, it is best to use a buggy with seats one behind the other. On Métro trains watch out for the doors, which spring open and close rapidly. Be aware, if you have small children, that certain stations, notably

Below left City bus in front of the Musée du Louvre
Below centre Waiting to board the Métro Below right Métro sign

Montparnasse–Bienvenüe, involve a lot of walking. If you happen to travel on the driverless line 14, be sure to take the front carriage so that the kids can play at being a train driver.

Tickets

The same tickets are valid for the Métro, RER in zone 1 and buses in zones 1 and 2. They are also valid for the Montmartre funicular. Single tickets are sold in Métro stations, at newsstands and in tobacconists (look for the red, lozenge-shaped *tabac* sign), but a block of 10, a *carnet*, available at Métro stations, is more economical. Children over four years old must have a child ticket. At 10 years an adult ticket is required. Each ticket is valid for 90 minutes, no matter how many transfers are made, but cannot be used for transfers between buses and the Métro system. There are on-the-spot inspections, so hang on to your tickets. Tourist travel passes, called Paris Visite, are available for adults and children, giving unlimited travel on the Métro, buses and RER within Paris for between one and five days. However, they are only worth buying if you plan to use public transport extensively. For more information consult the **Office du Tourisme et des Congrès de Paris** website.

Driving

It is not necessary – or ideal – to have a car to get around the city. If you do bring your own car to Paris you will need your driving licence, plus its registration and insurance documents. Carry these with you at all times when driving.

While RER and SNCF will get you to most out-of-town destinations, car hire is a useful option for exploring the countryside around **Fontainebleau** *(see pp236–7)*. Expect to pay €100–150 per day. The best deals are online, booked and paid for in advance, and all the main companies have offices in Paris. Alternatively, **Autolib'** provides a public self-service car rental system. To hire a car, you need a valid driving licence and passport, and most firms require a credit card. International driving licences are not needed for drivers from the EU, North America, Australia or New Zealand.

The French drive on the right and must yield to traffic merging from the right, except for cars already on a roundabout, which have right of way. The exception to this is the **Arc de Triomphe** *(see pp134–5)*, where cars must give way to those coming from the right on any one of the 12 roads that enter it. There are no road markings here, either, so a twirl around the famous arch will test your driving skills to the limit.

Children under 10 must not travel in the front seat but backwards-facing baby seats are allowed. Bring seatbelt adjusters for young children.

Taxis

Taxis can be hailed on the street but may not stop. *Station de taxis* or taxi ranks are marked with a blue sign. A white or green light on the taxi roof means it is available. Rates are based on the zone and time of day and there is a basic flag-fall charge as well, plus an additional charge for luggage. Many taxis will take up to two adults and two children only. There is no need to tip, but rounding up the fare is expected. A lot of drivers seem to have been inspired by the cult Luc Besson-scripted *Taxi* movie, so fasten your seatbelts!

Walking

The main sights of central Paris are so close together that adults will be tempted to walk from one to another. However, an exhausted, fractious child soon takes the fun out of a stroll. Bring a pushchair, even if the children have almost outgrown it, or hop on a bus. Be extra vigilant when crossing roads, and never assume that even a clearly marked pedestrian crossing will be respected.

Below left Taxis at a taxi rank outside Gare du Nord *Below right* Picturesque lake in the gardens of Versailles

Parking

There are numerous municipal car parks, most of which are open 24 hours a day, but which can cost up to €20 per day. Street parking is cheaper, but scarce, and you can expect to get a few bumps and scrapes. Street parking is often free over the weekend, after 7pm and in August, which is probably the only good time to have a car in Paris, as the city is relatively quiet. Never park where signs read *Parking (Stationnement) Interdit*, across delivery bays (marked *Livraison*) or on a taxi rank, as your car may be towed away. If this does happen, go to the nearest police station. Expect to pay a fine as well as a charge for every day the car is held.

By bike

Paris is an easy city to cycle in as it is generally flat, relatively small and has over 400 km (250 miles) of cycle lanes. **Vélib** is the municipal bike-hire scheme. The bikes are only for use by children over 14, however, and require a credit card with chip and pin. The website has a downloadable map of cycle lanes and details of when certain streets are pedestrianized. If there is a cycle lane you must use it or risk a fine. If you have small children, take to two wheels on Sundays and

public holidays, when streets are pedestrianized in the scheme "Paris Respire". If you feel that cycling with kids in a strange city is too risky, consider hiring bikes in the safe settings of the **Bois de Boulogne** *(see pp210–11)* or **Bois de Vincennes** *(see p204)*. But if you still want to see the sights on two wheels, the best option is a guided tour by bike.

By Rollerblade

Parisians are absolutely crazy about rollerblading and there are often organized mass excursions on blades on Friday nights and Sunday afternoons, which are great fun for families with older children.

Guided tours

A bus tour is a good way to introduce kids to the sights of Paris, especially at the beginning of a first visit to the city. That way, they can be involved in choosing what to see and do. All bus tours have multilingual commentaries. Open-top buses are the most fun, as long as the weather is good. **L'Open Tour** is a hop-on-hop-off service with tickets valid for three days, or **Les Cars Rouges** offers a nine-stop ticket valid for two days. A night-time tour is a magical and unforgettable experience.

There are lots more unusual ways to tour the city. Among the most fun is in an old Citroën 2CV, through **Paris Authentic**. Your guides are all enthusiastic young Parisians, but do not be surprised if your car breaks down and you have to get out and push. Touring Paris in a horse-drawn carriage will make most little girls feel like a princess, while everyone can pretend to be secret agents flying over the city in a helicopter. The views are breathtaking, especially at sunset. **Not a Tourist Destination** runs tours packed with "insider" tips on themes such as shopping, nightlife and food, as well as tours for kids. There are other companies offering special guided tours for children and/or families, too, often involving activities such as a treasure hunt.

Arrondissements

Paris is divided into 20 numbered districts called *arrondissements*. The numbering begins in the city centre and radiates out in a clockwise spiral, with the first four on the Right (north) Bank of the Seine and the next three on the Left Bank. Every street sign has its *arrondissement* number above the street name. Parisians usually refer to areas by their number, and this number forms the last two digits of Parisian postcodes.

Below left *Scootering under the Eiffel Tower*
Below right *Cycle tour group with guide on the banks of the Seine*

The Lowdown

Public transport

Buses, Trams, Métro, RER & RATP
32 46; www.ratp.fr
SNCF 36 35; www.sncf.fr

Tickets

Paris Convention and Visitors
Bureau www.parisinfo.com

Taxis and car services

Airport taxis 01 57 42 58 01;
www.parisairporttransfer.com
Alpha 01 45 85 85 85;
www.alphataxis.fr
Chauffeur Services Paris 01 47 52 22
23, 06 68 56 16 88; www.csparis.com
(services include stretch limos and tours)
Taxis Bleus 3609;
www.taxis-bleus.com
Taxis G7 www.taxisg7.com; private
hire car service passengers with
reduced mobility: 01 47 39 00 91
Uber www.uber.com/cities/paris

Car hire

Ada 08 25 16 91 69;
www.ada.fr
Autolib' 08 00 94 20 00;
www.autolib.eu
Avis 08 21 23 07 60; www.avis.fr
Budget 08 25 00 35 64;
www.budget.fr
easyCar www.easycar.com
Europcar 08 25 35 83 58;
www.europcar.fr
Hertz 08 25 86 18 61; www.hertz.fr
Rent-a-Car 08 91 70 02 00;
www.rentacar.fr

Parking

Parkings de Paris www.parkingsde
paris.com

Bike hire and tours

Bike About Tours 06 18 80 84 92;
www.bikeabouttours.com (private family
tours available)
Fat Tire Bike Tours
www.fattirebiketours.com (also offers
4-hour Segway tours)
Gepetto et Vélo 46 Rue Daubenton,
75005; 01 43 54 19 95;
www.gepetto-velos.com
Paris à Vélo C'est Sympa!
01 48 87 60 01;
www.parisvelosympa.com
Vélib www.velib.paris.fr

Rollerblade tours

Roller Squad Institute 01 56 61 99 61;
www.rsi.asso.fr (family tours on some
Sun afternoons)
Rollers et Coquillages 37 Blvd Bourdon
75019; www.rollers-coquillages.org
(excursions on Sun afternoons)

Bus tours

Les Cars Rouges 01 53 95 39 53;
www.carsrouges.com
Cityrama 01 44 55 61 00;
www.pariscityvision.com
L'Open Tour
www.parislopentour.com
Paris Bus Service 01 56 79 05 23;
www.paris-bus-service.com
Paris Vision 01 44 55 60 00;
www.pariscityvision.com

Walking tours

Not a Tourist Destination
01 71 50 97 97;
www.notatouristdestination.com
Paris Walking Tours
01 48 09 21 40;
www.paris-walks.com

Carriage tours

Paris Calèches 06 62 20 24 88;
www.pariscaleches.com

Car and minibus tours

Easy Dream 06 82 87 60 60;
www.easy-dream.com
Paris Authentic Pl Vendome,
75001; 06 64 50 44 19;
www.parisauthentic.com
Paris Euroscope 01 56 03 56 80;
www.euroscope.fr
Paris Trip 01 56 79 05 23;
www.paris-trip.com

Helicopter tours

Helipass www.helipass.com
(sightseeing flights over Versailles)

Tours for families and kids

French Adventures 01 46 80 17 66;
www.frenchadventures.com
(private tours for children or families,
including treasure and scavenger
hunts, games and workshops in
French only)
Muses et Musées 06 78 48 99 49;
www.musesetmusees.com
(self-guided activity and discovery tour
leaflets to purchase online; ages 7–13)
Paris d'Enfants 01 48 74 92 80;
www.parisdenfants.com
(40 activity-led tours for families with
5–12 or 11–15-year-olds; self-guided
tours with booklet and colouring
books in French only)
Paris Kid www.pariskid.com (cultural
excursions for 6–12-year-olds)
Parisphile 01 40 34 71 57 (tailored
guided tours for kids)

Below left Horse-drawn carriages setting out on a ride around the Champ-de-Mars
Below right L'Open Tour's open-top bus on a circuit of the city

A River View of Paris

The Seine and Paris are synonymous. The river flows majestically across the city for 14 km (9 miles) and is a Parisian's key point of reference: all street numbers are determined by how far they are from the river. The city was actually founded on an island in the Seine, the Ile de la Cité. It is still very much a working river, with commercial barges as well as tourist boats plying their way upstream and down.

Pont de Grenelle to Pont de la Concorde

Chaillot

Invalides

see next page

Pont de Grenelle to Pont de la Concorde

The river is at its most regal along this stretch, as it sweeps past the soaring Eiffel Tower, the striking Palais de Chaillot, the grandeur of Les Invalides and Pont Alexandre III, the most beautiful bridge in Paris.

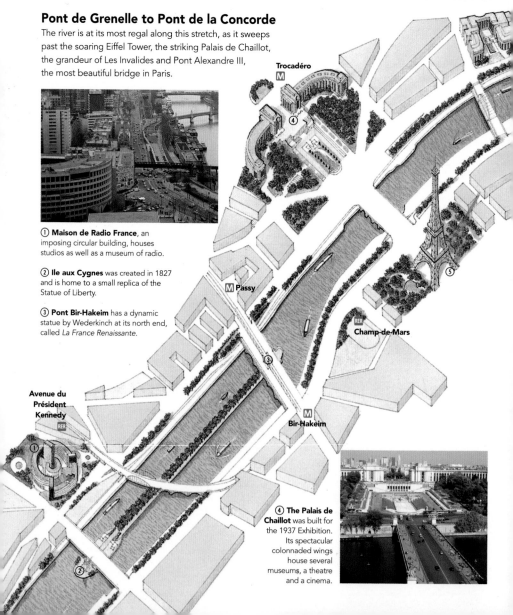

① **Maison de Radio France**, an imposing circular building, houses studios as well as a museum of radio.

② **Ile aux Cygnes** was created in 1827 and is home to a small replica of the Statue of Liberty.

③ **Pont Bir-Hakeim** has a dynamic statue by Wederkinch at its north end, called *La France Renaissante*.

Trocadéro Ⓜ

Ⓜ Passy

RER Champ-de-Mars

Avenue du Président Kennedy RER

Ⓜ Bir-Hakeim

④ **The Palais de Chaillot** was built for the 1937 Exhibition. Its spectacular colonnaded wings house several museums, a theatre and a cinema.

⑥ **Pont de l'Alma** has a statue beneath it, on its central pier, called *Le Zouave* (a type of light infantry soldier). If his feet are wet, the Seine is in danger of flooding. During the great flood of 1910, the water came up to his shoulders.

⑦ **The Liberty Flame**, at the entrance to the Alma Tunnel, is both an official monument to the French Resistance of World War II and an unofficial memorial to Diana, Princess of Wales, who died after a car crash in the tunnel in 1997.

⑧ **Pont Alexandre III** is the city's most ornate bridge, with lavish gilt and bronze decorations in the form of cherubs and winged horses. It links the Grand and Petit Palais on the north side with Les Invalides to the south, and the views from it are as splendid as the bridge itself.

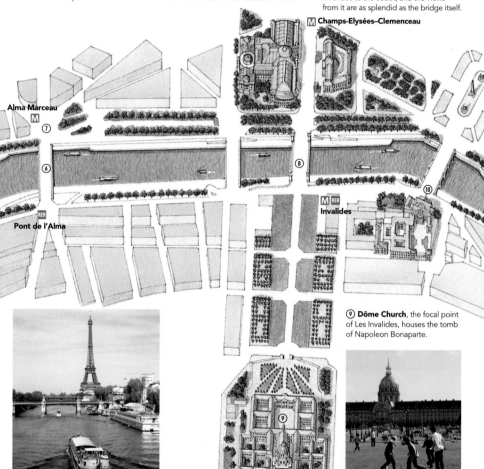

Ⓜ **Champs-Elysées–Clemenceau**

Alma Marceau Ⓜ

⑦

⑥

⑧

⑩

RER **Invalides** Ⓜ RER

RER

Pont de l'Alma

⑨ **Dôme Church**, the focal point of Les Invalides, houses the tomb of Napoleon Bonaparte.

⑤ **The Eiffel Tower**, Paris's most identifiable landmark, was built for the Exposition Universelle in 1889.

Paris or Venice?

It poured with rain all through the winter of 1909–10 and the Seine rose by 8.5 m (29 ft). Although the river didn't burst its banks, water flooded the city by rising up through stinky sewers and drains. Streets became rivers, and the brand new Métro was paralysed. The citizens of Paris were petrified by newspaper stories about crocodiles swimming out of their cages in the zoo. The waters didn't return to normal levels until March. After another major flood alert in 2003, about 100,000 works of art were moved out of the city, the largest relocation of art since World War II. It pays to keep an eye on *Le Zouave*!

⑩ **The Assemblée Nationale Palais-Bourbon** was originally built for Louis XIV's daughter. It has housed the lower chamber of the French Parliament since 1830.

A River View of Paris continued ▶

A River View of Paris, continued

Pont de la Concorde to Pont de Sully

Paris is at its most romantic here, as the Seine glides through the ancient heart of the city, passing on both sides of historic Ile de la Cité and charming Ile St-Louis, and brushing past the noble bulk of Notre-Dame cathedral. It is flanked by two great museums, the Louvre and Musée d'Orsay, by the gorgeous formal gardens of the Tuileries and – in summer, anyway – by the "seaside" beaches of Paris Plages.

Pont de la Concorde
to Pont de Sully

see previous page

Tuileries

Marais

Latin Quarter

⑪ **The Jardin des Tuileries** is a lovely formal garden first laid out in 1564 as the grounds of a palace built for Catherine de Médici, which was destroyed in 1871. There are outdoor restaurants and cafés, a round pond where children sail toy boats, and two art galleries – The Jeu de Paume and the Orangerie.

⑬ **The Louvre** stands on the site of a fortress built in 1170 by Philippe Auguste to guard Paris against his Norman enemies, along with a huge chain stretched across the Seine. The current building began life as a royal palace in the 15th century, and has been expanded in every century since then.

Assemblée Nationale

Quai d'Orsay

⑫ **The Musée d'Orsay**, a former railway station, was reborn in 1986 as a stunning museum whose collections include some of the greatest Impressionist art in the world.

⑭ **The Passerelle des Arts** is a 1984 steel reconstruction of an 1804 cast-iron footbridge, and has since become covered in "lovelocks" – padlocks affixed to the bridge by tourists.

⑮ **Pont Neuf**, completed in 1607, is the oldest of the city's 37 bridges, even though its name means "new bridge".

⑯ **Ile de la Cité**, sitting like a great ship on the Seine, is where the Paris we know today all began. Over 2,000 years ago, it was home to a tiny Asterix-style settlement inhabited by a Celtic tribe called the Parisii. Traces of their village, as well as Roman and medieval remains, can be seen in the crypt of Notre-Dame.

⑰ **The Conciergerie**, once the splendid palace of Philip the Fair, became a place of terror during the Revolution, when prisoners were held here prior to being taken to the guillotine for beheading.

⑱ **Notre-Dame** is figuratively and literally the heart of France – Kilometer Zero, from which distances are measured, lies just outside its main entrance.

⑲ **Pont de la Tournelle** is dominated by a dramatic modern statue of Saint Geneviève, the patron saint of Paris.

⑳ **Ile St-Louis** retains a villagey charm, with quirky little shops and restaurants, and elegant 17th-century houses. The best ice cream in Paris is to be found here, at Berthillon (see p68).

From Source to Sea

The River Seine rises 30 km (19 miles) northwest of Dijon in Burgundy, and flows into the English Channel at Le Havre in Normandy, a distance of 780 km (485 miles), which makes it the second-longest river in France, after the Loire. In Paris it can be as deep as 8 m (26 ft), but in ancient times it was much shallower and was edged by sandy beaches.

Pont Neuf Ⓜ

⑮

Châtelet Ⓜ

Hôtel de Ville Ⓜ

⑯

⑰ Cité Ⓜ

St-Michel Ⓜ RER

⑱

Ⓜ Pont Marie

⑳ Ⓜ

Sully Morland

⑲

Take to the Water

All aboard! A boat trip along the Seine is one of the highlights of the holiday for most kids. It's also a great introduction to the city, with views of many of the main sights that will definitely leave a lasting impression. There is a huge variety of river trips to choose between, from the Batobus shuttle service to luxury dinner cruises. On a smaller scale, the leafy old industrial Canal St-Martin can also be explored, by canal boat or barge.

Seine cruises and shuttle services

Bateaux Mouches is the most famous and the oldest river boat company in Paris, with its fleet of glass-topped boats. Cruises leave from near the Pont de l'Alma. The name Bateaux Mouches is synonymous with river boats in Paris. It has no connection with the French word for "fly", however – the earliest tourist boats were made in a district of Lyon called La Mouche. They were first used during the Exposition Universelle of 1867 and, until the development of the railways, were an important part of the transport system.

Bateaux Parisiens' sightseeing, lunch and dinner cruises depart from Port de la Bourdonnais, close by the Eiffel Tower. They provide an audio guide in French for children.

They also offer a special one-hour children's cruise, *La Croisière Enchantée* on which two elves recount some of the secrets of the city, though again only in French. There is limited parking at the boarding point, as well as a complex of shops and places to eat.

Vedettes de Paris also leave from close by the Eiffel Tower. They, too, have special tours for children in French, revealing the mysteries of Paris. The **Vedettes du Pont-Neuf** have quainter, smaller boats that depart from the Ile de la Cité. They also operate cruises on the Canal St-Martin and the River Marne.

Batobus is a hop-on-hop-off service, with tickets valid for up to five days. These river buses stop at the Eiffel Tower; Musée d'Orsay; St-Germain-des-Prés; Notre-Dame; Jardin des Plantes; Hôtel de Ville; the Louvre; and Champs-Elysées/

Pont Alexandre III. Note that these boats have little outside space and can get very hot in summer.

BOARDING POINTS
Boarding points for cruises and shuttles are easily identifiable and close to the main tourist attractions. Tickets can be bought at the quayside, although that can mean a long wait and/or disappointment at busy times, and there are often special discounts for online booking.

PRACTICALITIES
It's advisable to book ahead, especially in summer, and to arrive 30 minutes before the scheduled departure. Budget around €30–40 for a family of four. The basic sightseeing cruises last for an hour and there are commentaries in multiple languages. Bring hats, sunscreen and water in summer.

Below left Vedettes du Pont-Neuf pleasure boat on the Seine
Below right Summer crowds unwinding along the Quai de Bourbon near Notre-Dame

WHERE TO EAT AND DRINK

Many of the boat services offer lunch and dinner cruises. For families, the lunchtime cruises on the Bateaux Mouches or Bateaux Parisiens are good options with children's menus, or there are buffet meals on the Vedettes de Paris. The restaurant-boats run by the **Marina de Paris**, many of which depart from near the Musée d'Orsay, offer lunch and dinner cruises with a children's menu.

Other ways to enjoy the river

BY PRIVATE BOAT

To cruise the Seine in style, hire a private boat for an afternoon or morning through **Paris Connection**. Alternatively, the luxurious, family-friendly Hotel Plaza Athénée *(see p241)* has its own boat.

HOTELS WITH A SEINE-EYE VIEW

The swanky Hôtel Shangri-La *(see p242)* has suites with large balconies, one with a hot tub, that have panoramic views of the river. The more competitively priced Citadines St-Germain *(see p238)* looks out across the river to the Ile de la Cité, while the Novotel Eiffel Tower *(see p242)* on Quai de Grenelle also has fine river views.

RIVER WALKS AND PICNICS

There are great walks to be had along the banks of the Seine. Stroll from the Pont Alexandre III to Place de la Concorde past the houseboats. The views from the quayside of Ile de la Cité and Ile St-Louis are quintessentially Parisian, and the Pont des Arts and Square du Vert Galant are among the loveliest picnic spots in Paris. The Ile de la Grande Jatte near La Défense, immortalized by the artist Georges Seurat, is also a delightful place to picnic and unwind.

Canal cruises

Canauxrama operates a variety of boat cruises along the city's Canal St-Martin, which has nine locks, two swing bridges and eight romantic footbridges. Barges run from the Bassin de la Villette to the Port de l'Arsenal. There are activities for kids during some school holidays and it's a fun alternative if you already know the main sights. They also run day trips along the Marne that voyage out into suburbs as far as Bray-sur-Marne. **The Paris Canal Company** sails from Musée d'Orsay to La Villette, but it is a long cruise, so not ideal for smaller children, and it is pricey at around €50 for a family of four.

The Lowdown

River cruises

Bateaux Mouches Pont de la Conference, 75008; Métro: Alma Marceau; departures every 30–45 mins 10:15am–7pm; every 20 mins 7–10:30pm (winter every 45 mins–1 hr 11am–9pm); *www.bateaux-mouches.fr*

Bateaux Parisiens Port de la Bourdonnais, 75007; Métro: Bir Hakeim; departures every 30 mins 10am–10:30pm (to 8pm in winter); *La Croisière Enchantée:* Oct–Jul: 3:45pm Wed, Sat, Sun (also 2pm Wed Apr–Jun and holidays); *www.bateauxparisiens.com*

Batobus Port de la Bourdonnais, 75007; Métro: Bir Hakeim; departures every 20–25 mins; *www.batobus.com*

Vedettes de Paris Port de Suffren, 75007; Métro: Bir Hakeim; departures every 30–45 mins 10:30am–11pm; *www.vedettesdeparis.com*

Vedettes du Pont-Neuf Square du Vert Galant, 75001; Métro: Pont-Neuf; departures every 30mins–2hrs 10:30am–10:30pm (to 10pm in winter); *www.vedettesdupontneuf.fr*

Canal and other cruises

Canauxrama Bassin de la Villette, 13 Quai de la Loire, 75019; Métro: Jaurés or Bastille; *www.canauxrama.com*

Marina de Paris Port de Bercy, 75012; *www.marina-de-paris.com*

Paris Canal Company Bassin de la Villette, 19 Quai de la Loire, 75019; Métro: Jaurés; *www.pariscanal.com*

Paris Connection *www.parisconnection.fr*

Below left Boat cruise past the Quai du Marché-Neuf
Below right View along the charming Canal St-Martin

Practical Information

A little forward planning pays dividends when travelling with kids. Check when a sight is open before setting out – contact details and websites are listed in this book. Buy a *carnet* of tickets to save both money and time while using public transport *(see pp20–23)*. Make sure your travel insurance covers you for all eventualities, and make, and carry with you, a copy of your family's ID and passports in case the originals are stolen or lost.

Passports and visas

Citizens of EU countries can enter France for any length of time with a passport or national ID card; citizens of the USA, Canada, Australia or New Zealand do not require visas if staying for less than three months, but passports must be valid for three months beyond the end of the trip. If staying longer, a Schengen visa is required. Citizens of other nations should consult their country's French consulate.

Customs information

For EU citizens there are no limits on goods that can be taken into or out of France, provided they are for personal use. Visitors from outside the EU can import the following duty-free allowances: 200 cigarettes; 2 litres of wine plus 1 litre of spirits; 60 ml of perfume and 250 ml of eau de toilette; other items up to a value of €430 for air and sea travellers and €300 for other travellers. Non-EU residents can claim back Value-added Tax (VAT) if they spend more than €175.

Insurance

It is vital to take out travel insurance. At a minimum, this should cover cancellation, lost property, personal liability, legal expenses, medical cover and emergency flights home.

All EU nationals have access to the French social security system, which reimburses around 80 per cent of the cost of medical care; treatment must be paid for, then reclaimed later. To use the system, a free **European Health Insurance Card (EHIC)** is required; find out more on the **EHIC** website *(see p33)*. US visitors should check before leaving home that their health insurance covers foreign trips and includes repatriation.

Health

Almost every main street in France has a pharmacy; look for the green neon cross outside. All pharmacies will display the address of the closest *pharmacie de garde*, or duty pharmacy, that is open out of hours, or you can consult the online list. Pharmacists are trained to diagnose minor ailments, suggest treatments and can direct you to the nearest doctor. Suppositories are quite common for children's medicines in France. If that might be an issue, bring your own basic medicines.

There are very few health hazards in Paris; the tap water is safe to drink and no vaccinations are required. The city can get surprisingly hot in summer, so be

Below left *Parisian police at a busy intersection*
Below right *Shop on Rue des Francs Bourgeois in the Marais district*

prepared: a bottle of water or a small can of water spray and a hand-held fan will help cool down a fractious tot. Even in northern Europe the sun can be strong, so take precautions to avoid sunburn and heatstroke.

Personal safety and security

Paris is generally a safe city, but avoid poorly lit or isolated places. Beware of pickpockets in museums, on busy streets and on the Métro; use a hotel safe, if available, for documents and valuables; and only carry as much cash on you as you need.

In an emergency on the Métro or RER, call the station attendant by using the yellow telephone marked *Chef de Station* on the platforms.

Be very careful when crossing the road with children in Paris. Parisians frequently ignore traffic signals and pedestrian crossings, and often drive down one-way streets the wrong way. Remind children from countries that drive on the left that the French drive on the right.

PERSONAL PROPERTY
Make sure all items are insured. Be extra vigilant with bags, wallets, cameras and mobile phones when travelling with small children, as it is easy to get distracted. A waist-worn bag or money belt keeps hands free. If your passport is stolen you will need to contact your embassy or consulate.

POLICE
If you are a victim of crime, report the incident immediately at the nearest police station. You will need to make a statement called a *procès verbal*. Keep a certified copy of this for the insurance claim.

CHILD SAFETY
It is easy to get separated in a busy city. If older children have a mobile phone, make sure it is unlocked, turned on, fully charged and in credit, and that your mobile number has been entered with the country code, so they can call it despite being abroad. Make sure that small children know their full name, have ID and your mobile number on them, and know that the best person to ask for help if they get lost is a policeman or a female shop assistant.

MEDICAL EMERGENCY
Call for an ambulance from **SAMU** *(Service d'Aide Médicale Urgence)* or the **Sapeurs-Pompiers**, the fire brigade, which offers a first-aid and ambulance service.

Money

France is one of the 17 European nations using the Euro (€). All seven denominations of bank notes, from €5 to €500, are identical but coins, ranging from 1 cent to €2 pieces, show the country of origin. Kids might have fun trying to collect an example from every country.

There is no restriction on the amount of money visitors can bring into France.

BANKS AND BUREAUX DE CHANGE
There are ATMs all over Paris. Most banks in the centre will also change money, at better rates than a bureau de change, and they usually accept traveller's cheques. Banking hours vary widely and ATMs may run out of cash at peak times. Other bureaux de change are open 9am–6pm Mon–Sat and can be found along the Champs-Elysées and at main railway stations. American Express offices at the airports open early and close late.

CREDIT AND DEBIT CARDS
Carte Bleu, **Visa** and **MasterCard** are widely accepted, **American Express** less so. Cards issued in France are "chip-and-PIN" but if yours is not, ask for it to be swiped through the *bande magnétique*, or magnetic reader.

Below left *Families sightseeing near the Arc de Triomphe*
Below right *Using an ATM cash dispenser*

Opening hours

Most banks open 9am–4:30pm Tue–Fri, though hours vary between branches. Some branches also open on Saturday mornings. Post offices are open 8am–7pm Mon–Fri and on Saturday mornings. Most shops in Paris open 9am–7pm, but small shops often closed for lunch. Smaller supermarkets often close at 8pm, but the Monoprix supermarket on the Champs-Elysées is open until midnight Mon–Sat. Most shops are closed on Sunday. Many restaurants also close for a day at the beginning of the week, usually Monday. Many businesses, especially those in residential areas, close in August. As a general rule, museums and other sights are open 9am–5pm, often with a break for lunch, and tend to stay open late one evening per week. They are usually closed on Mondays or Tuesdays and public holidays. Ticket offices shut 30 minutes before closing time.

Media

There are kiosks and newsagents (*maisons de la presse*) all over the city, selling British, American and other foreign-language newspapers. There are lots of French magazines and comics for kids, mostly of a high standard. Many are very educational.

Most French hotels have TVs with at least a few satellite channels, but English-language stations will be mostly news and sport. French children's television is heavy on cartoons, which transcend the language barrier for the little ones.

Communications

French phone numbers have ten digits, all of which must be dialled. Some public telephones accept credit cards, otherwise a *télécarte*, or phone card, can be bought from a *tabac*, or tobacconist, at the Métro station, train station or post office. Very few boxes take coins.

MOBILE PHONES AND INTERNET

Most European mobile phones function normally in France; US cell phones need to be at least tri-band to work. Check with your service provider before using a mobile abroad, as charges can be very high – and keep an eye on older kids with their own mobiles. Use one of the various international call packages if you expect to be making more than a few calls. If your phone is unblocked you can buy a local SIM card from any tobacconist.

Internet access is widely available in Paris. Nearly all public places have free Wi-Fi.

POSTAL SERVICE

Sending postcards home is part of the fun for kids. *Timbres*, or stamps, can be bought from a tobacconist or any branch of the post office (La Poste). International mail is sent by air; allow up to five days for delivery.

Visitor information

The main **Paris Convention and Visitors' Bureau** (Office du Tourisme et des Congrès de Paris) is on Rue des Pyramides (Métro Pyramides) near the Louvre. They can assist with last-minute hotel bookings. The website has information for visitors.

Disabled facilities

Only line 14 of the Métro, some RER stops and some buses are accessible by wheelchair, but taxis are obliged by law to take wheelchair users. Most pavements are contoured to allow wheelchairs easier passage, but many restaur-ants are hard to access, especially toilets, which are often downstairs. Modern chain hotels are better equipped than characterful, historic ones. The Louvre, the Musée d'Orsay, the Château de Versailles and the Cité des Sciences are all easily accessible. The Visitors' Bureau website has a great deal of

Below left A Parisian newsstand selling newspapers, postcards and magazines
Below centre Window display in a department store

useful information, and the **Paris City Hall** produces a leaflet detailing all museum activities and tours for disabled people.

What to pack

The weather can be very variable so pack for rain in the summer and for very cold snaps in winter. Pack good walking shoes as Paris is a city that is a pleasure to explore on foot. Bring casual but smart clothes: Parisians dress well. Parisian supermarkets are well stocked with everything you might need to look after kids, and Monoprix, in particular, sells good-value children's clothes and shoes.

Time

France uses Central European Time (CET), which is 1 hour ahead of Greenwich Mean Time (GMT). Summer (Daylight Saving) Time comes into effect from 2am on the last Sunday in March, and ceases at 2am on the last Sunday in October. The French use the 24-hour clock.

Electricity

The voltage in France is 220 volts. Plugs have two round pins. The **BHV** store sells adaptors if you have forgotten to bring your own.

Babysitting

Many hotels can arrange babysitting but may need some advance warning. The **American Church in Paris** has a notice board with ads from English-speaking babysitters, or **Ma Babysitter Paris** has an online request form in English.

Toilets

There are plenty of public toilets in Paris, mostly modern, automated units. There are luxury pay toilets in the Carrousel du Louvre and the Printemps department store.

Etiquette

Children get a warm welcome all over Paris, in museums, hotels and restaurants, but it is important to remember that French parents and teachers are strict and expect children to be polite and respectful.

The French are quite formal. Remind your brood that they should address absolutely everyone, even the bus driver, with a cheerful "Bonjour Madame/Monsieur". It is worth memorizing even a very few basic phrases, and encourage kids to as well. The famous Parisian standoffishness is more often just exasperation at people who make no effort to speak their language.

Below left Charming children's clothes on display in a Parisian store
Below right Diners in a typical bistro

The Lowdown

Embassies and consulates
Australian Embassy 01 40 59 33 00; www.france.embassy.gov.au
British Embassy 01 44 51 31 00; www.ukinfrance.fco.gov.uk
US Embassy 01 43 12 22 22; http://france.usembassy.gov
For a full list see www.pagesjaunes.fr

Health
EHIC www.ehic.org.uk
24-hour pharmacies 6 Place de Clichy, 75009; 01 48 74 65 18 & 84 Avenue des Champs-Elysées, 75008; 01 45 62 02 41
Pharmacies de Garde www.pharmaciesdegarde.com

Emergency numbers
All services 112
Police 17 (emergencies); 08 91 01 22 22 (to locate your nearest police station)
SAMU (ambulance) 15
Sapeurs-Pompiers (fire and ambulance) 18
SOS Dentaires (emergency dentist) 01 43 37 51 00

Lost or stolen cards
American Express 01 47 77 72 00 (credit cards); 0800 832 820 (traveller's cheques)
MasterCard 0800 90 13 87
Visa/Carte Bleu 0800 901 179

Dialling codes
To call France from abroad from the UK, US and Ireland dial 00 33; from Australia 00 11 33. Omit the first 0 of the French number.
To call home from France dial 00, then the country code: UK 44; US and Canada 1; Ireland 353; Australia 61; New Zealand 64

Visitor information
Paris Convention and Visitors' Bureau www.parisinfo.com

Disabled facilities
Paris City Hall
www.paris.fr

Electricity
BHV 52–64 Rue de Rivoli, 75001

Babysitting
American Church in Paris 65 Quai d'Orsay, 75007; 01 40 62 05 00; www.acparis.org
Ma Babysitter Paris
www.baby-sitter-paris.fr

Where to Stay

Paris offers a wide range of family-friendly accommodation. It is virtually unheard of for a hotel not to accept children, and even the city's top hotels are keen to attract youngsters – in the Four Seasons Georges V they can bake madeleines for tea with the pastry chef! Not all hotels have facilities for small children, so check when booking, and always reserve a cot ahead of arrival. The listings (see pp238–47) are by area, as in the guide's sightseeing section.

Where to look

Paris's hotels tend to cluster by type. The most luxurious are to be found in the Tuileries quarter and near the Champs-Elysées. Small, characterful and boutique hotels are most likely to be in the Marais or on the Left Bank. Paris is divided into numbered arrondissements (see p250) and there are bargains to be found in the 10th (northeast of the Marais), in the 13th (south of the **Jardin des Plantes**; see p180) and the 14th (south of Montparnasse). Luxury also comes with a better price tag further from the centre. Most of the major chains have hotels outside the city centre, often a particularly good option for families, as the rooms tend to be larger and some have child-friendly facilities. **The Paris Convention and Visitors' Bureau** (see p32) offers an online reservation system.

What to expect to pay

Paris is a relatively compact city so opting for a cheaper hotel away from the centre will not lead to major commuting problems. A good chain-hotel family room can cost €120–250 a night, depending on location, facilities, day of the week and time of year.

Hotel rates are usually by room, not per person. Always ask for the family rate if booking two rooms. In most French hotels, children under the age of 12 stay free in their parents' room, and in **Novotels** children under 16 stay free, with breakfast included. Discounts are often available online, and the main chains regularly have online offers. Like most major business cities, Paris makes a good weekend destination for a family, when the room rates are often lower. Breakfast is not usually included

in the room rate and is not obligatory (allow €8–15 per adult). Wi-Fi is increasingly common, and in budget and moderately priced chain hotels it is often free.

Hotels

Hotels are graded from one star to palace according to the range of amenities provided, so star ratings may not be a reliable guide to the attractiveness of a place and the quality of service.

For families, a drawback of hotel accommodation in Paris is that most budget and mid-range hotels do not have a restaurant, exceptions being Novotels and other chains in the Accor group. Inexpensive hotels often do not have a lift, a problem with small children and pushchairs, but they do sometimes offer the most beautiful views over the

Below left Entrance to a Citadines aparthotel
Below centre Four Seasons George V *Below right* Bedroom in the Résidence Le Prince Regent

rooftops. Some also have shared bathrooms. Cheaper rooms generally have no view and look out on back courtyards.

France has some fantastically family-friendly chain hotels. Among the best are Novotel and **Ibis**, all part of the Accor group but with different identities. Novotel and **Ibis Styles** have the best family deals, especially online, and, although the decor may be bland, they offer exceptional facilities for families. Ibis and **Mercure** also have good facilities but are less family-orientated.

Aparthotels, whose rooms are small, self-contained apartments, are an ideal family option, combining the advantages of self-catering with the amenities of a hotel. A big bonus for a family is the laundry room. **Citadines** and **Adagio** are two excellent aparthotel chains.

Bed & breakfast

The French equivalent of B&Bs, *chambres d'hôtes*, is a national institution. It is a good family option, especially with older children who want to practise their French. Hosts often offer tips about where to go and what to do. If they offer dinner, the owners will sometimes dine with you.

However, this can often be a stylish, luxury option, especially in Paris, so prices vary widely. A number of agencies offer bed and breakfast.

Self-catering

This is an excellent option with children. Several agencies offer family-sized apartments, notably **RentApart** and **Haven in Paris**, which have five-star quality rentals. It is also possible to book self-catering accommodation for less than one week. House-swapping is a good option, too, through agencies such as **Home Link** and **Guardian Exchange**.

Hidden extras

By law, tax and service must be included in the price quoted or displayed at the reception desk. Tips are unnecessary except for exceptional service. Check whether the mini-bar is electronic before removing bottles to make space to store milk or snacks for the children. Garage parking is usually extra.

Booking

Try to reserve at least a month ahead, or longer for something special. Confirm a telephone

booking by email, and expect to pay a deposit of 25–30 per cent of the price. Try to arrive by 6pm or call to say you are on your way, or you may lose your booking.

Below left Hotel Le Pavillon de la Reine, Place des Vosges
Below right Interior of Hôtel Britannique, Avenue Victoria

Where to Eat

Things have moved on a bit since ancient Gauls like Obélix tucked into whole, roasted wild boar. French cuisine is arguably the world's finest, and food is as much part of the Paris experience as a trip up the Eiffel Tower. The city has a vast array of different places to eat, while visitors who opt to self-cater can make use of the wonderful street markets and specialist food shops (see pp38–9). Prices given in this guide allow for a two-course lunch (not dinner), for a family of four (two adults and two children), excluding wine but including soft drinks.

Restaurants

The French keep fairly strict dining hours: lunch from noon to 2pm and dinner from 7:30 or 8pm to 10 or 11pm. French children are used to eating out with adults and are generally very well behaved and nicely turned out. As a result, all ages are welcome, even in the city's finest restaurants. You will see whole families gathered round a table at 11pm, with no tears or tantrums going on. However, if you think your brood would not follow suit, there are plenty of places all over the city where a noisy table and spilt drinks will go totally unnoticed, or at least unremarked upon. Many visiting, non-French families find it best to eat their main meal out at lunchtime. Not only are prices lower, but Parisian dinner hours are simply too late for their young children.

Most restaurants have at least one prix fixe, or fixed price, menu of two, three or four courses: an entrée (first course), usually salads, vegetable or fish dishes, tarts and pâtés; a plat (main course), principally a meat, chicken or fish dish; and a dessert. A cheese course will be served before (or optionally instead of) dessert. On weekday lunchtimes a simpler menu, called a formule, is usually just two courses with a more limited choice. The plat du jour is the special of the day, often chalked up on a board.

Many restaurants offer a menu enfant, or children's menu – two or three small courses, often for kids under 10. Classic menu options are steak haché (a good-quality burger without the bun), beignets de poulet (chicken nuggets), jambon-frîtes (ham and chips) and omelette. Ice

cream is the usual dessert, sometimes called an eskimo.

A bistrot is a bit less formal than a restaurant, and often smaller and more moderately priced, while a brasserie is a larger, more bustling eatery, which tends to specialize in classics such as fruits de mer (seafood platters), French onion soup and steak and chips. They are often atmospheric, historic places and a bonus is that they are open all day.

A great option with kids is one of the city's many crêperies, which serve Breton pancakes with a choice of fillings, savoury on buckwheat galettes and sweet ones on crêpes.

Many cafés and bistrots have outdoor seating, ideal for a family with fidgety children.

It is acceptable everywhere to ask for a carafe d'eau, a free jug of tap water, to accompany your meal.

Below left Façade of restaurant, Rue du Faubourg Montmartre
Below right Outside tables at a café, Jardin des Tuileries

Tax and service are included in the bill by law, so tipping is optional, but it is customary to leave a little extra.

Chains

Paris has some very family-friendly chain restaurants, all with a relaxed environment and plenty to entertain the youngsters. Kids love **Chez Clément** (see p71), a chain of bistrot-style restaurants with three children's menus. Highchairs are available, and staff are happy to heat baby bottles and food. **Hippopotamus** is a child-friendly steak and burger chain that is open all hours, while **Café Indiana** serves burgers with a Mexican touch.

Cafés and tearooms

Paris is known for its cafés but, with kids, it is the salons de thé, or tea-rooms, that will score the highest. They serve a mouthwatering variety of cakes and biscuits, and range from **Ladurée** (see p135 & p172), famous for its macaroons, to small bakeries with a tearoom attached.

Ethnic flavours

France's colonial history means Paris is well served with North African restaurants, serving tasty couscous and tajines. There are Japanese, Cambodian and Vietnamese restaurants just off Avenue de l'Opéra; these can be a good option with children. Paris's China-town is in the 13th arrondissement, but there is also a gourmet Chinese restaurant, Shang Palace, in Hôtel Shangri-La (see p242). There are several good Indian restaurants in and around Passage Brady in the 10th arrondissement. Jewish restaurants are to be found in Marais. When all else fails, there are cheery, welcoming and eternally popular pizzerias all over Paris.

Special diets

There is a rather cavalier attitude to vegetarians and special diets in France. The pizza on the kids' menu often comes with ham, salads are sprinkled with bacon, vegetable soups are made with meat stock, and vegetables cooked with meat may be offered as a vegetarian alternative. Always ask the waiter what is in the dishes on the menu before ordering. Brasseries usually have salads and omelettes on the menu and ethnic restaurants are also a good option for vegetarians. Chestnuts, used in French cooking and in Corsican biscuits and cakes, may cause nut allergies.

Below left Mouthwatering macaroons, Ladurée
Below right Café with outdoor seating overlooking the Eiffel Tower

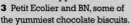
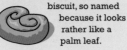

Drinks

For adults, there is a fantastic range of French wines to sample. In cafés, bars, *brasseries* and *bistrots*, and some restaurants, it is possible, and cheapest, to order wine by the carafe, usually referred to by size: the most common are 25 cl and 50 cl.

Just ask for a "café" and you will get a strong, black espresso coffee; a *café au lait* is a large white coffee. Herbal teas (*tisanes*) are also popular, and North African tearooms serve delicious, sweet Moroccan mint tea.

The brightly coloured drinks that are served up in cafés and restaurants are mixes of syrup and water, called *sirops à l'eau*. The emerald green is mint-flavoured and the red is grenadine.

On a hot day, there is nothing more refreshing than a *citron pressé*. This do-it-yourself drink is simply freshly squeezed lemon juice, a jug of water and sugar. Kids have fun mixing it up – it needs a lot of sugar not to be mouth-puckeringly sour.

Supermarkets

French supermarkets are excellent (*see p43*). Although French families buy all their basics, including wine, here, they shop for bread, cheese and cakes at specialist stores and go to the market at least once a week. **Monoprix** (*see p43*) is a leading chain, of which **Monop'** is a mini, town-centre version, as are **Carrefour Market** (*see p71 & p121*) and the majority of **Franprix** in central Paris. These are good places to buy picnic basics when in a hurry or on a budget.

Delicatessens

Ready-made food is easy to find in Paris. The city has countless delicatessens, charcuteries and *traiteurs* that make self-catering a gourmet experience. For a truly mouthwatering treat, do not miss the luxurious duo **Hédiard** (*see p139*) and **Fauchon** (*see p139*) in **Place de la Madeleine** (*see p139*); **Lafayette Gourmet** in **Galeries Lafayette** (*see p117*); **La Grande Epicerie** in **Le Bon Marché** (*see p162*); or **Dalloyau** (*see p138*) near the **Palais l'Elysée** (*see p138*), which has been selling wonderful food for over 300 years.

Markets

Paris has totally unmissable street markets selling some of the best food available in the capital. Most Parisians have their favourite market, so opinions on which is the best vary considerably. Rue Cler and Rue Montorgueil are always lively, while Rue du Mouffetard is a Paris icon, but among the best markets are the **Marché Président Wilson** (*Wed & Sat mornings*), **Marché Raspail** (*Tue, Fri & Sun*) and **Marché Edgar Quinet** (*Wed & Sat mornings*).

In season, look out for regional produce, such as asparagus from Argenteuil, carrots from Crécy, cherries from Montmorency, strawberries from Palaiseau and tomatoes from Montlhéry.

Cheese

The Ile de France produces perhaps France's most famous cheese, Brie (look for Brie de Mélun). Other local cheeses include nutty Coulommiers and Feuille de Dreux, which is ripened under chestnut leaves. Rue de Mouffetard is a good place to buy cheese, as is the famous *fromagerie* **Alléosse**, located near the **Arc de Triomphe** (*see pp134–5*). Which cheese to buy varies with the seasons. Eat goat's cheese in the spring, which is also the best time to buy Brie. Choose blue cheese in the autumn and melting Vacherin Mont d'Or at Christmas.

Below left Specials of the day chalked up outside a café
Below right Array of mouthwatering ice cream on display

Bread and cakes

There are many great French breads to try and, thanks to state protection, there are lots of local *boulangeries*. The French buy bread daily or even twice a day since it tends to go stale quickly as it contains no fat. **Poilâne** *(see p193)* is famed for its tasty sourdough bread, which makes great *tartines* (open sandwiches). **Sacha Finkelsztajn** sells Jewish breads, cheesecakes and strudels.

Pâtisseries sell an array of cakes and savoury snacks, perfect as picnic provisions. Start the day with a brioche, a croissant or a *pain au chocolat* (a chocolate-filled pastry). For a mid-morning snack most French kids are given a piece of chocolate tucked in a baguette. The place to buy macaroons is **Ladurée**. There is a particularly cosy branch, frequented by Parisians, in **St-Germain-des-Près** *(see p172)*.

Chocolates and sweets

Forget the museums and galleries, it is the chocolate shops the kids will want to see. Try a marzipan animal from **À la Mère de Famille** *(see p117)*, which opened its first branch in 1761 and has changed little since then. **Debauve & Gallais** created special chocolates for both Marie Antoinette and Napoleon III; their

most famous shop, which dates from 1818, is a registered historic monument. Kids can select sweets from the spectacular displays in two branches of **La Cure Gourmande** *(see p117)*. **Jadis et Gourmande** *(see p88)* in the Marais makes chocolate mobile phones, CDs, and even mini-Eiffel Towers. Look out for *bêtises de Cambrai* ("Cambrai naughties"), minty boiled sweets, the favourite of Astérix the Gaul.

The Lowdown

Chains
Café Indiana www.indianacafe.fr
Chez Clément www.chezclement.com (see also p71)
Hippopotamus www.hippopotamus.fr

Cafés and tearooms
Ladurée www.laduree.fr

Supermarkets
Carrefour Market www.carrefour.fr
Franprix www.franprix.fr
Monoprix/Monop' www.monoprix.fr

Delicatessens
Lafayette Gourmet www.galerieslafayette.com
La Grande Epicerie www.lagrandeepicerie.com

Markets
http://marche.equipement.paris.fr

Cheese
Alléosse www.fromage-alleosse.com

Bread and cakes
Poilâne www.poilane.com
Sacha Finkelsztajn www.laboutiquejaune.fr

Chocolates and sweets
La Cure Gourmande www.la-cure-gourmande.fr
Debauve & Gallais www.debauve-et-gallais.com
Jadis et Gourmande www.jadisetgourmande.fr
À la Mère de Famille www.lameredefamille.com

Kids in the kitchen
Café Le Nôtre www.lenotre.com

Kids in the kitchen

The **Café Le Notre** cooking school runs Wednesday afternoon workshops for kids. Book well in advance especially for Easter egg and *galette des rois* classes. Kids at the **Four Seasons George V** *(see p241)* can learn to make madeleines in the kitchen, while there are more formal classes at the **Ritz** *(see p111)*. **Chez Clément** *(see p71)* also runs cooking classes for kids.

Below left Interior of a restaurant perfect for fun, family dining
Below right Rows of ripe cheeses in a fromagier's window display

Shopping

Paris is a delightful city in which to shop, with lots of independent stores in some of the loveliest parts of town. There are many to interest kids, including some charming, classic toyshops. Travel light – always the best option with kids – as you will find everything you need here, and leave some room in the suitcase for souvenirs, as even the kitschest Eiffel Tower will end up in pride of place on the children's shelves and keep memories of the holiday alive.

Opening hours

Shops are usually open from 10am to 7pm Monday to Saturday. For Sunday shopping, try the **Marais**, the area around the **Champs-Elysées**, the **Carrousel du Louvre** (see p104) and **Bercy Village** (see p205). The **Monoprix** on the Champs-Elysées is open until midnight Monday to Saturday. Sales take place in January and June.

Where to shop

The old wine warehouses of Bercy Village are a lively place to shop and eat, with lots of things going on for kids. For something chic, there are designer outlets for children around the Champs-Elysées, where there are also branches of the leading international chains. The wide pavements make it easy to negotiate with a pushchair.

Montmartre and the Marais are full of quirky and interesting shops, and a pleasure to walk around. **Rue Vavin** and **Rue Brea**, near the Jardin du Luxembourg (see pp190–91), is an enclave of children's shops, while **Les Passages** (see p118) are quaint, 19th-century covered arcades full of fascinating little shops and are great on a rainy day.

Art, craft and hobbies

With so many small, specialist shops, Paris is a treasure trove for children who have hobbies. **La Maison de l'Astronomie** is packed with everything a stargazer needs, and also arranges field events. **Nature et Découvertes** (see p107) is the shop for science and nature buffs, with an endless supply of experimentation kits. It has a branch in the Carrousel du

Louvre, and organizes nature walks. **La Maison du Cerf Volant** near Bastille is the place for novelty kites. **Entrée des Fournisseurs**, in the Marais, sells a selection of knitting kits and cute buttons. Near the Ecole Nationale Supérieure des Beaux-Arts, **Esquisse** has a huge range of art materials, while **EOL**, near the Louvre, is a model-maker's paradise. Take young stamp collectors to the **Marché aux Timbres** (see p132) near the Rond-Point des Champs-Elysées on Thursdays, weekends and public holidays.

Books

There are lots of books about Paris for children, and many of the classic children's characters such as Astérix, Babar, Madeline and Petit Nicolas have had adventures in Paris. The books are widely

Below left Families shopping in Passage Verdeau *Below right* The famous English-language bookshop, Shakespeare and Company

Size Chart

Clothes sizes for children go by age in France.

Women's Clothes			Women's Shoes			Men's Clothes			Men's Shoes			Children's shoes		
British	French	US	British	French	US	British	French	US	British	French	US	British	French	US
4	32	0	3	36	5	34	44	34	6	39	7	7	24	7½
6	34	2	4	37	6	36	46	36	7	40	7½	8	25½	8½
8	36	4	5	38	7	38	48	38	7½	41	8	9	27	9½
10	38	6	6	39	8	40	50	40	8	42	8½	10	28	10½
12	40	8	7	40	9	42	52	42	9	43	9½	11	29	11½
14	42	10	8	41	10	44	54	44	10	44	10½	12	30	12½
16	44	12	9	42	11	46	56	46	11	45	11	13	32	13½
18	46	14				48	58	48	12	46	11½	1	33	1½
20	48	16										2	34	2½

available and make for great holiday bedtime reading.

Shakespeare and Company (see p65) is a Paris institution with a great atmosphere, just across the Seine from Notre-Dame. It sells new and second-hand books, including children's books, in English, in a medieval house with rickety staircases. **Boulinier** (see p177) is a great place for browsing through a vast collection of comic books and has a few second-hand books in English.

W H Smith, near the Jardin des Tuileries, may be less characterful but it has the largest collection of English-language books for kids in Paris. **Brentano's**, near Opéra Garnier (see p119), also has a good children's selection. **Chantelivre**, near **Le Bon Marché** department store, is an excellent bookshop, with a vast array of children's books in French. **Oxybul Junior** (see p191) is devoted to children's books and toys. It has branches in Bercy Village, near Rue Vavin and on Avenue Victor Hugo. They organize activities and story-tellings – in French – on Wednesdays and Saturdays.

Clothes and shoes

For chic Parisian kids there are many shops with unusual designs and classic clothes. Look for funky kids' clothes in **Monoprix** and **Du Pareil au Même**. Several boutiques have children's versions of adult clothes – little girls can look just like their mummies at **Eleven Paris, Antik Batik, Karl Marc John** and **Zadig & Voltaire**, all with branches in the Marais. Also in the Marais, **Petit Pan** has clothes with an Oriental touch, and workshops for budding designers. Designer outlets for kids include **Baby Dior** and **Rykiel Enfant**. There are more classic cuts at **Tartine et chocolat**, which has six shops in Paris, and **Petit Bateau**. For cheap chic try the **Bonpoint Stock** discount store near the Musée d'Orsay and, for classy shoes, **Six Pieds Trois Pouces** (see p170).

Below left Visitors inside the Carrousel du Louvre *Below right* Window display at a Bonpoint store

Hairdressers

Finish off the look with a French hairdo. There are some fun stylists in town with plenty of distractions to keep little ones occupied. **1, 2, 3 Ciseaux** is conveniently close to **Parc Monceau** (see p140), while **Simon** is in the little enclave of children's shops in Rue Vavin. There are also hairdressers in **Village Joué Club** and the **Bonton** concept store (see p93 and Toys, below).

Department stores

Paris has three department stores. The oldest is **Le Bon Marché** on the Left Bank, which has a reasonably good children's clothes' section and a kids' craft area. **Galeries Lafayette** (see p117) and **Printemps** sit next to each other just behind Opéra Garnier. Though pricey, they sell just about everything. They are not the easiest place to shop with kids but are worth a visit as they are 19th-century treasures. **Printemps** has a gorgeous roof terrace with lovely views across the city.

Games and DVDs

FNAC, with branches all over Paris, is the place to shop for anything to do with computers. The store on the Champs-Elysées sells only DVDs and computer games, but all branches have games, family and children's DVDs, as well as PCs, laptops and their accessories.

Lifestyle stores

Not So Big (see p81) is a concept store for children that sells clothes, toys and furniture. **Bonpoint** (see p191) has turned an old mansion near the Jardin du Luxembourg into a magical children's store complete with a tea room. Do not miss the quirky **Antoine et Lili** (see p123 and p203) stores, or the stylish **Colette** (see p106) near the Jardin des Tuileries. The striking Water Bar café is also here, and is a lovely place to relax after shopping.

Markets

There are some lovely trinkets to be found in Paris's open-air markets. The lively **Marché Edgar Quinet** (see p192), by the Tour Montparnasse (see p192) on Wednesday and Saturday mornings, has a good selection of handbags, jewellery and other items at pocket-money prices.

Paris is also famous for its flea markets. The largest, **Marché aux Puces de St-Ouen** (see p206) sells everything from T-shirts to rare and expensive antiques. The smaller **Marché aux Puces de Vanves** (see p215) is more fun for children, and offers better bargains (see also p38 for food markets).

Souvenirs

Paris abounds in quirky souvenirs and collectables that kids will find irresistible, from snow globes and fridge magnets to some highly imaginative memorabilia. How about an Eiffel Tower biscuit cutter? Or the famous monuments of Paris made out of pasta? And who can resist a light-up Eiffel Tower? The main monuments, galleries and museums have gift shops but prices are, unsurprisingly, slightly elevated at the Eiffel Tower. A great memento is a colouring book; look out for Je colorie Paris.

Toys

Probably the trendiest place in the city for children's toys, as well as clothing and accessories, is **Bonton**, a concept store with a chic and contemporary range of playthings for newborns and kids up to the age of 12. **Village Joué**

Below left Outside Le Bon Marché department store
Below right Antiques on display, Marché aux Puces de St-Ouen

Club is Paris's largest toy store, and quite affordable. It has taken over the entire, glass-roofed colonnade of the Passage des Princes in the **Boulevard des Italiens** *(see p118)*. Its birthday party selection is excellent. There are branches of the toy store **La Grande Récré** *(see p135)* across Paris, including an outlet just off the Champs-Elysées. Doll's house fans will adore **Pain d'Epices** *(see p117)* in Passage Jouffroy by the **Musée Grévin** *(see pp116–17)*. **L'Ours du Marais** sells only teddy bears.

Supermarkets

Everyday shopping is simple and convenient in Paris. Although supermarkets in the city centre are smaller than their out-of-town cousins, it is possible to buy, at the very least, a range of good-quality food and drinks *(see p38)*, as well as toiletries and baby products. Larger stores also sell electrical goods, household items, and anything else you would expect. All the city's branches of **Monoprix** have food halls and are an institution. Several supermarkets, notably **Carrefour Market**, are open late and on Sundays.

The Lowdown

Art, craft and hobbies
Entrée des Fournisseurs 8 Rue des Francs Bourgeois, 75003

EOL 3 Rue du Louvre, 75001; 01 43 54 01 43; www.eolmodelisme.com

Esquisse 3 Rue des Beaux-Arts, 75006; 01 43 26 06 86; www.esquisseparis.fr

La Maison de l'Astronomie 33–35, Rue de Rivoli, 75004; 01 42 77 99 55; www.maison-astronomie.com

La Maison du Cerf Volant 7 Rue de Prague, 75012; 01 44 68 00 75; www.lamaisonducerfvolant.com

Books
Brentano's 37 Ave de l'Opéra, 75002; 09 62 62 58 95

Chantelivre 13 Rue de Sèvres, 75006; 01 45 48 87 90; www.chantelivre.com

W H Smith 248 Rue de Rivoli, 75001; 01 44 77 88 99; www.whsmith.fr

Clothes
Antik Batik 26 Rue St-Sulpice, 75006; 01 44 07 68 53; www.antikbatik.fr

Bonpoint Stock 42 Rue de l'Université, 75007; 01 40 20 10 55; www.bonpoint.com

Christian Dior/Baby Dior 26–28 Ave Montaigne, 75008; 01 49 52 04 50; www.dior.com

Du Pareil au Même 14 Rue St-Placide, 75006; 01 45 44 04 40; www.dpam.com

Zadig & Voltaire 118 Rue Vieille du Temple, 75003; 01 42 78 69 92; www.zadig-et-voltaire.com

Karl Marc John 117 Rue Vieille du Temple, 75003; 09 72 33 95 44; www.karlmarcjohn.com

Eleven Paris 38 Rue des Rosiers, 75004; 01 42 71 52 13; www.elevenparis.com

Petit Bateau 9 Rue du 29 Juillet, 75001; 01 42 96 28 15; www.petit-bateau.com

Petit Pan 7 Rue de Prague, 75012; 09 54 18 50 39; www.petitpan.com

Rykiel Enfant www.soniarykiel.com

Tartine et chocolat 266 Blvd St-Germain, 75007; 01 45 56 10 45; www.tartine-et-chocolat.fr

Hairdressers
1, 2, 3 Ciseaux 10 Blvd de Courcelles, 75017; 01 42 12 03 60; www.123ciseaux.com

Simon 16 Rue Vavin, 75006; 01 53 10 08 12; www.simoncoiffeurdefamille.com

Department stores
Le Bon Marché www.lebonmarche.com

Galeries Lafayette www.galerieslafayette.com

Printemps www.printemps.com

Toys
La Grand Récré 8–12 Rue d'Amsterdam, 75009; 01 42 93 24 41; www.lagranderecre.fr

Bonton 122 Rue du Bac, 75007; 01 42 22 77 69; www.bonton.fr

Village Joué Club 3–5 Blvd des Italiens, 75002; 01 53 45 41 41; www.joueclub.fr

L'Ours du Marais Village Suisse, 9 Rue Alasseur, 75015; 01 42 77 60 43; www. oursdumarais.com

Supermarkets
Carrefour Market www.carrefour.fr

Monoprix www.monoprix.fr

Below left The stylish Galeries Lafayette department store
*Below centre Curios and antiques at a Paris flea market **Below right** Souvenirs for sale, Quai Aux Fleurs*

Entertainment

There is a wealth of opportunities to keep kids – and adults – entertained in Paris, from watching a fairytale ballet at the glamorous Opéra Garnier to being dazzled by a magic show in the Marais. There are circuses, where kids can also learn to perform under the Big Top; unforgettable movies to see; children's concerts and music workshops; and plenty of activities in the city's museums, especially on Wednesdays and during the school holidays.

Theatre

Some Paris theatres have children's matinees on Wednesdays and at weekends, notably **Théâtre du Gymnase**, **Théâtre Dunois**, **Café d'Edgar** and **Abricadabra Péniche Antipod**, a barge at **Parc de La Villette** (see pp202–3), which also runs theatre and circus workshops for kids. **Théâtre de l'Essaïon** specializes in classics such as *Alice in Wonderland*, while there are entertaining solo performances at **Le Point Virgule** and baffling magic shows at **Au Double Fond**.

Street theatre is to be found all over Paris, especially in spring during the festival **Le Printemps des Rues**, and in the 12th *arrondissement* at the **Festival Coulée Douce** in June.

Paris has a thriving dance scene and, although prices are steep, a night out at **Opéra Garnier** (see p119), to see a classical ballet or opera is something that none of the family will ever forget. For a change of culture, the **Institut du Monde Arabe** has North African dance shows and Arab music.

Cinema

France has a strong cinematic tradition, but there are plenty of international blockbusters on show as well. Many foreign-language films, especially those for children, are dubbed into French and marked VF *(Version Française)*. Films in their original language are VO *(Version Originale)*. New releases hit the screens on Wednesdays.

Look out for children's showings at **Cinémathèque Français** in **Bercy Village** (see p205) and the **Ecran des Enfants** at the **Centre Pompidou** (see pp80–81). The **Forum des Images** has special showings for under-10s and runs film festivals for kids, including the autumn series **Mon Premier Festival**.

Kids love watching movies at the 3D cinema **La Géode** in Parc de la Villette, which also hosts an open-air summer film fest. **Le Saint Lambert** specializes in children's films and comic strips in French, but most films for kids will not have English subtitles. You can take a tour behind the scenes as well as catch a movie at the famous **Le Grand Rex**, Paris's oldest cinema.

Circuses

Paris has some excellent traditional circuses, including two permanent ones, the historic **Cirque d'Hiver Bouglione**, and **Cirque Diana Moreno Bormann**, both in north-east Paris. In winter, **Cirque Pinder**, France's oldest travelling circus, sets

Below left Ornate decoration on the façade of Cirque d'Hiver
Below right Children performing in the Fête de la Musique

up in **Bois de Vincennes** *(see pp204–5)*. Kids can spend a day learning to juggle and walk the tightrope at **Le Cirque de Paris** and **Le Zèbre de Belleville**, also in northeast Paris.

Music

Philharmonie de Paris has workshops and concerts for kids all week, as does the **Théâtre du Châtelet**. The **Opéra National de Paris Bastille** runs a winter season of events for kids, and **Espace Léopold-Bellan** stages concerts on Wednesday afternoons.

There is music for free in the streets, squares and other venues all over Paris on 21 June, for the lively **Fête de la Musique**, and all summer in the city's parks.

Tickets and listings

Last-minute tickets can be bought at a considerable reduction from the **Kiosque Théâtre** on **Place de la Madeleine** *(see p139)* and opposite Gare Montparnasse. Listings of events are available at the **Office du Tourisme et des Congrès de Paris**, and there are useful websites, including **Lamuse**, which specializes in children's entertainment.

The Lowdown

Theatre

Abricadabra Péniche Antipod
www.penicheantipode.fr

Au Double Fond
www.doublefond.com

Café d'Edgar www.theatre-edgar.com

Festival Coulée Douce http://progeniture.free.fr

Institut du Monde Arabe
www.imarabe.org

l'Opéra Garnier
www.operadeparis.fr

Le Point Virgule
www.lepointvirgule.com

Le Printemps des Rues
www.leprintempsdesrues.com

Théâtre Dunois
www.theatredunois.org

Théâtre de l'Essaïon
www.essaion-theatre.com

Théâtre du Gymnase
www.theatredugymnase.com

Cinema

Cinémathèque Français www.cinematheque.fr

Ecran des Enfants www.centrepompidou.fr

Forum des Images www.forumdesimages.fr

La Géode www.lageode.fr.

Le Grand Rex
www.legrandrex.com

Mon Premier Festival
www.monpremierfestival.org

Le Saint Lambert 08 92 68 96 99

Circuses

Cirque Diana Moreno Bormann
www.cirque-diana-moreno.com

Cirque d'Hiver Bouglione
www.cirquedhiver.com

Cirque de Paris
www.cirque-paris.com

Cirque Pinder
www.cirquepinder.com

Le Zèbre de Belleville
www.lezebre.com

Music

Philharmonie de Paris
www.philharmoniedeparis.fr

Espace Léopold-Bellan
www.bellan.fr

Fête de la Musique
www.fetedelamusique.culture.fr

Opéra National de Paris Bastille
www.operadeparis.fr

Théâtre du Châtelet www.chatelet-theatre.com

Tickets and listings

Kiosque Théâtre
www.kiosquetheatre.com

Lamuse www.lamuse.fr

Office du Tourisme et des Congrès de Paris www.parisinfo.com

Below left Theatre ticket kiosk in Place de la Madeleine *Below centre* Le Grand Rex, Paris's most opulent cinema
Below right One of the innovative acts in the Festival Coulée Douce

The Parks of Paris

The parks of Paris are one of the many reasons the city is a perfect place to visit with children. There is much more to do in them than simply feed the ducks, too. Kids can sail wooden boats, ride on carousels or ponies, take in a puppet show, even come face-to-face with a woolly sheep. A bonus is that many of the top tourist sights are near some of the city's best parks – handy for letting off steam after a session of sightseeing.

Jardin des Tuileries

The Jardin des Tuileries (see p108) lies at the heart of the city, right beside the Louvre. In summer it has a funfair, but all year round there are trampolines and a carousel. For a classic Parisian childhood experience, wooden model boats can be hired to sail in the circular pond. There are several outdoor restaurants, too, which are great places to eat with kids. This is Paris's grandest park and the place for a leisurely stroll, but be warned – the lawns are strictly off limits.

Parc Monceau

Children can enjoy pony rides and eat candy floss in **Parc Monceau** (see p140), close to the Arc de Triomphe. They will have fun, too, discovering the Chinese pagoda, Dutch windmill and Egyptian pyramid. Huge mansions surround the park, some of which are fascinating museums such as the **Musée Nissim de Camondo** (see p140) and the **Musée Cernuschi** (see p140). This makes for a great day out, mixing culture and play.

Jardin des Plantes

One of the world's oldest botanical gardens, the **Jardin des Plantes** (see p180) is full of exotic species of flora. There is also a playground with a huge dinosaur, very appropriate as the garden is home to four great natural history museums with lots of fascinating dinosaur bones and other animal exhibits. Kids will love the small **Ménagerie** (see p181), or zoo.

Jardin du Luxembourg

Simply the best park in Paris for kids, the **Jardin du Luxembourg** (see pp190–91) is just a short walk from the Panthéon and is the place to really get a feel for the city. Parisian families come here to sail wooden boats on the round pond in front of the Senate and ride on the magical carousel, designed by Charles Garnier, the architect who built the **Opéra** (see p119). There are pony-rides for kids, boules courts, old men playing chess under the trees and a great puppet theatre – but there is a charge for the playground. Do not miss the charming beehives in the beekeeping school.

Champ-de-Mars

The Eiffel Tower stands at one end of this huge open space that was once a military parade ground. The **Champ-de-Mars** (see p156) also has a good-sized playground, a puppet theatre and, as a vast patch of grass,

it is the perfect place for letting off steam. Across the river at the **Trocadéro** (see pp144–5) there is another great garden – kids will especially love the giant fountains.

Further afield

Paris has two huge, leafy parks that sit on either side of the city, offering the kind of wide open spaces ideal for activities such as cycling or football. In the west, the big attraction for kids in the Bois de Boulogne is the **Jardin d'Acclimatation** (see pp210–11), an amusement park with rides, water chutes and farm animals. You can hire bikes to get around, as well as rowing boats to take out on the enormous lake.

Around two-thirds of Paris's 500,000 trees are in the **Bois de Vincennes** (see pp204–205). Among the activities for kids are a fairy tale château and a city farm to visit; puppet shows and free concerts, and bike and boat hire.

Below Miniature train from Porte Maillot to the Jardin d'Acclimatation

Above Families soaking up the sun, Jardin du Luxembourg **Left** *Before the show, Marionnettes du Champ-de-Mars* **Bottom left** *Sailing a boat, Jardin des Tuileries*

Off the tourist trail

Parc des Buttes-Chaumont *(see p204)*, east of Montmartre, has craggy cliffs, an island temple reached by a high arched bridge and an open-air *guinguette* café, **Rosa Bonheur** *(see p204)*. The island in the lake of **Parc Montsouris** *(see pp214–15)* features a grotto and waterfall, and Florida turtles can be spotted basking on its shore. Both parks have puppet theatres and sometimes offer pony rides.

Parks of the future

While the majority of the city's parks are 19th century, Paris has a number of modern parks that are popular with local families. A dragon slide is just one of the attractions of the futuristic **Parc de la Villette** *(see pp202–203)*, with its playful gardens and follies. It is also home to the **Cité des Sciences et de l'Industrie** *(see p202)*. Bring a skateboard or rollerblades when visiting **Parc de Bercy** *(see p205)*, to use in its modern-art skate park. There is a dramatic stepped cascade and a strange man-made canyon fountain, too. The fountains at **Parc André Citroën** *(see p213)* are great for cooling off on a hot day, but it is the giant tethered helium viewing balloon that will impress the kids.

Puppets in the park

Almost every Paris park has its own marionette theatre, known as *Les Guignols* after the leading character Guignol, a lovable rogue. The shows have not changed in 200 years and, although in French, have lots of visual humour that needs no translation.

Puppet theatres

Arrive early for performances, usually on Wed, Sat, Sun and public hols and often daily in school hols: €12–18

Les Guignols des Champs-Elysées, Rond-point des Champs-Elysées, 75008; 01 42 45 38 30; *www.theatreguignol.fr*

Guignol du Jardin d'Acclimatation Bois de Boulogne, 75016; 07 60 25 77 33; *www.jardindacclimatation.fr*

Guignol au Parc Floral Bois de Vincennes, 75012; 01 43 28 41 59; *www.guignolparcfloral.com*

Guignol de Paris Parc des Buttes-Chaumont, 75019; 01 40 30 97 60; *www.guignol-paris.com*

Marionnettes du Luxembourg Jardin du Luxembourg, 75006; 01 43 29 50 97 & 01 43 26 46 47; *www.marionnettesduluxembourg.fr*

Marionnettes de Montsouris Parc Montsouris, 75014; 01 46 63 08 09 & 06 07 77 85 42; *www.guignol-parcmontsouris.com*

Théâtre des Marionnettes de Paris Orée du Bois de Vincennes, 75012; 06 75 23 45 89; *www. lesmarionnettesdeparis.com*

Underground Paris

There is more to Paris than meets the eye. Underfoot, there is a warren of over 200 km (125 miles) of former quarry tunnels, and alongside the Métro and the sewers there are Gothic vaults, wine cellars, storage rooms, car parks and crypts, all layered one on top of the other like an enormous *millefeuille* gâteau. But the star of this subterranean show is the spooky Catacombes – enormous bone-pits full of the remains of millions of Parisians.

Paris: the great Gruyère cheese

Paris is built on limestone, a stone which reveals the secrets of its primeval formation, being riddled with fossils of ancient sea creatures. It was first quarried by the Romans to build their original city of Lutetia, and, over the centuries, the limestone beneath Paris has become riddled with tunnels and holes, just like a Gruyère cheese.

The old quarries under the Left Bank also supplied the stone used in some of the city's most famous monuments, such as **Notre-Dame** (*see pp64–5*) and the **Louvre** (*see pp104–107*). The quarries lay far beyond the city limits but, as Paris grew, it sprawled over the old and often hazardous tunnels. In 1774, part of what is now Avenue Denfert-Rochereau fell into the darkness below, prompting the authorities to commission inspectors to map the tunnels and shore them up. It was also decided to empty out the city's stinking, overcrowded cemeteries and turn part of the vast warren into an enormous bone store. Inspectors are still at work today, continually monitoring the safety of the old stone pillars that were installed, literally, to hold the city up.

The quarries were abandoned in the early 19th century but gypsum for plaster of Paris was mined in the northeast until 1873.

Crypts, vaults and bunkers

Many treasures were found while the city's network of underground car parks were being dug out, among them foundations of the Roman city discovered under the square in front of Notre-Dame and now displayed in the **Crypte Archéologique** (*see p65*). This crypt also has remnants of medieval streets and walls that pre-date the cathedral by several years. Some of the most ancient cellars in the city date back to Roman times, and vestiges of the city's first church, where Saint Denis is said to have prayed, are hidden underground at 14 Rue Pierre Nicole.

The crypts of churches, cathedrals and the **Panthéon** (*see pp188–9*) hold the remains of many of the most famous Parisians who ever lived. An especially spine-chilling encounter is to be had by taking a stroll past the bones of six million citizens, all laid out in macabre patterns in the **Catacombes** (*see p214*) to the south of the city.

Beneath Paris, too, there are bank vaults full of gold bars; wine

Below left. Atmospheric vaulted crypt of the Panthéon
Below right Gallo-Roman ruins, visible in the Crypte Archéologique

cellars stuffed with priceless bottles; bunkers from World War II, used by the Nazi occupiers and the French Resistance; as well as dozens of typically Parisian nightclubs.

Mushrooms and Métro stations

The end of quarrying in the early 19th century opened up a new business opportunity underground. Parisians realized that the damp tunnels were the perfect place to grow mushrooms – on horse manure, of which there was no shortage in 19th-century Paris. Mountains of *champignons de Paris* were grown underground until cultivation was moved out to the suburbs at the end of the 20th century.

Construction of the Métro began in 1900. With 297 stations, it is one of the world's densest systems, carrying more than five million passengers a day. The earliest Métro line ran close to the surface, but now they are deep underground too, and were joined in the 1970s by the RER. Do not miss Métro Abbesses, one of the few original Art Noveau stations, while Métro Louvre-Rivoli has replicas of ancient art from the museum above and Métro Bastille has art depicting historic events.

Stinky sewers

It is actually possible to visit part of the 2,350 km (1,460 miles) of sewers at **Les Egouts** *(see p157)*. Here, an endless stream of waste water flows in a channel down the centre of the tunnels, as drinking water gurgles through freshwater pipes that run along each side. It is stinky, but fun! The sewers run parallel to the overground world – blue and yellow "street" signs replicate the names of those above. Precious jewels, weapons, countless wallets and even a dead body have been found in these murky waters.

Fresher waters

The Bièvre was Paris's second river until it disappeared underground in 1912. It once ran through the 5th and 13th *arrondissements* and was another smelly place, where tanners and butchers worked. It still flows, however, and joins the Seine near Gare d'Austerlitz.

The reservoir beneath the **Opéra Garnier** *(see p119)*, which features in *The Phantom of the Opera*, really exists. The pool is home to some plump, pale catfish, which are fed mussels through a grille by the staff. It is also used by local firefighters to practise rescue missions that involve swimming in darkness.

Below left Touring the underground sewers of Les Egouts
Below right Human skulls and bones on display in the Catacombes

KIDS' CORNER

Look out for...
1 Line 14 on the Métro. It has no driver. Instead of a driver's cabin there is a glass window from which you can watch the tracks as you whizz ahead.
2 A hidden canal. Take a stroll along the Port d'Arsenal; here the Canal St-Martin disappears under Place de la Bastille. You can ride through it on a boat trip with Canauxrama *(see p29)*.
3 Walls and pictures built of skulls and bones. These were laid out in the Catacombes in the 18th century. Take a look if you dare.
4 The Banque de France on Rue La Vrillière. In its underground vaults are 2,642 tonnes (2,600 tons) of gold bars.

FALL OF HELL STREET
One day in 1774, there was a terrible groaning sound on the aptly named Rue d'Enfer (Hell Street) and half of it plunged into a gaping pit, soon known as the "Mouth of Hell".

Ghostly stations
There are abandoned stations that sit like little time capsules on the Paris Métro. If you keep your eyes peeled, you might spot one. When World War II broke out in 1939, the train drivers and guards were called up to fight and many stations were closed. Champ-de-Mars is a so-called "ghost station" on line 8 between La Motte Piquet–Grenelle and Ecole Militaire stations. St-Martin is another, on lines 8 and 9 between Strasbourg–St-Denis and République. Several of them are now hired out for film shoots.

The History of Paris

Taking a trip through the history of France is rather like riding a white-knuckle roller coaster that hurtles from dizzy peaks of triumph down into the depths of defeat and despair. Although Paris has not always been the capital city, for most of the last 1,000 years it has been the unquestioned hub, and heart, of the country. Parisians have always been a feisty lot, keen to keep control of their city and fiercely proud of revolting against tyranny and injustice.

Charles Martel – "the Hammer" – at the Battle of Poitiers in 732

Astérix versus Caesar

In 250 BC a bunch of Astérix-style Celtic tribesmen, the Parisii, built a stockade on what is now the Ile de la Cité. The Parisii were smashed by Julius Caesar's armies in 52 BC and the Romans occupied their city, naming it Lutetia, based on a Celtic word for a marshy place. The centre of the Roman city was where the Panthéon stands today.

Frankly brutal

As the Roman Empire crumbled, Paris was threatened by invading tribesmen from the east. First came Attila the Hun, then the Franks, who finally overthrew the Romans. In 481

their leader Clovis was crowned king, named his new domain Francia and made Paris his capital.

Then, in 732, the Arabs invaded France. The brilliant power behind the throne, Charles Martel, or "the Hammer", lived up to his name by pounding their forces. His grandson, Charlemagne, was a towering figure who ruled over such vast swathes of Europe that, in 800, he was made Holy Roman Emperor by the Pope.

Medieval Paris

Throughout the Middle Ages, the powerful strategic position of Paris made it an important centre of commerce, politics and learning. The medieval church also played a crucial part, establishing the Left Bank as an intellectual powerhouse, with the first university in northern Europe, and constructing the cathedrals of St-Denis and Notre-Dame. However, the city was a stinky, overcrowded place. When Philippe-Auguste became king in 1165 he was so sickened by the stench from the window of his new

Louvre fortress that he resolved to clean up the city. Open sewers were covered; marshlands were drained so the city could expand; and Paris was also wisely encircled by a huge, fortified defensive wall.

Meeting held in Notre-Dame in 1328, after the death of Charles the Fair

A long hundred years

By 1300 Paris was the biggest city in Europe, but it was a violent place that often rose up against the crown. In 1328 king Charles the Fair died leaving no direct heir. Both Edward III of England and Philippe de Valois had claims to the throne. So began

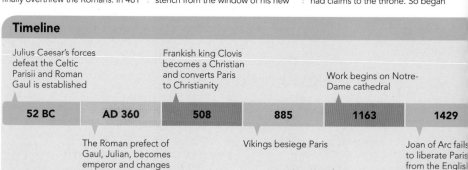

Timeline

Julius Caesar's forces defeat the Celtic Parisii and Roman Gaul is established		Frankish king Clovis becomes a Christian and converts Paris to Christianity		Work begins on Notre-Dame cathedral	
52 BC	**AD 360**	**508**	**885**	**1163**	**1429**
	The Roman prefect of Gaul, Julian, becomes emperor and changes Lutetia's name to Paris		Vikings besiege Paris		Joan of Arc fails to liberate Paris from the English

The Battle of Agincourt (1415), fought during the Hundred Years' War

the Hundred Years' War (in fact a series of wars that lasted 116 years). Paris was a place of food shortages, rising taxes, marauding mercenaries, civil wars, plague and, in the bitter winter of 1407, icefloes drifting down the Seine.

Having defeated the French at Agincourt in 1415, the English took the city and held onto it until 1436.

Renaissance and rifts

By the time its occupiers left, Paris was in ruins but, during the reign of François I, the Louvre was transformed into a glittering palace and the city blossomed and grew under the influence of the Renaissance.

Then, in 1562, growing religious tensions led to the Wars of Religion, the low point of which was the St Bartholomew's Day massacre of Parisian Protestants in 1572.

In 1589, the Protestant leader Henri of Navarre became heir to the throne but, to be accepted as King, he had to become a Catholic, joking "Paris is well worth a Mass". Peace returned, Protestants were granted freedom of worship and "Good King Henri" was a popular ruler.

But he faced constant danger from extremists on both sides, and in 1610 was stabbed to death.

A whole lot of Louis

Henri's eight-year-old son was crowned Louis XIII, but the power behind the throne was the ruthless Cardinal Richelieu. Taxes shot up, the peasants revolted and the nobles grumbled as their powers were curtailed. The next Louis, XIV, emptied the country's coffers waging war and transforming Paris into a "new Rome" fit for the Sun King.

His heir, Louis XV, was foolishly uninterested in France's discontent, while Paris buzzed with the new ideas of the Enlightenment. Louis XVI, too, lacked the wits to rule a bankrupt country. The poor went hungry, and the middle class raged at having no say in how the country was run. Then the ruined harvest of 1788 led to food riots in Paris. France was ripe for revolution.

Power to the people!

In the summer of 1789, it all boiled over and the Bastille was stormed (see Revolution!, pp54–5). Over the next few years, thousands of people were executed, among them Louis XVI. A young Corsican general, Napoleon Bonaparte, rallied the nation but, after waging war with the European powers, he lost his last battle at Waterloo in 1815 and the most tumultuous period in French history drew to a close.

The Hundred Years' War, which actually lasted 116 years, ends

End of the republic as Napoleon crowns himself Emperor of France at Notre-Dame

1453	1789	1804	1815

Beginning of the French Revolution

The Battle of Waterloo and the abdication of Napoleon

Long live the king!

In 1815, the French decided to give the monarchy another chance and it was time for another Louis. Louis XVI's elderly brother became King Louis XVIII. (Louis XVII never reigned – he died, aged ten, in prison.) He was succeeded by another brother, Charles X. Neither had learned the lessons of the Revolution and both tried to rule like absolute monarchs.

Unsurprisingly, the Parisians again revolted – the "July Revolution" of 1830 – and Charles fled to England, to be replaced by another relative, the Duc d'Orléans, Louis-Philippe.

With a population of 900,000, Paris was the second-largest city in Europe after London, but most people lived in disease-ridden slums. Grievances mounted and in February 1848 yet another revolution broke out. Louis-Philippe abdicated and fled, and a Second Republic was proclaimed. At the end of the year, presidential elections were held.

Portrait of French Emperor Louis-Napoleon Bonaparte, or Napoleon III

The Bonapartes are back

The victor, to the surprise of many, was Louis-Napoleon Bonaparte, the nephew of the late emperor. He soon followed in his uncle's footsteps by seizing dictatorial power in a *coup d'état* and proclaiming himself Emperor Napoleon III.

Under his rule, the appearance of Paris was transformed by Baron Haussmann, who replaced crowded, filthy, medieval streets with broad, intersecting avenues and boulevards. Parisians now had clean drinking water, street lighting and parks. The grand boulevards were soon filled with luxurious shops, but the city was still deeply divided. The poor were unable to afford the elegant new apartment buildings and were driven into the outlying districts, notably in the northeast of the city.

Fancy a rhino steak?

In 1870 Napoleon's rule came to an abrupt end when he declared war on Prussia, only to see his armies smashed. He abdicated and the Third Republic was established. By September the Prussian army had laid siege to Paris. Poor Parisians had to dig up corpses to grind the bones into gruel, while the rich munched their way through the city's zoos – rhino steaks went for a small fortune. Nonetheless, Parisians were furious when the government surrendered, and the city's working-class militia refused to hand in their guns, instead taking over Paris as a revolutionary Commune. The

government regrouped at Versailles and fierce fighting broke out as their troops retook the city. The Tuileries Palace and the town hall were destroyed and around 5,000 people were killed. In the aftermath, another 10,000 Communards were shot, 40,000 arrested and 5,000 deported.

But Paris soon bounced back. The Métro, cars, telephones and cinemas transformed life in the capital, and the economy prospered thanks to France's expanding empire. Paris became a glittering city, a mecca for artists, musicians and film-makers.

Tuileries Palace ablaze during the Communard uprising of May 1871

The war to end all wars

In August 1914, war broke out across Europe. The Germans once more invaded France, and panic spread through Paris as the enemy army, just 30 km (19 miles) from Paris, could be seen from the top of the Eiffel Tower.

Miraculously, the city was saved. Over four years of war Parisians suffered terrible losses at the front, while at home there were food shortages and then a devastating influenza epidemic. But, by the 1920s, Paris was once again at the

Timeline

"July Revolution" in Paris overthrows Charles X		Defeat of France in the Franco–Prussian War; establishment of the Paris Commune		World War I	
1830	**1851**	**1870–1**	**1889**	**1914–18**	**1939–45**
	Napoleon III declares the Second Empire		Eiffel Tower built for the Exposition Universelle		World War II: Par is occupied by th Nazis 1940–44

centre of artistic and literary life. France, however, was still divided and, when the Great Depression hit in 1929, extreme parties of both the right and the left flourished. The country's political divisions were a major factor in leaving France unprepared for a second war, which began in September 1939.

The darkest hour

On 14 June 1940, Paris fell with virtually no resistance. The right-wing government of Marshal Pétain signed an armistice with the Nazis and moved south to Vichy, in central France, while a little-known general, Charles de Gaulle, called on the French from his base in London to continue the fight.

Paris suffered four years of Nazi occupation and, in May 1941, the Vichy-run police began deporting Parisian Jews to Auschwitz.

In June 1944 the Allies landed in Normandy, and in August an uprising broke out in Paris, with barricades and running battles in the streets. On 26 August, de Gaulle entered the city to a rapturous welcome, and established a temporary government that lasted until 1946, when the Fourth Republic was established.

All change

Reconstruction was hard; there were ongoing divisions between left and right, and colonial conflicts in Indo-China and Algeria brought blood-shed to the streets of Paris. In 1958

President Charles de Gaulle speaking to the nation

the Fourth Republic collapsed and De Gaulle was returned to power. By 1968, growing social unrest and De Gaulle's authoritarian style of government sparked an uprising led by students and factory workers.

In the 1970s, under presidents Georges Pompidou and Valéry Giscard d'Estaing, Paris was again transformed. Modernism was all the rage, and the Pompidou Centre and Tour Montparnasse became new Parisian landmarks. In the 1980s, President Mitterrand gave the Louvre its glass pyramid and built a futuristic new district, La Défense.

In 1994 the Eurostar train service linked Paris direct to London via the Channel Tunnel. In 2002, France adopted the single-currency euro to replace the franc.

New challenges

François Hollande defeated Nicolas Sarkozy in the presidential elections in May 2012, to become the second Socialist Party president of the Fifth French Republic, after Mitterrand. But his policies are yet to lead to the level of reforms which many had hoped for.

ifth Republic is
stablished with
e Gaulle
s president

Nicolas Sarkozy
elected president

1958	1977	2007	2012

Jacques Chirac
becomes the first
elected mayor of
Paris since 1871

François Hollande
elected President

Revolution!

The French Revolution is one of the most important events in European history. So many people lost their heads to the guillotine that the streets literally ran with blood – Parisians even turned on their king and queen and chopped off their heads as well. In a tumultuous 26 years, France went from being an absolute monarchy to a republic, then to the seat of Napoleon's empire, and finally returned to a monarchy, this time a constitutional one.

Anyone for tennis?

Louis XVI needed cash. In order to hike up already crippling taxes, he was forced to convene the long-neglected French parliament, the Estates-General. This was made up of three tiers: the clergy, the nobility and the so-called Third Estate, which represented ordinary people.

This was seen by commoners as an opportunity to be heard, and they compiled huge books of complaints, which were brought to Versailles to be discussed.

When the reforms demanded by the Third Estate were blocked, their delegates declared themselves a National Assembly and, locked out of the main meeting hall on the king's orders, adjourned to a nearby indoor tennis court, the Jeu de Paume, where they swore the historic Tennis Court Oath not to disband until France had a proper constitution. A week later Louis backed down and a National Assembly was born.

The historic Tennis Court Oath, as depicted by Jacques-Louis David

Man the barricades!

As a constitution began to take shape, in Paris the debates and grievances on the streets turned into demonstrations and riots, as rumours ran wild that the king was about to send in the army to close down the National Assembly.

To forestall this, on 14 July, a mob stormed the hated Bastille prison in the belief that it was full of weapons (in fact, it held just seven prisoners). As the starving peasantry began to revolt in earnest, killing nobles and priests, the National Assembly quickly abolished the feudal system left over from the Middle Ages and proclaimed liberty and equality for all citizens.

Arguments about the new Constitution would go on for two years, with confrontations between different revolutionary factions.

Royals on the run

Many of the people were convinced the king and his supporters were still plotting to reverse the reforms. Parisians were starving and, in October, an angry crowd of women marched to Versailles to protest. They broke into the palace threatening to tear Louis and his queen, Marie Antoinette, to pieces.

The king was forced to sign the Declaration of the Rights of Man, and to return to Paris with his family, where they were held in the Tuileries Palace, as prisoners of the National Assembly. After almost two years in captivity, Louis, afraid for his family's safety, made a fatal error. They fled the capital for a royalist stronghold

King Louis XVI and Marie Antoinette

in the northeast, only to be captured just short of their destination, at Varennes, and brought back to Paris. Until this point most people had supported the idea of a constitutional monarch, but now the king was labelled a traitor.

Key dates

5 May 1789 The Estates-General convenes

20 June 1789 The Tennis Court Oath

14 July 1789 The storming of the Bastille begins the Revolution

26 August 1789 Declaration of the Rights of Man and the Citizen

6 October 1789 Versailles is stormed; Louis XVI and his family are returned to Paris as prisoners

21 June 1791 The royal family's "Flight to Varennes" is foiled

21 September 1792 The monarchy is formally abolished

1792–4 "The Terror"

21 January 1793 Louis XVI is found guilty of treason and executed

16 October 1793 Execution of Marie Antoinette

28 July 1794 Robespierre is guillotined; end of the Terror

9 November 1799 Napoleon seizes power after putting down a Royalist revolt

Prussian roulette

The rest of Europe was out to crush the Revolution, so the revolutionaries, fearing invasion, took a gamble and declared war on Prussia and Austria, in April 1792. It wasn't long before the enemy was almost at the gates of Paris. Louis, with his Austrian wife, was

The revolutionary army's victory over Prussia at Valmy

accused by the radicals of being a foreign stooge. A mob stormed the Tuileries and took the royal family to the medieval Temple prison. In September, in a riot of blood-letting, working-class Parisians went on the rampage, killing 1,200 prisoners before marching off to win the Battle of Valmy. Back home, a guillotine was erected in Place de la Concorde to deal with their internal enemies.

Everything changes

The Revolution wasn't just against the monarchy but also the power of the Catholic church, which was abolished. Notre-Dame was used as a warehouse. It was out with the old Christian calendar too. Each day was now made up of ten hours, each 100 minutes long, and a week was ten days long. Three weeks made up a month, and the twelve months were given new names related to the weather in northern France. This quirky calendar never really caught on, however, largely because such a long week meant there was only one day off in every ten. Meanwhile a new metric system of weights and measures was adopted and is still in use today.

Heads will roll

The Revolution took a radical turn, led by a ferocious faction called the Jacobins. A Committee of Public Safety, led by Danton, Marat and Robespierre, instigated "the Great Terror", in which 300,000 people were arrested and 20,000 executed in Paris alone. In January 1793, Louis XVI was taken to Place de la

Concorde and guillotined in front of a huge crowd. In October Marie Antoinette followed her husband to the scaffold, jeered by ghoulish spectators. However, in July 1794 the Jacobins were overthrown by a more moderate faction, and Robespierre and his cronies were sent to the guillotine themselves.

A rising star

Revolutionary France faced enemies from within as well as abroad, and was ever more dependent on its armies. In 1795 a royalist revolt was put down by a young Corsican general, Napoleon Bonaparte, who dispersed the mob by firing into it with cannons at point-blank range.

Napoleon was soon a national hero. His military successes in Italy and Egypt conquered new territories for France. In 1799 he seized power in a military coup and installed himself as First Consul. By 1804 he had crowned himself Emperor of France, at Notre-Dame.

The end of an era

For many years, Napoleon's power expanded across the continent. It was Russia that called a halt to his adventures, when his 1812 march towards Moscow went disastrously wrong. By 1814 the Russians, Prussians and British occupied Paris. Napoleon was exiled on the island of Elba but he soon returned, leading an army against the British at Waterloo. This was his final defeat, and he was again sent into exile on the island of St Helena, where he died in 1821.

Traditional artists' market in the Place du Tertre in Montmartre

Exploring
PARIS

Ile de la Cité
& Ile St-Louis

The illustrious history of Paris began on a humble boat-shaped island on the Seine, the Ile de la Cité. Once home to an Astérix-style village, the island grew with the arrival of the Romans, resumed its growth under the Franks and the Capetian kings and went on to become France's political and religious centre. Explore Roman remains, churches and parks, before crossing the Pont St-Louis to stroll around the Ile St-Louis.

Tuileries, Opéra & Montmartre

Champs-Elysées & Trocadéro

Beaubourg & the Marais

Eiffel Tower & Les Invalides

Ile de la Cité & Ile St-Louis

St-Germain & the Latin Quarter

Luxembourg & Montparnasse

Highlights

Notre-Dame
Visit the home of the famous hunchback, glare at the gargoyles and gaze out over the rooftops of Paris from the cathedral's towers (see pp64–5).

Crypte Archéologique
Step back in time and see the remains of the ancient Gaulish settlement, the Roman quayside and medieval houses (see p65).

Ile St-Louis
Graze along Rue St-Louis-en-l'Ile and taste the best ice cream in the city. Then picnic on the most romantic quaysides in Paris (see p68).

Paris Plages
In summer, the Seine's right bank turns into a real beach, with entertainers, cafés and all kinds of fun (see p68).

Conciergerie
Learn about French history's grizzly side on the site where hundreds of people were condemned to the guillotine (see pp70–71).

Pont Neuf
Stroll across the city's oldest bridge, browse the second-hand bookstores on the riverbank, or picnic in the Square du Vert-Galant on the tip of Ile de la Cité (see p72).

Above *Stunning stained glass in Sainte-Chapelle*
Left *Notre-Dame's legendary gargoyles keeping a watch over Paris from the cathedral's north tower*

The Best of
Ile de la Cité & Ile St-Louis

This is the historic centre of Paris, and should be the first stop on any itinerary. Although it is in the heart of the city, there is plenty to do outdoors. Visit a historic prison, parks, cathedrals and crypts, watch lively street entertainers, or enjoy picnics and fantastic food beside the river. Admire the city from Notre-Dame's towers, enjoy a drink on Quai Montebello and, if everyone is still awake, go for a moonlit stroll.

Kings, knights and history lovers

March like a Roman soldier across the **Petit Pont** (see p66) and salute Charlemagne, King of the Franks. Step back in time and hunt for the medieval street plan on the square in front of **Notre-Dame** (see p64–5). Gaze in wonder at the stained-glass windows in the **Sainte-Chapelle** (see p72), the most beautiful church in Paris, built by King Louis IX, then shudder in the shadow of **St-Germain l'Auxerrois** (see p73) on the Right Bank. When the cathedral's bell tolled in 1572 it signalled the start of the massacre of thousands of Protestants on St Bartholomew's Day. Walk across the **Pont Neuf** (see p72), the oldest bridge in the city, and meet Henri IV, who was the Protestants'

leader until he converted to Catholicism. Visit Marie Antoinette's ghost in her cell in the **Conciergerie** (see pp70–71) and be on your best behaviour outside Baron Haussmann's giant police headquarters. Learn about the horrors of World War II at the **Mémorial des Martyrs de la Déportation** (see p65).

Literary leanings

Read the Bible like a comic strip on the stained-glass windows of **Sainte-Chapelle** and on the chancel screen in **Notre-Dame**, or learn a few Latin phrases on the **Petit Pont**, where students studied in Latin in the open air in medieval times. Pick up a book to read or just stock up on old, new and second-hand ones,

Below The dazzling stained glass of the Sainte-Chapelle, depicting Bible stories in magnificent colour

Above The Seine flowing under the beautifully lit Pont Neuf with the Conciergerie in the background
Middle Colourful flowers on sale at the Marché aux Fleurs
Bottom Delicious cakes tempting window-shoppers

such as the *Babar the Elephant* series, from the legendary **Shakespeare and Company** *(see p65)*, a bookstore on the Left Bank. Both Victor Hugo's *Hunchback of Notre-Dame* and the cartoon strip adventure *Astérix and the Golden Sickle* are set in this area.

Hunger pangs

Walk down **Rue St-Louis-en-l'Ile** *(see p68)* for the town's best croissants, cheese and marzipan pigs, or pick up an ice cream cone at the famous **Berthillon** *(see p68)*. Savour a chocolate crêpe and admire the view on Quai de Bourbon, or stroll down the Quai Montebello to sip a cold drink at one of its cafés. Stock up for an outing by the Seine, one of the most romantic places in the world to picnic at any time of the day or night.

Out in the open

Take a break at **Place Dauphine** *(see p71)*, a good place to kick a ball around, or head for the **Square du Vert-Galant** *(see p72)*, which sticks out into the Seine like a boat's prow. Henri IV designed this square as a place simply to have fun. Admire the flowers in the **Marché aux Fleurs** *(see p67)* and whistle at the birds on a Sunday morning at the **Marché aux Oiseaux** *(see p67)*. In summer, cool off at **Paris Plages** *(see p68)* when the riverbank turns into a street party with deck chairs and real sand, plus a view of **Notre-Dame** and the **Conciergerie's** fairytale towers. In autumn, take a romantic stroll around the **Ile St-Louis** *(see p68)* at sunset. In winter, take to the ice outside the **Hôtel de Ville** *(see p69)*.

Notre-Dame and around

No fewer than 13 bridges, including the famous Pont Neuf, lead across to the Ile de la Cité and Ile St-Louis, the two small islands on the Seine that are both a pleasure to explore on foot. The views here are fantastic at any time of the day but are more magical in the evening when there are fewer tourists around. Many of the sights are outdoors, so choose a fine day and bring a picnic. On Sundays and public holidays, the Voie Georges Pompidou on the Seine's Right Bank is closed to traffic, and a haven for rollerbladers and cyclists.

Bookstore, reading library and literary meeting place Shakespeare and Company

Ile de la Cité & Ile St-Louis

Conciergerie p70

Notre-Dame p64

Statue of Charlemagne near Notre-Dame

Plants for sale at the Marché aux Fleurs, Paris's year-round flower market

The Lowdown

🚃 **Métro** Cité or St-Michel, line 4; Châtelet, lines 1, 4, 11 & 14; Pont Marie, line 7; Hôtel de Ville, line 1 or Pont Neuf, line 7. **RER** St-Michel, lines B & C or Châtelet les Halles, lines A, B & D. **Bus** 21, 38, 47, 58, 67, 70, 75, 76, 81, 85, 86, 87 & 96.

🚤 **River boat** Quai de Montebello & Quai de l'Hotel de Ville

🛒 **Supermarket** Franprix, 135 Rue St-Antoine, 75004; 35 Rue Berger, 75001; 31 Rue Mazarine, 75006; 2 Rue Marengo, 75001
Markets Marché aux Fleurs (flower market) and Marché aux Oiseaux (bird market) (see p67)

🎪 **Festivals** Fête du Pain (May); www.fetedupain.com. La Course des Garçons de Café (late Jun & early Jul); www.waitersrace.com. Christmas Crèche, Notre-Dame (Dec–Jan) & Eglise St-Germain-l'Auxerrois (Dec). Ice-skating rink, Pl de l'Hôtel de Ville (Dec)

➕ **Pharmacy** Pharmacie des Halles, 10 Blvd de Sébastopol, 75001; 01 42 72 03 23; open till midnight Mon–Sat, till 10pm Sun

🛝 **Nearest playgrounds** Square Jean XXIII, Pl du Parvis Notre-Dame, 75004; dawn–dusk (see p65). Square Albert Schweitzer, corner of Rue de l'Hotel de Ville and Rue des Nonnains d'Hyères, 75004; dawn–dusk (see p68). Square de la Tour St-Jacques, Rue de Rivoli, 75004; dawn–dusk (see p68)

Places of interest

SIGHTS
1. Notre-Dame
2. Statue of Charlemagne
3. Petit Pont
4. Marché aux Fleurs et aux Oiseaux & Quai de la Mégisserie
5. Ile St-Louis
6. Paris Plages on the Right Bank
7. Hôtel de Ville
8. Conciergerie
9. Sainte-Chapelle
10. Pont Neuf
11. St-Germain-l'Auxerrois

● EAT AND DRINK
1. Franprix
2. Café la Bûcherie
3. Le Paradis du Fruit
4. Metamorphosis
5. La Charlotte de l'Isle
6. La Tour d'Argent
7. Amorino
8. Boulangerie Pâtisserie des Deux Ponts
9. De Neuville
10. Le Flore en l'Ile
11. Berthillon
12. Boulangerie Martin
13. Boulangerie Heurtier
14. Café Livre
15. Miss Manon
16. L'Ebouillanté
17. Carrefour Market
18. Wanna Juice
19. Chez Clement
20. Chez Fernand
21. Au Bougnat
22. La Nouvelle Marinara
23. Le Fumoir

● SHOPPING
1. Shakespeare and Company
See also Conciergerie (p70)

● WHERE TO STAY
1. Citadines St-Germain-des-Prés
2. Hôtel Britannique
3. Hôtel du Jeu de Paume
4. Relais du Louvre
5. Résidence Le Petit Châtelet

0 metres 400
0 yards 400

PLACE G. POMPIDOU
St-Merri
RUE DU RENARD
RUE DE LA VERRERIE
R STE CROIX DE LA BRETONNERIE
R STE CROIX
ARCHIVES
RUE DES
RUE DU TEMPLE
R DE MOUSSY
R DU BOURG TIBOURG
RUE VIEILLE DU TEMPLE
RUE DES ROSIERS
R DU ROI DE SICILE
R F DUVAL
RUE PAVEE
Hôtel de Ville
Hôtel de Ville
PL DE L'HOTEL DE VILLE
RUE DE RIVOLI
PLACE ST GERVAIS
RUE FRANCOIS MIRON
St-Gervais St-Protais
R DES BARRES
RUE GEOFFROY L'ASNIER
RUE DE JOUY
RUE DE FOURCY
RUE DES NONNAINS D'HYERES
St-Paul
RUE ST ANTOINE
RUE CHARLEMAGNE
RUE SAINT PAUL
R NEUVE ST PIERRE
R DE L'AVE MARIA
R CHARLES V
R DES LIONS ST PAUL
R DU PETIT MUSC
R DE L'HOTEL DE VILLE
R DU FAUCONNIER
QUAI DE L'HOTEL DE VILLE
Quai de l'Hôtel de Ville
Pont Louis Philippe
VOIE GEORGES POMPIDOU
Pont Marie
La Seine
QUAI DES CELESTINS
BLVD HENRI IV
Pont St-Louis
QUAI DE BOURBON
RUE LE REGRATTIER
RUE ST-LOUIS
RUE DES DEUX PONTS
Pont Marie
QUAI D'ANJOU
SQUARE DE L'AVE MARIA
SQUARE H GALLI
Sully Morland
SQUARE JEAN XXII
QUAI D'ORLEANS
RUE BUDE
RUE POULLETIER
Ile St-Louis
ILE ST-LOUIS
QUAI DE BETHUNE
QUAI DE LA TOURNELLE
Pont de la Tournelle
PONT DE SULLY
SQUARE BARYE
Statue of Saint Geneviève
SQUARE DE L'ILE DE FRANCE
Pont St-Louis
QUAI DE LA TOURNELLE

① Notre-Dame
History, hunchbacks and gargoyles

Home to Victor Hugo's fictional hunchback, Quasimodo, Notre-Dame is over 850 years old. Built on the site of a Roman temple, it took over a century to complete and is covered with swooping buttresses and funny-faced gargoyles. During the Revolution it was looted and used as a wine warehouse. The cathedral has witnessed many dramatic events in French history – such as when, in 1804, Napoleon crowned himself emperor here instead of waiting for the Pope to do it for him.

Stained-glass rose window, Notre-Dame

Key Features

Biblical characters Covered in easily recognizable biblical characters, the façade was known as the "poor man's bible". When the cathedral was built, most Parisians were unable to read.

The spire Added by the architect Viollet-le-Duc in the 19th century, the spire soars to a height of 96 m (315 ft).

Rose windows Their colours are magnificent on a sunny day. Louis IX donated the southern window.

Crown of Thorns Viollet-le-Duc designed the gilded, diamond-encrusted shrine that holds this and other famous relics on display in the Treasury.

Gothic masterpiece Finished in 1330, the cathedral is 130 m (430 ft) tall and features flying buttresses, a large transept and 69-m (228-ft) high towers.

Gargoyles and chimeras Glare up at these creatures on the façade and in the tower where they sit hunched over.

Chancel screen In the centre of the church, the chancel screen tells the story of the life of Jesus like a medieval comic strip.

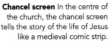

The Lowdown

Map reference 11 A6
Address 6 Pl du Parvis-Notre-Dame, Pl Jean-Paul II, 75004; 01 42 34 56 10; www. notredamedeparis.fr. Towers: 01 53 40 60 80 & 01 53 10 07 00; http://notre-dame-de-paris. monuments-nationaux.fr

Métro Cité or St-Michel, line 4, or Châtelet, lines 1, 4 & 14. **RER** St-Michel, lines B & C. **Bus** 21, 24, 27, 38, 47, 85 & 96. **River boat** Quai de Montebello

Open Cathedral: 8am–6:45pm; till 7:15pm Sat & Sun. Treasury: 9.30am–6pm; from 1:30pm Sun. Towers Apr–Sep: 10am–6:30pm

daily; Jul–Aug: 10am–6:30pm Mon–Fri; 10am–11pm Sat & Sun; Oct–Mar: 10am–5:30pm daily. For access to the towers, climb the 387 steps from Rue du Cloître.

Price Cathedral: free. Towers: €18–28; under 18s & under 26s with EU passport free. Treasury: €8–18

Skipping the queue Paris Museum Pass accepted. To avoid long queues for the towers, visit in the evening when there are fewer people, or early in the day before the crowds arrive.

Guided tours In English at 2pm Wed & Thu & at 2:30pm on Sat. English audio guide €5

Age range 3 plus; under 12s to be accompanied by adults

Activities Magic shows in Metamorphosis; 01 43 54 08 08

Allow 2–3 hours

Wheelchair access Limited

Toilets By the cathedral exit

Good family value?
Entry to Notre-Dame is free. Hence even if you spend a short time in it you will not feel short-changed. Kids love to climb up the towers and everyone loves the view.

Letting off steam

Twirl around the square in front of the cathedral like Esmeralda, the gypsy dancer in Victor Hugo's novel *Notre Dame de Paris* (1831), and stroll along the quayside. Square Jean XXIII, behind Notre-Dame, is a pretty park with a sandpit. In summer, head for the **Paris Plages on the Right Bank** *(see p68)*, when the main road along the river is transformed into "beaches" with real sand, water fountains and activities. In winter, go skating at the **Place de l'Hôtel de Ville** *(see p69)*.

Square Jean XXIII with Notre-Dame in the background

Eat and drink

Picnic: under €25; Snacks: €25–45; Real Meal: €45–90; Family treat: over €90 (based on a family of four)

PICNIC Franprix *(135 Rue St-Antoine, 75004)* sells picnic supplies, which can be enjoyed in the park alongside the cathedral.

SNACKS Café la Bûcherie *(41 Rue Bûcherie, 75005; 01 43 54 24 52; 7am–2am daily)* is a great spot to unwind with a drink and nibbles and has splendid views of Notre-Dame.

REAL MEAL Le Paradis du Fruit *(2 Place Saint Michel, 75006; 09 79 71 80 79)* is a family-friendly French chain that specializes in fresh juices and smoothies and also serves healthy but hearty dishes.

FAMILY TREAT Metamorphosis *(opposite 3 Quai Montebello, 75005; 01 43 54 08 08; www. metamorphosis-spectacle.fr; Apr– Sep: 7:30pm Tue–Sat, 12:30pm Sun)* serves classic French dishes aboard a moored barge, but the real draws are the magic shows that take place during dinner and Sunday brunch.

Shopping

Flick through English books in **Shakespeare and Company** *(37 Rue de la Bûcherie, 75005)* and in the green boxes of the Bouquinistes, who have been selling books on the Seine's banks since the 16th century. After the Revolution they peddled entire libraries that had been seized from noble families.

Find out more

DIGITAL The cathedral's website *www.notredameparis.fr/- Children-s-site* has a children's corner. Watch the video *General de Gaulle at Notre Dame on 26 August 1944* at *http://tinyurl.com/3jyujw5* and *King Babar hunting Father Christmas in Paris* in the Babar Christmas Special at *http://tinyurl. com/3v7gvto*. Discover Roman Paris at *www.paris.culture.fr/en/*
FILM Disney's *Hunchback of Notre Dame* (1996) will show kids how the cathedral dominated medieval Paris.

Next stop...

A CRYPT AND A MEMORIAL Visit the **Crypte Archéologique** *(Pl Jean Paul II, Parvis de Notre-Dame, 75004; 01 55 42 50 10; www.crypte. paris.fr)* in front of Notre-Dame. The city's Roman remains, as well as medieval shops and pavements, can be seen here. The **Mémorial des Martyrs de la Déportation** *(Sq de l'Ile de France, 75004; 01 46 33 87 56)* behind the cathedral commemorates the deportation of 200,000 men, women and children to Nazi concentration camps.

Gallo-Roman ruins inside the Crypte Archéologique

② Statue of Charlemagne
Master of all he surveyed

An imposing statue of Charlemagne (reigned 768–814) stands on the southern side of the square next to Notre-Dame. Charlemagne ruled over vast swathes of territory that today make up modern-day France and most of Central Europe, conquered by the Franks thanks to their powerful cavalry. His campaigns in Spain are recounted in the epic poem, *La Chanson de Roland* (The Song of Roland), the oldest surviving major work in French literature. Charlemagne was stately, fair-headed and tall, with a disproportionately thick neck; he fathered 20 children. A great patron of scholars from all over Europe, he himself never learnt to read or write. Although his statue occupies pride of place on Ile de la Cité, he only ever visited Paris twice; after the death of his father, Pepin, he moved the capital to Aix-la-Chapelle, or Aachen as it is known in German, where he liked to take the waters.

Letting off steam

The nearest bridge, Pont au Double, is a nice place to promenade and watch the rollerbladers swing by. It was originally built in 1623–34 to take patients to the Hôtel Dieu hospital; they were charged double

Charlemagne's statue stands tall in Square Jean XXIII, next to Notre-Dame

the normal crossing toll, hence the name. The bridge leads over to Square René Viviani on the Left Bank, which is good for a run-about and has free Wi-Fi. It is home to the oldest tree in Paris, planted in 1601. The tree's upper branches were blown off by a shell in World War I.

Stroll along the Seine like King Babar in search of Father Christmas but do not, like Madeline, end up in it – she was standing on the Pont au Double's balustrades when she fell.

③ Petit Pont
Follow in the footsteps of Babar and Madeline

The Romans built the first wooden bridge across the Seine at the exact spot where the modern Petit Pont spans the river, which is also the narrowest crossing point. The bridge was washed away by floods or destroyed by fire at least 14 times and was covered in teetering houses until 1719. The current bridge dates back to 1853. In Roman times, it linked the temples and villas on the Ile de la Cité to the town of Lutetia, which extended up to Mont-Ste-Geneviève, where the baths, the theatre and the

Book stalls along Quai de Montebello, with Notre-Dame in the background

The Lowdown

- 🌐 **Map reference** 11 A6
  Address PI du Parvis
  Notre-Dame, 75004
- 🚗 **Métro** Cité or St-Michel, line 4.
  RER St-Michel, lines B & C. **Bus** 21, 24, 27, 38, 47, 85 & 96. **River boat** Quai de Montebello
- 🍽 **Eat and drink** *Real meal* La Charlotte de l'Isle (24 Rue St-Louis-en-l'Ile, 75004; 01 43 54 25 83; http://lacharlottedelisle.fr; *puppet shows on Wed)* serves tea and cakes. *Family treat* La Tour d'Argent (15 Quai de la Tournelle, 75005; 01 43 54 23 31; www.latourdargent.com), founded in 1582, is an expensive restaurant that should interest older kids as it was the model for Gusteau's restaurant in the film *Ratatouille*. Diners having duck, raised on a farm in Challans, get a card with the bird's serial number.
- 🚻 **Toilets** By the cathedral exit

The Lowdown

- 🌐 **Map reference** 11 A6
  Address Quai Voltaire, 75005 to Quai de la Tournelle, 75006
- 🚗 **Métro** St-Michel, line 4. **RER** St-Michel, lines B & C. **Bus** 21, 38, 47, 58, 85 & 96. **River boat** Quai de Montebello
- 🍽 **Eat and drink** *Picnic* Amorino (47 Rue St-Louis-en-l'Ile, 75004; 01 44 07 48 08) is popular for ice cream and has shorter queues than the more famous Berthillon *(see p68)*. *Snacks* Boulangerie Pâtisserie des Deux Ponts (35 Rue des Deux Ponts, 75004) is a charming bakery, which sells croissants, bread and hot dogs in baguettes.
- 🚻 **Toilets** No

forum were located. More than 8,000 people lived in Lutetia, which was laid out on a regular grid plan. Rue St-Jacques, which runs south from the bridge, is one of the city's oldest streets, and follows the line of the main north-south axis of the Roman town, the *cardus maximus*.

The Seine's banks along Notre-Dame grace the pages of many children's books. Jean de Brunhoff's gentle King Babar and Ludwig Bemelmans' spunky heroine Madeline have both had adventures here.

Take cover

Across the Petit Pont from the square in front of Notre-Dame is the wonderfully eccentric bookstore **Shakespeare and Company** (see p65). After a shot of culture, unwind in one of the cafés nearby. On Monday nights, look out for famous authors, who are invited for a drink before the weekly reading in the shop.

④ Marché aux Fleurs et aux Oiseaux & Quai de la Mégisserie

Screeching parrots, butchers, doctors and detectives

Paris's biggest and best flower market spreads out daily on Ile de la Cité. On Sundays, caged birds and little bunnies join the exotic cacti and colourful flowers. Across the river on Quai de la Mégisserie is the city's pet-shop corner, full of ducks, chicks and other little creatures.

In the Middle Ages, the Place Louis Lépine was where the butchers carried out their trade, and the area stank to high heaven. There was also a small Jewish ghetto, while in Roman times, St Denis, the patron of Paris, was imprisoned here.

On the eastern side of the square is Hôtel Dieu, Paris's oldest hospital. Founded as early as the 7th century, it took care of the poor and sick, but often bred more diseases than it could cure, with up to five patients to a bed. Many important medical discoveries have been made here, and this was where one of the first surgeons, Ambroise Paré (1510–90), wielded his scalpel. Today it is home to the city's bustling Accident and Emergency Department.

Just southwest of the market is No. 36, Quai des Orfèvres, the headquarters of the Paris police force known as PJ 36. Founded in 1812, it provided the model for Scotland Yard and the FBI and inspired a whole gaggle of films and detective stories, including Inspector Maigret.

Hôtel Dieu, which was once an orphanage, is now a city hospital

Take cover

Gaze in wonder at the dizzyingly high ceiling and stunning stained glass inside **Sainte-Chapelle** (*see p72*), a Gothic masterpiece restored by Viollet-le-Duc and others in the mid-19th century.

The Lowdown

- 🌐 **Map ref** 10 G4
  Address Pl Louis-Lépine, 75004
- 🚗 **Métro** Cité, line 4. **RER** St-Michel, lines B & C. **Bus** 21, 38, 47, 58, 85 & 96. **River boat** Quai de Montebello
- 🕐 **Open** Marché aux Fleurs (flower market): 8am–7:30pm daily. Marché aux Oiseaux (bird market): 8am–7pm Sun
- 👫 **Age range** All ages
- 🍴 **Eat and drink** *Picnic* De Neuville (63 Rue St-Louis-en-l'Ile, 75004) sells chocolate bars spiced up with exotic flavours, and, in summer, ice cream. *Real meal* Le Flore en l'Ile (42 Quai d'Orleans, 75004; 01 43 29 88 27) is a good stop for lunch and also sells Berthillon (*see p68*) ice cream.
- 🚻 **Toilets** No

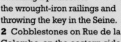

The Marché aux Fleurs, Paris's main flower market

Picnic under €25; **Snacks** €25–45; **Real meal** €45–90; **Family Treat** over €90 (based on a family of four)

Entertainers on Pont de Sully, at the eastern end of Ile St-Louis

⑤ Ile St-Louis

A village in the heart of a city

Until 1614, when the 13-year-old Louis XIII was persuaded that building some stylish town houses was a good idea, Ile St-Louis was known as the Ile des Vaches after the cows that grazed here. It remains a tranquil place with a village-like feel, thanks to its narrow streets. Rue St-Louis-en-l'Ile is a foody paradise, so there is a lot of grazing going on still. Lined with historic houses, it is a fun place to walk and peruse the shops. Look out for the dragons on No. 51, and No. 54, which was once a real tennis court.

Many famous people have lived on the Ile St-Louis, with its tree-lined quays, among them the philosopher Voltaire, the scientist Marie Curie and the French president from 1969–74, Georges Pompidou. In 1924, one resident, the poet Roger Dévigne, went as far as to declare it an independent republic.

Letting off steam

There is a playground on Square Albert Schweitzer and the pleasant garden of Square Barye, by Pont de Sully. Quai de Bourbon is a nice spot for a quick sit-down before walking across Pont des Tournelles to see the statue of the city's patron saint, Saint Geneviève, who, according to legend, saved Paris from destruction by Attila the Hun.

⑥ Paris Plages on the Right Bank

Sand, sun and deck chairs

Thanks to the modernizing zeal of President Pompidou, there has been a busy highway running along the Right Bank since the 1960s, but at the height of summer, for four weeks in July and August, everything changes. The cars disappear and the fun begins on this stretch of the Right Bank, running from the Louvre to Pont de Sully. Deck chairs line the Seine on an artificial sandy beach and there are street entertainers, water features, plenty of activities for children and a host of cafés. This area is closed to traffic on Sundays and public holidays all the year round.

The views here across from the river to the islands are beautiful and undeniably romantic. The Quai aux Fleurs, on the northeastern side of Île de la Cité, is famous for the medieval romance between 39-year-old scholar Pierre Abélard and 17-year-old Héloïse, the niece of a canon. When her uncle found out about the relationship he was furious, and locked her up in a convent. Their passionate letters of love and loss are legendary.

Close by is Square de la Tour St-Jacques. The tower is all that now remains of the Church of St-Jacques, which was destroyed in the Revolution.

Take cover

If the sun is too strong or the weather turns nasty, head east. The winding medieval streets of the **Marais** (see p81) are full of fascinating shops and lovely cafés.

The Lowdown

- 🌐 **Map reference** 10 H5
  Address Voie Georges Pompidou, 75004; www.paris.fr/parisplages
- 🚇 **Métro** Pont Neuf, line 4, Louvre–Rivoli or Hôtel de Ville, line 1. **Bus** 70, 74, 72 & 96 **River boat** Quai de l'Hôtel de Ville
- 🍴 **Eat and drink** *Picnic* Boulangerie Heurtier (*2 Rue de la Verrerie, 75004; 01 40 27 91 97; closed Mon*) sells gourmet sandwiches. *Real Meal* Café Livres (*10 Rue Saint Martin, 75004; 01 42 72 18 13; 9:30am–11pm Mon–Sat, 10am–8pm Sun*) offers tasty food.
- 🚻 **Toilets** In summer along the beach and on Pl de l'Hôtel de Ville

The Lowdown

- 🌐 **Map reference** 11 B6
  Address 75004
- 🚇 **Métro** Pont Marie, line 7. **RER** St-Michel, line C. **Bus** 67, 86 & 87 **River boat** Quai de Montebello
- 🍴 **Eat and drink** *Picnic* Berthillon (*29–31 Rue St-Louis-en-l'Ile, 75004; 01 43 54 31 61; www.berthillon.fr*) is famed for its ice cream. *Snacks* Boulangerie Martin (*40 Rue St-Louis-en-l'Ile, 75004; 01 43 54 69 48*) makes the best croissants in town.
- 🚻 **Toilets** No

Paris Plages, with deck chairs and parasols lined up along the Seine

Above Hôtel de Ville (Town Hall) across the Pont d'Arcole
Below right Bronze allegorical figure of Art, in front of the Hôtel de Ville

⑦ Hôtel de Ville

Rebuilding, organizing and getting down to business

The Hôtel de Ville, across Pont d'Arcole from Ile de la Cité, occupies what has been the site of the town hall since 1357, when the city merchants first took charge of organizing Paris. The original building was replaced with a grand, Renaissance-style city hall that took nearly a century (1533–1628) to build. This was burnt down during the Paris Commune of 1871, but its replacement was built in virtually the same style, covered in sculptures of famous Parisians made by some of the city's most renowned artists. The 18th-century mathematician Jean le Rond d'Alembert was sculpted by Auguste Rodin in a work that graces the front façade.

Since ancient times, the Right Bank was a place where business was conducted and goods were unloaded. Workers would come to the Place de l'Hôtel de Ville, then called Place de Grève, looking for work. The expression *en grève* (on strike) originally denoted someone who was not working.

In late June, the Place de l'Hôtel de Ville is the start- and end-point of the 8-km (5-mile) waiters' race, where restaurant staff race round the streets with full trays of drinks. To make it even harder, they run barefoot.

Letting off steam

The square in front of the Hôtel de Ville is a great place for kids. There is an old-fashioned carousel and, in winter, an ice-skating rink.

The Lowdown

- 🌐 **Map ref** 11 B5
  Address Pl de l'Hôtel de Ville, 75004; 01 42 76 00 40
- 🚇 **Métro** Hôtel de Ville, line 1.
  Bus 70, 74, 72, & 96. **River boat** Quai de l'Hôtel de Ville
- 🕐 **Open** Only for temporary exhibitions and Journées du Patrimoine (Heritage Days), celebrated annually in Sep
- 🚻 **Age range** All ages
- ♿ **Wheelchair access** Yes
- 🍽 **Eat and drink** Picnic Miss Manon (87 Rue St Antoine, 75004) is a delightful *boulangerie* (bakery), which offers an assortment of delicious sandwiches, quiches and cakes. Head to the Square de la Tour St-Jacques for a picnic. *Real meal* L'Ebouillanté (6 Rue des Barres, 75004; 01 42 74 70 52; noon–10pm; closed Mon), on a pedestrianized cobbled street behind the church of St-Gervais-et-St-Protais, sells delicious crêpes and tarte tatin.
- 🚻 **Toilets** On Pl de l'Hôtel de Ville

⑧ Conciergerie
Fairy tale towers fit for a torturer

If anywhere in Paris must be haunted, this is it. The Conciergerie is the oldest remaining part of France's original royal palace, rebuilt by Philippe le Bel, or Philip the Fair, around 1300. After Charles V moved to the Louvre, it became a rat-infested prison synonymous with death and torture under the watchful eye of a *concierge*, or steward. In 1793, the Revolutionary Tribunal condemned thousands to death here during the Reign of Terror. The Revolution's most prominent prisoners – including Marie Antoinette, Danton and Robespierre – all spent their final night here before being taken to the guillotine. The Conciergerie remained a prison until 1914.

Key Features

① **Cour des Femmes** Women had an outdoor space in the form of a courtyard in which they could get fresh air and even do their washing.

② **Chapelle des Girondins** The Girondins, a group of moderates, executed by the radical Jacobin revolutionaries, lend their name to this chapel.

③ **Marie Antoinette's Cell** A chapel marks the spot where the famous queen was held prisoner for nine months.

④ **Grooming Room** The Salle de Toilette is where prisoners were stripped of their belongings and had their hair shaved.

⑤ **Rue de Paris** Named after "Monsieur de Paris", the nickname of the executioner, this is where the poorest prisoners slept on straw crammed in tiny cells.

Prices given are for a family of four

Entrance/ Welcome desk

① ③② ④ ⑧ ⑦ ⑤ ⑥

Tour d'Argent

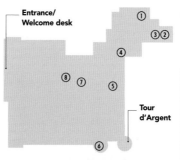

⑥ **Tour de César and Tour d'Argent** These are the remains of the former royal palace (not open to the public).

⑦ **Salle des Gens d'Armes** The largest surviving medieval hall in Europe, it was used as a dining room for the king's servants and could hold up to 2,000 people.

⑧ **Black marble table** This is a fragment of a 17th-century military constables' table.

The Lowdown

🌐 **Map reference** 10 G5
Address 2 Blvd du Palais, 75001; 01 53 40 60 80; www.conciergerie.monuments-nationaux.fr/en

🚗 **Métro** Cité or St-Michel, line 4. **RER** St-Michel, lines B & C. **Bus** 21, 24, 27, 38, 58, 81 & 85. **River boat** Quai de Montebello

🕐 **Open** 9:30am–6pm daily; closed 1 Jan, 1 May & 25 Dec

💶 **Price** €17; under 18s free; EU citizens under 26s free

👪 **Skipping the queue** Paris Museum Pass accepted and sold here; combined ticket with Sainte-Chapelle €13.50 per person

🎫 **Guided tours** Tours in English can be arranged three weeks in advance; 01 44 54 19 30

👫 **Age range** All ages

🕐 **Allow** 1 hour

♿ **Wheelchair access** No

☕ **Café** No

🛍 **Shop** In the Salle des Gens d'Armes; sells books and games

🚻 **Toilets** In the Tour d'Argent

Good family value?
History buffs will enjoy exploring this notorious prison. Read up about the Revolution beforehand as there is very little explanation aimed at children inside.

The ancient, leafy square of Place Dauphine

Letting off steam

After a lesson in history, watch people playing *boules* (a game played with metal balls) and kick a ball around in **Place Dauphine** (enter by Rue Henri-Robert, 75001), laid out by Henri IV to honour his son and heir, Louis. In the summer, admire the storybook towers of the Conciergerie and build sandcastles on the Right Bank during the popular **Paris Plages** (see p68).

Eat and drink

Picnic: under €25; Snacks: €25–45; Real meal: €45–90; Family treat: over €90 (based on a family of four)

PICNIC Carrefour Market (79 Rue de Seine, 75006; 01 43 25 65 03; www.carrefour.fr) is good for supplies. Place Dauphine or the Square du Vert-Galant (see p72) are the best places to picnic.
SNACKS Wanna Juice (65 Rue St-André des Arts, 75006; 01 46 34 11 90; www.wannajuice.com; 8:30am–7pm daily, from 10am Sat & Sun) for smoothies and light bites.
REAL MEAL Chez Clement (Pl St-André des Arts, 75006; 01 56 81 32 00; www.chezclement.com; 11:30am–11:30pm daily) has great children's menus. In summer enjoy eating outside on the terrace.
FAMILY TREAT Chez Fernand (9 Rue Christine, 75006; 01 43 25 18 55; noon–2:30pm, 7–11pm daily) is a neighbourhood bistro specialising in dishes from Normandy.

Shopping

Just across the Seine on the Left Bank is a lively shopping street, the Rue St-André des Arts, or head to the Right Bank for boutique shops along Rue de Rivoli.

Find out more

DIGITAL Find videos, games and puzzles for kids on the French Revolution at www.neok12.com/French-Revolution.htm. Games for children based around France's top tourist sights can be found at www.monuments-nationaux.fr/enfants/home_en.htm
FILM In *The Scarlet Pimpernel* (1934), a British aristocrat runs secret missions to rescue the condemned, including Louis XVII, in Robespierre's Paris. The cartoon version of Charles Dickens' novel *A Tale of Two Cities* (2002) is set in Paris and London during the Revolution.

Next stop...

CENTRE POMPIDOU After all that history it is fun to do something completely different. The crazy, post-modernist Centre Pompidou (see pp80–81) is a 15-minute walk across Pont au Change and up Boulevard Sébastopol. Marvel at the coloured pipes on the outside of the building. Enjoy watching some entertaining street theatre here before riding up the bubble-like escalators to admire the lovely views.

Street entertainers putting on a show at the Centre Pompidou

⑨ Sainte-Chapelle
Psychedelic heaven

The only French king to be made a saint, the devout Louis IX was a keen collector of relics. In 1239, he built the breathtakingly beautiful Sainte-Chapelle to house his prize acquisitions, including the Crown of Thorns now kept at Notre-Dame (*see p64*) and a fragment of Christ's Cross. The construction of this architectural masterpiece, which was built in just ten years, also served to express the absolute power of the king by the right of God.

Built in Flamboyant-Gothic style, the chapel has some of the finest medieval stained-glass windows in the world. A riot of dazzling electric colours on a sunny day, the 15 giant windows tell the stories of the Bible in a magical illuminated cartoon strip that soars up into the star-studded roof. The stunning 33-m (108-ft) high spire seems to point straight to heaven while the Rose Window ominously depicts the Day of Judgement.

Stunning interiors of the magnificent Sainte-Chapelle

The Lowdown

🌐 **Map reference** 10 G5
Address 6 Blvd du Palais, 75001; 01 53 40 60 80; *www.sainte-chapelle. monuments-nationaux.fr/en*

🚗 **Métro** Cité, line 4. **RER** St-Michel, lines B & C. **Bus** 27, 38, 85 & 96

🕐 **Open** 9:30am–6pm daily; Nov–Feb: till 5pm; 15 May–15 Sep: until 9pm Wed to see the chapel lit by the setting sun; closed 1 Jan, 1 May, Sep–Jun: 1–2:15pm & 25 Dec

💶 **Price** €18–28; under 18s free; EU citizens under 26 free

🏃 **Skipping the queue** Combined ticket with Conciergerie €12.50 per person; Paris Museum Pass accepted

🎫 **Guided tours** Can be arranged three weeks in advance; 01 44 54 19 33

👫 **Age range** 8 plus

🕐 **Allow** 30–45 minutes

♿ **Wheelchair access** Limited

🍽 **Eat and drink** *Family treat* Au Bougnat (*26 Rue Chanoinesse, 75004; 01 43 54 50 74; www. aubougnat.com; 8am–10pm daily*) is a bar–restaurant that serves excellent ravioli and duck.

👫 **Toilets** By the entrance, in the courtyard

Letting off steam
The pretty **Place Dauphine** (*see p71*), laid out in 1607 by Henri IV and named after the Dauphin, the future Louis XIII, is an elegant square in which to kick a ball around.

⑩ Pont Neuf
The old new bridge

Built in 1607 during the reign of Henri IV, the Pont Neuf, or New Bridge, is, ironically, the oldest surviving bridge in Paris. The first stone bridge to be built in the city, it was wider than any other bridge in Europe and also had a new invention – pavements. It soon became all the rage to stroll across it, among a bustling mix of entertainers, tradesmen, dentists and tricksters. In the middle of the bridge is a statue of Henri IV which, in 1618, was the first royal statue to

Pont Neuf, Paris's oldest bridge, spanning the Seine

be erected in the city. It was destroyed during the Revolution, but was recast in the 19th century. Steps from behind the statue lead to the Square du Vert-Galant, located at the spot where the Pont Neuf crosses Ile de la Cité, halfway across the river. The square was built by Henri IV, nicknamed *Vert-Galant* (Gay Blade), who enjoyed coming here for parties on summer evenings. Originally an island called the Ile des Juifs, this is where the leader of the Templars, Jacques de Molay, was burnt at the stake in 1314.

Letting off steam
One of the most magical spots in Paris, the Square du Vert-Galant is excellent for a picnic and a run around. Try to imagine what the locals felt like seeing the Vikings rowing towards them here in AD 845. This is also the point from which the **Vedettes du Pont Neuf** (*see p28*) pleasure boats depart.

The Lowdown

🌐 **Map reference** 10 G4
Address 75001

🚗 **Métro** Pont Neuf, line 7 or Cité, line 4. **RER** St-Michel, lines B & C. **Bus** 58 & 70

🍽 **Eat and drink** *Real meal* La Nouvelle Marinara (*46 Rue Dauphine 75006; 01 43 26 45 94; noon–3pm & 7–10pm daily*) is the best place to enjoy pizzas straight from a wood-fired oven.

⑪ St-Germain l'Auxerrois

Rivers of blood

A jewel of Gothic architecture with a fantastically elaborate doorway, the church of St-Germain l'Auxerrois was built in 1435. The church is famous for its association with the grisly St Bartholomew's Day Massacre. In 1572, the country was ruled by a weak and indecisive Catholic king, Charles IX, whose mother Catherine de Medici had plans to destroy the growing power of the Protestant community. On 23 August, the eve of the wedding of the Protestant Henri of Navarre, who would later become Henri IV, and Marguerite de Valois, she ordered the church bell to be tolled, which was a signal for a full-scale massacre to begin. Thousands of men, women and children who

had come to witness the wedding were murdered and the Seine turned red with Protestant blood.

Letting off steam

A copy of the original Napoleonic bridge, the **Pont des Arts** (*Quai du Louvre, Pl de l'Institut, 75006*) is a pedestrianized footbridge and a great place for families to enjoy a stroll and for young children to run along.

View of the imposing church of St-Germain l'Auxerrois

View of the Pont des Arts across River Seine

The Lowdown

🌐 **Map reference** 10 G4
Address 2 Pl de Louvre; 01 42 60 13 96

🚗 **Métro** Louvre Rivoli, line 1 or Pont Neuf, line 7. **RER** Châtelet-Les Halles, lines A, B & D. **Bus** 72, 74, 75, 76 81 & 85

🕐 **Open** 8am–7pm Mon–Fri, 9am–8pm Sat & Sun

ⓖ **Price** Free

👫 **Age range** 8 plus

⏱ **Allow** 15 minutes

♿ **Wheelchair access** Yes

🍴 **Eat and drink** *Family treat* Le Fumoir (*6 Rue de l'Admiral Coligny, 75001; 01 42 92 00 24; www.lefumoir.com; 11–2am daily*) is a cosy restaurant with vegetarian options and an excellent Sunday brunch. It offers snacks and pastries too.

🚻 **Toilets** No

Picnic under €25; **Snacks** €25–45; **Real meal** €45–90; **Family treat** over €90 (based on a family of four)

Beaubourg
& the Marais

The slaughterhouses and tanneries busy here in medieval times gave way to elegant mansions in the 17th century, as Henri IV decided to drain the area's marshes and build a city fit for kings. Today the lively Beaubourg quarter and charming Marais, with its tiny streets, are full of art, trendy shops, museums and lovely squares, including the stylish but family-friendly Place des Vosges.

Tuileries, Opéra & Montmartre

Champs-Elysées & Trocadéro

Beaubourg & the Marais

Eiffel Tower & Les Invalides

Ile de la Cité & Ile St-Louis

St-Germain & the Latin Quarter

Luxembourg & Montparnasse

Highlights

Centre Pompidou
Watch street theatre or ride up and down the crazy escalators (see pp80–81).

Musée des Arts et Métiers
Pay homage to the great inventors in this former monastery, now a museum dedicated to science, technology and engineering (see pp86–7).

Place des Vosges
Swashbuckle like d'Artagnan or fire over the barricades like Victor Hugo's young hero, Gavroche, in one of the most beautiful squares in the world (see pp92–3).

Musée Carnavalet
Learn how Paris grew from a village on an island in the Seine to become one of the most beautiful cities in the world in this fine museum (see p94).

Rue des Rosiers
Get a taste for Jewish cooking at one of the kosher restaurants in the Jewish quarter, one of Paris's most lively areas (see p96).

Place de la Bastille
Gawp at the empty space where the infamous prison stood and wonder how Egyptian mummies ended up under this huge traffic island (see p97).

Above Children's playground, Jardin du Port de l'Arsenal
Left Hand-painted historic porcelain dolls lovingly displayed at the Musée de la Poupée

The Best of
Beaubourg & the Marais

Steeped in history, the Marais is a jumble of winding streets dotted with mansions, trendy shops and restaurants, and small art museums – older children will love it. Spend a day visiting elegant courtyards and get a flavour of Parisian Jewish life here before heading to the Centre Pompidou, where there is always lots going on, inside and out. For some outdoor fun, stroll along the canal by the legendary Place de la Bastille.

Horrible histories

See the first boats to sail down the Seine and trace the history of the French Revolution at the **Musée Carnavalet** *(see p94)*, then head off in search of Philippe Auguste's medieval city walls, hidden in a school playground.

Be a knight and follow in the footsteps of the Templars in the **Square du Temple** *(see p87)* or swagger around like Henri IV through the courtyard of the **Hôtel de Sully** *(see p92)*, the home of his close friend and advisor, the Duke of Sully.

Stand on **Place de la Bastille** *(see p97)* to picture the start of the Revolution, then visit the house on **Place des Vosges** *(see pp92–3)* where Victor Hugo wrote *Les Miserables*, a story about poor people whose lives had hardly changed despite the Revolution, and who had a new monarchy to rebel against.

Walk around the Jewish quarter, **Rue des Rosiers** *(see p96)*, and find the plaque outside a school on Rue des Hospitalières-St-Gervais that commemorates the children deported during World War II. Learn more about the tragic fate of the French Jews at the sombre **Mémorial de la Shoah** *(see p96)*.

Right An early plane on show at the Musée des Arts et Métiers
Below Glass walkway in the Centre Pompidou

Above *Beautifully manicured gardens with flower beds, Musée Carnavalet*

Ethnic Paris

Take a culinary tour of the world. Sample Jewish cooking in the bakeries and restaurants along **Rue des Rosiers**. Savour cheesecake, strudel or herrings, or try a North African falafel. Buy a *Challah* bread for dinner and a spinning top for the Jewish festival of Hanukkah. Find out more at the **Musée d'Art et d'Histoire du Judaïsme** (see p89).

Explore **Passage Brady** (see p87), a covered arcade full of Indian restaurants and shops founded by immigrants from the former French colony of Pondicherry in India. Taste an authentic curry or buy ingredients to cook up something spicy at home.

Finish the tour by travelling on to Algeria, Morocco and Tunisia to enjoy delicious tagines in the restaurants near the **Musée des Arts et Métiers** (see pp86–7). This high-quality museum of science and industry covers topics such as photography, machinery and energy.

Shop, shop, shop

Shop for clothes and knick-knacks at **Merci** (see p93), which donates proceeds to charity. Chocolate lovers must pay a visit to the **Jadis et Gourmande** (see p88).

On a Sunday afternoon, walk around the busy Marais and get down to some trendy shopping on the popular Rue des Francs Bourgeois and the pedestrianized **Rue Montorgueil** (see p81), home to Paris's young designers. Step into the city's oldest bakery here, the *pâtisserie* **La Maison Stohrer** (see p83), where Rum Babas (rum-soaked cakes) were once prepared for Louis XIV. A haven for food lovers, this street is the perfect place in which to buy picnic supplies.

Art lessons

Be inspired by the best of modern art at the fascinating Musée National d'Art Moderne inside the **Centre Pompidou** (see pp80–81) or be dazzled by the centre's weird architecture, in the bustling piazza in front, and the colourful **Fontaine Igor Stravinsky** (see p82). The work of the city's great Jewish artists, including Chagall and Modigliani, is on show at the **Musée d'Art et d'Histoire du Judaïsme**.

Kids will enjoy seeing the paintings and sculptures of the great Pablo Picasso at the **Musée Picasso** (see p95). Also visit the **Musée Carnavalet**, which has 2,600 paintings, some of which are on the ceiling.

Left *Bread and cakes on display inside Paris's oldest bakery, La Maison Stohrer*

Centre Pompidou and around

Children love the buzz of the piazza in front of the Centre Pompidou. Full of street entertainers, the square is pedestrianized and safe for running around. Then there is the thrill of riding on the crazy escalators to admire the stunning view from the roof, which tops off the fantastic art on offer inside. There is a good mix of indoor and outdoor activities to suit all weathers, such as shopping in the bustling Rue Montorgueil or climbing the historic Tour de Jean Sans Peur. The sights in this area are all close together and easily explored on foot.

Beaubourg & the Marais

Musée des Arts et Métiers p86

Centre Pompidou

Place des Vosges p92

Outside tables at Dame Tartine, a popular restaurant with Parisians

Places of interest

SIGHTS

1. Centre Pompidou
2. Place Igor Stravinsky
3. Les Halles
4. Tour de Jean Sans Peur

● EAT AND DRINK

1. François Pralus
2. Berko
3. Les Piétons
4. Georges
5. Boulangerie Julien
6. Dame Tartine
7. La Maison Stohrer
8. Bistro Burger
9. Charles Chocolatier
10. Régis Colin

● SHOPPING

1. Not So Big
2. A La Poupée Merveilleuse

See also Centre Pompidou (p81)

● WHERE TO STAY

1. Novotel Les Halles

0 metres 300

0 yards 300

The interesting and colourful façade of the Centre Pompidou

The Lowdown

🚗 **Métro** Châtelet, lines 1, 4, 7 11 & 14; Les Halles, line 4; Etienne Marcel, line 4 or Hôtel de Ville, lines 1 & 11. **RER** Châtelet Les Halles, lines A, B & D. **Bus** 21, 29, 38, 47, 58, 67, 69, 70, 72, 74, 75, 76, 81, 85 & 96

🛒 **Supermarkets** Franprix: 25 Rue Montorgueil, 75001; 85 Rue Réaumur, 75002; 35 Rue Berger, 75001. Monop', 131 Rue St-Denis, 75001. **Market** Marché St-Eustache les Halles, Rue Montmartre, 75001; 12:30–8:30pm Thu, 7am–3pm Sun

➕ **Pharmacy** Pharmacie des Halles, 10 Blvd de Sébastopol, 75001; 01 42 72 03 23; open till midnight Mon–Sat, till 10pm Sun

🏝 **Nearest playground** Square de la Tour St-Jacques, Rue de Rivoli, 75004; dawn–dusk (see p82)

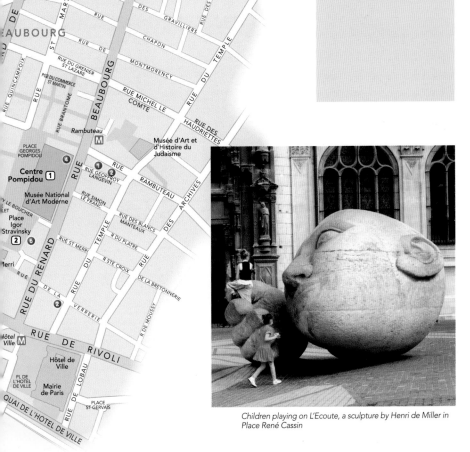

Children playing on L'Ecoute, a sculpture by Henri de Miller in Place René Cassin

① Centre Pompidou
Cubes, views and tubes

Georges Pompidou, French president from 1969 to 1974, loved all things modern, and chose Richard Rogers and Renzo Piano to create a dazzling new cultural centre. The result is the crazy glass and steel building – with its escalators, air-conditioning shafts and utilities pipes on the outside – that is the Centre Pompidou. It houses a huge public library as well as the Musée National d'Art Moderne, with cutting-edge modern art that is always on the move (its 100,000 pieces are rotated), in addition to temporary exhibitions.

Street entertainer

Key Features

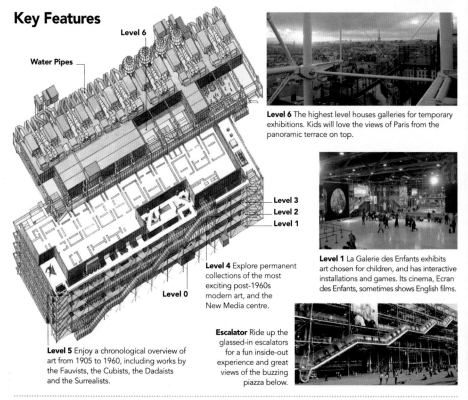

Level 6

Water Pipes

Level 3
Level 2
Level 1

Level 6 The highest level houses galleries for temporary exhibitions. Kids will love the views of Paris from the panoramic terrace on top.

Level 4 Explore permanent collections of the most exciting post-1960s modern art, and the New Media centre.

Level 0

Level 1 La Galerie des Enfants exhibits art chosen for children, and has interactive installations and games. Its cinema, Ecran des Enfants, sometimes shows English films.

Escalator Ride up the glassed-in escalators for a fun inside-out experience and great views of the buzzing piazza below.

Level 5 Enjoy a chronological overview of art from 1905 to 1960, including works by the Fauvists, the Cubists, the Dadaists and the Surrealists.

Letting off steam

Place Georges Pompidou, in front of the museum, is fun. Kids will love the sculptures of magical monsters on the Stravinsky Fountain in **Place Igor Stravinsky** (see p82).

Eat and drink

Picnic: under €25; Snacks: €25–45; Real meal: €45–90; Family treat: over €90 (based on a family of four)

PICNIC François Pralus (35 Rue Rambuteau, 75004; www. chocolats–pralus.com) is one of the city's best chocolatiers. The chocolate bars are made by Pralus himself. The busy Place Georges Pompidou is ideal for a picnic.
SNACKS Berko (23 Rue Rambuteau, 75004; 01 40 29 02 44) sells fabulous cupcakes in a range of fantastic flavours.
REAL MEAL Les Piétons (8 Rue des Lombards, 75004; 01 48 87 82 87; www.lespietons.com) is a Spanish tapas bar, on a pedestrianized street, which serves delicious paella and salads.

Performers entertain the crowd in the square in front of the Centre Pompidou

Prices given are for a family of four

The Lowdown

- 🌐 **Map reference** 11 B4
  Address Pl Georges Pompidou, 75004; 01 44 78 12 33; *www.centrepompidou.fr*

- 🚗 **Métro** Rambuteau, line 11 or Hôtel de Ville, line 1 & 11. **RER** Châtelet–Les Halles, lines A, B & D. **Bus** 21, 29, 38, 47, 58, 69, 70, 72, 74, 75, 81, 85 & 96

- 🕐 **Open** 11am–9pm Wed–Mon. Check *www.centrepompidou.fr* for night openings

- 💶 **Price** Exhibitions, museums and panoramic viewing point: €30–40 or €36–46 depending on the season; under 18s, and under 26s with EU passports, free. Panoramic viewing point only: €6–16; under 26s free. Écran des Enfants, inside Galerie des Enfants: €11–21

- 🧍 **Skipping the queue** Paris Museum Pass accepted. Free entry every first Sun of the month. Tickets for adults can be bought online or at the automatic machines. Under 18s and over 11s have to show their IDs at the desk for free tickets.

- 🚩 **Guided tours** Audio guides in English. Tours in French every Sat at 3:30pm and every

Sun at 4pm. The bookshop sells *My Little Pompidou*, a children's guide.

- 🧒 **Age range** 2 plus

- 🏃 **Activities** Toys and games, even for two-year-olds, at La Galerie des Enfants. Workshops on Wed & Sat; family activities on Sun & school hols. Films at Écran des Enfants, occasionally in English.

- ⏱ **Allow** 1–2 hours

- ♿ **Wheelchair access** Yes

- ☕ **Café** Café Mezzanine on level 1; Kiosque BPI on level 2 and the Georges restaurant on level 6: 01 44 78 47 99

- 🛍 **Shops** The Flammarion bookshop at the entrance sells guides in English, as well as art and activity books in French. The Design Boutique is in the entrance hall. There are other bookshops on levels 4 & 6.

- 🚻 **Toilets** In the main hall and on each floor

Good family value?
The Centre Pompidou is a flexible space. If kids are not interested in art, they can ride up the escalator for the view and enjoy street theatre in front of the museum.

Rows of lavishly decorated cupcakes behind the counter at Berko

FAMILY TREAT Georges *(Centre Pompidou; 01 44 78 47 99)*, the rooftop restaurant, has a large terrace with spectacular views across the city. The cuisine is mostly classic French but there are some Asian dishes as well.

Find out more
DIGITAL The Centre Pompidou has its own free app which is regularly updated, in English, French and Spanish.

FILM Watch *Mon Oncle* (1958). In this film, French film-maker Jacques Tati makes fun of Parisians who love anything modern – rather like Georges Pompidou.

Shopping
Not So Big *(38 Rue Tiquetonne, 75002; www.notsobig.fr)* is a concept store for kids. **A La Poupée Merveilleuse** *(9 Rue du Temple, 75004; www.a-la-poupee-merveilleuse-paris.fr)* sells party trinkets and games for kids.

Next stop…
THE MARAIS After a tour of the Centre Pompidou, explore the nearby Marais area, a maze of winding streets full of designer boutiques, art galleries, cafés and shops. Children can let off steam in the lovely Place des Vosges, then go north towards Rue Montorgueil, one of the trendiest streets in Paris, full of market stalls and bakeries.

Outdoor seating at Dame Tartine Bistro

② Place Igor Stravinsky

A Firebird drenched in water

Next to the Centre Pompidou, this bustling square enchants children and grown-ups alike with its colourful mechanical fountain. Opened in 1982, it was named after composer Igor Stravinsky. The Stravinsky Fountain has 16 moving, water-spraying sculptures inspired by his music. Niki de St-Phalle's bold, colourful shapes look good enough to eat, while her husband Jean Tinguely's creaking metal structures are darkly humoristic. Take time to stroll around the rectangular pool to see all of them, and especially look out for the splendid, golden-crested *Firebird* and the quirky figure of *La Mort* – or Death – with its grinning skull.

Take cover

Should the weather turn nasty, head back into the free areas of the **Centre Pompidou**, where levels zero and one have book and souvenir shops, and inviting cafés in which to linger.

③ Les Halles

A belly full of shops

Émile Zola called Les Halles the belly of Paris because of its once sprawling food market, created in 1181 by King Philippe Auguste. In 1969, the beautiful 19th-century glass pavilions were knocked down, also removing the last traditional working-class district from the city centre. The focus of the present Les Halles is a giant underground shopping centre, the Forum des Halles, which is taking on a new lease of life in a renovation programme that is due for completion in 2018. It is a good, if rather austere, place to shop – there are branches of all the main international and French chain shops here, but it can feel rather dreary.

There is also a swimming pool, the Piscine Suzanne Berlioux, and cinema complexes, among them the Forum des Images, where it is possible to watch thousands of films and archive footage in a multiscreen cinema.

The nearby Bourse du Commerce has an interesting fresco, painted in 1886 by Alexis-Joseph Mazerole, showing the four corners of the world, from the freezing cold of the Russian north to the jungles of Africa.

It is not advisable to visit the Les Halles area at night.

Letting off steam

Children can run around in the tiny playground near Square de Tour St-Jacques *(Rue de Rivoli, 75004)*. Alternatively have a dip in the pool of the Forum des Halles.

Entrance to the multiscreen cinema Forum des Images, Les Halles

The Lowdown

- 🌐 **Map** 11 B4
  Address 75004
- 🚇 **Métro** Rambuteau, line 11; Hôtel de Ville, lines 1 & 11 or Châtelet, lines 1, 11 & 14. **RER** Châtelet–Les Halles, lines A, B & D. **Bus** 21, 29, 38, 47, 58, 69, 70, 72, 74, 75, 81, 85 & 96
- ☕ **Eat and drink** *Picnic* Boulangerie Julien *(75 Rue St-Honoré, 75001; 01 42 36 24 83; www. boulangeriejulien.com; closed Sun)* has sandwiches, bread and croissants – they sell over a thousand a day! The bite-sized versions are perfect for children. Picnic in Place Igor Stravinsky. *Real meal* Dame Tartine *(2 Rue Brisemiche, 75004; 01 42 77 32 22; 10am–11pm daily)*, overlooking the Stravinsky Fountain, is a good place to relax while the kids are free to run around. It serves tasty *tartines*, soups and *crêpes*.
- 🚻 **Toilets** In Dame Tartine for diners

Rows of attractively decorated cakes and pastries in La Maison Stohrer

The Lowdown

🌐 **Map** 11 A3
Address: 75001;
www.forumdeshalles.com

🚗 **Métro** Les Halles, line 4, or Châtelet, lines 1, 7 & 11. **RER** Châtelet-les-Halles, lines A, B & D. **Bus** 38, 47, 75 & 76

🏃 **Activities** Children's workshops (in French) at Forum des Images (01 44 76 63 00; www. forumdesimages.fr). There is always plenty of street theatre to look out for. There are also games and films for under-12s.

♿ **Wheelchair access** Limited

☕ **Eat and drink** *Snacks* La Maison Stohrer (51 Rue Montorgueil, 75002; 7:30am–8:30pm daily) is one of the oldest and most famous patisseries, with a beautiful painted ceiling. The *Baba au Rhum* was invented here. *Real Meal* Bistro Burger (26 Rue Montorgueil, 75001; 01 44 82 56 64; noon–11pm daily) is a restaurant with quick service. The emphasis is on healthy burgers, and green beans can be chosen as an alternative to fries. The bistro offers small portions of larger meals and an excellent children's menu.

🚻 **Toilets** On level minus 3 and at the Porte Berger and Porte Rambuteau. Baby-changing facilities on level minus 3 near Porte Rambuteau

The 27-m (88-ft) tall Tour de Jean Sans Peur, a remnant of medieval Paris

④ Tour de Jean Sans Peur

Scared – no kidding

This tower is a rare remnant of medieval Paris. Jean sans Peur, the Duke of Burgundy, had his cousin Louis d'Orléans killed, which helped spark off the Hundred Years' War. Burgundy joined the English. Not exactly "sans peur", or fearless, as he claimed, the duke built an elaborate tower on top of his house to keep him safe from Louis' family and supporters, known as the Armagnacs. In spite of this, he was murdered in 1419. Children like the winding staircase, the beautiful carved, vaulted ceiling and Paris's oldest toilet. It is, however, not easy to negotiate the 140 steps to the top with smaller kids.

Letting off steam

Children will love the giant modern sculpted head, *L'Ecoute*, by Henri de Miller, in front of the St-Eustache church. They can even clamber up on the sculpture.

The Lowdown

🌐 **Map reference** 11 A3
Address 20 Rue Etienne Marcel, 75002; 01 40 26 20 28; *www.tourjeansanspeur.com*

🚗 **Métro** Etienne Marcel, line 4, or Les Halles, line 4. **RER** Châtelet-les-Halles, lines A, B & D. **Bus** 29

🕐 **Open** Summer: 1:30–6pm Wed– Sun; winter: Wed, Sat & Sun

💶 **Price** €10–16; under 7s free

👉 **Guided tours** In French for children

🏃 **Age range** 7 plus

🏃 **Activities** Activity leaflet in English for children under 13

⏱ **Allow** 30 minutes

☕ **Eat and drink** *Picnic* Charles Chocolatier (15 Rue Montorgueil, 75001; 01 45 08 57 77) specializes in dark chocolate. Try the *bûches* (chocolate logs). Picnic in the gardens in front of St-Eustache. *Snacks* Régis Colin (53 Rue Montmartre, 75002; 01 42 36 02 80; closed Sat & Sun) is an excellent bakery.

🚻 **Toilets** In the entrance hall on the ground floor

Musée des Arts et Métiers and around

Housed in an old abbey, the Musée des Arts et Métiers is a temple to science. Its pretty, enclosed courtyard is an ideal spot to unwind over a cold drink in summer. The area also has a lot of history to offer and, for Harry Potter fans, Paris's oldest house was once home to book-keeper and alchemist Nicolas Flamel (see p88). Sightseeing is concentrated in a very small area, and it is easy to get around on foot. The restaurants serve some of the city's best ethnic cuisine. The museum is 10 minutes on foot from the Centre Pompidou.

Porcelain dolls on display at the Musée de la Poupée

Places of interest

SIGHTS

1. Musée des Arts et Métiers
2. 51 Rue de Montmorency
3. Musée de la Poupée
4. Musée d'Art et d'Histoire du Judaïsme

● **EAT AND DRINK**

1. Marché aux Enfants Rouges
2. L'As du Fallafel
3. Passage Brady
4. Chez Omar
5. Bob's Kitchen
6. L'Auberge Nicolas Flamel
7. Jadis et Gourmande
8. Le Studio
9. Pain de Sucre
10. Breizh Café

● **SHOPPING**

1. Passage de Grand Cerf

● **WHERE TO STAY**

1. Bonne Nuit Paris
2. Hôtel du Nord – Le Pari Vélo

0 metres 300

0 yards 300

Early aeroplanes on display in the Musée des Arts et Métiers

The Lowdown

🚗 **Métro** Arts et Métiers, lines 3 & 11; Réaumur Sébastopol, lines 3 & 4; Rambuteau, line 11 or Hôtel de Ville, lines 1 & 11. **RER** Châtelet Les Halles, lines A, B & D. **Bus** 20, 29, 38, 39, 47 & 75

🛒 **Supermarkets** Monop', 65 Rue Turbigo, 75003; 01 44 54 37 63; 8am–midnight Mon–Sat. Franprix, 16 Rue Grenier St-Lazare, 75003; 8:30am–9pm Mon–Sat. Monoprix, 93 Blvd de Sébastopol, 75002; 01 42 33 36 15; 9am–10pm Mon–Sat **Market** Marché des Enfants Rouges (covered market), 39 Rue de Bretagne, 75003; 8:30am–1pm & 4–7:30pm Tue–Thu, 8:30am–1pm & 4–8pm Fri–Sat, 8:30am–2pm Sun

➕ **Pharmacy** Pharmacie des Halles, 10 Blvd de Sébastopol, 75001; 01 42 72 03 23; 8am–10pm Mon–Sat, 9am–10pm Sun

🛝 **Nearest playgrounds** Square du Temple, 64 Rue de Bretagne, 75003; dawn–dusk (see p87). Square Charles-Victor Langlois, Rue des Blancs Manteaux, 75004, dawn–dusk (see p89)

Phonograph in the Musée des Arts et Métiers

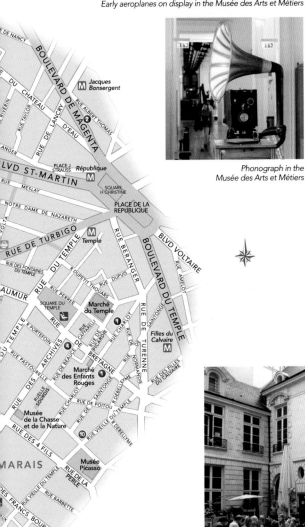

Alfresco dining at Le Studio

① Musée des Arts et Métiers
A temple to invention

A refreshing alternative to Paris's many art museums and palaces, this museum was founded in 1794 to showcase new and useful inventions. Housed in the old abbey of St-Martin-des-Champs, it is home to more than 2,000 inventions, chronologically organized into seven sections. There are explanations in English and interactive screens, but the majority of the museum is charmingly old-fashioned. Do not miss the church full of cars and planes.

Statue of Liberty outside Musée des Arts et Métiers

Key Features

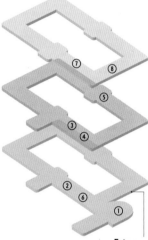

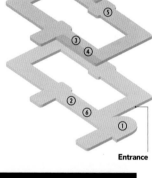

■ **Level 2** Scientific Instruments and Materials

■ **Level 1** Construction, Communication, Energy, Mechanics

■ **Level 0** Church, Transportation

⑤ **Television Receiver** René Barthélémy, a pioneer of French television, invented one of the first television receivers in 1931.

⑥ **Otto Safety Bicycle** Invented in 1879, with wheels side by side instead of one behind the other, this bicycle is only one among an extraordinary collection.

Entrance

① **Foucault's Pendulum** In 1851, this instrument proved the rotation of the Earth on its axis. See how it was done at noon and 5pm daily.

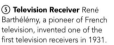

⑦ **Mechanical calculator** The mathematician Blaise Pascal invented the first mechanical calculator in 1642, while he was still a teenager.

② **Avion 3** French inventor Clément Ader designed the Avion 3, a plane inspired by a bat, first tried in 1897. Ader also invented the V8 Engine for the Paris–Madrid rally of 1903.

③ **Théâtre des Automates** Some of the mechanical toys here once belonged to Marie Antoinette. Catch a demonstration to see mechanical robots in motion.

④ **Machine de Marly** An engineering masterpiece, this machine was created in 1684 to bring water 162 m (532 ft) uphill to the fountains and lake at Versailles.

⑧ **Lavoisier's Laboratory** French chemist Antoine-Laurent de Lavoisier (1743–94) is known as the father of modern chemistry. He was guillotined during the Revolution, but his discoveries led to the birth of the chemical industry. His laboratory is reconstructed inside the museum.

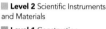

Prices given are for a family of four

The Lowdown

🌐 **Map reference** 11 B2
Address 60 Rue Réaumur, 75003; 01 53 01 82 00; www.arts-et-metiers.net

🚇 **Métro** Arts-et-Métiers, lines 3 & 11. **Bus** 20, 38, 39 & 47

🕐 **Open** 10am–6pm Tue–Sun, till 9:30pm Thu, closed 1 May & 25 Dec

€ **Price** €13–23; under 18s and under 26s with EU passport free

👫 **Skipping the queue** Paris Museum Pass accepted. Busiest at weekends but queues are unlikely as the museum is not on the tourist circuit.

🚩 **Guided tours** Audio guide in English for children: €5. The French parcours rapide (fast course) covers the most important 30 objects on show.

👫 **Age range** 6 plus

🤸 **Activities** The Théâtre des Automates has displays on the first and fourth Wed and third Sun of the month. Workshops in French on Sat during school hols and upon reservation for 4–14 year olds; 01 53 01 82 88. Family ticket: €22–32; 01 53 01 82 65

🕐 **Allow** 1–2 hours

♿ **Wheelchair access** Yes

☕ **Café** Café des Techniques (www.cafedestechniques.com), in the museum. Combined Sun brunch and museum ticket: €22.50; under 10s: €11

🚻 **Toilets** In the museum

Good family value?
Great fun for children of all ages. Plan your visit to coincide with the demonstration of Foucault's pendulum and the Théâtre des Automates' show.

Letting off steam
Once a fortified enclave of the Knights Templar, the pretty **Square du Temple** (64 Rue de Bretagne, 75003) has a lovely garden with an adjoining children's playground, and is a favourite picnic spot.

Family enjoying a picnic, Square du Temple

Eat and drink
Picnic: under €25; Snacks: €25–45; Real meal: €45–90; Family treat: over €90 (based on a family of four)

PICNIC Marché aux Enfants Rouges (39 Rue de Bretagne, 75003; closed Mon) offers a choice of cheeses, cold meats and fruits. Picnic in the Square du Temple.
SNACKS L'As du Fallafel (34 Rue des Rosiers, 75004; 01 48 87 63 60; closed Fri night & Sat), is a very popular restaurant serving falafels.
REAL MEAL Passage Brady (39 Blvd de Strasbourg, 75010), built in 1828, has wall-to-wall curry houses serving a little bit of Mumbai at affordable prices all day.

FAMILY TREAT Chez Omar (47 Rue de Bretagne, 75003; 01 42 72 36 26; open daily; cash only; no reservations), a Moroccan restaurant, is famous for its couscous.

Find out more
DIGITAL Brush up your knowledge of science at www.bbc.co.uk/schools/scienceclips/index_flash.shtml. For chemistry, check out www.chemistryforkids.net and www.physics4kids.com for physics. Watch the first great steps in aviation history on http://tinyurl.com/3e43juo.

Shopping
The area around Métro Etienne Marcel has trendy shops. The **Passage de Grand Cerf** just north of the Rue de Turbigo is a pretty, covered arcade dating from 1825.

Next stop...
AN ARCH AND A CRAZY BUILDING The museum is close to **Porte St-Denis** (Blvd St-Denis, 75003), the huge 17th-century arch that replaced one of the gates in the medieval city walls, once one of the entrances into Paris. Walk down Rue Beaubourg to the **Centre Pompidou** (see pp80–81).

(see pp80–81)

KIDS' CORNER

Look out for...
1 Hidden towers. Near the museum are two medieval towers on Rue de Vertbois and Rue St-Martin.
2 The first plane to cross the English Channel. Flown by Louis Bleriot in 1909, it hangs from the ceiling of the chapel in Musée des Arts et Métiers.
3 A racing car driven by a propeller in the Musée des Arts et Métiers' transportation gallery. Imagine the whooshing noise it would make!

FRENCH CALENDAR
The Revolutionaries invented a new calendar, the French Revolutionary Calendar. Year III, or 1794, the year the Musée des Arts et Métiers was founded, is engraved over the door of the courtyard and can be seen from the entrance.

Templar kingdom
The Knights Templar were a crusading order of knights who settled and built a massive fortress in the Marais area in the 12th century. A law unto themselves, they amassed a huge fortune and became some of Europe's first bankers. Their enemies started spreading rumours that they were involved in heresy and corruption. In 1307, King Philip IV, who was heavily indebted to the Knights, took advantage of the allegations to arrest their leaders, and tortured them to extract confessions. Before being burnt at the stake, one leader, Jacques de Morlay, cursed the king, saying he would die that year. Philip was indeed killed soon after in a hunting accident.

② 51 Rue de Montmorency

At the alchemist's table

Professor Dumbledore's friend, Nicolas Flamel, who puts in an appearance in the first Harry Potter book, was an alchemist who, according to legend, owned the Philosopher's Stone, a magical treasure that could turn base metals into gold and silver. Flamel lived at No. 51 Rue de Montmorency in the city's oldest surviving stone house, which now houses a restaurant that bears his name.

Flamel is also said to have discovered the elixir of life but, although he lived into his early eighties there is no evidence that he achieved immortality, and he had the foresight to design his own tombstone. Covered in strange signs and symbols, it is now on show in the Musée de Cluny (see pp176–7). In real life, Flamel made a fortune – not in a secret laboratory, but by buying and selling rare manuscripts.

The oldest stone house in Paris, at 51 Rue de Montmorency

The Lowdown

- 🌐 **Map reference** 11 B3
  Address L'Auberge Nicolas Flamel, 51 Rue de Montmorency, 75003; 01 42 71 77 78; www.auberge-nicolas-flamel.fr
- 🚇 **Metro** Etienne Marcel, line 4.
  Bus 29, 38 & 47
- 🕐 **Open** Noon–2:30pm & 7–10pm daily (reservations necessary)
- 🍽 **Eat and drink** *Real meal* Bob's Kitchen (74 Rue Gravilliers, 75003; 09 52 55 11 66) is great for a healthy wrap or an inexpensive brunch. *Family treat* L'Auberge Nicolas Flamel has a fixed price lunch menu and a children's menu too, and could be fun for junior gourmets and Harry Potter fans.
- 🚻 **Toilets** For diners only

Novelty chocolates at Jadis et Gourmande, a favourite with children

Rich and generous, he gave his fortune to the poor, who he and his wife Perenelle cared for and fed at No. 51. Somewhat ironically, the restaurant located here today is far too expensive for any needy Parisian.

Take cover

There is a crazy collection of stuffed animals and guns at the **Musée de la Chasse et de la Nature** (62 Rue des Archives, 75003; www.chassenature.org). Look out for the huge polar bear!

③ Musée de la Poupée

Magical miniatures

Paris was once famous for its dolls, and this tiny museum is set in an area where they used to be made. This lovely collection of dolls' houses and hand-made dolls from 19th-century France and around the world will delight little girls in particular. There is also a doll's hospital in the event of an emergency. Guido and Samy Odin, the father-and-son duo who own the museum, are available if any

The Lowdown

- 🌐 **Map reference** 11 B3
  Address Impasse Berhaud, 75003; 01 42 72 73 11; www.museedelapoupeeparis.com
- 🚗 **Métro** Rambuteau, line 11.
  Bus 29, 38 & 47
- 🕐 **Open** 10am–6pm, closed Sun, Mon & public hols
- 💶 **Price** €22–32; under 12s free on Sun morning
- 🚩 **Guided tours** €32–42
- 🚶 **Age range** 3 plus
- 🤸 **Activities** Workshops on Wed at 11am; storytelling on Wed at 2pm
- ⏱ **Allow** 30–45 minutes
- ♿ **Wheelchair access** Yes
- 🍽 **Eat and drink** *Picnic* Jadis et Gourmande (39 Rue des Archives, 75004; 01 48 04 08 03; www.jadisetgourmande.fr) makes everything imaginable in chocolate, from CDs to mobile phones and even the Eiffel Tower. Picnic in the Jardin d'Anne Frank. *Real meal* Le Studio (41 Rue du Temple, 75004; 01 42 74 10 38; www.the-studio.fr; 10am–midnight Tue–Sun, 5:30pm–midnight Mon) is a Tex-Mex restaurant with a terrace in a pretty enclosed courtyard with room for kids to run around.
- 🚻 **Toilets** On the ground floor

doll needs attention. A really well-stocked shop sells charming dolly clothes and toys. There are plenty of activities for children that transcend the language barrier.

Letting off steam

The museum is just by the gates to a little garden, the **Jardin d'Anne Frank**, which backs on to the Hôtel de St-Aignan, which houses the Musée d'Art et d'Histoire du Judaïsme. Look out for the locals' vegetable patch.

Elaborately dressed dolls in the Musée de la Poupée

④ Musée d'Art et d'Histoire du Judaïsme

Hanukkah lamps and festivals

Housed in a fabulous mansion typical of the Marais and close to the historic Jewish quarter around Rue des Rosiers (see p96), this museum celebrates the culture of French Jewry. France has the biggest Jewish population in Europe, and the collection traces its history from the Middle Ages to the present day. Children will be intrigued by the old-fashioned radio that plays the declaration of the foundation of the State of Israel in 1947, at the United Nations (in English). It is fun to visit during the big Jewish holidays, especially the festivals of Purim and Hanukkah, which are particularly celebrated with children in mind.

Some of the greatest painters of the early 20th century were Jewish, and the museum has a fine collection of the works of Expressionist artists such as Amedeo Modigliani, Chaim Soutine and Marc Chagall.

Letting off steam

Just behind the museum is the pretty Jardin d'Anne Frank. There is a small playground in **Square Charles-Victor Langlois** (Rue des Blancs-Manteaux, 75004) next to the church of Notre-Dame-des-Blancs-Manteaux. Look out for traces of an old tower on the ground.

Above Model of a synagogue, Jewish museum
Below Fragments of Jewish gravestones, Jewish museum

KIDS' CORNER

Look out for...
1 Strange signs and symbols on the façade of L'Auberge Nicholas Flamel.
2 Dolls – not just Barbies and cuddly babies, but dolls made of wood, china, wax and paper. They all live in the Musée de la Poupée.
3 Hanukkah candles. They come in all shapes and sizes at the Musée d'Art et d'Histoire du Judaïsme. Candles are lit every night during the eight-day festival to remember the Jewish uprising against the Greeks in the 2nd century BC. Lucky kids get a gift every time they are lit.

BON APPÉTIT
Guimauve, or marshmallow, is an important French word to know, and the chocolate marshmallows at Pain de Sucre on Rue Rambuteau are to die for. Look out for the état de choc (state of shock). Dare to try one!

Magic with metals
The story goes that one night, a poor man knocked on Nicolas Flamel's door and offered to sell him a magical book, Abraham the Jew. He told Flamel that if he deciphered the strange symbols in the book it would show him how to turn ordinary metals into gold and silver – and, more importantly, how to create a potion that would make him live for ever. Not surprisingly, Flamel bought the book and became a very wealthy man. Strangely, when treasure-hunters dug up his grave, it was found to be empty. There have been reported sightings of him over the years. Look out for a very, very old man!

The Lowdown

🌐 **Map reference** 11 B4
Address Hôtel de St-Aignan, 71 Rue de Temple, 75003; 01 53 01 86 60; www.mahj.org

🚗 **Métro** Rambuteau, line 11 & Hôtel de Ville, lines 1 & 11. **Bus** 29, 38, 47 & 75

💲 **Price** €13–23; under 18s and under 26s with EU passport free. Paris Museum Pass accepted

🕐 **Open** 11am–6pm Mon–Fri, 10am–6pm Sun

🚩 **Guided tours** Free audio guide in English

👫 **Age range** 8 plus

🎨 **Activities** Workshops related to Jewish hols; 01 53 01 86 62

⏱ **Allow** 1 hour

♿ **Wheelchair access** Yes

🍴 **Eat and drink** Picnic Pain de Sucre, (14 Rue Rambuteau, 75003; 01 45 74 68 92; closed Tue & Wed) sells melt-in-the-mouth marshmallows, and chocolate teddy bears; try the Zanzibar. Picnic at Square Charles-Victor Langlois. Real meal Breizh Café (109 Rue Vieille du Temple; 01 42 72 13 77; www.breizhcafe.com; closed Mon & Tue) serves delicious Breton crêpes.

🚻 **Toilets** By the central staircase

Place des Vosges and around

Beaubourg &
the Marais

Sunday is a lovely day to visit the Marais. The shops are open
and many of the streets north of Rue du Roi de Sicile are closed
to traffic and safe for kids. A little world of its own, the area is
easy to get around on foot and bursting with cafés for a light
snack and a rest, and a good deal of people-watching. It has
three museums for rainy-day entertainment and many squares,
including Place des Vosges, that are popular with local children.

Place des Vosges, the oldest planned square in Paris

| 0 metres | 250 |
| 0 yards | 250 |

Façade of the Hôtel de Sully,
on Rue St-Antoine

Places of interest

SIGHTS
1. Place des Vosges
2. Musée Carnavalet
3. Musée Picasso
4. Rue des Rosiers
5. Mémorial de la
   Shoah
6. Place de la Bastille

EAT & DRINK
1. Le Moulin de Rosa
2. Village St-Paul
3. Chez Janou
4. Carette des Vosges
5. Café du Centre
   Culturel Suédois
6. Le Loir dans
   la Théière
7. Chez Marianne
8. Sacha Finkelsztajn
9. Merci
10. Florence Kahn

11. Breakfast in America
12. Vins des Pyrénées
13. Café Français

SHOPPING
1. I Love My Blender
2. Bonton
3. Papier Tigre
4. Merci

WHERE TO STAY
1. Appartement
   d'Hôtes de la Folie
   Mericourt
2. Citadines Marais
   Bastille
3. Hotel Ibis Bastille
   Opéra
4. Hôtel Jeanne d'Arc
5. Le Pavillon
   de la Reine

Breads and pastries in the window of Boulangerie Murciano, Rue des Rosiers

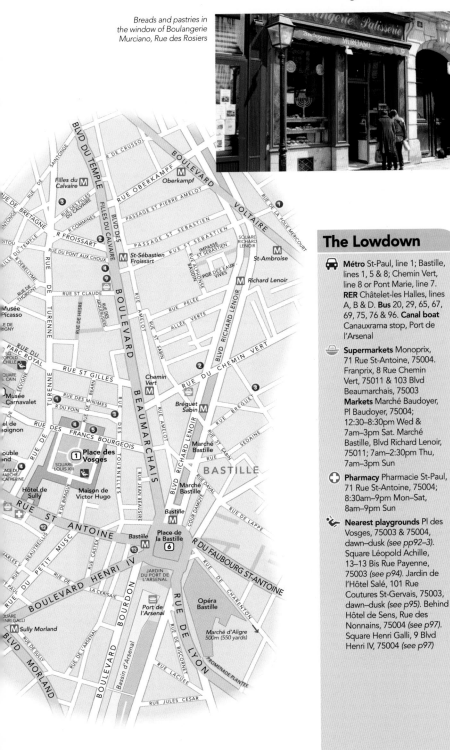

The Lowdown

🚗 **Métro** St-Paul, line 1; Bastille, lines 1, 5 & 8; Chemin Vert, line 8 or Pont Marie, line 7. **RER** Châtelet-les Halles, lines A, B & D. **Bus** 20, 29, 65, 67, 69, 75, 76 & 96. **Canal boat** Canauxrama stop, Port de l'Arsenal

🛒 **Supermarkets** Monoprix, 71 Rue St-Antoine, 75004. Franprix, 8 Rue Chemin Vert, 75011 & 103 Blvd Beaumarchais, 75003 **Markets** Marché Baudoyer, Pl Baudoyer, 75004; 12:30–8:30pm Wed & 7am–3pm Sat. Marché Bastille, Blvd Richard Lenoir, 75011; 7am–2:30pm Thu, 7am–3pm Sun

➕ **Pharmacy** Pharmacie St-Paul, 71 Rue St-Antoine, 75004; 8:30am–9pm Mon–Sat, 8am–9pm Sun

🛝 **Nearest playgrounds** Pl des Vosges, 75003 & 75004, dawn–dusk (see pp92–3). Square Léopold Achille, 13–13 Bis Rue Payenne, 75003 (see p94). Jardin de l'Hôtel Salé, 101 Rue Coutures St-Gervais, 75003, dawn–dusk (see p95). Behind Hôtel de Sens, Rue des Nonnains, 75004 (see p97). Square Henri Galli, 9 Blvd Henri IV, 75004 (see p97)

① Place des Vosges
All for one and one for all

One of the world's most beautiful squares, the perfectly symmetrical Place des Vosges is lined with rose-coloured houses with steep slate roofs and atmospheric vaulted arcades. At its heart is a tree-shaded square with a fountain and a play area where children can let off steam while families picnic. But it is also *Three Musketeers* territory – laid out by Henri IV in 1606, as the centre of a new district built on the marshes (*les marais*), it became the place to live during the era in which Dumas's book is set.

Inkwell in Maison de Victor Hugo

Key Features

No. 21 Cardinal Richelieu, once the most powerful man in France and the ultimate bad guy in *The Three Musketeers*, is a former resident. Centuries later, writer Alphonse Daudet (1840–97), author of the classic *Letters from My Windmill*, also stayed here.

Louis XIII's statue

Pavillon de la Reine and Pavillon du Roi The square is flanked by 36 identical houses, nine on each side. Two larger houses, the King's Pavilion and the Queen's Pavilion, sit on its northern and southern sides.

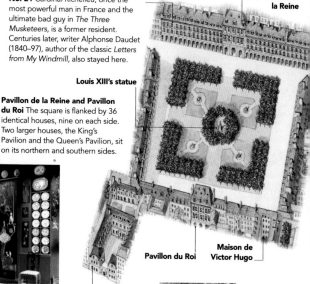

Pavillon de la Reine

Pavillon du Roi

Maison de Victor Hugo

Maison de Victor Hugo Author Victor Hugo lived at No. 6 with his wife and four children. He wrote a large part of his masterpiece *Les Misérables* here.

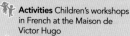
Hôtel de Sully

Statue of Louis XIII This statue of Henri IV's son sits at the centre of the square surrounded by lime and chestnut trees.

Hôtel de Sully Henri IV's former minister of finance, the Duc de Sully, lived in this beautiful mansion in the southwestern corner of the square. A hidden door located in the same corner leads to the mansion's delightful garden.

The Lowdown

🌐 **Map reference** 11 D5
Address 75003 & 75004.
Maison de Victor Hugo: 6 Pl des Vosges, 75004; 01 42 72 10 16; *www.maisonsvictorhugo.paris.fr*

🚇 **Métro** Bastille, line 1, 5 & 8; St-Paul, line 1 or Chemin Vert, line 8. **Bus** 20, 29, 65, 69 & 96

🕐 **Open** Maison de Victor Hugo: 10am–6pm, closed Mon & public hols

💶 **Price** Maison de Victor Hugo: free

🚩 **Guided tours** Maison de Victor Hugo: Audio guides (English)

👫 **Age range** Maison de Victor Hugo: 8 plus

🏃 **Activities** Children's workshops in French at the Maison de Victor Hugo

⏱ **Allow** Maison de Victor Hugo: 45–90 minutes

♿ **Wheelchair access** Yes

☕ **Café** Pl du Marché Ste-Catherine and Place des Vosges

🚻 **Toilets** In Maison de Victor Hugo

Good family value?
The pleasure in strolling around the square and playing in the park is that it does not cost a thing. To top it all, entry to Victor Hugo's house is free.

Canal boats along Port de l'Arsenal, with Colonne de Juillet in the distance

Letting off steam

The canalside Jardin du Port de l'Arsenal is another good place to stroll around, or picnic and watch the barges. **Nomades** *(37 Blvd Bourdon, 75004; www. nomadeshop.com; Tue–Sun)* organizes rollerblade tours of the city and rents out rollerblades.

Eat and drink

Picnic: under €25; Snacks: €25–45; Real meal: €45–90; Family treat: over €90 (based on a family of four)

PICNIC Le Moulin de Rosa *(32Rue de Turenne, 75003; 01 42 78 07 31; closed Sun)* sells particularly good brioche and tasty picnic savouries. Picnic in the Place des Vosges.
SNACKS Village St-Paul *(27 Rue St-Paul, 75004)* is an arty enclave of shops and restaurants hidden down a little passageway off Rue St-Paul. Enjoy drinks or a light meal in one of its cobbled courtyards.
REAL MEAL Chez Janou *(2 Rue Roger Verlomme, 75003; 01 42 72 28 41; www.chezjanou.com)* is a lively family bistro. The highlight for kids is the help-yourself chocolate mousse, served in a giant bowl.
FAMILY TREAT Carette des Vosges *(25 Pl des Vosges, 75003; 01 48 87 94 07)* has a beautiful setting on Place des Vosges and is a popular brunch spot. There is also a takeaway service at the counter.

Find out more

FILM Two Victor Hugo classics are captured on film in *Les Misérables* (1978) and Disney's *The Hunchback of Notre Dame* (1996). Alexander Dumas's heroes have inspired numerous films. Disney's 1993 and 2004 versions of *The Three Musketeers* – the latter a cartoon

version featuring Mickey Mouse, Donald Duck and Goofy – are both entertaining. Find out who the mysterious prisoner in the Bastille was, in *The Man in the Iron Mask* (1998).

Shopping

The Marais is one of the nicest parts of Paris for shopping with children. For books, **I Love My Blender** *(36 Rue du Temple, 75004; 01 42 77 50 32; closed Sun)* is a good option. The children's concept store **Bonton** *(5 Blvd des Filles du Calvaire, 75003; 01 42 72 34 69)* has a hairdresser, toys and cookery classes. **Papier Tigre** *(5 Rue des Filles du Calvaire, 75003; 01 48 04 00 21; www. papiertigre.fr)* has great stationery. **Merci** *(111 Blvd Beaumarchais, 75003; www.merci-merci.com)* donates its profits to charity, and has a good restaurant and café.

Take cover

Watch a magic show at the café **Le Double Fond** *(1 Pl du Marché Ste-Catherine, 75004; 01 44 71 40 20; www.double fond.com)*. Even the waiters are magicians, performing baffling sleights of hand at table as they serve.

Next stop...
MUSEUMS AND A PRISON

The Marais is home to museums, designer boutiques, art galleries and cafés. To relive the Revolution, go to **Musée Carnavalet** *(see p94)* and **Place de la Bastille** *(see p97)*.

Entrance to the courtyard of the Musée Carnavalet

Imposing façade of Musée Carnavalet, set in lovely gardens

② Musée Carnavalet

A house full of history

This museum tells the story of Paris and how it grew from a tiny village on an island in the river Seine to a city of more than 2 million people. It is a massive collection housed in two sumptuous mansions – the Hôtel Carnavalet and the Hôtel Le Peletier, which are among the grandest in the Marais.

Head for the Art Deco ballroom from the Hôtel Wendel and then head up to the second floor where the Revolutionary galleries are situated. There is a model of the Bastille made from the original prison stones, one of 83 that were sent to every part of the country. Also on show are Napoleon's toothbrush, some of the most famous Revolutionary proclamations

and a fascinating collection of personal belongings used by the royal family during their captivity.

On the ground floor, do not miss the models of medieval Paris and the ancient Roman city of Lutetia. There is a mammoth's tooth found in northern Paris and Neolithic canoes, some of the oldest boats in the world, in the orangerie.

Letting off steam

The museum has a lovely garden that is open to the public, with access from Rue des Francs Bourgeois in the summer. The Marais is full of tiny squares where children can run around. Just behind the museum, unwind in the tranquil **Square Georges Cain** (*Rue Payenne, 75003*), which has a fascinating collection of statues, or in **Square Léopold Achille** next door, which has a playground and a lawn also off Rue Payenne.

The Lowdown

- 🌐 **Map reference** 11 D5
  Address 16 Rue des Francs-Bourgeois, 75003; 01 44 59 58 58; *carnavalet.paris.fr*
- 🚇 **Métro** St-Paul, line 1 or Chemin Vert, line 8. **Bus** 29, 69, 76 & 96
- 🕐 **Open** 10am–6pm, closed Mon and public hols
- 💲 **Price** Free for permanent collection, but charges for special exhibitions
- 🚩 **Guided tours** In English for families; reserve a few weeks in advance. English audio guide €5
- 👫 **Age range** 5 plus
- 🎭 **Activities** Workshops and storytelling events in French: €5–14; 01 44 59 58 31/32; Wed, Sat, Sun & school hols.
- ⏱ **Allow** 1–2 hours
- ♿ **Wheelchair access** Yes, via 16 Rue des Francs-Bourgeois
- 🍴 **Eat and drink** *Snacks* Café du Centre Culturel Suédois (*11 Rue Payenne, 75003; 01 44 78 80 11; noon–6pm Tue–Sun*) is a cosy Swedish café serving Swedish food. It also has a pretty courtyard. *Real meal* Le Loir dans la Théière (*3 Rue des Rosiers, 75004; 01 42 72 90 61; 11:30am–7pm; Sat & Sun brunch from 10am*) serves traditional lunch dishes and cakes. Le Loir is named after the unfortunate dormouse who gets dunked in the teapot at the Mad Hatter's tea party in *Alice in Wonderland*. The lemon meringue and chocolate orange fondant are divine; it is also a good lunch option for vegetarians.
- 🚻 **Toilets** On the first floor

Murals on the wall of the re-created ballroom of Hôtel Wendel, Musée Carnavalet

Prices given are for a family of four

Statue in the pretty garden of Square Georges Cain

Light-filled interior in the Musée Picasso

In the Musée Carnavalet, look out for...

1 Louis XVI's chess set, the dauphin's tin soldiers and bingo game, and a curl of Marie Antoinette's hair.
2 Long, narrow canoes made from a single tree trunk. These canoes date back to way before Julius Caesar wrote the first description of the village of Lutetia (now Paris) in AD 52.
3 Writer Marcel Proust's bedroom. He wrote mostly in bed at night.

③ Musée Picasso
Crazy pots and funny faces

The dominant artist of the 20th century, Pablo Picasso was one of the greatest creative geniuses of all time. Born in Málaga, he lived and studied in Barcelona, Spain, before moving to France, where he spent most of his life. This collection of his work is the finest in the world, and was inherited by the state in lieu of the $50 million in death duties the family owed the state. The collection is housed in the beautiful Hôtel Salé, which was originally built for a salt-tax collector. The light and airy museum spans Picasso's lifetime and covers paintings, sculpture, ceramics and textiles. The collection begins with the artist's self portrait in blue. Painted in 1901, it shows how the poverty and loneliness that Picasso experienced during his early years in Paris had made his life hard.

This is an excellent museum to visit with kids, as they find Picasso's work intriguing and funny. Most kids really enjoy the crazy pots with funny faces in the basement and the vast array of mediums that he worked in.

The museum has been enlarged and modernized to exhibit more of the collection. Picasso enthusiasts can visit the Musée National d'Art Moderne in Centre Pompidou (*see pp80–81*), as well as the Musée de l'Orangerie (*see p108*), the Musée d'Art Moderne (*see p146*) and other institutions in Paris, to see important works by Pablo Picasso and other modern art.

Letting off steam

The **Jardin de l'Hôtel Sale** (*101 Rue Coutures St-Gervais, 75003*) has ping pong tables and a playground. There is a merry-go-round outside Métro St-Paul, which is a convenient treat at the end of a day out.

TOAST TO HIS HEALTH

According to his mother, Pablo Picasso's first words were "piz, piz", which is short for *lapiz* – Spanish for "pencil". His final words were "drink to me, drink to my health, you know I can't drink anymore". Toast the master the next time you sit down for a drink.

Cubed up

Picasso was one of the inventors of a new form of art called Cubism. In his paintings, he reduced the objects he saw to simple shapes like triangles and squares. Make your own Cubist artwork by cutting up photos from magazines or newspapers into angular shapes. Arrange them in different ways and glue them down on a piece of paper.

The Lowdown

- 🌐 **Map reference** 11 D4
  Address Hôtel Salé, 5 Rue de Thorigny, 75003; 01 42 71 25 21; www.musee-picasso.fr
- 🚇 **Métro** St-Paul, line 1 or Chemin Vert, line 8. **Bus** 29, 96, 69 & 75
- 🕐 **Open** Call or visit website
- 💶 **Price** €22; free for under-18s and under-26s with EU passport
- 🧍 **Age range** 3 plus
- ⏱ **Allow** 1–2 hours
- ♿ **Wheelchair access** Yes
- 🍴 **Eat and drink** *Picnic* Chez Marianne (*2 Rue des Hospitalières-*

St-Gervais, 75004; noon–midnight daily) is popular for its breads, falafel and Jewish cakes. Sacha Finkelstajn (27 Rue des Rosiers, 75004; mid-July–mid-August: 10am–7pm daily) sells Jewish pastries and deli dishes.
Snacks Merci (111 Blvd Beaumarchais, 75003; 01 42 77 78 92; www.merci-merci.com; 10am–7pm Mon-Sat) is a concept store; inside it is the Used-Book Café, which serves grilled cheese, soup and cakes. Cantine Merci, also inside the store, serves great vegetarian food and salads.
- 🚻 **Toilets** On the ground floor

Exhibits in the vaults of Le Musée de la Magie

④ Rue des Rosiers

Falafels, bagels and poppy-seed cake

There is nothing nicer on a sunny Sunday afternoon than a stroll down Rue des Rosiers, the hub of Paris's most traditional Jewish quarter. Kids love it, as its all about eating. The street is lined with bakeries selling bagels and cakes from Eastern Europe, and restaurants serving great Jewish fare, which are not to be missed, as well as shops full of candlesticks and other Jewish artifacts and antiques. At the end of the 19th century, Ashkenazi Jews from Eastern Europe fled from the Russian Empire and settled in the run-down, ramshackle area around Rue des Rosiers. In the 1950s and 1960s, Jews from North Africa joined them, bringing a completely different cuisine of falafels, hummus and tabbouleh, giving the place a deliciously cosmopolitan flavour. The street is immortalized in the hilarious, cult French comedy film, *The Mad Adventures of Rabbi Jacob* (1973).

Take cover

The magical **Musée de la Magie** (*11 Rue St-Paul, 75004; www. museedelamagie.com*) is a subterranean 16th-century vault full of interesting curios, optical illusions, interactive games and magic tricks. There are seven rooms stuffed with magic wands and mirrors, magicians' hats, secret boxes and all kinds of strange curios from the 18th century to the present day. There are regular magic shows and a great little shop full of tricks to play on friends and family.

The Lowdown

🌐 **Map reference** 11 C5
Address 75004

🚇 **Métro** St-Paul, line 1. **Bus** 67, 69, 76 & 96

🍴 **Eat and drink** *Picnic* Florence Kahn (*19 Rue des Rosiers, 75004; www.florence-kahn.fr*), a deli, sells Ashkenazi specialities such as gefilte (stuffed) fish and pletzels (onion- and poppy-seed covered flatbread), and the classic cheesecake *vatrouchka*. *Real Meal* Breakfast in America (*4 Rue Malher, 75004; www. breakfast-in-america.com*) is a burger bar serving burgers with fries, and all-day breakfasts with bacon and pancakes.

🚻 **Toilets** No

⑤ Mémorial de la Shoah

France's darkest hour

For a long time, the fate of the 76,000 Jews deported from France during World War II was largely ignored by the official historians and school textbooks, so the opening of this memorial and museum in 2005 was of major importance.

In the basement there is an eternal flame, a simple memorial to an unknown victim of the Holocaust – the Hebrew name for which is Shoah. The memorial provides fascinating details about the lives of victims under the Occupation. On a wall in the garden are the names of those who were murdered in Nazi death camps, among them 11,000 children. It is deeply moving.

The Lowdown

🌐 **Map** 11 C5
Address 17 Rue Geoffroy-l'Asnier, 75004; 01 42 77 44 72; *www.memorialdelashoah.org*

🚇 **Métro** St-Paul, line 1 or Pont Marie, line 7. **Bus** 67, 69, 76 & 96

🕐 **Open** 10am–6pm, till 10pm Thu, closed Sat, 1 Jan, 1 May, 14 Jul, 15 Aug, 25 Dec & Jewish hols

💶 **Price** Free

🚩 **Guided tours** In English on second Sun of the month. There is also a children's guided tour leaflet in French.

🚶 **Age range** 8 plus

🏃 **Activities** Children's workshops in French; 01 53 01 17 87; €12. The museum has an excellent children's website *www. grenierdesarah.org*. The films *Au Revoir Les Enfants* (1987), *La Rafle* (2010) and *The Great Dictator* (1940) and Judith Kerr's children's novel *When Hitler Stole Pink Rabbit* help to introduce the Holocaust to children.

⏱ **Allow** 45 minutes–2 hours

♿ **Wheelchair access** Yes

🛍 **Shop** La Librairie du Mémorial de la Shoah, in the museum

🍴 **Eat and drink** *Snacks* There is a coffee shop in the museum. Place du Marché Ste-Catherine, 75004 is a good spot for a relaxing drink. *Family treat* Vins des Pyrénées (*25 Rue Beautreillis, 75004; 01 42 72 64 94*) serves French cuisine in a classic 1930s setting. The good wine list will appeal to parents.

🚻 **Toilets** On each floor

Restaurants and shops in Rue des Rosiers, heart of the city's Jewish Quarter

Stone wall engraved with the names of 76,000 Jews at the Mémorial de la Shoah

Letting off steam

There is a little playground on **Rue des Nonnains**, behind the Hôtel de Sens, a beautiful Gothic mansion with magical towers. It now houses the Forney fine arts library. In the playground of the **Lycée Charlemagne** school on Rue des Jardins St-Paul, look out for part of the city wall built by King Philippe Auguste. Just north of the memorial is **Rue François Miron**, lined with fairytale buildings and enticing shops for kids. Children who like to cook will enjoy sniffing around in **Izrael**, an Ali Baba cavern full of exotic spices.

⑥ Place de la Bastille

Something missing?

The giant fortress prison that once stood at the Place de la Bastille was stormed by the people on 14 July 1789 and torn to pieces. Originally built in the 14th century, it was converted in the 17th century into a prison for political prisoners, who were usually held without trial. Despite the bad press, the prison was actually not that terrible by contemporary standards. At the centre of the square there now stands a tall green column commemorating a completely different Revolution, that of 1830. Napoleon planned to build a giant bronze elephant here but only a plaster model was ever put up, and that too was destroyed in 1846. The square is also home to the modern Opéra Bastille, and the area east of

the Place is very trendy, with lots of interesting boutiques, shops and cafés, as well as lovely 19th-century courtyards and the new marina, the Port de Plaisance de l'Arsenal, also known as Bassin de l'Arsenal.

Letting off steam

Stroll along the canalside at the **Bassin de l'Arsenal** (*Quai de la Rapée, Bastille*). A charming little park here, Square Henri Galli, preserves some remains of the earliest Bastille, and the original outline of the fortress is marked on the pavements on the corner of Boulevard Henri IV and Rue St-Antoine. The foundation stones of this once-notorious prison can still be seen – in the Bastille Métro station on the line 5 platforms.

The Lowdown

🌐 **Map** 12 E6
Address 75004

🚗 **Métro** Bastille, lines 1, 5 & 8. **Bus** 20, 29, 65, 69, 76, 86, 87 & 91

🍴 **Eat and drink** *Picnic* The lively street markets on Rue d'Aligre, 75012, will give the kids a flavour of French North Africa. Picnic in Place des Vosges or by the canal. *Real Meal* Café Français (*1–3 Pl de la Bastille, 75011; 01 40 29 04 02*) has an excellent bakery and is famous for its *palmier* pastries. There is a classic menu and a terrace, and it's open daily with entertainment for kids on Sundays.

🚻 **Toilets** No

The imposing Colonne de Juillet on Place de la Bastille

Tuileries, Opéra
& Montmartre

Originally built as a fortress, the captivating Musée du Louvre is now the world's biggest museum. Once the home of French kings, it stretches out along the river next to the lovely Jardin des Tuileries, and opposite the Palais Royal, the epicentre of the Revolution. North of here lie more museums, plus the shopping paradise of the splendid Grand Boulevards, and Montmartre, the original home of modern art.

Champs-Elysées & Trocadéro

Eiffel Tower & Les Invalides

Luxembourg & Montparnasse

Tuileries, Opéra & Montmartre

Beaubourg & the Marais

Ile de la Cité & Ile St-Louis

St-Germain & the Latin Quarter

Highlights

The Louvre
Meet mummies, including those of fish and cats, and smile at the *Mona Lisa* at the Musée du Louvre *(see pp104–7)*.

Jardin des Tuileries
Enjoy pony rides, sail wooden boats and have fun in the playgrounds here. Eat lunch under the trees and drink coffee at old-fashioned Café Renard *(see p108)*.

À la Mère de Famille
Do not miss the chocolates in this store on Rue du Faubourg Montmartre. The marzipan animals here have been tempting children since 1761 *(see p117)*.

Musée Grevin
Discover a waxwork world of celebrities. See the arrest of Louis XIV and meet the rich and famous *(see pp116–17)*.

Les Passages
Go shopping in these quaint, covered arcades, one of which is devoted to toys, children's clothes and books *(see p118)*.

Sacré-Coeur and Montmartre
Hop on the mini train for a climb uphill to bohemian Montmartre and its vineyard, and gaze out from the top of the cathedral, the highest point in the city *(see pp122–3 & p124)*.

Above *Children cooling their feet on a hot day in the Jardin du Palais Royal*
Left *Magnificent interiors of the Musée Grevin wax museum*

The Best of
Tuileries, Opéra & Montmartre

Paris's busy city centre spreads north from the Louvre to Montmartre. Shops, restaurants and cafés stand in harmony alongside innumerable museums, theatres and cinemas, fusing history, art and culture with entertainment and pleasure. This area comes alive in winter, when Parisians flock to the glittering Opéra. During the Christmas season, snowflakes over Sacré-Coeur add to Montmartre's charming village feel. In summer, unwind in the Palais Royal's peaceful garden or in the trendy Square des Batignolles.

A perfect Parisian adventure

Begin the day by gazing at mummies in the **Louvre** (see pp104–7). Sail wooden boats in the **Jardin des Tuileries** (see p108) followed by a picnic in the park or a meal in style at **Le Saut du Loup** (see p110), or under the trees at **Café Renard** (see p108).

After lunch, take bus no. 95 north to Place de Clichy (see p127), passing by the opera house, the **Opéra Garnier** (see p119). Walk to Place Pigalle and catch the little train up to **Sacré-Coeur** (see pp122–3). Kids will love the view, and a ride on the old-fashioned carousel.

Stroll down the hill past the old windmills on **Rue Lepic** (see p125). Have dinner and stock up on berlingots, traditional sweets, at **Coquelicot** (see p125) before heading home from Abbesses, the deepest Métro station in Paris.

Right One of the magnificent ceilings in the Opéra Garnier
Below Carousel with Sacré-Coeur in the background

Above *Works by Dalí, including the sculpture* The Profile of Time, *Espace Dalí* **Right** *The glass pyramid of the Louvre*

History, royals and revolutionaries

Go underground at the **Louvre** to check out the foundations of Philippe Auguste's medieval fortress and retrace the steps of the kings, queens and emperors of France through the magnificent royal apartments. Hop across the road to the **Palais Royal** (see p112), where the Revolution began in 1789. Take the kids on a journey through time in the footsteps of Napoleon's soldiers, starting under the arcades of the popular **Rue de Rivoli** (see p109), commissioned to celebrate one of his greatest victories, then see the army in action on the **Arc de Triomphe du Carrousel** (see p104) and on the huge column in **Place Vendôme** (see p111).

Cool off in the **Jardin des Tuileries**, but watch out for the little red dwarf who appears on the eve of a national disaster. Finish the day at the **Opéra Garnier**, which sits at the heart of the new, modern city built by Baron Haussmann in the 19th century. This is the place to feel like a true *belle époque* Parisian, strolling along the boulevards, enjoying the good things in life.

Art lessons

The **Louvre**, home to the most famous painting in the world, the *Mona Lisa*, never ceases to amaze. Ponder why the *Venus de Milo* has no arms and see art as propaganda in David's paintings of Napoleon.

Admire gorgeous jewellery at the **Musée des Art Décoratifs** (see p110) and gaze in awe at Monet's giant water-lily paintings at the **Musée de l'Orangerie** (see p108), before hopping on to bus no. 95 to another of his

favourites, the busy Gare St-Lazare, to sketch the trains from the Pont de l'Europe. From here walk up to Montmartre, past the former homes of some of the most famous artists who ever lived. Round off the day in the wonderful world of the Surrealist painter Salvador Dalí, at the **Espace Dalí** (see p124).

Shop till you drop

Shopping as entertainment began in the covered arcades of **Les Passages** (see p118), which are home to fantastic toy stores and tea-rooms. Check out Paris's two big stores, **Galeries Lafayette** (see p118) and **Printemps** (see p118), then lunch in **Printemps'** rooftop café. Be sure not to miss its state-of-the-art washrooms. Budding ballerinas can spend their pocket money in the shop at the Paris opera house, the **Opéra Garnier**. Wander around the unusual shops at the **Palais Royal**, find something chic at the **Carrousel du Louvre**, or buy something fun to take home in the streets of **Montmartre**.

The Louvre and around

The biggest museum in the world, the Louvre dazzles through the sheer scale and brilliance of its art collections. Kids will love the underground moats, the Egyptian gallery and the *Mona Lisa*. At night the Louvre looks spectacular, with the glass pyramid, which is the entrance to the museum, magically illuminated. The sights around the Louvre are concentrated in a small area, and there is a good mix of indoor and outdoor activities. There can be traffic in the late afternoon, during rush hour, so for a more peaceful walk choose a Sunday morning or public holiday.

Tuileries, Opéra & Montmarte

Sacré-Coeur
p122

Musée Grévin
p116

The Louvre

The Lowdown

🚗 **Métro** Concorde, lines 1, 8 & 12; Pyramides, lines 7 & 14; Tuileries, line 1; Louvre–Rivoli, line 1; Bourse, line 3; Palais Royal–Musée du Louvre, lines 1 & 7. **RER** Musée d'Orsay, line C or Châtelet les Halles, lines A, B & D. **Bus** 21, 24, 27, 39, 42, 48, 52, 67, 68, 69, 72, 73, 74, 75, 76, 81, 84, 85, 94 & 95. **River boat** Quai du Louvre

ℹ️ **Visitor information** 25 Rue des Pyramides, 75001; May–Oct: 9am–7pm Mon–Sun; Nov–Apr: 10am–7pm Mon–Sun; closed 1 May

🛒 **Supermarkets** Monoprix, 21 Ave de l'Opéra, 75001. Franprix, 9 Rue du Mail, 75001 & 20 Pl Marché St-Honoré, 75001 **Market** Marché St-Honoré, Pl du Marché St-Honoré, 75001; 12:30–8:30pm Wed, 7am–3pm Sat & Sun

🎡 **Festivals** Fêtes des Tuileries Funfair (Jul–Aug). Paris Plages (Jul–Aug) (*see pp68–9*)

➕ **Pharmacy** Pharmacie des Petits-Champs, 21 Rue des Petits-Champs, 75001; 01 42 96 97 20; 8am–8pm Mon–Fri, 9:30am–8pm Sat

🛝 **Nearest playground** Jardin des Tuileries, Rue de Rivoli, 75001; dawn–dusk daily (*see p108*)

🚻 **Toilets** Point WC, Carrousel du Louvre; baby change €2

Arcades along Rue de Rivoli

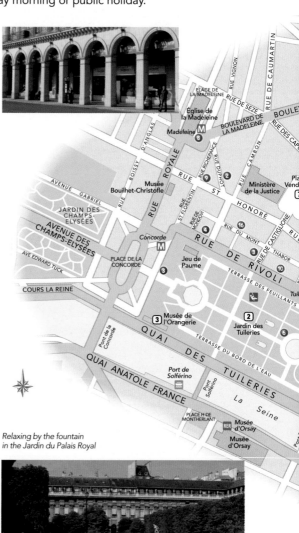

Relaxing by the fountain in the Jardin du Palais Royal

Places of interest

SIGHTS

1. The Louvre
2. Jardin des Tuileries
3. Musée de l'Orangerie
4. Rue de Rivoli
5. Musée des Arts Décoratifs
6. Joan of Arc Statue
7. Place Vendôme
8. Comédie Française
9. Palais Royal
10. Musée en Herbe

EAT AND DRINK

1. Gosselin
2. Mariage Frères
3. Café Marly
4. Colette Water Bar
5. 8 à Huit
6. Café Renard
7. Martin Yannick
8. Fauchon
9. Aux Délices de Manon
10. Angelina
11. Café Kitsuné
12. Saut du Loup
13. Pain Quotidien
14. La Sourdière
15. Le Zinc d'Honoré
16. Le Soufflé
17. Paul
18. Lai Lai Ken
19. Tétrel
20. Grand Véfour
21. Aki Boulangerie
22. A Priori Thé

SHOPPING

1. Apple Store
2. Nature et Découvertes
3. Librarie des Jardin
4. W H Smith
5. EOL

See also The Louvre p107

WHERE TO STAY

1. Hôtel du Louvre
2. Le Burgundy
3. The Westin Paris–Vendôme

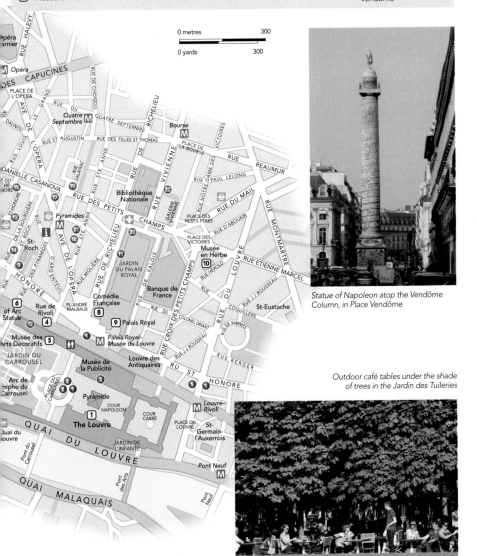

Statue of Napoleon atop the Vendôme Column, in Place Vendôme

Outdoor café tables under the shade of trees in the Jardin des Tuileries

① The Louvre
Mummies, mysterious ladies and medieval moats

Fascinating and beyond famous, the Louvre houses a stunning selection of art from the Middle Ages to 1848, as well as one of the biggest collections of ancient Egyptian treasures in the world. In all there are 35,000 things to see, and to look at them all would take about nine months. In over 800 years, it has metamorphosized from being a fortress to a palace, a stable, a granary and a home for squatters once the kings abandoned Paris. In 1793, after the Revolution, it opened as a museum to display the royal treasures.

Statues on top of the Arc de Triomphe du Carrousel

Key Features

① **Arc de Triomphe du Carrousel**
This triumphal arch was built to celebrate Napoleon's victories in 1805. Its marble columns are adorned with statues of soldiers of the Grand Armée.

② **Inverted pyramid** Made out of glass, this pyramid brings light to the subterranean complex, the Carrousel du Louvre, echoing that of the main entrance.

③ **Cours Visconti** The department of Islamic Art collection ranges from the 7th century to the fall of the Ottoman Empire. More than 3,000 objects are on display, in what is regarded as one of the world's best collections of Islamic Art.

⑤ **Medieval moat** The sheer size of the twin towers and the drawbridge in the moat will impress the kids and give them a taste of the vast fortified castle that once stood here.

⑥ **Glass Pyramid** The popular modern main entrance, designed by Chinese-American architect, I M Pei, was opened in 1989. It is made out of glass and so does not disturb the view of the historic buildings that surround it.

■ **Second Floor** French and Dutch paintings

■ **First Floor** French and Italian paintings, Decorative art and Islamic art

■ **Ground Floor** French and Italian sculpture, Egyptian, Greek and Near Eastern antiquities

■ **Lower Ground Floor** French and Italian sculpture and Islamic art

④ **Tapestries from the Gobelins factory** The museum's Decorative Arts collection, which covers a vast range of objects including jewellery, silver and glassware, also showcases a series of beautiful tapestries from the famous Gobelins factory.

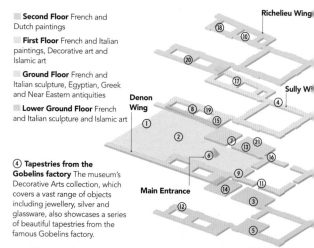

Richelieu Wing
Denon Wing
Sully W
Main Entrance

⑦ **Atrium** The light-filled atrium of IM Pei's glass pyramid houses the statues of the park of the Château de Marly.

⑧ **Mona Lisa** This famous painting once hung on both Louis XIV's and Napoleon's bedroom walls. Leonardo da Vinci never revealed the identity of this mysterious lady.

Prices given are for a family of four

⑨ **Venus di Milo** In this famous Ancient Greek statue Venus, the goddess of Love, may have lost her arms but this is still one of the most famous and beautiful statues in the world.

⑩ **François I** French kings and queens were crazy about Italian art and amassed much of the collection. See François I, in his magnificent Renaissance finery, his hand resting on his dagger, in the museum's French and Italian painting department.

⑪ **Giant Sphinx** Sphinxes were placed at the entrance of Egyptian temples to guard the mysteries of the powerful gods. The mythical monster here guards the museum's Ancient Egyptian antiquities collection.

KIDS' CORNER

A devilish pyramid

The modern glass pyramid in the courtyard is exactly 10 times smaller than the Pyramid of Cheops and contrary to belief it does not have 666 panes of glass. The number 666 is linked with the Devil and has sparked all sorts of rumours about the Louvre and shot it to fame in the popular book, and later film, *The Da Vinci Code*. In fact it has a completely uninteresting 673 panes.

FILCHING FACT FILE

Venus de Milo, the armless sculpture of the Goddess of Love, was discovered hidden under the ground by a Greek peasant while he was ransacking an ancient site on the island of Milos.

A thief in the museum

On a scorching hot summer Sunday in August 1911, the *Mona Lisa* was stolen by an Italian glazier who was working in the Louvre. The newspapers went wild and overnight it became the scandal of the year. The question now was not about the identity of the woman in the painting but where the stolen painting was located. Thousands queued to stare at the empty wall as a massive manhunt got underway. Two years later the glazier tried to sell the painting in Florence. He claimed to have kidnapped the painting to avenge the wagonloads of treasure hauled back to Italy by Napoleon Bonaparte.

The Lowdown

🌐 **Map reference** 10 F4
Address 75001; 01 40 20 53 17; www.louvre.fr.

🚗 **Métro** Palais Royal–Musée du-Louvre, lines 1 & 7. **Bus** 21, 24, 27, 39, 48, 68, 69, 72, 81 & 95. **River boat** Louvre–Quai du Louvre

🕐 **Open** 9am–5:45pm, till 9:45pm Wed & Fri, closed Tue, 1 Jan, 1 May & 25 Dec

€ **Price** €24–30; under 18s free; EU citizens under 26s free. Free first Sun of the month (Nov–Mar), 14 Jul & for under 26s from 6pm Fri

👪 **Skipping the queue** Paris Museum Pass accepted. Buy tickets in advance on the website, through TicketWeb or on FNAC. Tickets are valid for the entire day. Queues are shorter at the entrance by the Arc de Triomphe du Carrousel. Entry from 99 Rue de Rivoli is only for tickets bought in advance. If you have a pushchair walk to the front of the queue and staff will let you through.

🚩 **Guided tours** For adults in English; for children in French

during school hols Mon, Tue, Thu & Fri; 01 40 20 51 77; download themed tours; audio guide Louvre-Nintendo 3DSXL €5; under 18s €3. There is an Egyptian trail for kids in seven languages. The bookshop sells a variety of useful guides for children and families. Free maps are very useful.

🚻 **Age range** 5 plus

👫 **Activities** Workshops, films and talks for children & families in French; 01 40 20 51 77. Take a walk after dark in the Cour Carré, which is magical.

⏱ **Allow** At least 2–3 hours

♿ **Wheelchair access** Yes but limited

🛍 **Shop** The subterranean Carrousel du Louvre is a great place to browse the shops.

🚻 **Toilets** In the lobby and on all floors. Do not miss the Point WC in the Carrousel du Louvre

Good family value?

Plan the trip in advance using the website. On a first trip see the medieval moats, then visit the Egyptian collection and peep at the mysterious *Mona Lisa*.

① The Louvre continued ▶

The Louvre continued...
Mummies, mysterious ladies and medieval moats

⑫ The Dying Slave Michelangelo sculpted this work as part of a group of statues for the base of the tomb of Pope Julius II in Rome. These statues along with the 15th-century *Madonna and Child* by Donatello are displayed in the French and Italian sculpture collection.

⑬ Assyrian temple The Near Eastern antiquities collection is home to a re-created Assyrian temple. The ancient Assyrians believed that the winged bulls with human heads now on show in the Louvre would protect them against their enemies.

⑭ Marly Horses These dramatic early 18th-century statues of men restraining horses, which represent the struggle between man and beast, once stood in the garden of Louis XIV's Château de Marly but were later shifted to the Place de la Concorde.

⑮ Galerie d'Apollon With its gilded, panelled interior, this gallery looks like a jewel box, and is one too – it holds the crown jewels, including Empress Eugénie's crown, which has 2,490 diamonds.

⑯ Winged Victory of Samothrace One of the most famous Ancient Greek statues in the world, this belongs to the Hellenistic period (late 3rd to 2nd century BC), when statues began to get more naturalistic human forms. This statue was eventually restored.

⑰ Statue of Charlemagne The Decorative Arts collection spans many countries and centuries. It contains this rider, who is believed to be either Charlemagne or his grandson, Charles the Bald.

⑱ The Lacemaker The highlight of the museum's Dutch painting collection is Jan Vermeer's masterpiece, painted around 1665. His works give a glimpse into everyday life in the Netherlands.

Letting off steam
On the doorstep of the Louvre is one of Paris's oldest and most beautiful parks, the **Jardin des Tuileries** (see p108). Sail wooden boats, play in the playground and relax under the trees.

Eat and drink
Picnic: under €25; Snacks: €25–40; Real meal: €40–90; Family treat: over €90 (based on a family of four)

PICNIC Gosselin (*123–125 Rue St-Honoré, 75001; 01 45 08 03 59; www.gosselin.paris; 7am–8pm Sun–Fri*), is a bakery selling a selection of wholesome salads and sandwiches made from home-made bread.
SNACKS Mira (*Carrousel du Louvre, 01 55 35 12 60; open daily*) is a self-service Spanish tapas bar, which also serves a tasty paella.

Prices given are for a family of four

Lush greenery flanks the wide gravel walkways of the Jardin des Tuileries

REAL MEAL Colette Water Bar (*213 Rue St-Honoré, 75001; 01 55 35 33 90; 11am–7pm*) sells bottled water from around the world and bites to eat. Go for lunch or tea.
FAMILY TREAT Café Marly (*Richelieu wing, 93 Rue de Rivoli, 75001; 01 49 26 06 60; 8–1am; book in advance*) serves modern French fare.

Find out more
DIGITAL The Louvre website is fantastically child-friendly. Click on the cartoon figure of the first director Dominique Vivant Denon and check out "Tales of the Museum" at *www.louvre.fr*. There is more to discover about Ancient Egypt at *www.bbc.co.uk/history/ancient/ egyptians*. The museum shops also stock good CD-Roms, *One Minute at the Museum* and *The Louvre, Art for Kids*.
FILM Two excellent films for children are *One Minute at the Museum* and *The Amazing Museum*, both available in the museum shop. *Looney Tunes Louvre Come Back to Me* (1962) is more light-hearted. *The Da Vinci Code* (2006), a film adaptation of writer Dan Brown's bestselling novel of the same name, features the museum.

⑲ **Coronation of Napoleon** This 1807 painting by Jacques-Louis David is a piece of propaganda. Napoleon's family is shown, including his mother who was not even present for the ceremony. The artist also included himself – look for a man sketching in the balcony.

⑳ **The Raft of the Medusa** Thédore Géricault derived inspiration for this gigantic and moving work from the shipwreck of a French frigate in 1816.

㉑ **Code of Hammurabi** The King of Babylon wrote the first legal code in the world on a stone called a stele. Housed in the impressive Near Eastern antiquities collection, this is the world's oldest legal document.

Shopping

The underground Carrousel du Louvre is full of shops, including **Nature et Découvertes** (99 Rue de Rivoli, 75001), a branch of the scientific toyshop. Look out for scale models of the Louvre. The **Librarie des Jardins** (Jardin des Tuileries, 75001) sells children's books in English. **W H Smith** (248 Rue de Rivoli, 75001; www.whsmith. fr) has the best collection of English-language books for children in Paris. Fans of model-making should not miss **EOL** (3 Rue du Louvre, 75001; www.eolmodelisme.com).

a lovely place to take a stroll. Alternatively, walk over the **Pont des Arts** (see p73) and admire the view at sunset. In bad weather, head to **Aquarium de Paris – Cinéaqua** (see p144), a cutting-edge aquarium at Trocadéro, which is the perfect antidote to too much sightseeing.

Aquarium de Paris – Cinéaqua, one of the biggest aquariums in Paris

Next stop...

A BREATH OF FRESH AIR After a trip to the Louvre everyone needs to relax. In summer the gardens at the **Palais Royal** (see p114) are

Children's playground in the midst of the Jardin des Tuileries

② Jardin des Tuileries

A Parisian playground and a missing palace

Kids have been in love with the Jardin des Tuileries since it was opened to the public in the 17th century, supposedly after Charles Perrault, the author of the classic fairytale *Sleeping Beauty*, persuaded Louis XIV's minister Colbert that the people of Paris needed somewhere to let off steam. Designed in the 1660s by André Le Nôtre, who was responsible for the grounds at Versailles, these formal gardens create a beautiful green artery through the city centre, linking the Louvre with the Champs-Elysées.

The gardens were once an integral part of the now lost Palais des Tuileries, which was burned to the ground during the Commune of 1871. The palace originally stood at the top of the steps in front of the Arc du Carrousel built by Napoleon, thus forming a fourth side to the Louvre quadrangle.

There is a playground and a carousel, in addition to two ponds. Kids love sailing wooden boats in the big pond by the Louvre. In summer a large funfair moves in, with rides, stalls and a giant Ferris wheel.

Take cover

About 15 minutes' walk up Avenue de l'Opéra is a multimedia museum, **Paris Story** *(11 Rue Scribe, 75009; 01 42 66 62 06; www.paris-story. com; 10am–6pm daily)* with an audiovisual show that appeals to kids. Although slightly overpriced, it gives a good historical overview for children who know little about the history of France.

The Lowdown

- 🌐 **Map reference** 9 D3
  Address Rue de Rivoli, 75001; 01 40 20 90 43; www.paris.fr
- 🚗 **Métro** Tuileries, line 1; Concorde, lines 1, 8 & 12 or Palais Royal–Musée du Louvre, lines 1 & 7. **Bus** 21, 24, 27, 42, 68, 72, 73, 81, 84 & 94
- 🕐 **Open** 7:30am–7:30pm daily; Apr & May: till 9pm; summer: till 11pm
- 💲 **Price** Merry-go-round €2.50
- 👫 **Age range** All ages
- 🏃 **Activities** Free playground and funfair in summer
- ⏱ **Allow** 1–2 hours
- 🍽 **Eat and drink** *Picnic* Picnic 8 à Huit *(205 Rue St-Honoré, 75001; 8am–8pm Mon–Sat)* is good for picnic supplies. Picnic in the Jardin des Tuileries. *Real meal* Café Renard *(Jardin des Tuileries, 75001; 01 42 96 50 56; www. caferenard.fr; 9:30am–7pm; Jul–Aug: till 11pm)* is a century-old restaurant, with waiters in traditional outfits.
- 🚻 **Toilets** By the Place de la Concorde entrance

③ Musée de l'Orangerie

Monet and water lilies

Small and compact, the Musée de l'Orangerie is a lovely art museum for children. It houses works from the Walter-Guillaume collection, whuch spans art from the late Impressionist era to the inter-war period, including works by Cézanne, Matisse and Renoir. It is the sheer size of the gigantic paintings by Claude Monet, *Les Nymphéas* or water-lily paintings, which curve around the walls, that will make the biggest impression. Monet spent much of his old age painting this series in his garden in Giverny. Notice the thick paint and blurring of the image, which are partly the result of Monet's failing eyesight. The colours he used weave a magical, restful spell.

Letting off steam

The museum is located on the edge of the Jardin des Tuileries. The entrance to the gardens is just a few steps away to the north. Alternatively, walk across Place de la Concorde to the **Jardin des Champs-Elysées** (see p136).

Towering obelisk of Luxor in Place de la Concorde

Interactive exhibit featuring the Eiffel Tower, at Paris Story

Napoleon's grandest Parisian thoroughfare, and still fashionable, the Rue de Rivoli

The Lowdown

🌐 **Map reference** 9 C3
   Address Jardin des Tuileries, 75001; *www.musee-orangerie.fr*

🚗 **Métro** Concorde, lines 1, 8 & 12. **Bus** 24, 42, 52, 72, 73, 84 & 94

🕐 **Open** 9am–6pm, closed Tue, 1 May, 14 Jul am & 25 Dec

Ⓒ **Price** €15–25; under 18s free; EU citizens under 26 free

👫 **Skipping the queue** €26–36, joint ticket with Musée d'Orsay. Paris Museum Pass accepted

🚩 **Guided tours** Audio guide in English €5. The bookshop sells a kids' guide, *My Little Orangerie*

👫 **Age range** 5 plus

⏱ **Allow** 30 minutes

♿ **Wheelchair access** Yes

🍴 **Eat and drink** *Picnic* Martin Yannick (*302 Rue St-Honoré, 75001; closed Sat & Sun*) offers shortbread, the *sable* St-Roch. Picnic in the Jardin des Tuileries. *Snacks* Fauchon (*24–26 Pl de la Madeleine, 75008*) is the place to try a mini éclair glazed with Mona Lisa eyes.

👫 **Toilets** In the basement of the museum

④ Rue de Rivoli
A touch of Napoleonic grandeur

The elegant Rue de Rivoli was laid out in 1802 by Napoleon, part of his campaign to proclaim Paris as the capital of Europe. It is named after his victory over the Austrians at the Battle of Rivoli in 1797. It stretches from Place de la Concorde to the Marais, although the section that runs east from the Louvre, which has the biggest concentration of shops, was finished only in 1865. The new thoroughfare cut through a network of medieval streets in which a bomb had almost killed Napoleon in 1800. Be sure to take a stroll down the long arcades.

Letting off steam
Head to the **Jardin des Tuileries**. The arcaded stretch of the Rue de Rivoli, filled with a mix of shops selling luxury goods and tourist souvenirs, runs along the northern side of the gardens.

The Lowdown

🌐 **Map reference** 9 D2
   Address 75001 & 75004

🚗 **Métro** Tuileries, line 1; Louvre–Rivoli, line 1 or Hôtel de Ville, line 1. **RER** Châtelet–Les Halles, lines A, B & D. **Bus** 67, 69, 72, 74, 75 & 76

🍴 **Eat and drink** *Snacks* Aux Délices de Manon (*400 Rue St-Honoré, 75001; 01 42 60 83 03; www.delicesdemanon.com*) is a friendly café and takeaway. *Family treat* Angelina (*226 Rue de Rivoli, 75001; 01 42 60 82 00; www.angelina-paris.fr; 9am–7pm*), a 19th-century tearoom, is legendary for its hot chocolate and Mont Blanc meringues.

👫 **Toilets** The luxurious Point WC in the Carrousel du Louvre

Le Nôtre's grand formal gardens in the Jardin des Tuileries

KIDS' CORNER

Look out for...
1 The Jeu de Paume, opposite the Musée de l'Orangerie, is where the king used to play indoor tennis. The name means "palm game" because it was played with bare hands then!
2 A moat. The fortress of Charles V was surrounded by a large moat that ran along the bottom of the stairs and into the Tuileries from the Place du Carrousel.
3 Monet's famous paintings of water lilies in the Musée de l'Orangerie. Can you see which tree often features in them?

Answer at the bottom of the page.

TELLING TALES
The first author to write a book of fairytales, Charles Perrault published his stories, including *Sleeping Beauty*, *Cinderella*, *Puss in Boots* and *Little Red Riding Hood*, in 1697. Although these tales had been known and told for generations, they had never been written down. Perrault first wrote the book for his children.

The Little Red Man of the Tuileries
The Palais des Tuileries was said to be haunted by a red hobgoblin who appeared whenever there was about to be a national catastrophe. The sinister dwarf was seen by Catherine de Médici before the deaths of three of her six children. Henri IV also saw him just before he was assassinated. The goblin was last seen in the flames of the palace as it burned to the ground in 1871.

Answer: **3** Weeping willows.

The Musée des Arts Décoratifs with the Saut du Loup café in the foreground

⑤ Musée des Arts Décoratifs

Glittering jewels, dolls and posters

Learn how to live and dress in style through the four museums housed in the eclectic Musée des Arts Décoratifs. The **Galerie des Jouets** has around 12,000 toys from the 19th and early 20th centuries, including a beautiful collection of dolls. The **Galerie des Bijoux** has a stunning jewellery collection, including over-the-top Baroque bling and delicate elf brooches in Art Nouveau style. Look out for the 10 rooms that show how the rich lived from 1400 to the early 20th century. The **Musée de la Publicité** (Advertising Museum) showcases 40,000 historic advertising posters, and also has a cinema room with designer seating, where visitors can watch advertising films. Try also to catch one of the dazzling temporary exhibitions of clothes shown in the **Musée de la Mode**.

Letting off steam

Cross Place André Malraux to reach the **Jardin du Palais Royal**, a good spot for running around.

A relaxing corner in the Jardin du Palais Royal

The Lowdown

- 🌐 **Map reference** 10 E3
  Address 107 Rue de Rivoli, 75001; 01 44 55 57 50; www.lesartsdecoratifs.fr
- 🚗 **Métro** Palais Royal–Musée du Louvre, lines 1 & 7 or Pyramides, lines 7 & 14. **Bus** 21, 27, 39, 48, 68, 69, 72, 81 & 95
- 🕐 **Open** 11am–6pm Tue–Sun, till 9pm Thu (for temporary exhibitions)
- 💶 **Price** €19–29; under 18s and EU citizens under 26 free
- 👫 **Skipping the queue** The museum does not attract huge crowds
- 🎫 **Guided tours** Free audio guide; family tours in French; call for details
- 👫 **Age range** 6 plus
- 👫 **Activities** Children's workshops Wed afternoons & school hols 10am & 2pm; 01 44 55 59 25
- ⏱ **Allow** 1–2 hours
- ♿ **Wheelchair access** Yes
- 🍴 **Eat and drink** *Snacks* Café Kitsuné (51 Galerie Montpensier, 75001; 01 40 15 62 31; closed Mon) is a cute coffee shop from the clothes label Kitsuné. *Real meal* Saut du Loup (107 Rue de Rivoli; 01 42 25 49 55; www.lesautduloup.fr; noon–midnight), accessed via the museum, is great for cakes and ice cream on the terrace in summer. The menu is modern French cuisine. Kids can play on the lawns.
- 👫 **Toilets** On the ground floor

⑥ Joan of Arc Statue

A knight in shining armour

Erected in 1880, this glittering golden equestrian statue of Joan of Arc (Jeanne d'Arc) stands on Place des Pyramides. During the Hundred Years' War, Joan of Arc gazed down on Paris from the small hill that is now Place André Malraux – La Butte des Moulin, or Windmill Hill – hoping that her army of 12,000 men would drive the English out of the city. It was here that she was wounded in the leg by an arrow. Canonized in 1920, Joan of Arc is one of the patron saints of France along with St Denis and St Louis.

The Lowdown

- 🌐 **Map reference** 10 E3
  Address Pl des Pyramides, 75001
- 🚗 **Métro** Tuileries, line 1 or Pyramides, lines 7 & 14. **Bus** 48, 69 & 72
- 👫 **Age range** All ages
- 🍴 **Eat and drink** *Real meal* Pain Quotidien (18 Pl du Marché St-Honoré, 75001; www.lepainquotidien.com; 8am–10pm), is a reliable bet for a light meal or simply for coffee and chocolate spread on toast. *Family treat* La Sourdière (4 Rue de la Sourdière, 75001; 01 42 60 12 87) offers good traditional bistro food.
- 👫 **Toilets** No

Gleaming Joan of Arc in the middle of Place des Pyramides

Napoleonic details on the Vendôme Column in Place Vendôme

Letting off steam

The statue is right by the gate to the **Jardin des Tuileries** *(see p108)* and only moments from the gardens of the arcaded **Jardin du Palais Royal**, whose courtyard contains black-and-white-striped columns perfect for jumping off.

⑦ Place Vendôme

Paris's chicest square

Built in 1699 to reflect the glory of the equestrian statue of Louis XIV that was placed in the centre, Place Vendôme failed to impress the revolutionaries. They melted the statue to make cannons to fight off invading armies. In 1806, a giant column, based on Trajan's Column in Rome, was constructed using captured enemy cannons. It proclaimed Napoleon's army's exploits in a spiral strip around the outside. This too was torn down by revolutionaries in 1871, and a copy now stands in its place. Perhaps the most chic spot in Paris, this square is beautiful at night. It has also witnessed famous events such as the marriage of Napoleon to Josephine at No. 3. The Ritz hotel at No. 15 has had a long list of famous guests including Ernest Hemingway, Edward VII, Charlie Chaplin and Princess Diana.

Letting off steam

Nearby is the **Jardin des Tuileries** with lawns, fountains and a popular playground. Let the kids be mini-Parisians, sailing wooden boats on the pond.

Elegant arcaded façades on Place Vendôme, housing exclusive shops

The Lowdown

- 🌐 **Map reference** 10 E2
  Address 75001
- 🚗 **Métro** Tuileries, line 1.
  Bus 67, 74, 81 & 85
- 🚻 **Age range** All ages
- 🍽 **Eat and drink** *Real meal* Le Zinc d'Honoré (36 Pl du Marché St-Honoré, 75001; 01 49 27 05 00; open daily) serves steak with potato gratin or fries. *Family treat* Le Soufflé (36 Rue du Mont Thabor, 75001; 01 42 60 27 19; www.lesouffle.fr; closed Sun) is the perfect place to sample sweet and savoury soufflés.
- 🚻 **Toilets** No

Picnic under €25; Snacks €25–45; Real meal €45–90; Family treat over €90 (based on a family of four)

⑧ Comédie Française
A staged death

Founded by King Louis XIV in 1680, the Comédie Française is often known by its earlier name, Maison de Molière, after the troupe of actors brought together by the famous French playwright, Molière. Its productions in period costume are sensational, although best appreciated by those who understand French. The present building was built in 1900 after a severe fire destroyed the original structure. Look out for the armchair in which Molière died, a few hours after collapsing dramatically on stage while performing his aptly named play, *Le Malade Imaginaire – The Imaginary Invalid*. He did not receive the last rites, since two

Colonnaded façade of the Comédie Française

priests refused to visit him while a third arrived too late. The theatre then was a drunken, violent and riotous place, and actors were considered the ultimate lowlife. In 1673, a dissatisfied audience even tried to burn the theatre down.

Letting off steam
Walk up **Rue de Richelieu** to look at the fountain decorated with a statue of Molière and then enjoy a run around the **Palais Royal**.

⑨ Palais Royal
The king of the castle and the dirty rascal

Built in 1624, Palais Royal was originally the home of Cardinal Richelieu, who, during the reign of Louis XIII, was considered the most powerful man in France. Later, the palace became the childhood home of Louis XIV. In the 1780s, Louis XVI's brother, the Duke of Orléans, enclosed the gardens with arcades and filled them with plenty of cafés, shops and theatres. Unlike Versailles it was

somewhere everyone could come and enjoy themselves. As a result it was often quite rowdy and dangerous. The restaurants and coffee houses were the seedbed of the Revolution, which began when Camille Desmoulins called the city to arms in one of the cafés here the night before the Bastille was stormed. The arcades continue to house several fine restaurants as well as lots of intriguing shops selling stamps, toy soldiers, music boxes and medals.

Letting off steam
The delightful **Jardin du Palais Royal** is the perfect place to picnic. Bring a ball and a skipping rope or buy one in the toyshop by the Grand Véfour restaurant. Watch out for the pond – Louis XIV almost drowned here as a child.

Unwinding at a café in the graceful Place du Palais Royal

The Lowdown

🌐 **Map reference** 10 F3
Address Pl de Palais Royal, 75001

🚇 **Métro** Palais Royal–Musée du Louvre, lines 1 & 7; Pyramides, lines 7 & 14 or Bourse, line 3.
Bus 21, 24, 27, 29, 39, 48, 68, 69, 72, 81 & 95

♿ **Wheelchair access** Yes

🍴 **Eat and drink** *Picnic* Tétrel (44 Rue des Petits Champs, 75002) offers the most famous sweets in France. Try Asterix's favourite *les bêtises de Cambrai* (the naughtiness of Cambrai). Picnic in the Jardin du Palais Royal. *Family treat* Le Grand Véfour (17 Rue du Beaujolais, 75001; 01 42 96 56 27; 12:30–2pm, 8–10pm, closed Sat, Sun & Aug), one of the first grand restaurants in France, is under the direction of Michelin-starred chef Guy Martin. Sit in Napoleon's seat and soak up the history here.

🚻 **Toilets** No

The Lowdown

🌐 **Map reference** 10 F3
Address 2 Rue de Richelieu, 75001; 08 25 10 16 80; www.comedie-francaise.fr

🚗 **Métro** Palais Royal–Musée du Louvre, lines 1 & 7.
Bus 21, 24, 27, 39, 48, 68, 69, 72, 81 & 95

🕐 **Open** Check website for performance timings

💲 **Price** €16–26 for tickets

👫 **Age range** 11 plus

♿ **Wheelchair access** Yes

🍴 **Eat and drink** *Picnic* Paul (25 Ave de l'Opéra, 75002; 01 42 60 78 22) serves croissants, sandwiches and salads. Picnic in the Palais Royal. *Real meal* Lai Lai Ken (7 Rue Ste-Anne, 75001; 01 40 15 96 90; 9am–6pm daily) is a fun, canteen-style Japanese café.

🚻 **Toilets** For theatregoers only

Well-manicured lawns of the Jardin du Palais Royal

Innovative artwork by Keith Haring, on display at the Musée en Herbe

⑩ Musée en Herbe

Sticking and glueing, Picasso-style

The inspirational Musée en Herbe, an art museum especially designed to introduce children to the world of art through reproductions of famous pictures and interactive games, was groundbreaking when it was set up in 1975. The museum presents art shows and workshops for children, based on the works of celebrated artists. Kids will enjoy the sticking and glueing activities while learning to appreciate art. There are workshops for toddlers, a gallery for aspiring young artists and a space for temporary exhibitions. Most of the permanent exhibits set out to showcase innovative work that plays with perspective or colour combinations.

Letting off steam

Stroll up to the square of **Place des Victoires**. Take the exit by Le Grand Véfour and turn right – it is a 5-minute walk. If the weather is bad, wander in the 19th-century arcade, **Galerie Vivienne**, which is close to the square.

Equestrian statue of Louis XIV in Place des Victoires

The Lowdown

🌐 **Map reference** 10 G2
Address 21 Rue Hérold, 75001; 01 40 67 97 66; www.musee-en-herbe.com

🚗 **Métro** Les Halles, line 4 or Palais Royal–Musée du Louvre, lines 1 & 7. **RER** Châtelet les Halles, lines A, B & D. **Bus** 29, 48, 67, 74 & 85

🕐 **Open** 10am–7pm daily, until 9pm Thu

💶 **Price** €32–52; depends on the activity chosen

Guided tours 01 40 67 97 66; book in advance

Age range All ages

Activities Workshops in French; 01 40 67 97 66; reservation recommended

⏱ **Allow** 1–2 hours

♿ **Wheelchair access** Yes

🍽 **Eat and drink** *Picnic* Aki Boulangerie (*11 Rue St-Anne, 75001; 01 42 97 54 27; closed Sun*), in the Little Japan district of Paris, is a French bakery which prepares snacks with a Japanese twist. Worth trying is the crusty sandwich filled with *tonkatsu* (breaded pork). Picnic in the Jardin du Palais Royal. *Real meal* A Priori Thé (*35 Galerie Vivienne, 75002; 01 42 97 48 75; noon–6pm daily*) is a good stop for lunch, with desserts in half portions. It is famous for its cheesecake.

Toilets Yes

Musée Grévin and around

Spotting the who's who of the celebrity world in the Musée Grévin, then gorging on a sumptuous bar of chocolate in one of the city's oldest sweet shops, À la Mère de Famille, is a wonderful, fun way to spend a rainy day in Paris with children. Les Passages, the covered arcades just off Boulevard Montmartre, are full of enchanting shops and cafés, which the kids will love. All the attractions are indoors and within easy walking distance of each other.

Tuileries, Opéra & Montmartre

Sacré-Coeur p122

Musée Grévin

The Louvre p104

Places of interest

SIGHTS
1. Musée Grévin
2. Les Passages
3. Les Grands Boulevards
4. Opéra Garnier

● **EAT AND DRINK**
1. À la Mère de Famille
2. Krep
3. Le Bouillon Chartier
4. La Boule Rouge
5. Stanz, Les Ateliers du Bagel
6. L'Arbre à Cannelle
7. Déli-Cieux
8. Brasserie Printemps
9. Monoprix
10. Chez Clément
See also Musée Grévin (p116)

● **SHOPPING**
1. Citadium
2. La Cure Gourmande
3. Pain d'Epices
4. La Boîte à Joujoux
5. Le Petit Roi
6. Rue Drouot
7. Galeries Lafayette
8. Printemps

● **WHERE TO STAY**
1. Hôtel Chopin
2. Hôtel de la Cité Rougemont
3. Park Hyatt Vendôme
4. Résidhome Paris-Opéra

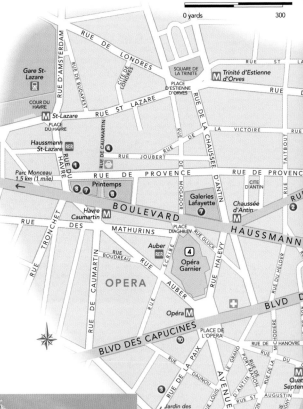

0 metres 300
0 yards 300

Symbol of the opulence of the Second Empire, Opéra Garnier

Interior of the popular bistro, Le Bouillon Chartier

The Lowdown

🚗 **Métro** Richelieu-Drouot, lines 8 & 9; Grands Boulevards, lines 8 & 9; Bourse, line 3 or Opéra, lines 3, 7 & 8. **RER** Haussmann St-Lazare, line E; Auber, line A. **Bus** 20, 21, 22, 24, 27, 29, 32, 39, 42, 48, 53, 66, 67, 68, 74, 81, 85 & 95

ℹ️ **Visitor information** 25 Rue des Pyramides, 75001; May–Oct: 9am–7pm Mon–Sun; Nov–Apr: 10am–7pm Mon–Sun; closed 1 May

🛒 **Supermarkets** Franprix, 5 Rue Geoffroy Marie, 75009; Monoprix, 56 Rue des Caumartin, 75009. **Markets** Marché du Bourse, Pl de la Bourse, 75002; 12:30–8:30pm Tue & Fri

🎉 **Festivals** Christmas windows, a fantasy-land window display as part of Christmas decorations and window fittings, Printemps & Galeries Lafayette (Dec)

➕ **Pharmacy** Pharmacie Centre Opéra, 6 Blvd des Capucines, 75009; 01 42 65 88 29; open till 12:30am

🛝 **Nearest playground** Square de Montholon, Rue Lafayette, 75009; dawn–dusk (see p117)

Map labels: RUE DE BELLEFOND, RUE DE MAUBEUGE, RUE MAYRAN, RUE ROCHAMBEAU, SQUARE DE MONTHOLON, RUE LAMARTINE, RUE DE MONTHOLON, RUE PAPILLON, RUE BUFFAULT, Cadet Ⓜ, RUE LAFAYETTE, RUE BLEUE, RUE DE TREVISE, RUE POISSONNIERE, ATEAUDUN, Dame .orette Ⓜ, VICTOIRE, RUE DU FAUBOURG, RUE CADET, RUE SAULNIER, RUE DES DEUX SŒURS, RUE LE PELETIER, Le Peletier Ⓜ, Folies Bergère, CITE, RUE A THOMAS, RUE DU FAUBOURG POISSONNIERE, FAYETTE, RUE DE PROVENCE, PASSAGE VERDEAU, RUE RICHER, RUE STE CECILE, RUE DU CONSERVATOIRE, RUE CHAUCHAT, RUE DROUOT, RUE MONTMARTRE, RUE GEOFFROY MARIE, BOULEVARD, RUE DE MONTYON, RUE LAFFITTE, RUE LE PELETIER, RUE ROSSINI, Les Passages ②, RUE BERGERE, RUE ROUGEMONT, es Grands oulevards ③, Richelieu-Drouot, Musée Grévin ①, CITE BERGERE, Ⓜ BLVD MONTMARTRE, LIENS, La Tête dans les Nuages, PGE DES PRINCES, RUE D'AMBOISE, Grands Boulevards Ⓜ, BLVD POISSONNIERE, Les Passages ②, PGE DES PANORAMAS, RUE D'UZES, RUE FAVART, RUE, ST, RUE VIVIENNE, R MONTMARTRE, MARC, FEYDEAU, RUE DE RICHELIEU, RUE DE LA BOURSE, PL DE LA BOURSE, MBRE, Bourse des Valeurs, Bourse Ⓜ, LLES, ST THOMAS, PL DE LA BOURSE, RUE COLBERT, RUE VIVIENNE, RUE DE LA BANQUE, Bibliothèque Nationale, GALERIE COLBERT, GALERIE VIVIENNE, JARDIN U PALAIS ROYAL

Paris's historic waxworks museum, Musée Grévin

① Musée Grévin

Glass eyes, great events and ghoulish murders

This is the best place for spotting celebrities captured in wax – kings and queens, pop stars and footballers. Comparisons with London's Madame Tussauds are inevitable but Grévin is less gruesome and more authentic. The museum is famous for its historical scenes, among them a gory portrayal of the Revolution, and depictions of the big events of the 20th century. But what steals the show is the museum's splendid Baroque building, home to the original light and sound show from the 1900 Universal Exhibition.

Sign outside the Musée Grévin

Key Features

① **Palais des Mirages** The play of sound, light and mirrors in this giant kaleidoscope is amazing, and each glance upwards reveals a new perspective.

■ **First Floor** Hall of Mirrors, The Tout-Paris Theatre

■ **Ground Floor** Marble Staircase, Workshop, The Grévin Collection, Hall of Columns

■ **Lower Floor** Gift Shop

■ **Basement** The History of France, The 20th Century

② **Le Théâtre Tout-Paris** Mingle with celebrities in this stunning theatre and have a paparazzi take your picture with the likes of Brad Pitt and George Clooney. The stars change over the years – those on the wane head for the melting pot.

③ **Grand Escalier de Marbre** Make a grand entrance as you ascend the mirrored marble staircase, and be bowled over by the beauty of the interiors.

④ **Les Clichés du 20e siècle** See the great events of the 20th century in this section, including Neil Armstrong taking his first steps on the Moon.

Entrance

⑤ **Secrets d'Atelier** Learn the secrets of how a waxwork is created in the special exhibition – it takes six months and a team of 10 artists to make one model.

⑥ **Salle des Colonnes** The panelled columns in this hall are carved out of rosewood and decorated with gold and marble. Also housed inside are some of the museum's best waxwork models.

⑦ **Histoire de France** Step back in time. This section has historical tableaux of icons from the past.

The Lowdown

🌐 **Map reference** 4 G6
Address 10 Blvd Montmartre, 75009; 01 47 70 85 05; www.grevin.com

🚗 **Métro** Grands Boulevards or Richelieu-Drouot, lines 8 & 9 or Bourse, line 3. **Bus** 20, 39, 48, 67, 74 & 85

🕐 **Open** 10am–5.30pm Mon–Fri, till 7pm Sat & Sun, public & school hols; from 9am autumn & Christmas school hols, closed for the five days after Christmas

💶 **Price** €43–79; under 6s free

👪 **Skipping the queue** Paris Museum Pass accepted. Buy tickets in advance on the website or from FNAC and Virgin stores. If you don't get the chance to do either of these, then go at lunchtime.

🚩 **Guided tours** Tours in French at 2:30pm on Sat & Sun, closed school hols: €20 per child; book in advance; 01 47 70 83 97

👫 **Age range** 6 plus.

👫 **Activities** Kids love to spot the famous people on display. Carry a camera and get snapped hobnobbing with the stars.

⏱ **Allow** 1 hour 30 minutes

♿ **Wheelchair access** Yes

☕ **Café** Café Grévin close by

🚻 **Toilets** At several locations

Good family value?
Although it is a fun break from art galleries and highbrow museums, the Musée Grévin is not a cheap place to visit.

Chocolates and sweets on display, À la Mère de Famille

Letting off steam
You'll find a playground and ping-pong tables in the pretty park in **Square de Montholon** (80 Rue Lafayette, 75009), a 10-minute walk to the northeast. For a serious run around take the Métro and head for the **Jardin des Tuileries** (see p108) or **Parc Monceau** (see pp140–41).

Eat and drink
Picnic: under €25; Snacks: €25–45; Real meal: €45–90; Family treat: over €90 (based on a family of four)

PICNIC À la Mère de Famille (35 Rue du Faubourg Montmartre, 75009; 01 47 70 83 69; www.lameredefamille.com) opened in 1761 and sells everything to satisfy a sweet tooth. Walk over to Square de Montholon for a picnic.
SNACKS Krep (11 Rue La Fayette, 75009) serves sweet or savoury crêpes to eat in or takeaway.
REAL MEAL Le Bouillon Chartier (7 Rue du Faubourg Montmartre, 75009; 01 47 70 86 29; www.restaurant-chartier.com; 11:30am–10pm) is a French bistro with waiters dressed in white aprons. It is a popular spot with local families. Get there at noon on the dot, or 6:30pm to avoid the queues in high season.
FAMILY TREAT La Boule Rouge (1 Rue de la Boule Rouge, 75009; 01 47 70 43 90; noon–3pm & 7–11:30pm Mon–Sat) is a good restaurant in which to sample delicious North African cuisine.

Find out more
DIGITAL Watch Michael Jackson meet his wax model at http://tinyurl.com/3tjzkw5, and Pauvre Pierrot, the first cartoon film ever made and shown at the Musée Grévin at http://tinyurl.com/26fl8qn.

Shopping
Citadium (50–56 Rue de Caumartin, 75009) offers a good selection of cutting-edge streetwear. Passage Jouffroy, next to the museum, is a children's paradise. Stock up with chocolate olives, nougat toffees and *navettes* (boat-shaped biscuits) at **La Cure Gourmande**. Buy everything to kit out a doll's house at **Pain d'Epices** or **La Boîte à Joujoux**. **Le Petit Roi** sells second-hand cartoon books. Stamp collectors should head for **Rue Drouot**. Perhaps the best-known department stores in Paris, **Galeries Lafayette**, with its great food hall, and elegant **Printemps**, are both on Boulevard Haussmann.

Exterior of Printemps department store, on Boulevard Haussmann

Next stop...
CHOCOLATES AND MOVIES Discover the secrets of chocolate at **Choco-Story** (28 Blvd Bonne Nouvelle, 75010; 01 42 29 68 60; 10am–6pm daily), a museum offering the delicious opportunity to taste different varieties. Then watch a film in the old cinema, **Les Etoiles du Rex** (1 Blvd Poissonnière, 75002; 01 45 08 93 40; www.legrandrex.com). Built in 1932, it is the biggest in Europe, with 2,800 seats.

The Passage Verdeau, one of Paris's lovely 19th-century shopping arcades

② Les Passages
A mini world in a hidden city

Les Passages were the world's first shopping malls, and today they make up a hidden labyrinth of historic arcades crisscrossing the area between the Palais Royal and Boulevard Montmartre.

In their 19th-century heyday there were over 150 of these glass-covered walkways, created to cater for the emerging middle classes, who had money to spend and a taste for shopping, but did not want to dirty their shoes. At the time, the streets of Paris were still almost medieval, without pavements and sewers.

Today, the principal and most interesting arcades are the Passage des Panoramas, Galérie Vivienne,

The Lowdown

🌐 **Map reference** 4 G6
Address 75002

🚗 **Métro** Grands Boulevards or Richelieu-Drouot, lines 8 & 9 or Bourse line 3. **Bus** 20, 39, 48, 67, 74 & 85

🍽 **Eat and drink** *Snacks* Stanz, Les Ateliers du Bagel *(56 Rue la Fayette, 75009; 09 80 88 88 40)* serves up sweet or savoury freshly prepared bagels all day long – and is particularly good for breakfast or brunch. *Real meal* L'Arbre à Cannelle *(57 Passages des Panoramas, 75002; 01 45 08 55 87; 6:30–11pm Wed–Sat)* is a restaurant and tearoom.

🚻 **Toilets** No

Prices given are for a family of four

Galérie Colbert, Galérie Vero-Dodat and the Passage des Princes.

Les Passages offer a glimpse into a more elegant past, an oasis of calm and a secret treasure. They're also great fun to explore with children, being full of intriguing shops, delightful cafés and quirky surprises. Best of all, for kids, the Passage des Princes is entirely given over to the **Village Joué Club** *(see p42)*, the city's biggest and most amazing toyshop.

Letting off steam

Save Passage des Princes until last and then let the kids loose in **Village Joué Club**'s myriad themed areas, full of every toy and game they can imagine – and more.

③ Les Grands Boulevards
A shopaholic's paradise

The eight original Grands Boulevards – Madeleine, Capucines, Italiens, Montmartre, Poissonnière, Bonne Nouvelle, St-Denis and St-Martin – were laid out by Louis XIV around the line of the obsolete city walls. The word *boulevard* comes from the Middle Dutch *bulwerc*, which means rampart. In the 19th century, Baron Haussmann sliced through the city in several directions, destroying a labyrinth of stinking streets. He added the vast Avenue de l'Opéra, which Charles Garnier, the architect of the opera, insisted should have no trees that might obscure the view of his masterpiece. The opera is at the heart of the area while, just behind it, on Boulevard Haussmann, are two other 19th-century masterpieces, two stunning department stores

crammed with luxuries: Galeries Lafayette, which looks like an opera house itself, and Printemps.

Letting off steam

Stroll down to the peaceful gardens at the former royal palace, the **Palais Royal** *(Pl du Palais Royal, 75001)* at the southern end of Avenue de l'Opéra.

Children playing football in the Jardin du Palais Royal

The Lowdown

🌐 **Map reference** 4 G6
Address 75002 & 75009

🚗 **Métro** Opéra, lines 3, 7 & 8; Richelieu-Drouot or Grands Boulevards, lines 8 & 9. **RER** Auber, line A. **Bus** 21, 22, 27, 29, 42, 53, 66, 68, 81 & 95

🍽 **Eat and drink** *Snacks* Déli-Cieux *(Printemps, 64 Blvd Haussmann, 75009; www.printemps.com; 9:35am–8pm, till 10pm Thu)*, the roof-garden restaurant in the department store, has panoramic views across the city and serves French dishes. *Family treat* Brasserie Printemps *(01 42 82 58 84; 9:35am–8pm, till 10pm Thu)*, on the sixth floor of Printemps, serves French cuisine. Eat under its colourful stained-glass cupola.

🚻 **Toilets** Inside Printemps & Galeries Lafayette

Boulevard des Capucines, one of the original Grands Boulevards

④ Opéra Garnier

Phantoms, ballerinas and bees

Decorated like a giant birthday cake, the Opéra National de Paris Garnier, or Palais Garnier, was designed by Charles Garnier in 1860. Its opulent splendour and red velvet boxes exude the sensuous and slightly sinister atmosphere of the story *Fort Comme la Mort* (1889) by writer Guy de Maupassant. The red and gold auditorium is lit by a gigantic crystal chandelier that crushed the audience below when it fell down in 1896. This event, as well as the building's underground lake and vast cellars, inspired Gaston Leroux's novel *Phantom of the Opera*. Junior *Angelina Ballerina* fans will enjoy twirling their way down the staircase. There is an excellent shop, the Boutique de l'Opéra National, so bring the piggy bank.

Letting off steam

Walk down Rue de la Paix from Place de l'Opéra towards the river and **Jardin des Tuileries** (*Pl de la Concorde, 75001; daily dawn–dusk*) for some open space after all the traffic and commotion around the Grands Boulevards.

Section of the ornately sculpted façade of Opéra Garnier

Bust of Charles Garnier, its architect, above one of the entrances to the Opéra

The Lowdown

🌐 **Map reference** 4 E6
   Address 1 Pl de l'Opéra, 75009; 08 92 89 90 90; www.operadeparis.fr

🚇 **Métro** Opéra, lines 3, 7, 8. **RER** Auber, line A. **Bus** 21, 22, 27, 29, 42, 53, 66, 68, 81 & 95

🕐 **Open** 10am–5pm daily; Jul–Sep: till 6pm; matinée days: till 1pm; closed 1 Jan, 1 May & 25 Dec

💲 **Price** €30–40; under 10s free. Entry ticket offers a reduction to the Musée d'Orsay, valid for a week after the visit

🎫 **Skipping the queue** Visit during lunchtime

🚩 **Guided tours** In English at 11:30am & 2:30pm on Wed, Sat & Sun and everyday during school hols; €38–46 for a family; 1 hour 30 minutes

👫 **Age range** 5 plus

♿ **Wheelchair access** Yes

🛍️ **Shop** Boutique de l'Opéra National in the main gallery

🤹 **Activities** Family workshops in French; 01 40 01 19 88. Watch the classic World War II comedy *La Grande Vadrouille* (1966), set partly in the opera house, and the silent movie *Phantom of the Opera* (1925). The opera has a season aimed at young people.

🕐 **Allow** 45 minutes–1 hour

☕ **Eat and drink** *Picnic* Monoprix (*21 Ave de l'Opéra, 75009*) is a good stop to pick up supplies for a picnic in the Jardin des Tuileries. *Real meal* Chez Clément (*17 Blvd des Capucines, 75002; 01 53 43 82 00; www.chezclement.com*) serves tasty meals and is child-friendly.

👫 **Toilets** On all levels

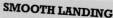

Picnic under €25; **Snacks** €25–45; **Real meal** €45–90; **Family treat** over €90 (based on a family of four)

Sacré-Coeur and around

Children love the sparkly white basilica of Sacré-Coeur, and, although Montmartre is packed with tourists, that has its own appeal – after all, souvenirs such as fridge magnets and postcards are what kids like. The easiest way to get to the heart of things is to take the little tourist train or the funicular; climbing the steps can be tiring. Walk back down Rue Lepic for the real Montmartre experience. On Sundays, traffic is restricted on Rue des Martyrs and across Montmartre, adding to the peaceful, village-like feel.

Places of interest

SIGHTS

1 Sacré-Coeur
2 Place du Tertre & Montmartre Vineyard
3 Espace Dalí Montmartre
4 Rue Lepic
5 Cimetière de Montmartre
6 Europe
7 Les Batignolles

● **EAT & DRINK**

1 Chloé.S.
2 Arnaud Larher
3 Un Zèbre à Montmartre
4 Le Miroir
5 Au Rendez-vous des Amis
6 Le Café qui Parle
7 Sorbet Dilai
8 Le Moulin de la Galette
9 Le Grenier à Pain
10 Coquelicot
11 Musée de la Vie Romantique
12 La Scuderia del Mulino
13 Boulangerie Lemaire
14 Nirvana
15 Méli Mélo
16 Le Club des 5

● **SHOPPING**

1 Antoine et Lili
2 La Case de Cousin Paul
3 La Chaise Longue

● **WHERE TO STAY**

1 Adagio Apartments Montmartre
2 Hôtel Alba Opéra
3 Hôtel des Trois Poussins
4 Ibis Berthier Porte de Clichy
5 Loft Paris
6 Paris Oasis
7 Résidhome Paris-Opéra
8 Terrass Hôtel
9 Tim Hotel

View of Sacré-Coeur from Square Louise Michel

The Lowdown

🚗 **Métro** Abbesses, line 12; Anvers, line 2; Pigalle, lines 2 &12; Pl de Clichy, lines 2 & 13; Brochant, line 13; La Fourche, line 13 or Rome, line 2. **RER** Haussmann St-Lazare, lines A & E. **Bus** 30, 31, 53, 54, 66, 67, 68, 80, 81, 85, 95 & Montmartrobus 64. **Train** Funiculaire de Montmartre, Tourist train: Montmartrain.

ℹ️ **Visitor information** Near Métro Anvers, 72 Blvd de Rochechouart, 75018; 10am–6pm daily, closed 1 Jan, 1 May & 25 Dec

🛒 **Supermarkets** Carrefour, 17 Rue Clignancourt, 75018 & 63 Blvd de Rochechouart, 75009. Monoprix, 52 Rue Fontaine, 75009. Simply Market, 7–9 Blvd des Batignolles, 75008. Monop' Pigalle, 1–3 Pl Pigalle, 75009. 8 à Huit, 48 Rue d'Orsel, 75018 & 24 Rue Lepic, 75018. Franprix, 24 Rue La Condamine, 75017. **Markets** Marché Batignolles (covered market), 96 Rue Lemercier, 75017; 8:30am– 1pm & 3:30–8pm Tue–Fri, 8:30am–8pm Sat, 8:30am– 2pm Sun. Marché Pl d'Anvers, 75009; 3–8pm Fri

🎡 **Festivals** Lavagem do Sacré-Coeur, a religious procession by the city's Brazilian community (early Jul). Fête des Vendanges, grape harvest in Montmartre Vineyard; (Oct). Christmas crèche, Sacré-Coeur basilica (Dec)

➕ **Pharmacy** Pharmacie Européenne, 6 Pl du Clichy, 75009; 01 48 74 65 18

🛝 **Nearest playgrounds** Parc de la Turlure, Rue de la Bonne, 75018 (see p122). Square Louise Michel, 75018 between Pl St-Pierre and the Sacré-Coeur (see p122) Square Suzanne Buisson, Rue Girardon, 75018 (see p124). Square Berlioz, Pl Adolphe Max, 75009 (see p126). Square des Batignolles, 75017 (see p127). Parc Clichy-Batignolles Martin Luther King (see p127).

🚻 **Toilets** Public WC; Pl Suzanne Valadon, 75018

Parc de la Turlure, an oasis behind Sacré-Coeur

Cosy interior of Les Club des 5, a favourite with children

① Sacré-Coeur
A big white meringue

Perched on the highest point in Paris, Sacré-Coeur is the city's second-highest building after the Eiffel Tower. Paris lies at its feet, and kids will love the view from above. Built as a "penance" to expiate the sins of France, and especially the 1871 Paris Commune, it was intended to symbolize the restoration of conservative, Catholic values. Hence, many of the Neo-Byzantine design elements incorporate nationalist themes. It is, however, also seen as a symbol of the repression of the uprising of 1871, which both started and came to a bloody climax here.

Stained-glass rose window, Sacré-Coeur

Key Features

Bell tower Added in 1904, the belltower houses the 19-tonne (17-ton) Savoyarde bell. It is one of the heaviest bells in existence.

Tall dome There are incredible views of up to 40 km (24 miles) from the 129-m (423-ft) high dome. They are especially stunning at sunset.

Spiral staircase

Stained-glass gallery

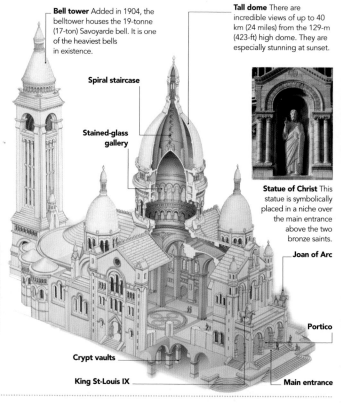

Great Mosaic of Christ This glittering mosaic, dominating the chancel vault, is one of the largest in the world and represents France's devotion to the Sacred Heart.

Statue of Christ This statue is symbolically placed in a niche over the main entrance above the two bronze saints.

Joan of Arc

Portico

Bronze doors Beautifully decorated with relief sculptures, the doors in the portico entrance illustrate the story of the life of Jesus.

Crypt vaults

King St-Louis IX

Main entrance

Letting off steam

In Montmartre, the kids are spoilt for choice. The pretty gardens of **Square Willette** slope down in front of Sacré-Coeur and there is a carousel at the bottom of the hill. There is also **Square Louise Michel**, between Place St-Pierre and the Sacré-Coeur. Behind the cathedral is the **Parc de la Turlure**, where the Turlure windmill once stood. It is a peaceful place to picnic.

Prices given are for a family of four

Eat and drink

Picnic: under €25; Snacks: €25–45; Real meal: €45–90; Family treat: over €90 (based on a family of four)

PICNIC Arnaud Larher *(53 Rue Caulaincourt, 75018; 01 42 57 68 05; www.arnaud-larher. com; closed Sun afternoon & Mon)* is one of the few prize-winning chocolatiers to make milk chocolates. Families can walk up to Parc de la Turlure for a picnic.

SNACKS Chloé.S. *(40 Rue JB Pigalle, 75009; 01 48 78 12 65; 11am–7:30pm; closed Mon)* is every girl's dream. Decorated in an all-pink doll's house-style, it makes for a pretty stop for cupcakes, tea and bagels.

REAL MEAL Un Zèbre à Montmartre *(38 Rue Lepic, 75018; 01 42 23 97 80; 9–2am daily)* is a laid-back little restaurant, which serves a great chocolate mousse.

The Lowdown

 Map reference 4 G2
Address 35 Rue du Chevalier de la Barre, 75018; 01 53 41 89 00; www.sacre-coeur-montmartre.com

 Métro Abbesses, line 12; Anvers, line 2 or Pigalle, lines 2 & 12. Catch the funicular, using the same tickets, or the tourist train (www.promotrain.fr), from Pl Pigalle. **Bus** 30, 31, 80 & 85

 Open 6am–10:30pm daily. Dome: 9am–7pm; winter: till 6pm. Crypt: opening times vary

 Price Basilica: free. Crypt: €10. Dome: €16–26

 Skipping the queue Sacré-Coeur is a very busy

place, but it is less crowded in the evening, when the basilica is at its most magnificent and romantic.

 Guided tours No

Age range All ages

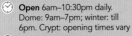 **Allow** 30 minutes–1 hour

Wheelchair access Limited

Café No

Toilets By the exit

Good family value?
Montmartre's charms are for free, and the view from the basilica's steps is almost as good as from the top of the dome. Inside the basilica, silence is the rule.

FAMILY TREAT Le Miroir (94 Rue des Martyrs, 75018; 01 46 06 50 73; closed Aug), a casual bistro, serves delicious lamb with chanterelle mushrooms and little pots de crème vanille (pots of vanilla cream).

Shopping
Montmartre has lots of interesting shops selling original gift items, homewares and clothes. Do not miss the outfits and accessories at **Antoine et Lili** (90 Rue des Martyrs, 75018; www.antoineetlili.com) or the garlands of fancy lights (choose your own colour combination) in **La Case de Cousin Paul** (4 Rue Tardieu, 75018; www.lacasede cousinpaul.com). **La Chaise Longue** (91 Rue des Martyrs, 75018; www. lachaiselongue.fr) is also a fun place to browse for home decor items.

The Moulin Rouge cabaret with its iconic red windmill

Find out more
DIGITAL Watch rock band U2's music video Two Hearts Beat as One, shot in front of the basilica and around Montmartre, at http:// tinyurl.com/b8epuk
FILM Moulin Rouge (2001) is a romantic musical with Nicole Kidman. The films set here reflect life's grittier side and are better for older kids. Louis Feuillade's Fantômas films (1913–14), set in and around Place Pigalle, depict the criminal exploits of a slick but dastardly villain. Watch a clip http://tinyurl.com/coho3of

Next stop...
MOULIN ROUGE One of the world's most famous cabarets, the **Moulin Rouge** (82 Blvd de Clichy, 75018; 01 53 09 82 82; www.moulinrouge.fr) was built in 1885 and is topped off with a red windmill. Its name is synonymous with the high-kicking dance, the cancan, and was made famous in Henri de Toulouse-Lautrec's drawings and posters. The building is worth a look from the outside, and if families fancy a show, 6–12-year-olds can get in to matinees half-price on two Sundays a month. The tourist train that leaves from Place Pigalle passes right in front and heads up to Sacré-Coeur.

② Place du Tertre and Montmartre Vineyard

The roof of Paris

"Tertre" means a little hill and, at 130 m (430 ft), this square is one of the highest spots in Paris. It was once the site of a gallows but, in the 19th century, artists began to sell their work here. It is still full of painters peddling their wares. To visit Montmartre without going for a wander in the quieter narrow, cobbled streets behind Place du Tertre is to miss out on the spirit of the area. The Montmartre Vineyard on Rue St-Vincent is one such peaceful corner and is all that is left of the acres of vineyards that once grew on the hill. It is particularly lovely in autumn, and can be viewed through the surrounding fence. Pull away the tourist veneer and Montmartre has a lot of character and a strong local community, which celebrates the wine harvest in style every October.

Take cover
Musée de Montmartre
(12 Rue Cortot, 75018; www. museedemontmartre.fr) is a charming museum in an old house with lots of memorabilia of artists such as Henri de Toulouse-Lautrec

View of the Montmartre Vineyard from Square Roland Dorgelès

who lived and worked here. There is also a fairly accurate scale model of the old village of Montmartre, which kids may like. **Halle St Pierre** at the foot of the *butte (2 Rue Ronsard; 01 42 58 72 89; www. hallesaintpierre.org)* is an interesting art space with children's workshops.

③ Espace Dalí Montmartre

The dreams of the man with the weird moustache

Espace Dalí Montmartre is the only place to get a look at some actual works of art in the area, and although it is a bit commercial, it is a fun place to visit with kids. The museum has an interesting collection of sculptures and other objects by the Surrealist Spanish artist, Salvador Dalí (1904–89). Children will find his dreamlike models of melting watches, the table with human feet and the collection of crazy sculptures entertaining and intriguing. Although there are a few pictures in the

The Lowdown

- **Map reference** 4 G1 & 4 G2
  Address 75018
- **Métro** Abbesses, line 12. **Bus** Montmartrobus 64 runs from Pl Pigalle to the top of Montmartre.
- **Open** Montmartre vineyard: closed to visitors
- **Skipping the queue** Pl du Tertre is very popular with visitors, so go in the evening or the early morning when it is less crowded.
- **Age range** All ages
- **Allow** 1 hour
- **Eat and drink** *Snacks* Au Rendez-vous des Amis *(23 Rue Gabrielle, 75018)*, a cosy café-bar, is a good stop for a drink. *Real Meal* Le Café qui Parle *(24 Rue Caulaincourt, 75018; 01 46 06 06 88; 8:30am–11pm; no reservations for brunch)* is great for brunch on Sat, Sun and public hols.
- **Toilets** No

The Lowdown

- **Map reference** 4 F2
  Address 11 Rue Poulbot, 75018; 01 42 64 40 10; www.daliparis.com
- **Métro** Anvers, line 2 or Abbesses, line 12. **Bus** 54, 80 and Montmartrobus 64
- **Open** 10am–6pm daily
- **Price** €34–44; under 8s free
- **Guided tours** For kids in French; 01 42 64 40 21
- **Age range** 5 plus
- **Activities** Activity sheets for kids in English
- **Allow** 45 minutes
- **Eat and drink** *Snacks* Sorbet Dilai *(1 Rue Tardieu, 75018)* sells ice creams and sorbets. *Family treat* Le Moulin de la Galette *(83 Rue Lepic, 75018; 01 46 06 84 77; www.lemoulindelagalette.fr; noon–11pm)* is touristy, but it is possible to eat out in the garden in summer, which families will love.
- **Toilets** At the exit

museum, the sculptures, furniture, graphics and film show how Surrealist artists worked in all mediums.

Letting off steam

Take the funicular from the foot of Montmartre *(Rue Tardieu)* to Sacré-Coeur, which offers a fantastic view of the city. Local children play in **Square Suzanne Buisson** *(Rue Girardon, 75018)*, which is located behind Moulin de la Galette. A statue of Saint Denis stands in the middle of the garden. This is a good place to get a feel of the real Montmartre.

Le Moulin de la Galette restaurant with Moulin Radet in the background

④ Rue Lepic

Montmartre from top to bottom

The best way to see Montmartre with children is to take the little tourist train from Place Pigalle and then walk back down Rue Lepic, which is a great place to shop and eat. At the top of the street there are two windmills that once milled flour. In 1870 they were converted into a dance hall and restaurant and immortalized in the painting *Dance at the Moulin de la Galette* by Pierre-Auguste Renoir. The artist Vincent van Gogh and his brother Theo once lived at No. 54. Just behind Place des Abbesses is the pretty Place Emile Goudeau, where Pablo Picasso painted the ground-breaking Cubist picture, *Les Demoiselles d'Avignon*, in 1907.

Head home from the Abbesses Métro station. Built in 1912, it is one of the prettiest, and has one of only three original Hector

Above Entrance to Abbesses, the deepest Métro station in Paris
Below People enjoying a meal outside Coquelicot on a sunny day

Guimard-designed Art Nouveau glass entrances left in Paris. It is also the deepest station in the city.

Letting off steam
There is a tiny square, **Square Jehan Rictus**, close to Place des Abbesses, which is known for its *"mur des je t'aime"* (wall of love).

A BRAVE FIGHT
In 1814, when the Russians occupied Montmartre, the brothers who owned the windmill Moulin de Blute Fin at 74 Rue Lepic fought back bravely. One of them was killed, and the Cossacks nailed his body to its sails.

Dada Dalí
A lot of people thought the artist Salvador Dalí was crazy. He was a great showman, and had an enormous moustache with twirly waxed ends that he claimed were antennae that helped him connect with cosmic forces. A Surrealist, Dalí lived a life as strange and magical as his art, once almost suffocating when he tried to give a lecture in a diving suit. He even died in a surreal way; he refused to drink anything after his wife Gala died, believing that he would simply dry out, and that later a drop of water would bring him back to life.

The Lowdown

🌐 **Map ref** 4 F2
Address Rue Lepic, 75018

🚇 **Métro** Abbesses, line 12. **Bus** 54, 80 & Montmartrobus 64

👫 **Age range** All ages

⏱ **Allow** 30 minutes–1 hour

🍴 **Eat and drink** *Picnic* Le Grenier à Pain (*38 Rue des Abbesses, 75018; closed Tue & Wed*) is a bakery, which sells tasty cakes and sandwiches. They won the 2010 Golden Bagette award. Head to the gardens in front of Sacré-Coeur, or walk up Rue Lepic to Square Suzanne Buisson, which is not touristy and is popular with local families. *Snacks* Coquelicot (*24 Rue des Abbesses, 75018; 01 46 06 18 77; 7:30am–8pm*) has simple dishes such as boiled eggs and poached egg in brioche, a good selection of takeaway food and a scrummy cake counter.

🚻 **Toilets** No

⑤ Cimetière de Montmartre

Take a walk with the dead

Built below street level in the hollow of an old quarry, this cemetery has become a popular tourist destination because of the famous artists and writers buried here. Although it was originally used as a mass grave during the Revolution, it is now an evocative and peaceful place. Maple trees shade the tombs of legends such as the Russian dancer Vaslav Nijinsky, who lived in a flat in Montmartre. It is also the final resting place of Louise Weber, better known as "La Goulue", the cancan dancer famously painted

The atmospheric Cimetière de Montmartre

Entrance to the Musée de Montmartre on Rue Cortot

The Lowdown

🌐 **Map reference** 4 E2
   Address 20 Ave Rachel, 75018

🚇 **Métro** Pl du Clichy, lines 2 & 13.
   Bus 30, 54, 68, 74, 80, 81 & 95

🕐 **Open** 8am–5:30pm; from 8:30am weekends; Mar–Nov: to 6pm

Ⓖ **Price** Free

👫 **Age range** All ages

🕐 **Allow** 45 minutes–1 hour

♿ **Wheelchair access** Limited

🍽 **Eat and drink** Snacks Musée de la Vie Romantique (16 Rue Chaptal, 75009; 01 55 31 95 67; mid-Apr–mid-Oct: 10am–6pm; closed Mon), once home of the writer Georges Sand, has a café in its peaceful, leafy gardens, good for tea or a light lunch. Real Meal La Scuderia del Mulino (106 Blvd de Clichy, 75018; 01 42 62 38 31; noon–2:30pm & 6:30pm–midnight) sells good pizza. The restaurant may look touristy, but it is popular with locals and has friendly staff.

👫 **Toilets** No

by Toulouse-Lautrec. Other tombs include those of painters Edgar Degas and Francis Picabia, author Alexandre Dumas and New Wave film-maker François Truffaut, whose autobiographical movie *Les 400 Coups* (1959) is set locally.

Take cover

Close by is the **Musée de Montmartre** *(see p124)*, housed in a charming 17th-century building, which gives a glimpse of what the area was once like.

⑥ Europe

A baron's dream

The rigid order of Baron Haussmann's redevelopment of Paris in the middle of the 19th century is nowhere more clear than in the angular streets of the area known as Europe. Haussmann annexed the villages of Monceau, Batignolles and Clichy to the city of Paris. Each of the streets south of Place de Clichy is named after a European capital. A short walk

Painting of Gare St-Lazare by Claude Monet, on display in the Musée d'Orsay

The Lowdown

🌐 **Map reference** 3 C4
   Address 75009

🚇 **Métro** Pl du Clichy, lines 2 & 13.
   Bus 54, 67, 68, 80, 81 & 95

🍽 **Eat and drink** Snacks Boulangerie Lemaire (22 Rue de Moscou, 75008) sells good cakes, quiches and sandwiches. Family treat Nirvana (6 Rue de Moscou, 75008; 01 45 22 27 12; closed Sun) is the best Indian restaurant in Paris. Do not miss the aubergine curry, and be sure to try the cheese naan (a round, flat, leavened bread).

👫 **Toilets** Inside the Printemps department store (84 Blvd Haussmann, 75009)

down Rue de Saint-Pétersbourg is Rue d'Edimbourg, where the Impressionist painter Claude Monet briefly lived. From the nearby Place de l'Europe he made a series of paintings of the comings and goings of puffing steam trains and busy passengers at the bustling Gare St-Lazare, which then represented something strikingly modern – look out for the pictures at the Musée d'Orsay (see pp170–71). The square is still a young trainspotter's delight, with a view down on to the tracks and platforms of the oldest station in the city.

Letting off steam

Square Berlioz (Pl Adolphe Max, 75009), across Rue de Clichy to the south of Boulevard Clichy, is a pretty square with a quiet little playground.

⑦ Les Batignolles
A village enclave

The old working-class district of Batignolles became part of Paris in 1860 and rallied behind the Commune in 1871. It was a cheap place to live, and many famous artists and writers moved here, among them Edouard Manet.

Today, this peaceful but trendy enclave is a good place to get a taste of real Parisian life. There are some lovely cafés, interesting shops and two great parks, as well as an organic market and a bric-a-brac market during the weekend. Walk from Place du Clichy along Boulevard des Batignolles and then up the pleasant shopping street, Rue des Batignolles. Then head to the cafés and restaurants in Place Docteur Félix Lobligeoius. It is a lovely place to end the day on a summer evening as it is completely off the tourist track.

The fun and funky interior style of Le Club des 5

Letting off steam

Pretty **Square des Batignolles** is a classic little Parisian park with ducks, a waterfall, table tennis and swings. It also has free Wi-Fi. Across the road on Rue Cardinet is the large, ultramodern **Parc Martin Luther King**, which is a better option for older children and is full of skateboarders.

The beautiful gardens in Square des Batignolles

The Lowdown

🌐 **Map reference** 3 C3
Address 75017

🚇 **Métro** Brochant, line 13; La Fourche, line 13 or Rome, line 2. **Bus** 30, 31, 53 & 66

🍴 **Eat and drink** *Snacks* Méli Mélo (52 Rue des Batignolles, 75017; 01 53 11 09 81; 11:30am–7:30pm weekdays, 3:30–7:30pm Sat & Sun) sells soup, sandwiches and ice cream. It is also possible to create an individual salad to eat in or take-away. *Real Meal* Le Club des 5 (57 Rue des Batignolles, 75017; 01 53 04 94 73; www.leclubdes5.fr; 7:30–11pm Mon, noon–2:30pm & 7:30–11pm Tue–Fri, noon–4:30pm Sat & Sun) is known for its burgers, which are among the best in town. Kids will love the crazy collage walls of cartoon and TV characters.

🚻 **Toilets**: No

Picnic under €25; **Snacks** €25–45; **Real meal** €45–90; **Family treat** over €90 (based on a family of four)

Champs-Elysées
& Trocadéro

Symbol of France, the Arc de Triomphe stands at the top of the spectacular Champs-Elysées, the wide pavements of which are full of cafés and shops embodying luxury and elegance. This famous avenue leads all the way down to the Place de la Concorde, past grand buildings and tree-lined gardens. Down by the river, to the west, lie the museums of the Trocadéro, treasure troves of nature, humankind and architecture.

Highlights

Arc de Triomphe
Admire this monumental arch, which stands 50 m (164 ft) tall. It is the starting point for victory celebrations (see pp134–5).

Ladurée, Drugstore Publicis and Dalloyau
Try multi-coloured macaroons at *belle époque* patisserie Ladurée. Bite into club sandwiches at Drugstore Publicis and cakes at Dalloyau (see p135 & p138).

Champs-Elysées
Stroll down the most famous avenue in the world like a local, dressed to impress in your Sunday best (see pp134–5).

Aquarium de Paris – Cinéaqua
Escape from all the frenzy to this subterranean aquarium and cinema – the perfect antidote to tourism and tired feet (see p144).

Musée Guimet
Discover treasures from the East at this museum. See goddesses with a thousand arms, demons with multiple heads and a secret Japanese garden (see p146).

Trocadéro
Let off steam in style, running around the fountains under the watchful gaze of the Eiffel Tower (see pp144–5).

Left The cafés of the Champs-Elysées are classic spots for admiring the Parisian scene
Above left Detail on a pillar by architect Jacques Hittorff in Place de la Concorde

The Best of
Champs-Elysées & Trocadéro

The Arc de Triomphe has some classy neighbours, among them the French president, visiting movie stars and the city's most well-heeled families. Study how to eat, dress and live it up Parisian-style in the area's chocolate shops, cafés, parks, puppet shows and designer boutiques. The luxury hotels here are among the world's most child-friendly. This part of the city has museums too, most of them largely off the tourist trail.

Powerful Paris

Admire the feats of the French Army at the **Arc de Triomphe** (see pp134–5). Just under the roof are 30 shields, each bearing the name of a victorious battle Napoleon fought either in Europe or North Africa. If it is 14 July, do not miss the military parade with soldiers, tanks and planes. Read General de Gaulle's call to arms on the pavement under the arch before heading down the Champs-Elysées to see his statue on Place Clemenceau.

Walk past the president's front door at the **Palais de l'Elysée** (see p138) or continue down the avenue to be overwhelmed by the views of **Place de la Concorde** (see p138), and by its history – this is where the guillotine was in action during the Revolution.

Star-studded Paris

Count the stars at the **Arc de Triomphe**. Gaze down from here at the boulevards that slice up Paris in the shape of a star, then look up at the **Eiffel Tower** (see pp154–5), which twinkles at night. Feel like King Babar while lunching at the **Petit Palais** (see p136) and pretend to be a Russian tsar strolling across the **Pont Alexandre III** (see p136).

Shop for a pineapple at **Hédiard** (see p139), or go window-shopping on the super-haute-couture Rue du Faubourg-St-Honoré, running parallel to the designer-filled Champs-Elysées, before sipping tea in elegant Galerie des Gobelins of the hotel **Plaza Athénée** (see p137). Round off the day with dinner at **114 Faubourg** (see p138) at Le Bristol.

Below Pont Alexandre III, Paris's most ornate bridge

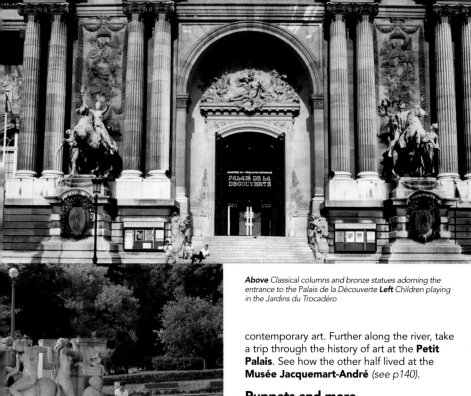

Above Classical columns and bronze statues adorning the entrance to the Palais de la Découverte Left Children playing in the Jardins du Trocadéro

Get an education

Kick off with a tour of the **Trocadéro** *(see pp144–5)* and discover where we all came from at the **Musée de l'Homme** *(see p144)*. Set sail with the French Navy at the **Musée de la Marine** *(see p144)* and learn about aquatic life at **Aquarium de Paris – Cinéaqua** *(see p144)*. The **Cité de l'Architecture et du Patrimoine** *(see p144)*, where the most famous buildings in France are scaled down to size, is great for a crash course on architecture. In another nearby cluster of museums, meet the demons from the temple of Angkor Wat at the **Musée Guimet** *(see p146)* or check out the fascinating dresses at the **Musée Galliéra** *(see p147)*. At the **Palais de la Découverte** *(see p137)*, watch lightning strike overhead, learn how ants talk to each other, and wonder at the secrets of the heavens. Go to **Palais de Tokyo** *(see p146)* to see some electrifying modern and

contemporary art. Further along the river, take a trip through the history of art at the **Petit Palais**. See how the other half lived at the **Musée Jacquemart-André** *(see p140)*.

Puppets and more

Let off steam in style in the city's smartest park, **Parc Monceau** *(see p140)*, or laugh at the puppets at the **Théâtre Guignol** *(see p136)* on the Champs-Elysées. Start a stamp collection at the **Marché aux Timbres** *(see p132)* before going for a ride on the carousel at the Trocadéro. Dream about madeleines, savour an éclair from **Dalloyau** *(see p138)* and drool over the food counters at **Fauchon** *(see p139)*. For kids who love Disney characters, the **Disney Store** *(see p135)* is a fun place to go. Top it all off with books, toys and more at **Oxybul Éveil & Jeux** *(see p145)*.

Right Asian art on display at the Musée Guimet

Arc de Triomphe and around

Champs-Elysées
& Trocadéro

Arc de
Triomphe

Palais de Chaillot
p144

Of all the grand avenues that characterize the exclusive area around the Arc de Triomphe, none defines it better than the Champs-Elysées. With its wide pavements, lined with cafés, it is perfect for strolling, and there is always something going on, even on Sundays and during the evening. It is quite long, so it might be useful for little feet to jump on a bus, or take the Métro. North of the Champs-Elysées is a residential area, which closes down when local families are on holiday in August.

Pont Alexander III, connecting the Left Bank to the Grand Palais

The Lowdown

🚇 **Métro** Charles de Gaulle-Etoile, lines 1, 2 & 6; Champs-Elysées-Clemenceau, lines 1 & 13; Franklin D Roosevelt, lines 1 & 9; St-Philippe-du-Roule, line 9; Madeleine, lines 8, 12 & 14; Concorde, lines 1, 8 & 12; Miromesnil, lines 9 & 13; Monceau, line 2 or Courcelles, line 2. **RER** Charles de Gaulle-Etoile, line A; Invalides, line C. **Bus** 22, 24, 28, 30, 31, 38, 42, 43, 49, 52, 54, 63, 72, 73, 80, 83, 84, 92, 93 & 94. **River boat** Port des Champs-Elysées

🛒 **Supermarkets** Monoprix, 122 Rue de la Boétie, 75008. Franprix, 1 Rue Penthièvre, 75008. Monop', 9 Blvd Madeleine, 75001. **Markets** Marché des Ternes (covered food market), 8 Rue Lebon, 75017; 7:30am–1pm & 4–7:30pm Tue–Sat, 7:30am–1pm Sun. Marché Treilhard (covered food market), 1 Rue Corvetto, 75008; 8:30am–1pm, 4–7:30pm Tue–Sat; 8:30am–1pm Sun. Marché Aguesseau, the smallest food market in

Paris, Pl de la Madeleine, 75008; 7am–2:30pm Tue, Fri. Marché aux Timbres (stamp market), Ave Gabriel, 75008; 9am–7pm Thu, Sat, Sun, public hols; winter: till 4:30pm. Christmas Market, Champs-Elysées; mid-Nov–Dec

🎪 **Festivals** Paris Marathon (Apr). La Defilé, a huge military parade (14 Jul). Tour de France (Jul); www.letour.fr. Armistice Day (11 Nov).

➕ **Pharmacy** Dhéry, 84 Ave des Champs-Elysées; 01 45 62 02 41

🛝 **Nearest playgrounds** Jardin des Champs-Elysées, Ave des Champs-Elysées, 75008; dawn–dusk daily (see p136). Parc Monceau, Blvd de Courcelles, 75008; 7am–10pm (see p140). Jardin des Tuileries, Rue de Rivoli, 75001; 7:30am–7pm (see p138).

🚻 **Toilets** Point WC, 26 Ave des Champs-Elysées, 75008; baby-changing facilities €2

Macaroons in the window display of Ladurée, an elegant tearoom

Places of interest

SIGHTS

1. Arc de Triomphe
2. Grand Palais and Petit Palais
3. Pont Alexandre III
4. Palais de la Découverte
5. Palais de l'Elysée
6. Place de la Concorde
7. Place de la Madeleine
8. Musée Jacquemart-André
9. Parc Monceau
10. St-Alexandre-Nevsky Cathedral

● EAT AND DRINK

1. Monoprix, 52 Champs-Elysées
2. Aubrac Corner
3. Ladurée, 75 Champs-Elysées
4. Drugstore Publicis
5. Mini Palais
6. Café Lênotre
7. Le Relais Plaza
8. Dragons Elysées
9. Dalloyau
10. 114 Faubourg
11. Cojean
12. Ladurée, 16 Rue Royale
13. Galler
14. Bread and Roses
15. Sushi Shop
16. Boulangerie du Parc Monceau
17. Gus L'Atelier Gourmand
18. A La Ville de Petrograd
19. Daru

See also Grand Palais and Petit Palais (p136), Palais de la Découverte (p137) and Musée Jacquemart-André (p140)

● SHOPPING

1. Paul & Joe
2. Christian Dior
3. Mon Plus Beau Souvenir
4. FNAC
5. Paris St-Germain
6. Disney Store
7. La Grande Récré

See also Arc de Triomphe (p134)

● WHERE TO STAY

1. Adagio Haussmann
2. Four Seasons George V
3. Hôtel du Collectionneur
4. Hôtel Keppler
5. Hotel de la Trémoille
6. Le Bristol
7. Plaza Athénée

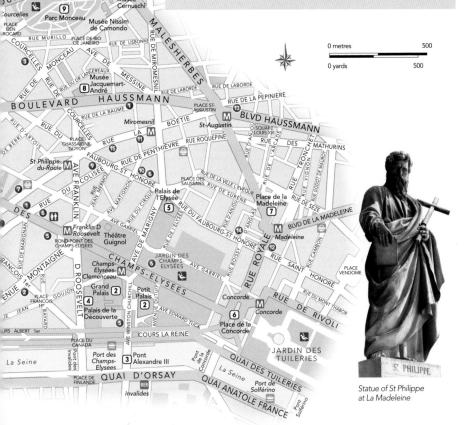

0 metres 500
0 yards 500

Statue of St Philippe at La Madeleine

① Arc de Triomphe

Generals, stars and parades

After defeating the Austrian and Russian troops at the Battle of Austerlitz in 1805, Napoleon commissioned a triumphal arch in the Roman style. However, no sooner were the foundations for the arch laid, than his empire began to collapse. The arch was finally completed in 1836. Four years later, Napoleon's remains passed under it, on the way to his final resting place at Les Invalides. Since then, both occupying armies and liberating troops have marched through it.

Arc de Triomphe ceiling detail

The Lowdown

- **Map reference** 2 E4
  Address Pl Charles de Gaulle, 75008; 01 55 37 73 77; *www.arc-de-triomphe.monuments-nationaux.fr*
- **Métro** Charles de Gaulle-Etoile, lines 1, 2 & 6. **RER** Charles de Gaulle-Etoile, line A; access via the underpass. **Bus** 22, 30, 31, 52, 73 & 92
- **Open** Apr–Sep: 10am–11pm & Oct–Mar: 10am–10:30pm; closed 1 Jan, 1 & 8 May am, 14 Jul am, 11 Nov am & 25 Dec
- **Price** €19; under 18s and EU citizens under 26 free
- **Skipping the queue** It is best to visit in the evening to watch the sunset. Paris Museum Pass accepted and sold.
- **Guided tours** Tours in English can be arranged by calling 01 44 54 19 30
- **Age range** All ages
- **Activities** Ceremony to relight the eternal flame at 6:30pm daily. Annual military parade 14 Jul
- **Allow** 1 hour
- **Wheelchair access** Yes, but limited. No access to the roof/views
- **Shop** The shop in the visitors' centre at the top of the stairs by the entrance sells souvenirs including a great colouring-in book, *Je colorie Paris*.
- **Toilets** In museum area

Good family value?

There is a lot to do and look at, considering it is "just" an arch. Bring binoculars, to make the most of the friezes and the view.

Key Features

Spectacular views Baron Haussmann's star-shaped towngrid is easy to admire from the roof, as is the crazy traffic whizzing around the roundabout below.

The Battle of Austerlitz The frieze on the arch's northern side shows Napoleon's troops breaking the frozen lakes to drown thousands of enemy soldiers.

Triumph of Napoleon A relief on the left base celebrates the peace brought by the Treaty of Vienna in 1810.

Military heroes The names of the generals who served in Napoleon's army are engraved on the inner façades of the small arches. The names of those who died on the battlefield are underlined.

Tomb of the Unknown Soldier An unknown soldier lies buried under the centre of the arch, one among the 1.5 million French soldiers who died during World War I.

Napoleon's victories Thirty shields just below the arch's roof bear the names of the victorious battles fought by Napoleon.

Tree-lined path in the Jardins des Champs-Elysées

Letting off steam

If the Champs-Elysées seems too busy, opt for a 10-minute ride on bus No. 30, or take an easy walk to **Parc Monceau** (see p140), which has a popular playground. Or take a bus down the avenue to the Rond-Point des Champs-Elysées for the tree-lined **Jardin des Champs-Elysées**, with fountains and pavillions.

Eat and drink

Picnic: under €25; Snacks: €25–45; Real meal: €45–90; Family treat: over €90 (based on a family of four)

PICNIC Monoprix (52 Champs-Elysées, 75008; open until midnight) has basic supplies. Picnic in the Jardin des Champs-Elysées.
SNACKS Aubrac Corner (37 Rue Marbeuf, 75008; 01 45 61 45 35) is a bright little café, which serves fast food, burgers, sandwiches and hot meals, all with flavours from the southwest of France. It offers the option of eat in or takeaway.
SNACKS Ladurée (75 Champs-Elysées, 75008; www.laduree.fr; 7:30am–11pm Mon–Fri, 8:30–12:30am Sat, 8:30am–11pm Sun) serves the best macaroons in Paris in its *belle époque* tearooms.

Mouthwatering multicoloured macaroons on display in Ladurée

FAMILY TREAT Drugstore Publicis (133 Champs-Elysées, 75008; 01 44 43 77 64; www.publicisdrugstore. com; 8am–2am Mon–Fri, 10am–2am Sat & Sun) has a brasserie, which serves giant club sandwiches. It also has a stylish bar.

Shopping

Kit the kids out in style on the Champs-Elysées, where there are plenty of children's designer outlets. Visit **Paul & Joe** (2 Ave Montaigne, 75008), which designer Sophie Albou named after her two sons, and check out the children's collection at **Christian Dior** (28 Ave Montaigne, 75008) . With chandeliers and a velvet-curtained changing room **Mon Plus Beau Souvenir** (144 Rue de Courcelles, 75017) is another place to shop for designer labels. International chain stores have crept in among the high-end boutiques on the Champs-Elysées, and there are computer games and DVDs at **FNAC** (No. 74). Football fans should head for the **Paris St-Germain** shop (No. 27). There are plenty of toys at the **Disney Store** (No. 44) and **La Grande Récré** (126 Rue de la Boétie, 75008).

Find out more

DIGITAL Watch a documentary about the Battle of Austerlitz on www.history.com/videos/the-battle-of-austerlitz
FILM Teenage twins live it up by the Palais de l'Elysée in Passport to Paris (1999).

Next stop...

PETIT PALAIS AND PALAIS DE LA DÉCOUVERTE Check out the art at the Petit Palais (see p136), or discover the world of science at the Palais de la Découverte (see p137).

Sculptures on display inside the stunning portico of the Petit Palais

② Grand Palais and Petit Palais

Babar the elephant's garlanded, glittering palace

Built for the Exposition Universelle in 1900, the Grand Palais and the Petit Palais both house temporary art exhibitions and shows. The **Petit Palais** also has an excellent and varied permanent art collection, with Impressionist and Art Nouveau paintings, but the building itself almost steals the show. Decorated with painted ceilings and swirling white garlands, glittering angels on the roof and palm trees in the garden, it looks very much like the palace of Babar, the beloved French children's book character.

On the opposite side of the road is the larger **Grand Palais**, which took more steel girders to build than the Eiffel Tower. The western section of the palace houses the Palais de la Découverte (see p137).

Letting off steam
In the **Jardins des Champs-Elysées**, across the road, there is plenty of space to run around. In the northwest corner, puppet shows are still staged in Paris's oldest puppet theatre, **Théâtre Guignol** (Rond-Point des Champs-Elysées, 75008; 01 42 45 38 30; www.theatreguignol.fr; Wed, Sat, Sun & school hols 3pm, 4pm & 5pm), which opened in 1818.

Children enjoying a puppet show at the famous Théâtre Guignol

Gilt-bronze statues atop the pillars on Pont Alexandre III

③ Pont Alexandre III

Winged horses on the Tsar's bridge

Next to the Petit Palais stands the prettiest bridge in Paris, the glittering Pont Alexandre III, which looks like it belongs in a fairytale – covered in cupids, cherubs and winged horses. Its design does not really match the character of its namesake, Tsar Alexander III, who ruled Russia with an iron fist, but it was built in his honour to celebrate an alliance between France and Russia. The foundation stone of the bridge was laid by Alexander's son, Nicholas II, in 1896. It has featured in several films, including the James Bond adventure *A View to a Kill* (1985) and the cartoon *Anastasia* (1997).

Letting off steam
Stroll along the Seine from Pont Alexandre III to **Place de la Concorde** (see p138). Check out the houseboats here and imagine what it would be like to live in them.

Statue of Cupid with his bow and arrow on Pont Alexandre III

The Lowdown

🌐 **Map reference** 9 A2
Address Petit Palais: Ave Winston Churchill, 75008; 01 53 43 40 00; www.petitpalais.paris.fr. Grand Palais: www.grandpalais.fr

🚇 **Métro** Champs-Elysées-Clemenceau, lines 1 & 13. **RER** Charles de Gaulle-Etoile, line A. **Bus** 28, 42, 52, 72, 73, 80, 83 & 93

🕐 **Open** Petit Palais 10am–6pm, till 8pm Thu, closed Mon & public hols. Grand Palais: timings vary according to the exhibition.

💶 **Price** Petit Palais: permanent collection free; Grand Palais: charges for temporary exhibits

🚩 **Guided tours** Yes, in addition to children's audio guide

👫 **Age range** 5 plus

👫 **Activities** Children's activity leaflets and storytelling events in French

⏱ **Allow** 45 minutes–1 hour

♿ **Wheelchair access** Yes

🍽 **Eat and drink** *Real meal* Eat sandwiches and cakes in the café of the Petit Palais, under the golden garlands of leaves on the terrace. *Family treat* Mini Palais (Ave Winston Churchill, 75008; 01 42 56 42 42; 10–2am daily), run by Michelin-starred chef Eric Fréchon, has a terrace in summer.

🚻 **Toilets** By the café in the Petit Palais and on the ground floor of the Grand Palais

The Lowdown

🌐 **Map reference** 9 A3
Address 75008

🚗 **Métro** Champs-Elysées-Clémenceau, lines 1 & 13.
RER Invalides, line C. **Bus** 28, 42, 72, 73, 83 & 93

⑤ **Price** Free

👫 **Age range** All ages

⏱ **Allow** 15 minutes

☕ **Eat and drink** *Family treat* Café Lênotre *(10 Ave des Champs-Elysées, 75008; 01 42 65 85 10; closed three weeks in Aug)* is a good place to eat outside on the terrace in summer. This restaurant-tearoom-bar is a great spot for tea especially, as the cakes are delicious. Be sure to try the *mille-feuille* with its layers of light puff pastry. Classical French cuisine is also served. *Family treat* Le Relais Plaza *(www.plaza-athenee-paris. fr; noon–2:45pm & 7–11:30pm)*, The restaurant of the Hôtel Plaza Athénée has been feeding movie stars since 1936. The chefs are happy to prepare whatever the kids fancy – at a price. Tea is served in the lobby of the hotel.

④ Palais de la Découverte
A "palace" of discoveries

How do ants communicate? What is an invertebrate? How does a battery work? The Palais de la Découverte science museum is the place to find answers to some of life's puzzling questions. A wide range of exhibits covers all aspects of scientific study. The museum was founded by a doctor in the 1930s with the aim of popularizing science. Check out the rat-run, then escape into space in the planetarium. The museum shop has a great array of exciting gadgets and toys. Nearby Avenue

The Lowdown

🌐 **Map reference** 9 A2
Address Ave Franklin D Roosevelt, 75008; 01 56 43 20 21; www.palais-decouverte.fr

🚗 **Métro** Champs-Elysées-Clémenceau lines 1 & 13 or Franklin D Roosevelt lines 1 & 9.
RER Invalides, line C. **Bus** 28, 42, 52, 63, 72, 73, 80, 83 & 93

🕐 **Open** 9:30am–6pm Tue–Sat, 10am–7pm Sun, closed public hols

⑤ **Price** €28–38; under 6s free. Planetarium (per person): €3. Reduced price for under 25s

👫 **Age range** 6 plus

🏃 **Activities** Workshops in French for 8–12-year-olds during school hols for €1.50

⏱ **Allow** 2 hours

♿ **Wheelchair access** Yes

☕ **Eat and drink** *Picnic* The science museum has a sandwich bar for snacks. Picnic by the Seine or in the Jardin des Champs-Elysées. *Family treat* Dragons Elysées *(11 Rue de Berri, 75008; 01 42 89 85 10; noon–2:30pm & 7–11:30pm)*, is a fun place for kids as the floor is a giant aquarium. The restaurant serves Chinese cuisine. Enjoy lunch here on weekdays when the set menu is a very good deal.

👫 **Toilets** By the café

Montaigne is a street dedicated to high fashion. The enormous Louis Vuitton store on the Champs-Elysées is the flagship shop of just one of the many great fashion houses that have a presence here.

Letting off steam
The ultramodern car showroom **Rendez-vous Toyota** *(79 Ave des Champs-Elysées, 75008)* is crammed with interesting interactive activities for adults and children alike.

The Dragons Elysées, with its underfloor aquarium

Picnic under €25; **Snacks** €25–45; **Real meal** €45–90; **Family treat** over €90 (based on a family of four)

⑤ Palais de l'Elysée

Is the President at home?

The official residence of the French president since 1873, the Palais de l'Elysée was built for a count in 1718 in what was then a leafy outpost of the city. During the Revolution, it was turned into a warehouse, a factory and then a dance hall. In 1814, when the Russians occupied Paris, Napoleon signed his abdication here in the Salle d'Argent, before Tsar Alexander I moved in, leaving his Cossacks to camp in the Champs-Elysées. Today, the president of the Republic lives in a modern apartment on the first floor, facing the Rue de l'Elysée.

Letting off steam

Behind the palace are the **Jardins des Champs-Elysées** *(see p135)*, with a playground and free Wi-Fi.

The Lowdown

- 🌐 **Map reference** 9 B1
  Address 55 Rue du Faubourg-St-Honoré, 75008; *www.elysee.fr*
- 🚌 **Métro** St-Philippe-du-Roule, line 9 or Madeleine, lines 8, 12 & 14. **Bus** 24, 28, 38, 42, 49, 52, 80 & 84
- 🕐 **Open** Closed to the public
- 🍔 **Eat and drink** *Picnic* Dalloyau, (*101 Rue du Faubourg St-Honoré, 75008; www.dalloyau.fr*) is named after the family that runs it, who cooked the whitest bread ever for Louis XIV. Try the cake that they invented, called *l'Opéra*. Picnic in the Jardin des Champs-Elysées. *Family treat* 114 Faubourg (*01 53 43 43 00; www.lebristolparis.com; noon–2:30pm & 7–10:30pm*), Hôtel Bristol's restaurant, serves waffles with smoked salmon.
- 🚻 **Toilets** No

Fountain of River Commerce and Navigation in the Place de la Concorde

⑥ Place de la Concorde

Revolutionary guillotine and an Egyptian obelisk

The magnificent Place de la Concorde provides stunning views along the Champs-Elysées – north to the Madeleine church, east to the Louvre and south across the river to the Assemblée Nationale. Take the children after dark, when it appears truly magical.

Originally named Place Louis XV, the square was laid out in 1757. During the Revolution it became Place de la Révolution, and was the main location for the guillotine. In 1792–4, the square literally ran with blood in an orgy of killing when over a thousand people, including Louis XVI and his queen, Marie Antoinette, were executed here. After the horrors of the Revolution, the square was renamed Concorde, or "harmony", in the hope of more peaceful times ahead. On the northwestern corner of the square is one of the most luxurious hotels in the city, the Hôtel Crillon. The identical, imposing building on the northeastern side is the Navy Ministry. The obelisk located in the middle of the square was made 3,200 years ago, and is the oldest monument in Paris. At one time, the obelisk stood in the Temple of Ramses in Luxor, but it was given to the French people by the Pasha of Egypt in 1829. In exchange for this gift, the pasha received a clock that did not work.

Letting off steam

On the northeastern side of the square is the **Jardins des Tuileries** *(see p108)*, where kids can enjoy pony rides.

The Lowdown

- 🌐 **Map reference** 9 C2
  Address 75008
- 🚌 **Métro** Concorde, lines 1 & 8
  Bus 24, 42, 52, 72, 73, 84, & 94
- 🎠 **Activities** The giant Ferris wheel from Nov–Jan. Summer funfair in the Jardin des Tuileries
- 🍔 **Eat and drink** *Snacks* Cojean (*11 Ave Delcassé, 75008*) is a great spot for healthy sandwiches, salads, fresh juices and mini portions for kids. There is the option of eating in or takeaway. *Real meal* Ladurée (*16 Rue Royale, 75008; www.laduree.fr; 8:30am–7pm, 10am–7pm Sat, closed Sun*), which opened in 1862, is a luxury tearoom.
- 🚻 **Toilets** At the entrance to the Jardin des Tuileries

Hôtel Bristol on the exclusive Rue du Faubourg St-Honoré

Prices given are for a family of four

Sumptuous savoury dishes at the city's most famous food shop, Fauchon

⑦ Place de la Madeleine

The Ten Commandments, fruit jellies and dainty cakes

In 1764, work began on La Madeleine, the church dedicated to Mary Magdalene and located in the centre of the square named after it. But the Revolution got in the way and it was only consecrated in 1845, after years of changing plans for its design and usage, which included a stock exchange, a ballroom, a market and a public library. The final design, which mirrors the Assemblée Nationale across the Seine, on the other side of Place de la Concorde, was ordered by Napoleon. He wanted a Roman-style temple, dedicated to the glory of his army, which is why it has no bell and does not face towards Jerusalem like other churches. Look out for the Ten Commandments on its bronze doors.

The square is also home to two luxurious delicatessens, which have restaurants as well. Fauchon at No. 26 offers an array of éclairs and picnic boxes, while Hédiard at No. 21 was the first shop in France to sell tropical fruit; it also offers fruit jellies and cakes. Alexander Dumas, who wrote *The Three Musketeers* (1844), was the first to try their fresh pineapples.

Letting off steam

It is a 10-minute walk to **Square Louis XVI**, on the corner of Rue d'Anjou and Boulevard Haussmann, which has benches to sit on and pathways to run along, as well as a slide and games for kids. Once the Madeleine's cemetery, this was where victims of the guillotine – including Louis XVI and Marie Antoinette – were buried.

Towering corinthian columns adorning La Madeleine, Place de la Madeleine

The Lowdown

🌐 **Map reference** 9 D1
Address 75008; 01 44 51 69 00 (La Madeleine); www.eglise-lamadeleine.com

🚇 **Métro** Madeleine, lines 8, 12 & 14. **Bus** 24, 42, 52, 72, 73, 84 & 94

🕐 **Open** La Madeleine: 9:30am–7pm

💰 **Price** Free

👫 **Age range** All ages

🧍 **Activities** Sunday morning service in the church

⏱ **Allow** 20 minutes

🍽 **Eat and drink** *Picnic* Galler (114 Blvd Haussmann, 75008; 01 45 22 33 49; www.galler.com; 10am–7pm Mon–Sat) creates chocolates mixed with crushed flower petals. Picnic in the Parc Monceau. *Real meal* Bread and Roses (25 Rue Boissy d'Anglas, 75008; 01 47 42 40 00, www.breadandroses.fr; 8am–10pm, till 8pm Sat; closed Sun) is a great spot for lunch, with delicious *tartines* (open sandwiches), quiche, speciality breads and soup.

🚻 **Toilets** Next to the church

Picnic under €25; **Snacks** €25–45; **Real meal** €45–90; **Family treat** over €90 (based on a family of four)

The grandiose Winter Garden of the Musée Jacquemart-André

⑧ Musée Jacquemart-André

Spend, spend, spend!

In 1860, the tiny village of Monceau was annexed to the city of Paris as part of a massive rebuilding project organized by Baron Haussmann, and some of the richest people in France bought land here. Heir to a banking fortune, Edouard André moved here in 1875 and spent a fortune building up one of the most lavish and sumptuous private homes in Paris. His wife Nélie Jacquemart, a society portrait painter, was a shopaholic art collector who travelled around the world amassing paintings, frescoes and sculptures. The couple often threw splendid parties to show off their spectacular collection of Renaissance and 17th- and 18th-century art, which can still be seen here today. The museum is also an excellent place for children to learn about the luxurious lifestyle of the aristocracy at a time when many Parisians endured grinding poverty.

Letting off steam

Explore the leafy **Parc Monceau**, full of surprises, and with a sandpit for the little ones. The kiosk in the park sells balls, buckets, spades and toys.

The elegant drawing room of the Musée Jacquemart-André

⑨ Parc Monceau

Monuments and a massive tree

With its golden-topped gates, Parc Monceau is Paris's most elegant park and a favourite with well-dressed local children and their nannies. It is the sort of place where Petit Nicolas, the cheeky schoolboy hero of Sempé's classic stories, would spend the afternoons, and where writer Marcel Proust liked to take a stroll. The park was created in 1769 by the Duke of Chartres, Philippe d'Orléans, who wanted to have his own English-style garden with curvy paths and funny monuments. Look out for an Egyptian pyramid and a statue dedicated to the famous pianist Frédéric Chopin, who died in Paris in 1849. The biggest tree in Paris, an Oriental plane, is also located here. Its trunk measures a whopping 7 m (23 ft) round.

Take cover

Near the eastern gate on Avenue Vélasquez is the **Musée Cernuschi** (www.cernuschi.paris.fr). The museum houses a collection of Far Eastern treasures, and is free of charge. Nearby, the **Musée Nissim de Camondo** (*63 Rue de Monceau, 75008; www.lesartsdecoratifs.fr/francais/nissim-de-camondo*) was once the home of a Jewish family who moved to Paris in 1869 after building a powerful financial empire in Constantinople. Walk through the kitchen and servants' quarters up to the stylish salons, full of fine art and antiques.

Relaxing near the Pavillon de Chartres, the main entrance to Parc Monceau

The Lowdown

🌐 **Map reference** 2 H4
Address 158 Blvd Haussmann, 75008; 01 45 62 11 59; www.musee-jacquemart-andre.com

🚗 **Métro** Miromesnil, lines 9 & 13 or St-Philippe-du-Roule, line 9. **Bus** 22, 28, 43, 52, 54, 80, 83, 84 & 93

🕐 **Open** 10am–6pm daily

💲 **Price** €24–44; under 7s free; one child between 7–17 years free for every three visitors

🚩 **Guided tours** Audio guide in English

🧍 **Age range** 6 plus

🧍 **Activities** Family Fun Programme every afternoon in Jul and Aug. Children's activity booklet in English available

🕐 **Allow** 1–2 hours

♿ **Wheelchair access** Yes

🍴 **Eat and drink** *Snacks* Sushi Shop (*59 Rue de la Boétie, 75008; 08 26 82 66 28; 11am–3pm & 6–11:15pm Mon–Fri*) has an excellent Japanese menu with a French twist. There is a great sushi selection, as well as maki rolls, sashimi and some good vegetarian options. It also offers the choice of eating in or takeaway. *Real meal* The museum café (*11:45am–5:30pm; weekend brunch 11am–3pm*) is a popular spot for a luxury Sunday brunch or tea and has a special kids' menu.

🚻 **Toilets** On the ground floor

The Lowdown

- **Map reference** 2 H2
  Address Blvd de Courcelles, 75008
- **Métro** Monceau, line 2. **Bus** 30, 84 & 94
- **Open** 7am–10pm; winter: till 8pm
- **Price** Free
- **Age range** All ages
- **Activities** Playground, merry-go-round and mini-skatepark. Free Wi-Fi
- **Allow** 30 minutes upwards
- **Eat and drink** *Picnic* Boulangerie du Parc Monceau *(Rue de Prony, 75017; 01 42 27 41 25)* doubles as a café, and has takeaway food such as sandwiches, quiches and cakes. Picnic in Parc Monceau. *Real meal* Gus L'Atelier Gourmand *(62 Rue Prony, 75017; 01 47 66 13 22; 10:30am–9pm Mon–Fri, till midnight Thu),* a delicatessen restaurant, serves cold meats, quiches and traditional hot dishes as well as a salad pick-and-mix and tea.
- **Toilets** In the rotunda, by the main entrance on Blvd de Courcelles

⑩ St-Alexandre-Nevsky Cathedral

Fantastic onion domes and fragrant incense

The onion domes and incense of the Russian Orthodox St-Alexandre-Nevsky Cathedral bring a breeze from the East and a hint of the exotic to Paris. In the 19th century, many Russians, including aristocrats, writers, painters and revolutionaries, flocked to Paris. In the 1860s, the community had grown so large that a Russian orthodox church was built and the tsar decided there was need for a Paris office for his notorious secret police. After the Russian Revolution in 1917, many aristocrats fled to France.

Letting off steam

Just minutes away is **Parc Monceau,** which is a great spot for a picnic and a run about. This park features many magnificent trees and rare plants.

The Lowdown

- **Map reference** 2 F3
  Address 12 Rue Daru, 75008; 01 42 27 37 34
- **Métro** Courcelles, line 2. **Bus** 30
- **Open** Variable, depending on services
- **Price** Free
- **Age range** 8 plus
- **Allow** 15–30 minutes
- **Wheelchair access** No
- **Eat and drink** *Family treat* A La Ville de Petrograd *(13 Rue Daru, 75008; 01 48 88 07 70; noon–3pm & 7pm–midnight Mon–Sat)* is a restaurant offering *blinis* (wheatflour pancakes), Russian tea and appetizing desserts. *Family treat* Daru *(19 Rue Daru, 75008; 01 42 27 23 60; www.daru.fr; 10am–11pm Mon–Sat)* was founded by a member of Nicholas II's guard in 1918 and serves *blinis,* Russian caviar, salmon, eggs, *borscht* (soup made with beetroot), pickles and smoked sturgeon. There is also a delicatessen.
- **Toilets** On request

Image of Christ on the exterior of the St-Alexandre-Nevsky Cathedral

A colonnaded pool in Parc Monceau, one of the chicest parks in Paris

Palais de Chaillot and around

The area known as the Trocadéro, centred on the Palais de Chaillot, is crammed with fascinating museums that are slightly off the tourist trail, and is a good option for a rainy day. The grand layout testifies to the area's World Fair heritage; the Modernist Palais de Chaillot was built for the Exposition Internationale in 1937, replacing the old Palais de Trocadéro, created for the one in 1878. The immediate vicinity is full of offices; for shopping and nice cafés, head up to Avenue Victor Hugo. Be aware that the area closes down in August, when the locals go on holiday.

Champs-Elysées & Trocadero

Arc de Triomphe p134

Palais de Chaillot

Places of interest

0 metres 400
0 yards 400

SIGHTS
1. Palais de Chaillot
2. Musée Guimet
3. Palais de Tokyo & Musée d'Art Moderne
4. Musée Galliéra

EAT AND DRINK
1. Carton
2. Paul
3. Zen Café
4. L'Astrance
5. Noura
6. Tokyo Eat
7. Béchu
8. Hôtel Shangri-La

See also Musée Guimet
and Musée d'Art Moderne (p146)

SHOPPING
1. Oxybul Éveil & Jeux

See also Palais de Chaillot (p144)

WHERE TO STAY
1. Citadines Trocadéro
2. Hôtel Baltimore
3. Hôtel Elysées Regencia
4. Hôtel Residence Foch
5. Jays
6. Hôtel Shangri-La

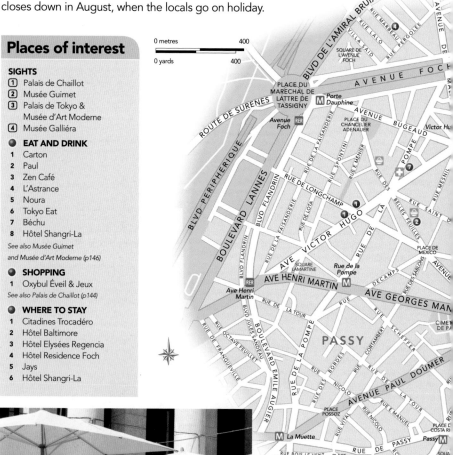

Relaxing in a café outside Palais de Tokyo

 The Lowdown

🚗 **Métro** Trocadéro, lines 6 & 9; Iéna, line 9 or Alma-Marceau, line 9. **RER** Champs de Mars–Tour Eiffel, line C or Pont de l'Alma, line C. **Bus** 22, 30, 32, 42, 63, 72, 80, 82 & 92. **River boat** Quai de la Bourdonnais

🛒 **Supermarkets** Casino, 16 Rue des Belles Feuilles, 75016. Monoprix, 24 Rue Belles Feuilles, 75016. Franprix, 56 Rue de Longchamp, 75016. **Markets** Marché Passy (covered market), Pl de Passy; 8am–1pm & 4–7pm Tue–Fri, 8:30–1pm & 3:30–7pm Sat, 8am–1pm Sun. Marché St-Didier, between Rue Mesnil and St-Didier: 7:30am–2pm Tue, Thu–Sat (covered market). Marché Président Wilson, Ave du Président Wilson, 75016; 7am–2:30pm Wed & Sat

🎪 **Festival** Trocadéro Christmas Village, Pl du Trocadéro (Dec)

➕ **Pharmacy** Pharmacie Basire, 143 Rue de la Pompe & 118 bis Ave Victor Hugo; 01 47 27 88 49; www.pharmacie-basire.com; open 9am–9pm Mon; 8am–9pm Tue–Sat, closed Sun and bank hols

🛝 **Nearest playground** Jardins du Trocadéro, 75016; dawn–dusk (see p145)

Gilded bronze statue near Palais de Chaillot, with the Eiffel Tower in the background

Panoramic view of Paris from the Eiffel Tower

① Palais de Chaillot
Fishy films and fountains

From humble beginnings as a pastoral village, this part of Paris is now dominated by the monumental Palais de Chaillot, universally known by locals as the Trocadéro. It is the best place from which to gaze at the Eiffel Tower, but also somewhere to take a crash course in architecture, French maritime heritage and the history of humankind, by visiting its museums. That done, relax at Aquarium de Paris – Cinéaqua, touring its aquarium or taking in a film.

Statue of Marshal Foch, Place du Trocadéro

Key Features

Marshal Foch The imposing statue of Ferdinand Foch, who led the Allies to victory in 1918, stands here. He prophesied that it was not a peace, but only an armistice that would last 20 years.

Palais de Chaillot The two curving wings of the monumental building are separated by a large terrace that offers a great view over the Trocadéro gardens and the Seine.

The Musée de la Marine Come here to see perfect little model ships, the pretty prow of Marie Antoinette's rowing boat and Napoleon's sparkling barge.

Cité de l'Architecture et du Patrimoine See France's most famous buildings in miniature at this museum, in the palace's east wing.

Aquarium de Paris – Cinéaqua

Trocadéro fountains

Jardins du Trocadéro

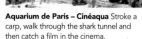

Musée de l'Homme The museum has one of the world's best prehistoric collections as well as temporary exhibitions.

Trocadéro fountains Cannons of water fire towards the Eiffel Tower and are lit at night – a spectacular sight.

Aquarium de Paris – Cinéaqua Stroke a carp, walk through the shark tunnel and then catch a film in the cinema.

The Lowdown

🌐 **Map reference** 7 D1
Address 17 Pl du Trocadéro, 75016; www.mnhn.fr. Musée de l'Homme. Musée de la Marine: 01 53 65 69 69; www.musee-marine.fr. Cité de l'Architecture et du Patrimoine: 1 Pl du Trocadéro, 75016; 01 58 51 52 00; www.citechaillot.fr. Aquarium de Paris – Cinéaqua: 01 40 69 23 23; www.cineaqua.com

🚇 **Métro** Trocadéro, lines 6 & 9. **RER** Champs de Mars–Tour Eiffel, line C. **Bus** 22, 30, 32, 63, 72 & 82. **River boat** Quai de la Bourdonnais

🕐 **Open** Musée de la Marine: 11am–6pm, till 7pm Sat & Sun; closed Tue, 1 Jan, 1 May & 25 Dec. Cité de l'Architecture et du Patrimoine: 11am–7pm, till 9pm Thu; closed Tue, 1 Jan, 1 May & 25 Dec. Aquarium de Paris – Cinéaqua: 10am–7pm, closed 14 Jul

💶 **Price** Musée de la Marine: €14–24; under 18s, and under 26s with EU passport free. Cité de l'Architecture et du Patrimoine: €16–26; under 18s, and under 26s with EU passport free. Aquarium de Paris – Cinéaqua: adults €40–50; 13–17 years €16–26; under 13s €13–23; under 3s free

🏃 **Skipping the queue** Paris Museum Pass accepted.

🎧 **Guided tours** The museums have audio guides in English.

👫 **Age range** All ages

👫 **Activities** Workshops and activity leaflets in French

⏱ **Allow** Half a day

🍴 **Eat and drink** In the Cité de l'Architecture et du Patrimoine & Cinéaqua

Letting off steam

The **Jardins du Trocadéro** run down to the Seine alongside the most fantastic fountain in Paris. There is a playground and a vintage merry-go-round. During weekends there are street entertainers moon-walking and break-dancing on the esplanade.

Eat and drink

Picnic: under €25; Snacks: €25–45; Real meal: €45–90; Family treat: over €90 (based on a family of four)

PICNIC Carton *(150 Ave Victor Hugo, 75016)* sells lemon *pavé* and chocolate *feuilleté*. Picnic by the fountains in the Jardins du Trocadéro.
SNACKS Paul *(12 Rue de Bellefeuilles, 75016; 01 47 55 92 14)*, this French bakery chain is a reliable place for a lunchtime sandwich, a morning croissant or an afternoon cake.
REAL MEAL Zen Café *(Aquarium de Paris – Cinéaqua, 5 Ave Albert de Mun; 01 40 69 23 90; www. cineaqua.com; open for breakfast, lunch and tea daily, for brunch on Sun)* offers salads, sandwiches and Bento boxes. One of its walls is part of the Aquarium de Paris.

Old-fashioned merry-go-round in the Jardins du Trocadéro

 Shops In the museums

Toilets Inside the Cité de l'Architecture et du Patrimoine; inside the two museums; near the cinema area and the activities area in Aquarium de Paris – Cinéaqua

Good family value?

Though Cinéaqua is expensive, it has something for everyone. At the Musée de la Marine the explanations are only in French, so take an audio guide.

Elegant interior of fine dining restaurant L'Astrance

FAMILY TREAT L'Astrance *(4 Rue Beethoven, 75016; 01 40 50 84 40; closed Sat–Mon)* serves French fare with a global twist in an elegant setting. Reservations need to be made at least one month in advance.

Shopping

Avenue Victor Hugo has children's shops, cake shops and toyshops, the best of which is **Oxybul Éveil & Jeux** *(148 Ave Victor Hugo, 75116)*.

Find out more

DIGITAL Watch the video *Hitler in Paris* at *http://tinyurl.com/cqpbtyf*, the 1937 World Fair at *http://tinyurl.com/3j3f6uy* and baby sharks at *http://tinyurl.com/3nvbtmm*. Check out *www.bbc.co.uk/oceans* to explore the world's oceans, *www.academickids.com* to learn about prehistory, and *www.archkidecture.org* for awesome buildings.

Next stop...

EIFFEL TOWER After taking a look at the **Eiffel Tower** *(see pp154–5)* from the Palais de Chaillot, walk across the Seine on Pont d'Iéna and whizz up to the top of the tower.

View of the Eiffel Tower from the Palais de Chaillot

Exhibits in the Musée Guimet

② Musée Guimet
Dragons and demons

Treasures from the temple of Angkor Wat, including the seven-headed snake demon called the Giants Way, are on display in this museum of Asian art and culture. Originally 200 m (657 ft) tall, the idol was brought to Paris for the Exposition Universelle of 1878. Most of the collection on show was put together by Emile Guimet, who spent his vast fortune travelling in Asia collecting pieces for his personal museum. *Mulan* fans will enjoy exploring the Chinese collection. Do not miss the goddess Avalokiteshvara, who has a thousand arms.

The Lowdown

🌐 **Map reference** 2 E6
Address 6 Pl d'Iéna, 75016; 01 56 52 53 00; www.guimet.fr

🚇 **Métro** Iéna, line 9. **Bus** 22, 30, 32, 63 & 82

🕐 **Open** 10am–6pm, closed Tue, and 1 Jan, 1 May & 25 Dec

💶 **Price** €15–26; under 18s, and under 26s with EU passport, free

🎟️ **Skipping the queue** Paris Museum Pass accepted

🎧 **Guided tours** Audio guide in English; storytelling tour in French

👫 **Age range** 5 plus

👨‍👧 **Activities** Activity leaflets and workshops in French; 01 56 52 53 45. Japanese tea ceremony: €12; 01 56 52 53 45

⏱️ **Allow** 2 hours

♿ **Wheelchair access** Yes

🍴 **Eat and drink** *Real meal* The museum café serves French and Asian cuisine; 01 47 23 58 03. *Family treat* Noura (27 Ave Marceau, 75016; 01 47 20 33 33) serves Middle Eastern classics.

👫 **Toilets** In the basement

Bas-relief created by Alfred Janniot, along a wall of the Palais de Tokyo

Letting off steam

Unwind in the Japanese garden around the **Musée du Panthéon Bouddhique** (*19 Ave d'Iéna, 75016*), an oasis of waterfalls, pools and bamboo swaying in the wind.

③ Palais de Tokyo & Musée d'Art Moderne
Technicolour cows and an electricity fairy

The Palais de Tokyo was built for the World Fair of 1937, when it was the electricity pavilion, and gets its name from the nearby Quai de Tokyo, now Avenue of New York.

The Palais de Tokyo's east wing houses the light and airy Musée d'Art Moderne, a good spot to introduce kids to modern art since the works are laid out chronologically. See the world turned upside down by the Fauvists, the "Wild Beasts", who painted blue cows, red trees and pink grass. Move on to see the world squared up by the Cubists. The museum also has two giant canvasses of *The Dance* by Henri Matisse.

Tucked away in a room of its own is one of the biggest paintings in the world. Raoul Dufy's *La Fée*

Electricité (The Electricity Fairy), which was commissioned by the Parisian Electricity Board in 1936, tells the story of electricity from Zeus and his fire bolts to Edison.

The other wing of the Palais de Tokyo is the city's trendiest contemporary art venue, where the temporary exhibitions are always cutting-edge and eye-opening.

Letting off steam

Take the stairs leading from Avenue du Président Wilson to Rue de la Manutention and walk to the little garden next to the Palais de Tokyo.

The Lowdown

🌐 **Map reference** 8 E1
Address Musée d'Art Moderne: 11 Ave du Président Wilson 75016; 01 53 67 40 00; www.mam.paris.fr. Palais de Tokyo: 13 Ave du Président Wilson, 75016; 01 81 97 35 88; www.palaisdetokyo.com

🚇 **Métro** Iéna, line 9 or Alma-Marceau, line 9. **RER** Pont de l'Alma, line C. **Bus** 32, 42, 63, 72, 80, 82 & 92

🕐 **Open** Musée d'Art Moderne: 10am–6pm (until 10pm for temporary exhibitions), closed Mon and public hols. Palais de Tokyo: noon–midnight, closed Tue, 1 Jan, 1 May & 25 Dec

💶 **Price** Musée d'Art Moderne: free for the permanent collection. Palais de Tokyo: €10–20, joint ticket and restaurant deal. Under 18s free

🎧 **Guided tours** Audio guide in English

👫 **Age range** 5 plus

👨‍👧 **Activities** Workshops available; see website for more details. Storytelling and tours in the Palais de Tokyo are sometimes available in English; 01 47 23 35 16. Workshops for kids in French at the Musée d'Art Moderne; 01 53 67 40 80

⏱️ **Allow** 2–3 hours

♿ **Wheelchair access** Yes

🍴 **Eat and drink** *Snacks* The Musée d'Art Moderne's café has a terrace overlooking the Eiffel Tower and serves a varied menu. *Family treat* Tokyo Eat (*Palais de Tokyo, 13 Ave du Président Wilson, 75016; 01 47 20 00 29; closed Tue*) tempts with exciting fusion food and stylish ice creams, served under funky UFO-style lights. A resident DJ adds to the buzz.

👫 **Toilets** In both the museums

④ Musée Galliéra

Dresses, handbags and hats

Just a stone's throw away from Paris's famous fashion houses, this museum is located in the elegant 19th-century Palais Galliéra, a Renaissance-style building built by Gustave Eiffel for Duchesse Maria de Ferrari Galliéra.

On display are mountains of fascinating dresses, underwear, hats, handbags, umbrellas, kids' clothes and dolls' wardrobes from the 18th century to the present day. Some of the outfits have been worn by famous people, such as Marie Antoinette and Empress Josephine, while others have been donated by fashionable women, including Baronne Hélène de Rothschild and Princess Grace of Monaco. The museum displays these creations in rotation, twice in a year, through temporary exhibitions.

Letting off steam

The museum has a pretty garden while the terrace in front of the **Palais de Tokyo** (13 Ave du Président Wilson, 75116; 01 47 23 54 01) is where local kids practise skateboarding.

The **Cimetière de Passy** (2 Rue du Commandant Schloesing, 75016) is the last resting place of some of the most famous names in the history of Paris, such as the composer Debussy and the painter Edouard Manet. Eminent politicians and aristocrats are also buried there. With excellent views of the Eiffel Tower (see pp154–5), it is a pleasant place for a stroll.

Poster advertising an exhibition of Givenchy couture at the Musée Galliéra

The Lowdown

🌐 **Map reference** 2 E6
Address 10 Ave Pierre 1er de Serbie, 75116; 01 56 52 86 00; www.galliera.paris.fr

🚇 **Métro** Iéna, line 9 or Alma-Marceau, line 9. **Bus** 32, 42, 63, 72, 80, 82 & 92

🕐 **Open** 10am–1pm, 2–5:30pm Tue, 10am–1pm Wed–Fri

🚩 **Guided tours** Audio guide in English

👫 **Age range** 5 plus

🤸 **Activities** Workshops, guided tours and activity leaflets in French

⏱️ **Allow** 1 hour

♿ **Wheelchair access** Yes

☕ **Eat and drink** *Snacks* Béchu (118 Ave Victor Hugo, 75016; 7am–8:30pm; closed Mon) is good for a teatime treat. Try the *Victor Hugo*, a chocolate cake with a meringue in the middle. *Family treat* Hôtel Shangri-La (10 Ave d'Iéna, 75016; 01 53 67 19 98) serves outstanding Asian and French cuisine.

🚻 **Toilets** On the ground floor

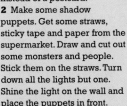

Rear façade of the Musée Galliéra, with a fountain

Eiffel Tower
& Les Invalides

A monumental part of Paris, the area around Les Invalides, on the Left Bank of the Seine, is determined to leave an impression. Everything from the Dôme church at the imposing Hôtel des Invalides to the sprawling 18th-century buildings of the Ecole Militaire at the end of the sweeping Champ-de-Mars is outstanding. Overlooking it all stands Paris's towering steel lady, the Eiffel Tower.

Tuileries, Opéra & Montmartre

Champs-Elysées & Trocadéro

Beaubourg & the Marais

Eiffel Tower & Les Invalides

Ile de la Cité & Ile St-Louis

St-Germain & the Latin Quarter

Luxembourg & Montparnasse

Highlights

Eiffel Tower
Climb to the top of the spectacular tower and gaze down at the beautiful city below (see pp154–5).

Les Egouts
Look out for the endearing little stars of *Ratatouille* and the heroes of *Les Misérables* on a tour of Paris's famous sewers (see p157).

Champ-de-Mars
Watch an entertaining puppet show before enjoying a ride on the ponies and running around the playground in these vast, lawned gardens (see p156).

musée du quai Branly
Step into a world of African dancers, strange masks and totem poles in this fascinating museum (see p156).

Les Invalides
Visit the spectacular church where Napoleon lies buried, next to one of the best military museums in the world (see pp160–61).

Musée Rodin
Lunch in the lovely garden at the museum, then admire the marvellous sculptures of Auguste Rodin while enjoying an ice cream (see p162).

Above left Detail of the ceiling in the Assemblée Nationale Palais-Bourbon
Left Summer crowds on the Champ-de-Mars, beneath the famous Eiffel Tower

The Best of
Eiffel Tower & Les Invalides

Indulge in being a proper tourist here – there is no other way to approach the Eiffel Tower, so give in to trinket-buying and posing for photos in front of it. The other prominent landmark in the area, the imposing Hôtel des Invalides, is also a must, whether for a peek at Napoleon's tomb or hours of gazing at historic guns and model forts. Art of all kinds can be enjoyed both indoors and outdoors, best of all in the gardens of the Musée Rodin.

A perfect Parisian day

Begin the morning by visiting the **Musée Rodin** (*see p162*) and admire the work of the greatest French sculptor of the 19th century, Auguste Rodin, followed by lunch in the garden café.

Afterwards, head to the **Champ-de-Mars** (*see p156*), checking out the shops along the way. Watch a puppet show at the **Marionettes du Champ-de-Mars** (*see p156*) before braving some strong smells and the dirty underside of the city on a tour of Paris's sewers, **Les Egouts** (*see p157*).

On a summer evening, picnic under the magnificent **Eiffel Tower** (*see pp154–5*). Then race to the top to enjoy spectacular views of the city twinkling below. Finish in style with a delicious meal at **58 Tour Eiffel** (*see p155*) on the second floor.

Right *Colourful hot-air balloons in the Champ-de-Mars*
Below *Auguste Rodin's* The Thinker *in the Musée Rodin*

Above Fascinating artifacts on display at the musée du quai Branly Below Glittering gilded Dôme church of Les Invalides

Military might

Admire the guns in the gardens of the **Hôtel des Invalides** *(see p160)* before tracing the history of warfare from the Stone Age to World War II at the **Musée de l'Armée** *(see p160)*. March around the **Cour d'Honneur** *(see p160)*, which is still used as a parade ground, and salute Napoleon's statue. Pop into the Dôme church to pay a visit to his sarcophagus as well as the tomb of the leader of the Allied forces in World War I, General Foch.

At the **Musées des Plans-Reliefs** *(see p160)*, marvel at the skills of Louis XIV's master fortress builder, Sébastien le Prestre de Vauban, who revolutionized siege warfare. Learn more about the heroes of the Resistance during World War II at the **Musée de L'Ordre de la Libération** *(see p160)*. Head to the **Hôtel Matignon** on Rue de Varenne, the official residence of the French prime minister. He is able to enjoy what is one of the biggest private gardens in town.

Walk across the Champ-de-Mars to the imposing Royal Military Academy of Louis XV, the **Ecole Militaire** *(see p162)*. At the age of 16, newly arrived from Corsica, Napoleon Bonaparte was a cadet here. Modern-day French peacekeeping troops have played an important role around the world, notably during the war in Bosnia. Learn more about France's role in world politics at Place de Fontenoy, the headquarters of the United Nations Educational, Scientific and Cultural Organization, **UNESCO** *(see p156)*.

A world of art

Discover indigenous art and artifacts from Asia, Africa, Oceania and the Americas in the fascinating **musée du quai Branly** *(see p156)*, and listen to recordings of the many weird and wonderful instruments also on display. Wander south across the **Champ-de-Mars** and pause for thought at **Le Mur de la Paix** *(see p156)*, the Wall of Peace outside the **Ecole Militaire**, then admire the massive mural by Pablo Picasso, ceramics by Jean Miró and sculptures by Henry Moore at the headquarters of **UNESCO**.

Fall in love with the works of Auguste Rodin in his former home, studio and gardens, now the delightful **Musée Rodin**. Then stroll over to the Dôme church at the **Hôtel des Invalides** and prepare to be dazzled by *The Glory of Paradise*, painted on the circular, domed ceiling by Charles de la Fosse in 1692.

Eiffel Tower and around

From the moment kids arrive in Paris they want to get to the top of the Eiffel Tower. In summer be prepared for big crowds. If the plan is to have a picnic, buy supplies beforehand, since shops here are few and far between; for the same reason it is best to bring snacks, as the kiosks are expensive. Exploring this area requires a lot of walking so, for small children, be sure to bring a pushchair. On Sundays and public holidays, Quai Branly is closed to traffic and is a fun place to rollerblade or take a stroll.

Eiffel Tower &
Les Invalides

Eiffel
Tower   Les Invalides
p160

Places of interest

SIGHTS
1. Eiffel Tower
2. Champ-de-Mars
3. musée du quai Branly
4. Les Egouts

EAT AND DRINK
1. Boulangerie Secco
2. Les Buffets de la Tour Eiffel
3. Thé aux 3 Cerises
4. 58 Tour Eiffel
5. Millet Traiteur
6. Tribeca
7. Michel Chaudun
8. Les Deux Abeilles

See also musée du quai Branly (p156)

WHERE TO STAY
1. Adagio Paris Tour Eiffel
2. Hôtel Ares Eiffel
3. Novotel Eiffel Tower

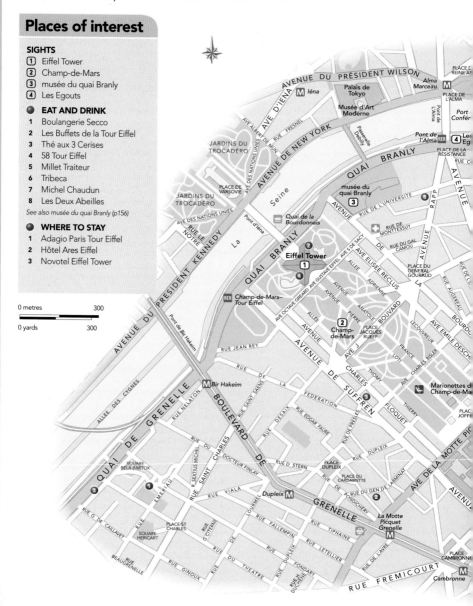

Subterranean tours of Les
Egouts, Paris's sewers

A puppet show in progress at the Marionettes du
Champ-de-Mars

Children's play area in the Champ-de-
Mars, in front of the Eiffel Tower

The Lowdown

🚗 **Métro** Bir Hakeim, line 6;
Trocadéro, lines 6 & 9; Ecole
Militaire, line 8 or Iéna &
Alma Marceau, lines 9. **RER**
Champ de Mars–Tour Eiffel,
line C or Pont de l'Alma, line
C. **Bus** 28, 42, 63, 69, 72,
80, 82, 87 & 92. **River boat**
Quai de la Bourdonnais

🛒 **Supermarkets** Monoprix, 2
Rue du Commerce, 75015.
Franprix, 107 Ave de la
Bourdonnais, 75007 & 27
Rue Cler, 75007
Market Marché Saxe Breteuil,
Ave de Saxe, 75007;
7am–2:30pm Thu, Sat

🎊 **Festivals** Famillathlon: family
sports day in the Champ-de-
Mars; www.famillathlon.org
(Sep). Ice-skating at the Eiffel
Tower (some years;
mid-Dec–end Jan)

➕ **Pharmacy** Pharmacie de la
Tour Eiffel, 24 Rue de
Monttessuy, 75007; 8am–8pm
Mon–Fri, 9am–8pm Sat

🛝 **Nearest playground** There
is a large playground with
a sandpit at the southern end
of the Champ-de-Mars,
75007; dawn–dusk daily
(see p156)

① Eiffel Tower
The iron lady of Paris

There is something irresistible about the Meccano-style star of the Paris skyline. It is a magnet for children, whose main ambition is to get to the top as fast as possible. In 1886, a competition was held to build a tower at the gates of the Exposition Universelle of 1889, to commemorate 100 years since the Revolution. Gustave Eiffel emerged as the winner from among 170 entries, which included a giant watering can and an enormous guillotine. Far from an instant hit, the Eiffel Tower (Tour Eiffel) was lucky not to be torn down later.

Colourful scale models of the Eiffel Tower

The Lowdown

🌐 **Map reference** 8 E3
Address Champ-de-Mars, 75007; 08 92 70 12 39; *www.toureiffel.paris*

🚗 **Métro** Bir Hakeim, line 6 or Trocadéro, lines 6 & 9. **RER** Champ-de-Mars–Tour Eiffel, line C. **Bus** 42, 69, 82 & 87. **River boat** Port de la Bourdonnais

🕐 **Open** 9:30am–11pm; mid-Jun–Aug: 9am–midnight; Easter weekend: to midnight

💶 **Price** Summit: approx. €50. Second level (lift): approx. €30; 4–11-year-olds: €4; under 4s free

👪 **Skipping the queue** The queues are shorter at night – or buy tickets online in advance

🚩 **Guided tours** Download guide with iPhone apps

👫 **Age range** All ages, but small children may find the tower above the second level frightening

🤸 **Activities** Download kids' quiz book from *www. eiffel-tower.com*

⏱ **Allow** 1.5 hours – or 3 hours in high season

♿ **Wheelchair access** Yes, but first and second levels only

☕ **Café** On first & second levels

🚻 **Toilets** On every floor

Good family value?
It may be pricey but kids will love it. It is best to visit the tower at the end of a trip to Paris so that children can spot from above the sights they have visited.

Key Features

Viewing gallery On a clear day it is possible to see Chartres Cathedral, 80 km (50 miles) away.

Bust of Eiffel Eiffel was sculpted by Antoine Bourdelle in 1929 and the bust was placed below the tower in his memory.

Double-decker lifts These vintage lifts ply their way up and down to and from the second floor.

Eiffel's staircase See a piece of the original staircase that was taken down in 1983 to make way for new lifts. Gustave Eiffel would walk up to the top to his office.

Champ-de-Mars A former parade ground, these long gardens stretch from the tower's base to the Ecole Militaire (military school).

Third level The viewing gallery is 276 m (906 ft) above the ground. Mr Eiffel had an office here.

Sparkling Eiffel Every evening since the millennium, a 200,000-watt lighting system makes the Eiffel Tower sparkle for 5 minutes every hour, on the hour, until 1am.

Crisscross girders The complex pattern of the girders helps to stabilize the tower on windy days. The metal parts can expand up to 12 cm (5 inch) on hot days.

Second level At 115 m (376 ft), this level is separated from the first by 359 steps, or a few minutes in the lift.

First level At a height of 57 m (187 ft), this level can be reached by lift or by 360 steps. It has a glass floor giving fabulous views and a new exhibition space.

Bust of Eiffel

The Eiffel Tower with the Champ-de-Mars in the foreground

Letting off steam

Some years, in winter, there is an ice-skating rink on the first level but the best place to burn off some energy, all year round, is on the well-manicured expanses of **Champ-de-Mars** (see p156), the park that stretches out from beneath the tower.

Eat and drink

Picnic: under €25; Snacks: €25–45; Real meal: €45–90; Family treat: over €90 (based on a family of four)

PICNIC Boulangerie Secco (20 Rue Jean Nicot, 75007; closed Sun & Mon) is famous for its seasonal selection of pastries. Picnic in the Champ-de-Mars.

SNACKS Les Buffets de la Tour Eiffel is situated on the ground floor and the first and second floors of the tower. It offers pizzas, salads and sandwiches as well as pastries, ice cream and hot and cold drinks.

REAL MEAL Thé aux 3 Cerises (47 Ave de Suffren, 75007; 01 42 73 92 97; noon–6pm Tue–Fri, noon–7pm Sat & Sun) serves delicious meals, such as brie on toast. Kids can enjoy a delicious hot chocolate with whipped cream.

Contemporary decor at 58 Tour Eiffel, the first-floor restaurant

FAMILY TREAT 58 Tour Eiffel (08 25 56 66 62; www.restaurants-toureiffel.com; 11:30am–4:30pm & 6:30–11:30pm) is located on the first floor. Lunch is the best option, when the menu is lighter and prices more competitive.

Find out more

DIGITAL On *http://tinyurl.com/2g5beua*, watch daredevil French inline skater Taïg Khris set the world record for the highest roller-skate jump, at 40 m (131 ft), from the first floor of the Eiffel Tower in 2010. Find out about more towers on *www.great-towers.com* and play games with the Eiffel Tower on *www.tour-eiffel.fr*

FILM Check out James Bond in action on the tower in *A View to a Kill* (1985), Chuckie and his friends in *Rugrats in Paris* (1996) and the cartoon heroes of *Looney Tunes Back in Action* (2003). It appears in *Zazie dans le Métro* (1960), *The Aristocats* (1970) and *Ratatouille* (2007). Ludwig Bemelmans' heroine Madeline lives in a leafy street nearby in *Madeline* (1998).

Shopping

The only thing to buy next to the Eiffel Tower is a model of it. The original models were made of scrap metal from the tower, but now they come in all colours and materials.

Next stop...

NOTRE-DAME Take a river cruise from the Eiffel Tower past various famous sights, ending up at the other ultimate Paris icon, **Notre-Dame** (see pp64–5).

Puppet show at the old-fashioned Marionettes du Champ-de-Mars

② Champ-de-Mars
War, peace and puppets

Once a military parade ground, the vast Champ-de-Mars with its long sweeping pathways is perfect for riding a bike and kicking a ball about. It was here that a grudging Louis XVI was forced to accept the new constitution on 14 July 1790. Today, watch a Punch-and-Judy-style puppet show at the Marionettes du Champ-de-Mars, the old-fashioned theatre on the northeastern side of the park, which is fun even if the kids do not speak a word of French. At Le Mur de la Paix, the Wall of Peace monument, near the Ecole Militaire, leave a message of peace in the cracks.

Take cover
The headquarters of the United Nations Educational, Scientific and Cultural Organization, **UNESCO** (Pl de Fontenoy, 75007), has a huge mural inside by Pablo Picasso.

③ musée du quai Branly
Skulls, masks and magic

Opened in 2006, the **musée du quai Branly** is home to an amazing ethnographic collection. The exhibits are presented in striking, original ways, often through film and music, which makes them especially accessible to children. The museum is crammed with fascinating objects

from all over the world. Follow in the footsteps of the great explorers, such as André Thévet who was sent by the King of France to found a colony in South America in 1555, or the team who drove a Citroën car 30,000 km (18,641 miles) across Asia in 1931. Among the treasures they brought back was a beautiful painted saddle from Uzbekistan. Discover the shrunken heads from the South Seas but also look out for the 1,000-year-old wooden statue from Africa. It is both a man and a woman, with unborn twins in its stomach.

Letting off steam
The musée du quai Branly is situated in a modern garden. In summer there are several events here for children. Look out for the wall of plants which makes up part of the outside of the building, and enjoy a picnic beside the fountains in the gardens.

Artifacts from Africa on display in the musée du quai Branly

The Lowdown

🌐 **Map reference** 8 F3
Address 75007

🚇 **Métro** Ecole Militaire, line 8 or Bir Hakeim, line 6. **RER** Champ-de-Mars–Tour Eiffel, line C. **Bus** 28, 42, 63, 80 & 82

🚻 **Age range** All ages

👫 **Activities** Marionettes du Champ-de-Mars; 01 48 56 01 44; €3.50. Shows 3pm & 5pm Wed, Sat & Sun. Watch the fireworks let off at Trocadéro on 14 July

🍽 **Eat and drink** *Snacks* Millet Traiteur (103 Rue St-Dominique, 75007; 01 45 51 49 80; 8:30am–8pm Tue–Sat, 8am–5pm Sun) is good for delicious cakes and pastries. *Real meal* Tribeca (36 Rue Cler, 75007; 01 45 55 12 01; 8:30–1am daily) is a simple pizzeria with a terrace. It is a good place to stop for a light meal, and the service is great, too.

👫 **Toilets** At the Marionnettes du Champ-de-Mars and on 22 Ave Charles Floquet

The Lowdown

🌐 **Map reference** 8 F2
Address 37 quai Branly, 75007; 01 56 61 70 00; www.quaibranly.fr

🚇 **Métro** Iéna or Alma Marceau, line 9. **RER** Pont de l'Alma, line C. **Bus** 42, 63, 80, 92 & 72. **River boat** Port de la Bourdonnais

🕐 **Open** 11am–7pm, till 9pm Thu, Fri & Sat, closed Mon & various days in Feb & Apr

💲 **Price** €17–27; under 18s free

👫 **Skipping the queue** Paris Museum Pass accepted

🎧 **Guided tours** English audio guide for adults and children €20–25, duration 45 minutes

👫 **Age range** 6 plus

👫 **Activities** Download the English activity booklet from the website, as key objects are difficult to locate in the museum. The bookshop sells a children's guide,

My little quai Branly. Workshops & tours in English; 01 56 61 71 72; €32–42; check availability

⏱ **Allow** 2 hours

♿ **Wheelchair access** Yes

🍽 **Eat and drink** *Real meal* Café Branly (01 47 53 68 01; 9am–6pm, till 8pm Thu–Sat, closed Mon), the museum café, has great views from the outside tables of the Eiffel Tower and is located in a lovely garden. *Family treat* Les Ombres (27 Quai Branly; 01 47 53 68 00; www.lesombres-restaurant.com; open daily; book in advance), on the roof of the museum, is a gourmet experience with stunning views. The lunch is of exceptionally good value.

👫 **Toilets** By the museum entrance and on levels 2 & 3

④ Les Egouts
What is that smell?

Victor Hugo made the sewers of Paris famous in his well-known novel, *Les Misérables*. Kids, however, will probably think Remy the rat, the star of *Ratatouille*, put them on the map. A feat of 19th-century engineering, the sewers run parallel to the streets above for 2,400 km (1,490 miles), and would stretch as far as Istanbul. Between 1800 and 1850, the population of Paris doubled to over a million but the city had very few underground sewers. In the 1850s, Baron Haussmann transformed standards of living by building a remarkable hidden parallel city and it was soon a must-see for visitors, among them Tsar Alexander II of Russia. Today, visitors can take a tour of the sewers and discover the

mysteries of underground Paris. All of the tours are limited to an area around the Quai d'Orsay entrance, and are on foot.

Letting off steam
There is a shortage of playgrounds in this part of Paris so head back into the **Champ-de-Mars** for a run around. The quickest way to get there is to walk down Avenue Rapp.

The Lowdown

- 🌐 **Map reference** 8 F1
  Address Pont de l'Alma, opposite 93 Quai d'Orsay, 75007; 01 53 68 27 81
- 🚗 **Métro** Alma Marceau, line 9. **RER** Pont de l'Alma, line C. **Bus** 63 & 80
- 🕐 **Open** 11am–5pm; winter: till 4pm; closed Thu, Fri, public hols, two weeks in Jan & during heavy rainfall
- 💰 **Price** €16–26; under 6s free
- 👫 **Skipping the queue** Paris Museum Pass accepted
- 🚩 **Guided tours** Yes
- 👫 **Age range** 5 plus
- 🕐 **Allow** 1 hour
- ♿ **Wheelchair access** No
- 🍴 **Eat and drink** *Picnic* Michel Chaudun (*149 Rue de l'Université, 75007; closed Sun*), the famous chocolatier, has a giant chocolate Tutankhamun in a glass case made in 1965. Picnic in the Champ-de-Mars. *Snacks* Les Deux Abeilles (*189 Rue de l'Université, 75007; 01 45 55 64 04; 9am–7pm; reserve a table; closed Sun*) serves salads, soups and quiche, followed by raspberry soufflé tart.
- 🚻 **Toilets** Near the shop

Above Relaxing on a sunny day on the Champ-de-Mars Below A history tour of Paris's atmospheric sewers, Les Egouts

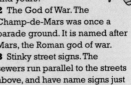

Les Invalides and around

The shimmering golden dome of Les Invalides towers over the lawns that stretch from the equally magnificent Pont Alexandre III, and is bound to impress the kids. Mini military buffs can run past the cannons to explore one of the best collections of guns and armour in the world. Afterwards relax in the garden of the Musée Rodin, just across the road, a great place to unwind. Exploring this area involves plenty of walking, so small children will need pushchairs.

Eiffel Tower & Les Invalides

Eiffel Tower p154 • Les Invalides

Places of interest

SIGHTS

1. Les Invalides
2. Ecole Militaire
3. Musée Rodin
4. Assemblée Nationale Palais-Bourbon

● EAT AND DRINK

1. Boulangerie Deschamps
2. Les Trois Coeurs
3. Coutume Café
4. Les Cocottes de Christian Constant
5. Aux Délices de Mimi
6. Le Basile
7. Besnier Père et Fils
8. Le Bon Marché
9. Le Bac à Glaces
10. Kayser

See also Les Invalides (p160)

● SHOPPING

1. Deyrolle
2. Papillon
3. À la Mère de Famille

See also Les Invalides (p160)

● WHERE TO STAY

1. Hôtel Mayet
2. Hôtel du Palais Bourbon

Neo-Classical façade of the Assemblée Nationale Palais-Bourbon

The Thinker, one of Rodin's most celebrated sculptures, at the Musée Rodin

The Lowdown

Métro Invalides, lines 8 & 13; Varenne, line 13; La Tour Maubourg, line 8; St-François Xavier, line 13; Ecole Militaire, line 8 or Assemblée Nationale, line 12. **RER** Invalides, line C or Musée d'Orsay, line C. **Bus** 28, 63, 69, 80, 82, 83, 84, 87, 92, 93 & 94

Supermarkets Carrefour, 84 Rue St-Dominique, 75007. Franprix, 27 Rue Cler, 75007; 11 Rue Casimir Perrier, 75007 & 107 Ave La Bourdonnais, 75007

Pharmacy Pharmacie des Invalides, 25 Blvd de La Tour Maubourg, 75007

Nearest playgrounds Champ-de-Mars, 75007; dawn–dusk daily (see p156). Playground to the south of Les Invalides; dawn–dusk daily (see p161). Square d'Ajaccio, Blvd des Invalides, 75007; dawn–dusk daily (see p161)

Outdoor café in the Musée Rodin

① Les Invalides
Guns, generals and potatoes

Louis XIV built the Hôtel des Invalides in 1671–76, for the thousands of soldiers who were wounded and disabled in his endless campaigns. At its centre rises the glittering dome of the Eglise du Dôme, the final resting place of Napoleon Bonaparte. More about him, as well as wars and weapons from medieval times to World War II, can be found in the museums surrounding the church. One of the best collections of military history in the world, it is a must for toy soldier enthusiasts.

General de Gaulle's Liberation Order and compass

Key Features

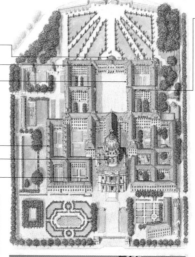

North entrance

Musée de l'Armée

Cour d'Honneur This courtyard is still used for military parades. Napoleon's statue, known as the Little Corporal, stands nearby.

Musée de l'Ordre de la Libération

Eglise du Dôme

South entrance

Musées des Plans-Reliefs Scale models and maps of the most famous fortifications in France are housed here.

Mighty cannons The gardens designed by de Cotte in 1704 are lined with rows of 17th- and 18th-century bronze cannons.

Musée de l'Armée Occupying the main part of the Hôtel des Invalides, this museum has the third-largest collection of armoury in the world plus galleries on the wars that ravaged France between 1870 and 1945.

Eglise du Dôme Napoleon Bonaparte lies buried in the crypt here, inside six coffins like a Russian matryoshka doll.

Musée de l'Ordre de la Libération This museum documents the daring feats of resistance during World War II.

The Lowdown

🌐 **Map reference** 9 A5
Address 129 Rue de Grenelle, 75007; www.musee-armee.fr

🚇 **Métro** La Tour Maubourg, line 8; Invalides, lines 8 & 13; Varenne, line 13 or St-François Xavier, line 13. **RER** Invalides, line C. **Bus** 28, 63, 69, 80, 82, 83, 87, 92 & 93

🕐 **Open** Musée de l'Armée: Apr–Oct: 10am–6pm; Nov–Mar: till 5pm; closed first Mon of the month & 1 Jan, 1 May & 25 Dec

💶 **Price** €15–19; under 18s free; EU citizens under 26 free. €25–35 on Tue eve, after 5pm

in summer and after 4pm in winter; free on 14 Jul

🧍 **Skipping the queue** Paris Museum Pass accepted. Ticket gives access to the Musée de l'Armée, Napoleon's Tomb, Musées des Plans-Reliefs and Musée de l'Ordre de la Libération.

🎧 **Guided tours** Multimedia guides €6 for adults and €4 for children; tours in English for children

👫 **Age range** 7 plus

🏃 **Activities** A variety of kids' workshops and activities in French; 01 44 42 51 73

⏱ **Allow** 2–3 hours

♿ **Wheelchair access** Yes, for the Musée de l'Armée

☕ **Café** Near the south entrance

🛍 **Shop** The museum shop by the south entrance has books in English

🚻 **Toilets** Near the ticket office and in the shop

Good family value?
Although it is very good value for what is on offer, guns and soldiers are not necessarily going to entertain the whole family.

Prices given are for a family of four

Children's playground to the south of Les Invalides

Letting off steam

Run off steam on the lawns in front of the Hôtel des Invalides or in the little playground in the green central section of the tree-lined Avenue de Breteuil, just south of here. **Square d'Ajaccio** *(Blvd des Invalides, 75007)*, just northeast of the Hôtel des Invalides, has a sandpit and games for kids. For a more serious park experience there is the nearby **Champ-de-Mars** *(see p156)*.

Eat and drink

Picnic: under €25; Snacks: €25–45; Real meal: €45–90; Family treat: over €90 (based on a family of four)

PICNIC Boulangerie Deschamps *(43 Ave de Saxe, 75007; closed Mon, Tue)* has tasty tarts, quiches and chocolate croissants. Picnic in the Champ-de-Mars.

SNACKS Les Trois Coeurs *(111 Rue St-Dominique, 75007; 01 45 51 24 41)* is perfect for supplies for an upmarket picnic.

REAL MEAL Coutume Café *(47 Rue de Babylone, 75007)* is renowned for its excellent coffee and its healthy, seasonal food.

FAMILY TREAT Les Cocottes de Christian Constant *(135 Rue St-Dominique, 75007; 01 47 53 73 34; noon–11pm daily)*, a Michelin-starred restaurant, is where chef Christian Constant whips up good-value gourmet food in a relaxed diner-style atmosphere.

Find out more

DIGITAL Discover the lives of Napoleon and Charles de Gaulle at *www.napoleon.org/en/kids* and *www.charles-de-gaulle.org*. There are documentaries about Napoleon at *http://tinyurl.com/4y9dx42*. A number of computer games are

also available, the best of which are *Napoleon: Total War* (2010) and *Napoleon's Campaigns* (2008). **FILM** *Waterloo* (1970) is a great family watch. *Monsieur N* (2007) is good for older children.

Shopping

Deyrolle *(46 Rue du Bac, 75007)*, the famous taxidermist, opened in 1831 and is a bizarre menagerie of lions and creepy crawlies. **Papillon** *(82 Rue de Grenelle, 75007)*, a clothes shop, is part of the Bonton stable. **À la Mère de Famille** *(47 Rue Cler, 75007)* is an irresistible chocolate shop.

Next stop...

PUPPETS AND GARDENS Follow up the serious museum experience with some fresh air. Have a picnic and catch a puppet show in the **Champ-de-Mars**, or stroll across the beautiful **Pont Alexandre III** *(see p136)* with its glittering statues. From here walk along the Seine past the houseboats to the tranquil **Jardin des Tuileries** *(see p108)* and unwind in the playground.

Paris's prettiest bridge, Pont Alexandre III, leading to Les Invalides

② Ecole Militaire
Stripes, salutes and scandals

The Royal Military Academy of Louis XV was founded in 1750 to educate cadet officers from poor families. Its most famous pupil was undoubtedly Napoleon Bonaparte, who studied here as a teenager, graduating in just one year instead of two. The academy is not open to the public but dominates the southern end of the Champ-de-Mars (see p156), which pupils originally used as a parade ground and as a spot to grow vegetables for the school canteen. It was here, in 1895, that Captain Dreyfus was stripped of his army command; an event that developed into the scandalous Dreyfus Affair, which rocked the government and divided the nation.

Letting off steam

After admiring the exterior of the building the ideal place to run about is the huge expanse of the **Champ-de-Mars**.

Picnicking on the Champ-de-Mars with the Ecole Militaire in the background

The Lowdown

🌐 **Map reference** 8 G5
  Address 1 Pl Joffre, 75007

🚇 **Métro** Ecôle Militaire, line 8.
  Bus 28, 80, 82, 87 & 92

🕐 **Open** Closed to the public

☕ **Eat and drink** *Picnic* Aux Délices de Mimi (*178 Rue de Grenelle, 75007; closed Sun*) is a delightful patisserie, which offers pastries and cakes. Picnic in the Champ-de-Mars. *Real meal* Le Basile (*34 Rue de Grenelle, 75007; 01 42 22 59 46; 7am–11pm Mon–Sat, 9am–7pm Sun*) is a '60s-style café that offers sandwiches, hamburgers and quiche.

🚻 **Toilets** No

Stately façade of the Musée Rodin

③ Musée Rodin
People in bronze and plaster

The spacious garden of the Musée Rodin steals the show at this museum dedicated to Auguste Rodin (1840–1917), the greatest French sculptor of the 19th century. Dotted around this peaceful, walled-in haven stand the masterpieces *The Thinker*, *The Burghers of Calais* and *The Gates of Hell*. Rodin's style was more natural than the Classicist ideals people were used to and his controversial portrayal of the author Honoré de Balzac, also here, was ridiculed in the press when it was unveiled in 1898. It all makes for a perfect taster of Rodin's work in a brilliantly family-friendly environment, where the kids can get close to famous art with an ice cream in hand. Inside, in the elegant 18th-century Hôtel Biron where Rodin lived as an old man, works spanning his whole career are presented chronologically, including the delightful and very popular *The Kiss*. There is also a room devoted to the art of his lover, sculptor Camille Claudel.

Letting off steam

Bring a bucket and spade and create your own sculptures in the sandpit of the Rodin museum's garden. Some of the most beautiful gardens in Paris belong to religious orders, one of the best being the **Jardin Catherine Labouré** (*33 Rue de Babylone, 75007*), with its long, vine-covered pergolas, kitchen garden and little playground. It is about a 10-minute walk from the Musée Rodin.

The Lowdown

🌐 **Map reference** 9 B5
  Address 79 Rue de Varenne 75007; 01 44 18 61 10; www.musee-rodin.fr

🚇 **Métro** Varenne, line 13.
  RER Invalides, line C. **Bus** 69, 82, 87 & 92

🕐 **Open** 10am–5:45pm (to 8:45pm Wed), closed Mon, 1 Jan, 1 May & 25 Dec

💰 **Price** Family ticket €11.30; under 18s free; EU citizens under 26 free. Garden: €1–10

👫 **Skipping the queue** Paris Museum Pass accepted. Keep the entry ticket and get a reduced price at the Musée Maillol (*61 Rue de Grenelle, 75007*).

🚩 **Guided tours** Audio guide available in English. Family audio tour in English for children aged 6–12.

👫 **Age range** 5 plus

⏱ **Allow** 1–2 hours

♿ **Wheelchair access** Limited

🍴 **Eat and drink** *Picnic* Besnier Père et Fils (*40 Rue de Bourgogne, 75007; closed Sat & Sun*) sells excellent brioches (sweet French bread). Picnic in the Champ-de-Mars. *Snacks* Le Bon Marché (*24 Rue de Sèvres, 75007; closed Sun*), the oldest department store in Paris, has an excellent food hall, La Grande Epicerie de Paris (*www.lagrandeepicerie.com*).

👫 **Toilets** In the garden café

④ Assemblée Nationale Palais-Bourbon

Laying down the law

The 18th-century Palais Bourbon, built for one of the daughters of Louis XIV, has been home to the lower house of the French parliament since 1830. During World War II, it became the Nazi administration's seat of government. The colonnaded façade was added in 1806 to mirror the façade of La Madeleine (see p139) across the river. Inside there is a post office, a café and even a hairdresser. The president is not allowed inside in case he tries to influence the way the deputies vote. Next door is the Ministry of Foreign Affairs, known as the Quai d'Orsay.

Entrance hall of the Assemblée Nationale Palais-Bourbon

Letting off steam

There is a garden in front of the **Basilique Ste-Clotilde** (23 Rue Les Cases, 75007), a 10-minute walk down Boulevard St-Germain. Cross Place Jacques Bainville then go east along Rue St-Dominique. In 1830, the Virgin Mary is said to have appeared to a nun, Catherine Labouré, at **Chapelle Notre-Dame de la Médaille Miraculeuse** on Rue du Bac. Picnic in the park named after her, on Rue de Babylone.

The Lowdown

- 🌐 **Map reference** 9 B3
  Address 33 Quai d'Orsay; 01 40 63 60 00; www. assemblee-nationale.fr
- 🚇 **Métro** Assemblée Nationale, line 12 or Invalides, line 8. **RER** Musée d'Orsay, line C. **Bus** 83, 84, 86 & 94
- 🕐 **Open** Watch a debate when the parliament is in session. Question time is on Tue & Wed. Bring a passport or ID card. Check website for details
- 💰 **Price** Free
- 🚩 **Guided tours** 3pm Sat but apply 2–3 months in advance by writing to a French MP; see website for details
- 🚻 **Age range** 10 plus
- ♿ **Wheelchair access** Limited
- 🍴 **Eat and drink** *Snacks* Le Bac à Glaces (109 Rue de Bac, 75007; tearoom: closed Sun) is a great stop for chocolate sorbet and crêpes. *Real meal* Kayser (18 Rue du Bac, 75007; 01 42 61 27 63 7am–8pm) is a good *boulangerie* for lunch. The menu features risottos, *tartines* and salads.
- 🚻 **Toilets** No

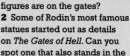
Parliament in session at the Assemblée Nationale Palais-Bourbon

Picnic under €25; **Snacks** €25–45; **Real meal** €45–90; **Family treat** over €90 (based on a family of four)

St-Germain
& the Latin Quarter

A centre for learning in the Middle Ages, the Latin Quarter, along the Left Bank of the Seine, has at its heart a warren of winding streets. The long Boulevard St-Germain slices through it, stretching from west of the Musée d'Orsay to the Institut du Monde Arabe. Families can relax in the Jardin des Plantes before enjoying a picnic in the Arènes de Lutèce, followed by a stroll through the street market in Rue Mouffetard.

Tuileries, Opéra & Montmartre

Champs-Elysées & Trocadéro

Beaubourg & the Marais

Eiffel Tower & Les Invalides

Ile de la Cité & Ile St-Louis

St-Germain & the Latin Quarter

Luxembourg & Montparnasse

Highlights

Musée d'Orsay
Be impressed by the Impressionists and their varying styles through the masterpieces of Monet, Manet, Renoir, Van Gogh and their contemporaries (see pp170–71).

Cafés of St-Germain-des-Prés
Stop for a *citron pressé* at the meeting places of French intellectuals: Café de Flore and Les Deux Magots (see pp172–3).

Institut du Monde Arabe
Marvel at the views from the Institute while savouring a plate of *couscous* or sticky cakes in its rooftop restaurant (see p178).

Musée de Cluny
Look out for the stone heads of the 12 Kings of Judah and the well-preserved Roman baths at this museum (see pp176–7).

Arènes de Lutèce
Enjoy a game of football in the place where Roman gladiators once fought to the death (see p178).

Muséum National d'Histoire Naturelle & Jardin des Plantes
See the displays of stuffed animals at the museum before heading to the zoo located in the gardens, to meet them for real (see pp180–81).

Above left Stained-glass window in the church of St-Germain-des-Prés
Left The spectacular main hall of the Musée d'Orsay, converted from a 19th-century railway station into a museum

The Best of
St-Germain & the Latin Quarter

The haunt of intellectuals and students, the Left Bank has an atmosphere that is both scholarly and relaxed, and is full of cafés, from the famous ones of St-Germain-des-Prés to the more laid-back spots near the university. The Musée d'Orsay is a beautiful introduction to Impressionism, while the districts further south are among the most family-friendly in the city, taking in the zoo, the natural history museum and a market on Rue Mouffetard.

Avant-garde Paris

Through the ages this area has attracted revolutionary philosophers, political thinkers, intellectuals, experimenting artists, authors and jazz musicians, all contributing to its experimental avant-garde reputation. Take a walk to see if the vibe is still there – keep an ear out for some street jazz, browse through the shelves of one of the many small bookshops here, and settle into a table at **Café de Flore** or **Les Deux Magots** (see p172).

Medieval life

Visit the oldest church in Paris, **St-Germain-des-Prés** (see p172), which was begun in AD 542. Next, explore the medieval core of Paris, the **Quartier Latin** (see p178), with its winding, narrow streets, including the Rue du Chat-qui-Pêche, only 1.80 m (6 ft) wide.

Right Skeletons at the Muséum National d'Histoire Naturelle
Below The bustling terrace of Les Deux Magots

Above *Place de la Contrescarpe, lined with popular cafés, at the top of Rue Mouffetard*

Stroll down Rue de Dragon and imagine what it would have been like in the Middle Ages, when rubbish and all sorts of disgusting things were thrown out of the windows. Famous writer Victor Hugo, who campaigned to preserve the old city of Paris from demolition, once lived here.

Gaze at a wide range of treasures fit for a princess alongside the swords and shields wielded by valiant knights at the **Musée de Cluny** *(see p176)*. Picnic in its medieval garden, then walk down **Rue du Fouarre** *(see p178)*, where students at the university of the **Sorbonne** *(see p178)* studied in the Middle Ages.

Animal magic

The excellent **Musée de Cluny** is full of weird and wonderful creatures, embroidered or carved in wood or stone. Spot a unicorn, winged lions, centaurs and an organ-playing pig before heading off for a sumptuous meal at **Les Editeurs** *(see p177)*. The walls of this lovely bistro are lined with more than 5,000 books.

For real wildlife, visit the oldest zoo in Paris in the **Jardin des Plantes** *(see p180)*. If it rains, see the stuffed versions, looking like they are just stepping off Noah's Ark, in the nearby **Muséum National d'Histoire Naturelle** *(see pp180–81)*.

Art mecca

Trace the history of medieval art in the **Musée de Cluny**. Next, visit the **Musée Eugène Delacroix** *(see p173)* and admire the paintings

of the Romantic painter Eugène Delacroix, displayed in a charming house with a garden in **St-Germain-des-Prés**. Walk past the **Ecole Nationale Supérieure des Beaux-Arts** *(see p173)* on Rue Bonaparte. Look out for Picasso's statue of his friend Guillaume Apollinaire outside the church of **St-Germain-des-Prés**.

Marvel at the superb Impressionist paintings and fanciful Art Nouveau furniture on show in the enchanting **Musée d'Orsay**, which is a converted railway station.

Compare them with the beautiful art of the Arab world, showcased in the **Institut du Monde Arabe** *(see p178)*.

Right *Medieval tapestry in the Musée de Cluny*

Musée d'Orsay and around

The Musée d'Orsay is an excellent place to introduce young art lovers to the bright colours and zest for life portrayed in Impressionist paintings. This neighbourhood is a good rainy-day option with kids, as the sights are all indoors and between them lie the shops and cafés of the Left Bank. The sights are spread over a large area, so do not try to cover all of it on foot – use the river boat, RER or bus, or jump in a taxi to travel between the museum and St-Germain.

St-Germain & the Latin Quarter

Musée d'Orsay

Musée de Cluny p176

Places of interest

SIGHTS

1. Musée d'Orsay
2. St-Germain-des-Prés
3. Cafés of St-Germain-des-Prés
4. Musée Eugène Delacroix

EAT AND DRINK

1. Boulangerie du Bac
2. Kayser
3. Eggs and Co
4. Les Climats
5. Grom
6. Ladurée
7. Le Bonaparte
8. Café de Flore
9. Paul
10. Crêperie des Canettes

SHOPPING

1. Stock Bonpoint
2. Six Pieds Trois Puces

See also Musée d'Orsay (p171)

WHERE TO STAY

1. Hôtel de Buci
2. Hôtel de Fleurie
3. Hôtel de l'Université
4. Relais Christine

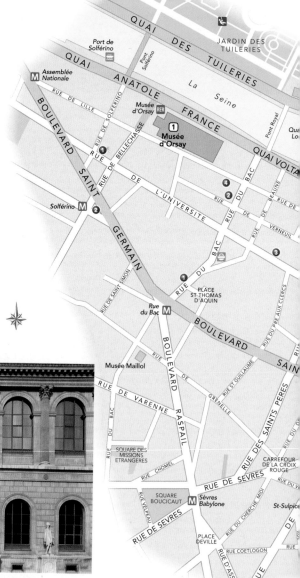

Façade of the Ecole Nationale Supérieure des Beaux-Arts

Children's playground at the Jardin des Tuileries

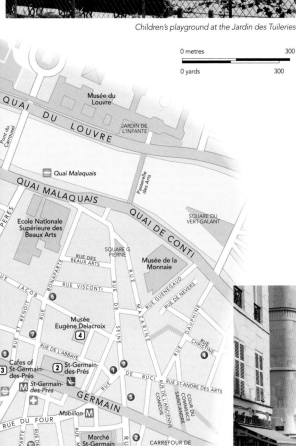

0 metres 300
0 yards 300

The Lowdown

🚗 **Métro** St Germain-des-Prés, line 4 or Solférino, line 12. **RER** Musée d'Orsay, line C. **Bus** 24, 39, 63, 68, 69, 70, 73, 83, 84, 86, 94, 95 & 96. **River boat** Quai de Solférino & Quai Malaquais

ℹ️ **Visitor information** 25 Rue des Pyramides, 75001; May–Oct: 9am–7pm, from 10am Nov–Apr; closed 1 May

🛒 **Supermarkets** Monoprix, 50 Rue de Rennes, 75006 & 35 Rue du Bac, 75007 **Markets** Marché St-Germain (covered market), 4/6 Rue Lobineau, 75006; 8am–8pm Tue–Sat, 8am–1:30pm Sun. Marché Raspail (outdoor market), Blvd Raspail, 75007; 7am–2:30pm Tue & Fri; 9am–3pm Sun (organic produce only)

🎪 **Festival** Christmas Village, Pl St-Germain-des-Prés (Dec)

➕ **Pharmacy** Pharmacie St-Germain-des-Prés, 45 Rue Bonaparte, 75006; 01 43 26 52 92; 9am–midnight daily

🛝 **Nearest playgrounds** Jardin des Tuileries, Rue de Rivoli, 75001; 7:30am–7pm (or sunset) (see p108). Playground with a sandpit on Square Félix Desruelles, 168 Blvd St-Germain, 75006; dawn–dusk daily

Strolling along the Rue de l'Abbaye near St-Germain-des-Prés

① Musée d'Orsay
All aboard for world-class art

Home to some of the most famous Impressionist paintings in the world, the light and airy Musée d'Orsay used to be a steam-train station, but it had to close because its platforms were too short for modern trains. The giant station clock is still here, and the halls are still bustling, but now with art lovers of all ages, who flock here to see the amazing collection of paintings, artistic oddities and gorgeous Art Nouveau objects. Kids as young as five come here on school trips, jumping on the glass floor that covers a scale model of the Opéra quarter.

Clock in the Main Hall

Key Artists

① **Van Gogh** *Bedroom at Arles* was one of Van Gogh's favourite paintings. He also painted more than 40 self-portraits. Spot one hanging over the bed in the painting.

② **Georges Seurat and Paul Signac** These artists were pioneers of the style called Pointillism, using tiny dots of colour that blend together to form an image when viewed from a distance. See Seurat's *Le Cirque* (The Circus) and Signac's *Femmes au Puits* (Women at the Well).

③ **François Pompon** Get nose to nose with the *Ours Blanc*, a huge polar bear sculpted between 1923 and 1933.

④ **Henri Matisse** In 1905, critics were shocked by the works of Matisse and his friends, which used bright, clashing colours, and called the artists *fauves* (wild beasts), from which Fauvism took its name. Look out for Matisse's *Luxe, Calme et Volupté*.

⑤ **Honoré Daumier** *The Washerwoman* depicts one of the many women who would spend their days washing laundry in the Seine.

■ **Le Pavillon Amont** Art from European schools.

■ **Upper Floor** Impressionism.

■ **Middle Floor** Art Nouveau, Symbolist, Post- and Neo-Impressionist and other decorative art and sculptures from the late 19th century.

■ **Ground Floor** Pre- and early Impressionist paintings and mid-19th-century sculpture.

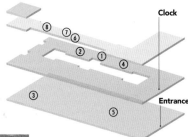

⑥ **Pierre-Auguste Renoir** Poor and excluded from the official art world, painters such as Renoir spent a lot of time in working-class bars and cafés painting real people. Look out for his *Dancing at the Moulin de la Galette.*

Letting off steam

Head across the river to the **Jardin des Tuileries** (see p108) to sail wooden boats on the pond. There is also a good free playground here.

Musée d'Orsay, housed in a converted iron-and-glass railway station

Prices given are for a family of four

Eat and drink

Picnic: under €25; Snacks: €25–45; Real meal: €45–90; Family treat: over €90 (based on a family of four)

PICNIC Boulangerie du Bac *(52 Rue du Bac, 75007; 01 45 48 98 23)* is a neighbourhood bakery popular with locals, selling delicious baked goods such as quiches and tarts as well as cakes.
SNACKS Kayser *(18 Rue du Bac, 75007; closed Mon)*, a popular bakery, has sandwiches, quiches, cakes and pastries to takeaway.
REAL MEAL Eggs & Co *(11 Rue Bernard Palissy; 01 45 44 02 52; 10am–6pm daily)* offers eggs in all shapes and sizes.

FAMILY TREAT Les Climats *(41 Rue de Lille, 75007; 01 58 62 10 08)* serves a very good luxury brunch. The Michelin-starred restaurant is housed in an Art Nouveau post office and has a terrace.

Shopping

Stock Bonpoint *(67 Rue de l'Université, 75007; www.bonpoint. com)* has great reductions for kids on previous season's clothes.
Six Pieds Trois Pouces *(223 Blvd St-Germain, 75007; 01 45 44 03 72; www.sixpiedstroispouces. com)* offers a good variety of stylish and trendy children's shoes.

The Lowdown

- 🌐 **Map reference** 9 D4
- **Address** 1 Rue de la Légion d'Honneur, 75007; 01 40 49 49 78; www.musee-orsay.fr/en
- 🚗 **Métro** Solférino, line 12. **RER** Musée d'Orsay, line C. **Bus** 24, 63, 68, 69, 73, 83, 84 & 94
- 🕐 **Open** 9:30am–6pm, till 9:45pm Thu, 1 May & 25 Dec
- 💲 **Price** €22–39; under 18s free; EU citizens under 26 free
- 👪 **Skipping the queue** Paris Museum Pass accepted. Joint ticket with Musée L'Orangerie. Avoid Tue when the museum is one of the few in the city that is open. Buy tickets online in advance.
- 🚩 **Guided tours** For adults in English; for families and children in French. Audio guide available. The bookshop offers children's guides, *My Little Orsay* and *A Trip to the Orsay Museum*.

- 👫 **Age range** 5 plus
- 🤸 **Activities** Workshops & activities for children in French; 01 53 63 04 63. Lovely colouring books available in the museum shop for budding artists
- ⏱ **Allow** At least 2 hours
- ♿ **Wheelchair access** Yes
- ☕ **Café** On the ground floor; the restaurant on the middle floor has good views of the clock
- 🏷 **Shop** The museum bookshop in the entrance hall has a special kids' section
- 🚻 **Toilets** On the ground floor

Good family value?
The art featured is very accessible to children. Introduce kids to the lives and pictures of the artists displayed here in advance. The ticket gives a reduced rate at the Palais Garnier and the Opéra House for a week after the visit.

⑧ **Edgar Degas** Interested in movement, Degas focused much of his work around two very diverse subjects – racehorses and dancers, the latter beautifully observed in his painting *The Ballet Class*.

⑦ **Claude Monet** The Impressionists wanted to catch the moment. Monet was fascinated by how light changed at different times of the year especially when it snowed. *The Cart* is one of his many works on show at the museum.

Find out more

DIGITAL Download colouring pages from *www.nowyouknowabout.com* and watch a BBC mini-series about the history of Impressionism on *http://tinyurl.com/3jwqsz3*
FILM *Now You Know About Artists* (2006), a documentary film especially for children, is based on the great painters. *Degas and the Dancer* (1998) is the story behind the artist's famous statuette.

Next stop...

MUSÉE RODIN Take advantage of the family ticket for €10 at Musée Rodin (*see p162*), which enables access for two adults and two children under 18. But the big draw is the beautiful garden, which has a lovely café and a sandpit to keep kids occupied. It is a walk of just over 10 minutes.

Outdoor café in the attractive gardens of the Musée Rodin

Tower of St-Germain-des-Prés, with one of the oldest belfries in France

② St-Germain-des-Prés

The oldest church in Paris

The church of St-Germain-des-Prés once stood at the centre of a large abbey that was for many years located beyond the city walls. Founded in the 6th century by Childebert I, the son of Clovis, King of the Franks, the abbey was an important centre of intellectual life for the French Catholic church and also the burial place for the kings of France before the founding of the basilica of St-Denis. The church originally had three towers but the

two located on the eastern side were badly damaged during the Revolution. The other tower still survives, housing one of the oldest belfries in France. The interior of the church is an interesting mix of architectural styles, with some 6th-century marble columns, Gothic vaulting and Romanesque arches. Among the notables buried inside are John Casimir, king of Poland, and the father of modern philosophy, René Descartes. Look out for a statue of the goddess Isis at the entrance of the church.

Letting off steam

There is a small playground with a sandpit on the southern side of the church. The nearby Pont des Arts footbridge is a lovely spot for a picnic. There is a nice swimming pool, **Piscine St-Germain** (*12 Rue Lobineau, 75006; 01 56 81 25 40*), but be aware that swimming hats are obligatory in Paris and the opening hours of the pool are rather erratic, especially during term time.

The Lowdown

- 🌐 **Map reference** 10 E6
  Address 3 Pl St-Germain-des-Prés, 75006; 01 55 42 81 33; www.eglise-sgp.org
- 🚇 **Métro** St-Germain-des-Prés, line 4. **Bus** 39, 95 70, 63, & 86
- 🕐 **Open** 8am–7:45pm Mon–Sat, 9am–8pm Sun
- 💲 **Price** Free
- ♿ **Wheelchair access** Yes
- 🍽 **Eat and drink** *Picnic* Grom (*81 Rue de Seine, 75006*) offers excellent ice cream. Their dark chocolate and extra-noir chocolate flavours are not to be missed. Picnic in Jardin du Luxembourg or opt to sit and eat a sandwich by the church. *Snacks* Ladurée (*21 Rue Bonaparte; 01 44 07 64 87; www.laduree.fr*) serves the best macaroons in the city. This branch is far less touristy than the other two in the 8th arrondissement.
- 🚻 **Toilets** Public WC, 186 Blvd St-Germain, 75006

Bustling crowds at Grom, a branch of the popular Italian chain

③ Cafés of St-Germain-des-Prés

Coffee for culture vultures

The café is a vital part of Parisian life and people of all ages come here for conversation, discussion and gossip over a coffee, apéritif or *citron pressé*; it is a great place to introduce kids to Parisian culture.

In the mid-20th century St-Germain was a buzzing place where American authors and jazz musicians mingled with local artists, writers and philosophers. Ernest Hemingway, Bud Powell, Pablo Picasso, Alfred Camus, Jean-Paul Sartre and Simone de Beauvoir all quenched their thirst in the cafés that cluster around the belfry of St-German-des-Prés. The most famous ones are Café de Flore; Les Deux Magots, which takes its name from the two statues of Chinese merchants inside; and Brasserie Lipp, a distinguished restaurant-brasserie with beautiful Art Deco tiles.

Although many tourists come here today the cafés are popular with Parisians too, and still form part of literary Paris. Nearby are two ancient streets: Rue Dragon,

The Lowdown

- 🌐 **Map reference** 10 E6
  Address Brasserie Lipp, 151 Blvd St-Germain 75006. Café de Flore, 172 Blvd St-Germain 75006. Les Deux Magots, 6 Pl St-Germain des-Prés, 75006
- 🚇 **Métro** St-Germain-des-Prés, line 4. **Bus** 63 & 95
- 💲 **Price** All the cafés are expensive, especially the terraces at Café de Flore and Les Deux Magots
- 👪 **Age range** All ages
- ♿ **Wheelchair access** Limited
- 🍽 **Eat and drink** *Real meal* Le Bonaparte (*42 Rue Bonaparte, 75006; 01 43 26 42 81*), next to Les Deux Magots, is an affordable place to enjoy a drink, a sandwich or a salad. *Family treat* Café de Flore (*172 Blvd St-Germain, 75006; 01 45 48 55 26; www.cafedeflore.fr*) serves quiches, sandwiches, omelettes and onion soup. The café still has a literary clientele.
- 🚻 **Toilets** In the cafés

Relaxing in one of Paris's most popular parks, Jardin du Luxembourg

where Victor Hugo once lived; and Rue Servandoni, where Alexandre Dumas's musketeer hero d'Artagnan lived at No. 12 then 7 Rue des Fossoyeurs.

Letting off steam

Walk down Rue Bonaparte to the delightful **Jardin du Luxembourg** *(see pp190–91)* for a real Parisian experience.

Interior of Café de Flore, the former meeting place of intellectuals

④ Musée Eugène Delacroix
A romantic daredevil

The leader of the French Romantic movement in painting, Eugène Delacroix lived his life like a hero in a 19th-century novel. He lived in this apartment, with its charming little courtyard garden, when he was decorating the ceiling of the nearby church of St-Sulpice. Some of his famous works, among them *The Entombment of Christ*, are on display in the museum. There is also a collection of personal items, including things he brought back from a visit to Morocco in 1832. This journey also inspired him to introduce images of wild animals and Arab civilization in his work.

Letting off steam

Take a stroll in the peaceful **Cour du Mûrier** *(14 Rue Bonaparte, 75006)*, which is now the garden of the Ecole Nationale Supérieure des Beaux-Arts.

The Lowdown

🌐 **Map reference** 10 F5
Address 6 Rue Furstemberg, 75006; www.musee-delacroix.fr

🚗 **Métro** St-Germain-des-Prés, line 4. **Bus** 39, 63, 70, 86, 95, & 96

🕐 **Open** 9:30am–5:30pm, closed Tue, 1 Jan, 1 May & 25 Dec

🎫 **Price** €10–20; under 18s free; EU citizens under 26 free

🎟️ **Skipping the queue** On weekday mornings the museum is often deserted, and never busy.

👫 **Age range** 8 plus

⏱️ **Allow** 45 minutes–1 hour

♿ **Wheelchair access** No

🍴 **Eat and drink** *Picnic* Paul *(77 Rue de Seine, 75006; 7:30am–9pm daily)* is an ideal place for sandwiches, quiches, cakes and pastries. It offers the option to takeaway. On a nice day head for Square du Vert-Galant at the western end of Ile de la Cité for a picnic. *Real meal* Crêperie des Canettes *(10 Rue des Canettes, 75006; 01 43 26 27 65; www.creperiedescanettes.fr; noon–4pm Mon–Sat & 7pm–midnight, closed Aug)* serves sweet and savoury crêpes and salads.

👫 **Toilets** On ground floor

Musée de Cluny and around

Step into the world of knights and princesses at the Musée National du Moyen Age, better known as the Musée de Cluny. Then head for Paris's zoo, the Ménagerie, in the Jardin des Plantes, a good place to spend an afternoon. Whatever the weather, this area has a mix of indoor and outdoor activities and is well served by Métro and bus – do not try to cover all of it on foot. Weekends are pleasant here as there is less traffic, especially around the market in Rue Mouffetard, close to the Jardin des Plantes, which is closed to cars on Sundays and public holidays.

St-Germain & the Latin Quarter

Musée d'Orsay p170

Musée de Cluny

Charming façade of the Musée de Cluny

Places of interest

SIGHTS
1. Musée de Cluny
2. Quartier Latin
3. Arènes de Lutèce
4. Rue Mouffetard
5. Jardin des Plantes
6. Muséum National d'Histoire Naturelle
7. Ménagerie

EAT AND DRINK
1. Al Dar
2. La Boulangerie de Papa
3. Le Coffee Parisien
4. Les Editeurs
5. Le Zyriab
6. Kayser
7. Aux Cerises de Lutèce
8. Vegan Folie's
9. Le Pot O'Lait
10. Le Boulanger du Monge
11. L'Arbre à Canelle
12. Mosquée de Paris
13. Le Quartier Latin

14. Gelati d'Alberto
15. Restaurant Marty

SHOPPING
1. Boulinier
2. Album
3. Magie
4. Il était une fois
5. Au Plat d'Etain
See also Musée de Cluny (p176)

WHERE TO STAY
1. Grand Hôtel des Balcons
2. Hôtel des Grands Ecoles
3. Hotel Design Sorbonne
4. Hôtel du College de France
5. Hôtel Marignan
6. Hôtel Résidence Henri IV
7. Hôtel St-Jacques
8. Résidence des Arts
9. Résidence le Prince Regent
10. Seven Hôtel
11. The Five

Interior of the Moorish café within Mosquée de Paris

Fruit and vegetables on sale at the street market in Rue Mouffetard

The Lowdown

Métro Cluny-La-Sorbonne, line 10; St-Michel, line 4; Odéon, lines 4 & 10; Maubert Mutualité, line 10; Jussieu, lines 7 & 10; Cardinal Lemoine, line 10; Monge, line 7; Censier Daubenton, line 7 or Gare d'Austerlitz, lines 5 & 10. **RER** St-Michel, lines B & C or Gare d'Austerlitz, line C. **Bus** 21, 24, 27, 38, 47, 57, 61, 63, 67, 84, 85, 86, 87, 89, 91. **River boat** Stop on Quai St-Bernard for Jardin des Plantes and Quai de Montebello for Latin Quarter

Supermarkets Monop', 35 Blvd St-Michel, 75005. Carrefour, 34 Rue Monge, 75005. Franprix, 82 Rue Mouffetard, 75005

Markets Marché Maubert, Pl Maubert, 75005; 7am–2:30pm Tue & Thu (to 3pm Sat). Marché Monge, Pl Monge, 75005; 7am–2:30pm Wed & Fri, 7am–3pm Sun

Pharmacy Pharmacie Bader, 12 Blvd St-Michel, 75005; 01 43 26 92 66; 9am–9pm Mon–Sat, 11am–9pm Sun

Nearest playground Jardin du Musée de Cluny, Blvd St-Germain, 75005 (see p177); Arènes de Lutèce, Rue de Navarre, 75005 (see p178); Jardin des Plantes, 57 Rue Cuvier, 75005 (see p180); Jardin du Luxembourg, Blvd St-Michel, 75006 (see pp190–91)

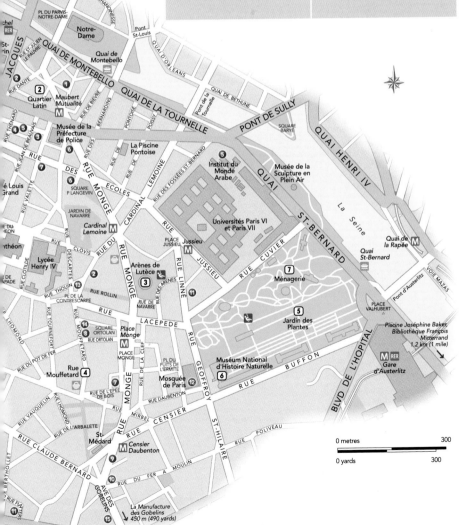

① Musée de Cluny
Knights, princesses and unicorns

In the late Middle Ages the rich abbots of powerful Cluny Abbey built a beautiful mansion decorated with sculpted animals, incorporating the remains of the largest Roman baths in Paris. Located in the heart of the Latin Quarter, once part of the Roman town of Lutetia, it now houses the finest museum of the Middle Ages in France, with stunning collections of medieval art on show. The unique Thermes de Cluny (Roman baths) are also part of the museum. Harry Potter fans will love to see the tombstone of Dumbledore's friend Nicolas Flamel, covered in mysterious symbols.

Detail on an ornate silver cross

Key Features

■ **First Floor** Lady with the Unicorn tapestry series and the chapel

■ **Ground Floor** Tapestries, stained-glass windows, Gallery of the Kings of Judah and Gallo-Roman artifacts

■ **Gallo-Roman Ruins** Roman Baths, with Frigidarium, Caldarium and Tepidarium (cold, hot and tepid baths)

Courtyard

Entrance

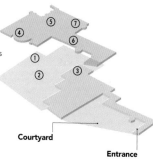

④ **Lady with the Unicorn** This exquisite tapestry is over 500 years old and part of an outstanding set of six.

⑤ **Ivories and Goldsmithing** The Gold Rose in this collection, created in the Middle Ages, is the oldest in conservation in the world.

① **Roman Baths** Built in AD 200, the baths are the best Roman ruins in Paris and were once decorated with mosaics and marble.

② **Frigidarium** The largest cold bath in the country, this is the only Roman building with a roof in north France. Spot two stone ships – the originals once sailed on the Seine.

③ **Gallery of the Kings** This gallery houses 21 of the 28 decapitated stone heads of the Kings of Judah that once decorated the façade of Notre-Dame.

⑥ **Stained-glass windows** Fragments of the brightly coloured stained-glass windows moved here from Sainte-Chapelle tell the Biblical story of Samson in the form of a cartoon strip.

⑦ **Chapel** Constructed in the Flamboyant style, it has a beautiful vaulted ceiling. It was used as a dissection room after the Revolution.

The Lowdown

🌐 **Map reference** 14 G1
Address 6 Pl Paul-Painlevé, 75005; 01 53 73 78 00; *www.musee-moyenage.fr*

🚗 **Métro** Cluny-La-Sorbonne, line 10; St-Michel, line 4 or Odéon, lines 4 & 10. **RER** St-Michel, line B. **Bus** 21, 27, 38, 63, 85, 86 & 87

🕐 **Open** 9:15am–5:45pm, closed Tue, 1 Jan, 1 May & 25 Dec; garden: 8am–9pm; winter: till 5:45pm

💲 **Price** €17–27; under 18s free; EU citizens under 26 free

👫 **Skipping the queue** Paris Museum Pass accepted

🚩 **Guided tours** In French for families on weekends and school hols; audio guide for adults in English; children's audio and mini activity guides both in French.

👫 **Age range** All ages

👫 **Activities** Workshops in French for families on Wed & school hols; 01 53 73 78 16; medieval music concerts

🕐 **Allow** 2 hours

♿ **Wheelchair access** No

☕ **Café** No

🛍 **Shop** A good selection of books for children in French and English is available from the shop near the ticket desk.

👫 **Toilets** Near the ticket desk

Good family value?
Art and history buffs will appreciate a trip to the museum. Kids will enjoy exploring the Roman baths, which are well worth the visit.

Prices given are for a family of four

Garden of the Musée de la Sculpture en Plein Air, in a delightful setting by the Seine

Letting off steam

The museum has a lovely medieval garden with a children's glade. Nearby is one of the best swimming pools in Paris, **La Piscine Pontoise** *(19 Rue de Pontoise, 75005; 01 55 42 77 88)*, which has a changing room overlooking the pool. Further away is an open-air sculpture park, the **Musée de la Sculpture en Plein Air** *(Quai St-Bernard, 75005)*, usually called Jardin Tino Rossi after the Corsican singer. It is a good spot for a picnic, with views across the river.

Eat and drink

Picnic: under €25; Snacks: €25–45; Real meal: €45–90; Family treat: over €90 (based on a family of four)

PICNIC Al Dar *(8–10 Rue Frédéric Sauton, 75005; 01 43 25 17 15; noon–3pm & 7pm–midnight)*, a Lebanese deli, is attached to a great little restaurant. Enjoy a peaceful picnic in the museum garden.

SNACKS La Boulangerie de Papa *(1 Rue de la Harpe, 75005; 01 43 54 66 16)* serves sandwiches, crêpes and cakes.

REAL MEAL Le Coffee Parisien *(4 Rue Princesse, 75006; 01 43 54 18 18; noon–midnight daily)* is an American diner for great burgers.

FAMILY TREAT Les Editeurs *(4 Carrefour de l'Odéon, 75006; 01 43 26 67 76; 8–2am; www.lesediteurs.fr)* is a cosy bistro, good for brunch in particular. Its walls are lined with around 5,000 books.

Shopping

Comic-book enthusiasts should head to **Boulinier** *(20 Blvd St-Michel, 75006)*. More comics and designer gadgets are available

at **Album** *(8 Rue Dante, 75006)*. The world's oldest magic shop, **Magie** *(8 Rue des Carmes, 75006; www.mayette.com)*, also offers lessons in magic. **Il était une fois** *(1 Rue Cassette, 75006; 01 45 48 21 10; www.iletaitunefois-paris.fr)* is a treasure trove for children's costumes and toys. Another good stop is **Au Plat d'Etain** *(16 Rue Guisarde, 75006; www.auplat detain.com)*, which has been selling tin soldiers since 1775.

Find out more

DIGITAL Interactive games and lots of fun facts and information about the Middle Ages can be found at *www.kidsonthenet.org.uk*. *Age of Empires* (2009), a popular computer game series, challenges players to lead a medieval army to victory. **FILM** *Les Visiteurs* (1993) is a French comedy in which a medieval knight and his servant are accidentally sent into the 20th century by a befuddled Merlin-like wizard. Watch *Astérix the Gaul* (1967) to find out what Paris was like as Lutetia. *Harry Potter and the Philosopher's Stone* (2001) reveals more about Nicolas Flamel (*see p88*), a real-life author in the Middle Ages who gained a reputation as an alchemist.

Next stop...

MEDIEVAL PARIS Walk across the Seine to **Notre-Dame** *(see pp64–5)* and get eye-to-eye with medieval Paris in the **Crypte Archéologique** *(see pp64–5)* there. It is a 10-minute walk to the **Arènes de Lutèce** *(see p178)*, the old Roman amphitheatre, which is a good spot in which to enjoy a picnic and kick a football about.

② Quartier Latin

Downtown Lutetia

Once the core of the Roman city, the Latin Quarter has a maze of cobbled streets and narrow passageways to explore. Since the Middle Ages, it has been associated with scholarly learning and for centuries it was obligatory for all who studied and worked at the Sorbonne university, founded in 1257, to speak only Latin – hence its name. Students often studied outside on straw, laid down

Attractive façade of the Chapelle de la Sorbonne

The Lowdown

- 🌐 **Map reference** 15 B1
  Address 75005
- 🚗 **Métro** Cluny-La-Sorbonne, line 10; St-Michel, line 4 or Maubert Mutualité, line 10. **RER** St-Michel, line C. **Bus** 24, 47, 63, 86 & 87
- 👫 **Skipping the queue** Visit on a Sun morning or early evening
- 👫 **Age range** All ages
- ⏱ **Allow** 1–2 hours
- ♿ **Wheelchair access** Yes
- 🍴 **Eat and drink** *Snacks* La Boulangerie de Papa (*1 Rue de la Harpe, 75005; 01 43 54 66 16*) is popular with local families and students. *Family treat* Le Zyriab (*1 Rue des Fossées-St-Bernard, 75005; 01 40 51 38 38; www.noura.com; closed Mon*), located on the roof of the Institut du Monde Arabe, has fine views and is great for afternoon tea. It is a good choice for vegetarians.
- 👫 **Toilets** Public WC,123 Rue St-Jacques, 75005

in Rue du Fouarre (Straw Street). Several universities are still based here and although few students can afford to live in the area any more, it remains quaint. Admire the exterior of the Chapelle de la Sorbonne and take a stroll along Rue St Julien le Pauvre to Quai Montebello, then take Rue de la Harpe to head back to the Musée de Cluny.

Take cover

The **Musée de la Préfecture de Police** (*4 Rue de la Montagne Ste-Geneviève; 9am–5pm Mon–Fri*) is a rather old-fashioned museum with curiosities on show such as the arrest warrant for the revolutionary Danton and weapons used by criminals.

③ Arènes de Lutèce

Gladiators, *boules* and footballs

Before the arrival of the Romans, Paris was a small sleepy village situated on an island in the Seine. In the 2nd century, the Romans built one of the biggest amphitheatres in Gaul; it could hold up to 15,000 spectators. This arena was the venue not only for gladiatorial fights but also theatrical shows, which were unique to Gaul. After the fall of the Roman Empire, a section of the amphitheatre was shifted to reinforce the city's defences. It was then used as a cemetery, until it was filled in completely. It was rediscovered when the area was

redeveloped in the 19th century. Today, it is a lovely park where kids can play football and old men enjoy a game of *boules*.

Take cover

Travel to the Arab world at the **Institut du Monde Arabe** (*1 Rue des Fossées-St-Bernard, 75005; www.imarabe.org*), housed in a magnificent modern building with stunning glass windows. There is a small museum here along with a literary café and restaurant with views across to Notre-Dame.

The Lowdown

- 🌐 **Map reference** 15 B3
  Address Rue de Navarre, 75005
- 🚗 **Métro** Jussieu, lines 7 & 10; Cardinal Lemoine, line 10 or Monge, line 7. **Bus** 47, 67 & 89
- ⏱ **Open** 9am–5:30pm; summer: till 9:30pm
- 💲 **Price** Free
- 👫 **Age range** All ages
- ⏱ **Allow** 15 minutes–1 hour
- 🍴 **Eat and drink** *Picnic* Kayser (*14 Rue Monge, 75005; closed Sun*) is one of the city's most famous bakeries and serves great sandwiches and savoury snacks. Picnic on the steps of the amphitheatre. *Snacks* Aux Cerises de Lutèce (*86 Rue Monge, 75005; 01 43 31 67 51; 11am–7pm Tue–Sat*) is a little café that looks like granny's kitchen. Sample the delicious cakes here.
- 👫 **Toilets** On the eastern side of the park

A children's play area in the Arènes de Lutèce

People enjoying the spring sunshine in Place de la Contrescarpe

Copies of old advertisements on sale in Rue Mouffetard

④ Rue Mouffetard
Cakes and entertainment

Winding down the hill south of the Panthéon (see pp188–9), on the route of the old Roman road out of the city, is the lively, cobbled street Rue Mouffetard. Most of the buildings here date from the 17th and 18th centuries. For kids the main attraction is the tantalizing line-up of patisseries, *fromageries* and ice-cream vendors. The area is also known for its wonderful daily market and the African market on Rue Daubenton. At the top of the street, close to the Lycée Henri IV, is Place de la Contrascarpe, a village-like square. Full of cafés, it is a busy spot in the evening.

Letting off steam

There is a little park on Rue Ortolan, **Square Ortolan**, which is a good place for a quick picnic.

The Lowdown

- 🌐 **Map reference** 15 A3
  Address 75005
- 🚗 **Métro** Monge, line 7 or Censier Daubenton, line 7. **Bus** 27, 47 & 84
- 🕐 **Open** Market: 10am–1pm Tue–Sat, 8am–1pm Sun
- 👫 **Age range** All ages
- 🧍 **Activities** Lots of street entertainers
- 🍴 **Eat and drink** *Snacks* Vegan Folie's (53 Rue Mouffetard, 75005; 01 43 37 21 89; closed Mon) serves sweet and savoury organic cupcakes. *Real meal* Le Pot O'Lait (41 Rue Censier, 75005; 01 42 17 15 69; www.lepotolait.com; closed Sun & Mon) offers excellent crêpes. There is a fixed price children's menu.
- 🚻 **Toilets** No

Market stalls and vendors lining the narrow Rue Mouffetard

Picnic under €25; **Snacks** €25–45; **Real meal** €45–90; **Family treat** over €90 (based on a family of four)

Skeletons of dinosaurs on display at the Muséum National d'Histoire Naturelle

⑤ Jardin des Plantes

Plants from the four corners of the world

Originally laid out as a medicinal herb garden for Louis XIII in 1626, the Jardin des Plantes was first opened to the public in 1640. Perhaps not quite as exciting for kids as the neighbouring zoo and natural history museum, the botanical garden itself offers a welcome breath of greenery and space, a puzzling maze and a huge dinosaur climbing frame in a sandpit. *Les Grandes Serres*, the garden's greenhouses, are full of exotic plants from faraway places, while the pretty *Jardin Alpin*, an Alpine garden, has a collection of around 3,000 mountain flowers.

Take cover

Watch craftsmen at work at **La Manufacture des Gobelins** (*42 Ave des Gobelins, 75013; guided tours: 2–3pm Tue–Thu)*, an old 17th-century tapestry factory where Flemish weavers made tapestries for Versailles. It is a short ride away on the Métro, down to Gobelins station.

A greenhouse full of exotic species in the Jardin des Plantes

The Lowdown

🌐 **Map reference** 15 C3
Address 57 Rue Cuvier, 75005; entrances also on Rue Buffon, Rue Geoffry-St-Hilaire & Pl Valhubert; www.mnhn.fr

🚇 **Métro** Gare d'Austerlitz, lines 10 & 5; Jussieu, lines 7 & 10 or Monge, line 7. **RER** Gare d'Austerlitz, line C.
Bus 24, 57, 61, 63, 67, 89 & 91

🕐 **Open** 8am–5:30pm daily; summer: till 7:30pm. Jardin Alpin: Apr–Oct: 8am–4:40pm Mon–Fri, 1:30–6pm Sat, Sun & public hols; closed Nov–Mar. Les Grandes Serres: 10am–6pm Wed–Mon

💰 **Price** Main park: free. Jardin Alpin: free entry Mon–Fri; €8–18 Sat, Sun & public hols. Les Grandes Serres: €20–30; under 4s free

👫 **Skipping the queue** A two-day pass (€90–100) to all attractions in the Jardin des Plantes also gives discounts in shops and restaurants

👫 **Age range** All ages

⏱ **Allow** 45 minutes–2 hours

🍴 **Eat and drink** *Picnic* Le Boulanger de Monge (*123 Rue Monge, 75005; www.leboulangerdemonge.com; closed Mon)* is a good local organic baker. Settle down for a picnic in the park. *Snacks* L'Arbre à Canelle (*14 Rue Linné, 75005; 01 43 31 68 31)* is good for sandwiches and a light meal. The small café in the park is a pleasant place to stop for a drink.

👫 **Toilets** By the entrance to the zoo

⑥ Muséum National d'Histoire Naturelle

Animal crackers

Kids will love this museum, where they can get nose-to-nose with an antelope or see some truly fantastic skeletons. Housed in four separate buildings, the Muséum National d'Histoire Naturelle has been a centre for scientific research since its foundation in 1793. The main draw for children is the parade of stuffed animals in the Grande Galerie de l'Evolution, which is a veritable Noah's Ark. The Galerie des Enfants,

The Lowdown

🌐 **Map reference** 15 C3
Address 36 Rue Geoffroy St-Hilaire, 75005; 01 40 79 54 79/56 01; www.mnhn.fr

🚇 **Métro** Gare d'Austerlitz, lines 5 & 10; Censier Daubenton, line 7 or Jussieu, line 7. **RER** Gare d'Austerlitz, line C. **Bus** 24, 57, 61, 63, 67, 89 & 91

🕐 **Open** 10am–6pm, closed Tue, 1 May & 25 Dec

💰 **Price** Grande Galerie de l'Evolution, Galeries de Paléontologie & Galerie de Minéralogie: €24–34 per gallery; under 4s free; Galerie des Enfants: €32; under 4s free

👫 **Skipping the queue** A two-day pass (€90–100) to all attractions in the Jardin des Plantes also gives discounts in the shops and restaurants. Avoid Wed afternoons when under 11s are off school.

👣 **Guided tours** In French, on Saturdays by reservation; 08 26 10 42 00

👫 **Age range** All ages

👫 **Activities** Workshops during school hols

⏱ **Allow** 1–2 hours

♿ **Wheelchair access** Yes

🍴 **Eat and drink** *Snacks* Mosquée de Paris (*2 Pl du Puits de l'Ermite, 75005; 01 43 31 38 20; www.la-mosquee.com)* houses a Moorish café, which is the perfect place to get an Oriental sugar fix. *Real meal* Le Quartier Latin (*1 Rue Mouffetard, 75005; 01 40 51 04 61)* serves Italian cuisine – the apple tart is a hit.

👫 **Toilets** In the basement of the Galeries de Paléontologie & the Grande Galerie de l'Evolution

Tiny, rare amphibians in the micro-zoo of the Ménagerie

formerly the Salle de Découverte, explains issues about the natural world in an inventive manner. There are modern interactive activities as well as specimens of endangered and extinct species. In the Galeries de Paléontologie et d'Anatomie is an amazing collection of skeletons, from whales to dinosaurs, while the Galerie de Minéralogie is home to gems and some truly giant crystals.

Letting off steam

Return to the **Jardin des Plantes** (*see opposite*) for a botanical picnic and plenty of play areas.

⑦ Ménagerie
Bison, bears, monkeys and creepy crawlies

The characterful Ménagerie is the oldest public zoo in the world and was founded in 1793 to house the survivors from the Royal Ménagerie at Versailles – all four of them. The state gathered animals from circuses as well as street performers to add to the collection. This lovely, intimate zoo, classically Parisian in style, is home to mostly small mammals and creepy crawlies. although there are also some big cats and minute mites, the latter to be seen in the micro-zoo.

The Lowdown

🌐 **Map reference** 15 C3
Address 57 Rue Cuvier, 75005; 01 40 79 37 94; www.mnhn.fr

🚇 **Métro** Gare d'Austerlitz, lines 10 & 5; Jussieu, lines 7 & 10 or Monge, line 7. **RER** Gare d'Austerlitz, line C. **Bus** 24, 57, 61, 63, 67, 89 & 91

🕐 **Open** 9am–5pm daily; summer: till 6pm

💶 **Price** €36–46; under 4s free

🎫 **Skipping the queue** A two-day pass (€90–100) to all attractions in the Jardin des Plantes also gives discounts in shops and restaurants

🚩 **Guided tours** Every Wed €4 per person

👫 **Age range** All ages

⏱ **Allow** 2 hours

🍴 **Eat and drink** *Picnic* Gelati d'Alberto (45 Rue Mouffetard, 75005) is an ice cream shop loved by children for its flower-shaped scoops. Picnic in the zoo or in the nearby Jardin des Plantes. *Family treat* Restaurant Marty (20 Ave des Gobelins, 75005; 01 43 31 39 51; www.restaurantmarty. com) is famous for its 1920–30s decor and its excellent seafood.

🚻 **Toilets** By the entrance

Letting off steam

Take a pleasant walk by the Seine along the **Quai François Mauriac** and see the interesting old industrial wharfs and the modern Bibliothèque François Mitterrand, both of which give a refreshingly different perspective to the city. There is a lovely swimming pool set in a barge on the Seine, the **Piscine Joséphine Baker** (*Quai François Mauriac, 75013; 01 56 61 96 50; open daily*). It takes water from the Seine – treated before use – and has a paddling pool for small children. In summer the roof retracts and the pool is in the open air.

Quai François Mauriac on the banks of the Seine

Picnic under €25; **Snacks** €25–45; **Real meal** €45–90; **Family treat** over €90 (based on a family of four)

Luxembourg
& Montparnasse

The enchanting Jardin du Luxembourg is a Parisian park straight out of a storybook, with its vintage carousel, wooden sailing boats and miniature carriage rides for kids. It is at the heart of an affluent neighbourhood, dominated by the elegant 18th-century dome of the Panthéon and the starkly modern Tour Montparnasse. The area is a joy to explore, with its entertaining mix of old and new, quaint and chic.

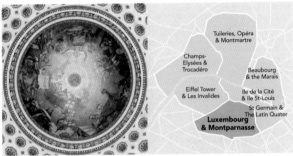

Tuileries, Opéra & Montmartre

Champs-Elysées & Trocadéro

Beaubourg & the Marais

Eiffel Tower & Les Invalides

Ile de la Cité & Ile St-Louis

St Germain & The Latin Quater

Luxembourg & Montparnasse

Highlights

Panthéon & Cimetière du Montparnasse
Get a lesson in history in the crypt of the church then stroll down to the cemetery which, according to legend, has a vampire stalking its alleyways (see pp188–9 & p192).

Le Bon Marché
Buy delicious picnic fare at La Grande Epicerie, the food hall in the city's oldest department store (see p194).

Jardin du Luxembourg & Palais du Luxembourg
Ride a carousel in the gardens before sailing a boat in front of the palace (see p190).

Rue Vavin
Shop for chic clothes, wonderful toys and interesting books on this street located near the Jardin du Luxembourg (see p191).

Tour Montparnasse
Shoot to the top of the city's tallest skyscraper, which boasts Europe's fastest lift, at 56 floors in 38 seconds (see p192).

Musée de la Poste & Musée Pasteur
Learn about France's postal service then head to the institute founded by Louis Pasteur, who discovered how to pasteurize milk (see pp194–5).

Above left The Panthéon's decorative dome lantern, which allows only a little light to filter into the church's centre
Left The Jardin du Luxembourg with the Palais du Luxembourg in the background

The Best of
Luxembourg & Montparnasse

Quiet gardens, cute toyshops and quaint cafés add to the charms of the Luxembourg and Montparnasse quarters. Watch planes take off at Orly Airport from the Tour Montparnasse, or meet some famous dead people at the Cimetière du Montparnasse. Enjoy the views from the top of the Panthéon, then relax in the Jardin du Luxembourg, one of Paris's most beautiful parks. End the day shopping in the area's street markets.

Be a little Madeline

Start the day shopping for a dress on **Rue Vavin** (see p191). Be sure to pick up a copy of author Ludwig Bemelmans's book *Madeline* at the **Oxybul Junior** (see p191) store along the way. Sail wooden boats in the **Jardin du Luxembourg** (see pp190–91) before taking a ride in a princess-style carriage.

Enjoy a hearty lunch at **Bread and Roses** (see p191) on Rue de Fleurus. Afterwards, pay a visit to a great female role model at **Musée Curie** (see p189). Carry a red balloon up the windy outside staircase to the top of the **Panthéon** (see pp188–9), let it go and watch it float across the city. Walk back to Rue du Cherche Midi to sample *punitions* (bite-sized crunchy biscuits) at **Poilâne** (see p193).

Left Façade of the Pantheon, with its 22 Corinthian columns
Below Sailing a wooden boat in the Jardin du Luxembourg

Above Children enjoying the playground adjoining the rooftop Jardin Atlantique

Shoppers' heaven

Stroll down **Rue Vavin** buying clothes, toys and books. Pick up bargain jewellery and handbags before choosing something tasty for lunch at the **Marché Edgar Quinet** (see p192).

Step into Monoprix in the shadow of the Tour Montparnasse for some affordable shopping therapy before walking up Rue de Rennes to buy books, DVDs and computer games in the giant **FNAC**.

Buy the best bread in town at **Poilâne** then head to **Le Bon Marché** (see p194), the city's oldest department store, and its splendid food hall, **La Grande Epicerie** (see p194), a perfect place to pick up something appetizing for the family's dinner.

Impressive art

Marvel at one of the biggest horses in town in the **Musée Antoine Bourdelle** (see p193) and admire the sculptures in the garden at the **Musée Zadkine** (see p192).

Learn about the history of France through the giant paintings on display at the **Panthéon** and get a closer look at the Statue of Liberty in the **Jardin du Luxembourg**, also home to the atmospheric Fontaine Médicis.

Lunch at **La Coupole** (see p193) where artists whiled away hours in conversation and heated arguments. Relish goodies from Paris's best bakery, **Eric Kayser** (see p191), which has many branches in the city.

In famous footsteps

Meet some of the most celebrated Frenchmen and one French-Polish lady, the Nobel Prize-winning scientist Marie Curie, in the crypt of the **Panthéon**, before taking a walk down Rue Pierre et Marie Curie, named

after the celebrated scientist Marie Curie and her husband. Count the number of statues of famous people in the **Jardin du Luxembourg**.

Stop for a drink or a bite to eat at **La Closerie des Lilas** (see p191) in Boulevard du Montparnasse, where the writer Emile Zola lunched with the artist Paul Cezanne while Russian revolutionaries played chess on the terrace. Then walk across to explore the **Cimetière du Montparnasse** (see p192), which is crammed with the sculptured tombs of prominent singers, actors and writers.

Next, head to Gare Montparnasse, where German forces surrendered to General Leclerc in 1944. Visit the memorial dedicated to him and the Resistance leader Jean Moulin, in the **Jardin Atlantique** (see p194).

Before stopping for a hot chocolate, pay homage to Louis Pasteur, the man who made milk safe to drink, at the **Musée Pasteur** (see p195).

Above right Sculptures at the Musée Antoine Bourdelle
Below right Bustling La Coupole restaurant lit up at night

Panthéon, Jardin du Luxembourg and around

Choose a nice day to explore this part of town, as the main attraction is the Jardin du Luxembourg, Paris's best park. Kids will also enjoy the views from the Panthéon's colonnaded outdoor gallery and from Tour Montparnasse. If approaching the area by metro, aim to avoid the vast interchange Montparnasse Bienvenüe, which involves a lot of tunnel walking. On Sundays and public holidays from March to November, Rue Auguste Comte and Avenue de l'Observatoire, to the south of the Jardin du Luxembourg, are full of pedestrians and rollerbladers.

Busy thoroughfare with the Panthéon in the background

Places of interest

SIGHTS
1. Panthéon
2. Jardin du Luxembourg
3. Musée Zadkine
4. Tour Montparnasse
5. Musée Antoine Bourdelle
6. Musée de la Poste
7. Musée Jean Moulin
8. Musée Pasteur

EAT AND DRINK
1. Boulangerie Pâtisserie des Arènes
2. La Brioche Dorée
3. Loulou Friendly Diner
4. Le Comptoir du Panthéon
5. Eric Kayser
6. Bonpoint Concept Store
7. Bread and Roses
8. La Closerie des Lilas
9. Jean Charles Rochoux
10. Bagels and Brownies
11. Marché Edgar Quinet
12. Poilâne
13. Les Cedres du Liban
14. Le Bon Marché
15. Marino Pietro Pizza
16. Mansard Vincent
17. Crêperie du Manoir Breton
18. Des Gâteaux et du Pain
19. Le Baribal

See also Tour Montparnasse (p192)

SHOPPING
1. Le Ciel est à Tout le Monde
2. L'Epée de Bois
3. Catimini
4. Petit Bateau
5. Oxybul Junior
6. IKKS
7. Tikibou

WHERE TO STAY
1. Hôtel Apollon
2. Hôtel Aviatic
3. Hôtel des Academies et des Arts
4. Hôtel des Grands Hommes
5. Hôtel du Panthéon
6. Hôtel du Parc
7. Hôtel Louis II
8. Hôtel Petit Belloy St Germain
9. Hôtel Residence Quintinie Square
10. Hôtel Victoria Palace
11. La Belle Juliette
12. Novotel Montparnasse
13. Novotel Vaugirard
14. Pullmann Montparnasse
15. Villa des Artistes
16. Villa Madame

Model of an
aeroplane
in the Musée
de la Poste

The Lowdown

🚗 **Métro** Montparnasse
Bienvenüe, lines 4, 6, 12 &
13; Vavin, line 4; Maubert
Mutualité or Cardinal
Lemoine, line 10; Odéon,
lines 4 & 10; Notre-Dame
des Champs, line 12; Edgar
Quinet, line 6; Falguière, line
12 or Pasteur, lines 6 & 12.
RER Luxembourg, line B; Port
Royal, line B. **Bus** 21, 27, 28,
38, 58, 82, 83, 84, 85, 88, 89,
91, 92, 94, 95 & 96. The
airport bus for Orly leaves
from Denfert-Rochereau

🛒 **Supermarkets** Monop',
35 Blvd St-Michel. Monoprix,
31 Rue du Départ, 75014.
Franprix, 71 Rue de
Rennes, 75006.
Markets Marché Port Royal,
Blvd Port Royal, 75006;
7am–2:30pm Tue & Thu,
7am–3pm Sat

🎪 **Festivals** Christmas markets: Pl
St-Sulpice, 75006 & Parvis de
la Gare Montparnasse, 75015.
Ice-skating rink: Parvis de la
Gare Montparnasse (Dec)

➕ **Pharmacy** Pharmacie des Arts,
106 Blvd du Montparnasse,
75014; 01 43 35 44 88; open
daily till midnight

🛝 **Nearest playgrounds** Jardin
du Luxembourg, Blvd
St-Michel, 75001; daily
7:30am–dusk; winter:
8am–dusk; entrance free
(see pp190–91). Square Paul
Langevin, Rue des Ecoles &
Rue Monge, 75005; daily
7am–dusk; winter: 8am–dusk;
free Wi-Fi. Square Gaston
Baty, Rue Poinsot, 75014,
behind the Monoprix
supermarket; daily 7am–dusk;
winter: 8am–dusk (see p192).
Jardin Atlantique, Gare
Montparnasse, 75015;
8:30am–9:30pm daily (see
p195). Pl Adolphe Chérioux,
75015, near the Vaugirard
Métro; daily 7am–dusk;
winter: 8am–dusk (see p195)

🚻 **Toilets** Inside Le Bon Marché
(see p194); Public WC, 36
Blvd Edgar Quinet, 75014
and inside Gare
Montparnasse

Summer crowds at the sumptuous Jardin du Luxembourg

① Panthéon
Pendulums, panoramas and a Pole

The sheer size of the Panthéon is stunning. This Roman-looking temple was commissioned to be built as a church by Louis XV in 1757. However, money for the grandiose project soon ran out, as France teetered on the brink of bankruptcy. By the time it was finished the Revolution was in full swing and churches were out of fashion. It was rededicated as a temple of reason then became the secular resting place of famous people such as Victor Hugo, Emile Zola, Alexandre Dumas and Marie Curie.

Interior of the dome lantern, Panthéon

Key Features

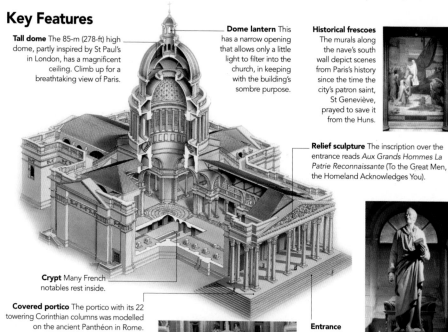

Dome lantern This has a narrow opening that allows only a little light to filter into the church, in keeping with the building's sombre purpose.

Tall dome The 85-m (278-ft) high dome, partly inspired by St Paul's in London, has a magnificent ceiling. Climb up for a breathtaking view of Paris.

Historical frescoes The murals along the nave's south wall depict scenes from Paris's history since the time the city's patron saint, St Geneviève, prayed to save it from the Huns.

Relief sculpture The inscription over the entrance reads *Aux Grands Hommes La Patrie Reconnaissante* (To the Great Men, the Homeland Acknowledges You).

Crypt Many French notables rest inside.

Covered portico The portico with its 22 towering Corinthian columns was modelled on the ancient Panthéon in Rome.

Giant pendulum This hangs from the ceiling and marks the spot where the 19th-century physicist Léon Foucault carried out his first experiments to prove the rotation of the Earth on its axis.

Entrance

Statue of Voltaire This stands in front of his tomb in the crypt. There was a rumour that his remains had been stolen but the tomb was opened and they were indeed there.

The Lowdown

🌐 **Map reference** 14 H2
Address Pl du Panthéon, 75005; 01 44 32 18 00; http://pantheon.monuments-nationaux.fr

🚗 **Métro** Maubert Mutualité or Cardinal Lemoine, line 10. **RER** Luxembourg, line B **Bus** 21, 27, 38, 82, 84, 85 & 89

🕐 **Open** Daily, Apr–Sep: 10am–6:30pm; Oct–Mar: 10am–6pm; closed 1 May, 25 Dec & 1 Jan

Colonnade: closed for renovation until 2016

💶 **Price** €15; under 18s, and under 26s with EU passports free

👫 **Skipping the queue** Paris Museum Pass accepted and sold

🎫 **Guided tours** In English upon reservation: 01 44 54 19 30.

👫 **Age range** All ages

👫 **Activities** Kids' leaflet in French

⏱ **Allow** 2 hours
♿ **Wheelchair access** No
☕ **Café** No
🚻 **Toilets** By the entrance

Good family value?
Take the kids along for a lesson on the heroes buried in the crypt. The sheer enormity of the building will leave them awestruck.

The classically designed park, Jardin du Luxembourg

Letting off steam

Head straight down the hill to the **Jardin du Luxembourg** (Blvd St-Michel, 75006), one of Paris's most beautiful parks, or to the **Arènes de Lutèce** (49 Rue Monge, 75005; 01 43 31 46 34) to watch people play boules. Just behind the Panthéon is the most exclusive school in Paris, the Lycée Henri IV. Its swimming pool, **Piscine Jean Taris** (16 Rue Thouin, 75005; 01 55 42 81 90), is open to the public.

Eat and drink

Picnic: under €25; Snacks: €25–45; Real meal: €45–90; Family treat: over €90 (based on a family of four)

PICNIC Boulangerie Pâtisserie des Arènes (31 Rue Monge, 75005; 01 43 26 29 29; closed Wed) sells mouthwatering cakes and pastries. Picnic in the Arènes de Lutèce.

SNACKS La Brioche Dorée (20 Blvd St-Michel, 75006; 01 56 81 03 12), a bakery chain, offers sandwiches, quiches and cakes to eat in or takeaway.

REAL MEAL Loulou Friendly Diner (90 Blvd St-Germain, 75005; 01 46 34 86 64; 8am–1am daily) is an American-style diner serving burgers, bagels and salads.

FAMILY TREAT Le Comptoir du Panthéon (5 Rue Soufflot, 75005; 01 43 26 90 62; 11am–11:30pm (bar until 2am), just scrapes into the top price band, with food to match many other more expensive venues.

The laboratory where scientist Marie Curie worked, Musée Curie

Find out more

DIGITAL Watch films about the life of Marie Curie, including a cartoon version at http://tinyurl.com/3ry5uvl. There are also films on the French Resistance and Jean Moulin, including his interment in the Panthéon.

FILM Watch Alexandre Dumas's famous novels on the big screen: *The Count of Monte Cristo* (2002 & 2005 with Gérard Depardieu), *The Man in the Iron Mask* (2000) and *The Three Musketeers* (1993). Also watch the cartoon version *Dogtanian and the Three Muskehounds* (2004). *Now You Know About Scientists* (2010) tells the stories of Marie Curie and Louis Pasteur.

Shopping

There are two good toyshops in the area: **Le Ciel est à Tout le Monde** (10 Rue Gay Lussac, 75005) and **L'Epée de Bois** (12 Rue de L'Epée de Bois, 75005), which means the Wooden Sword and mostly sells wooden toys.

Next stop…

A CHURCH AND A LABORATORY
Next to the Panthéon is the Church of **St-Etienne-du-Mont** where the city's patron saint, St Geneviève, was buried – until her remains were destroyed in the Revolution, leaving only her finger for posterity. The Panthéon sits on top of the hill named in her honour, Montagne St-Geneviève.

In Rue Clovis, just behind the Panthéon, is part of Philippe Auguste's medieval wall and the Lycée Henri IV, whose former pupils include Jean-Paul Sartre and Simone Weil. Marie Curie worked just around the corner. Visit her laboratory at **Musée Curie** (11 Rue Pierre et Marie Curie, 75005; www.curie.fr).

② Jardin du Luxembourg
Merry-go-round in a children's paradise

The Jardin du Luxembourg is Paris's most gorgeous park and, for younger children, a garden of delights. Especially addictive is trying to spear rings with a wooden sword while riding on the park's charming merry-go-round, designed by Charles Garnier of Opéra fame. The gardens surround the Palais du Luxembourg, the home of the second chamber of the French parliament, the Senate. The Musée du Luxembourg hosts temporary exhibitions.

Statue of Liberty in the garden

Key Features

Musée de Luxembourg

Palais du Luxembourg

Fine statues Over 100 statues were erected in the gardens in the 19th century, among them a mini version of the Statue of Liberty.

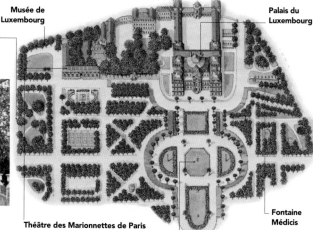

Fontaine Médicis This 17th-century fountain is built to look like a grotto, a popular feature in Italian Renaissance gardens. Find the statue of a Cyclops here.

Théâtre des Marionnettes de Paris Kids will enjoy shows at this theatre even if they do not understand French.

Fontaine Médicis

Octagonal lake Just in front of the palace, this is the best place to watch a gaggle of ducks swimming or children sailing model wooden boats like the storybook character Madeline.

Fontaine de l'Observatoire At the garden's southern tip, this fountain is one of the loveliest in Paris. Four female statues hold up a globe, and there are figures of dolphins, horses and a turtle, too.

The Lowdown

🌐 **Map reference** 14 F2
Address Jardin du Luxembourg: Blvd St-Michel, 75006; 01 42 34 23 89. Palais du Luxembourg: 15 Rue de Vaugirard, 75006; 01 42 34 20 60. Musée du Luxembourg: 19 Rue de Vaugirard, 75006; www.museeduluxembourg.fr. Théâtre des Marionnettes de Paris: 01 43 26 46 47

🚇 **Métro** Odéon, lines 4 & 10; Vavin, line 4 or Notre-Dame-des-Champs, line 12. **RER** Luxembourg, line B. **Bus** 21, 27, 38, 58, 82, 84, 85 & 89

🕐 **Open** Jardin du Luxembourg: 7am–dusk, winter: 8am–dusk. Musée du Luxembourg: 10am–7:30pm, till 10pm Mon & Fri, closed 1 May & 25 Dec. Théâtre des Marionnettes de Paris: Wed, Sat, Sun & school hols. Playground Poussin Vert du Luxembourg, to the south of the garden: 10am–dusk daily

💰 **Price** Jardin du Luxembourg: free. Musée du Luxembourg: €37–47, under 16s free. Théâtre des Marionnettes de Paris: €18–28. Poussin Vert du Luxembourg: €9–19

🧍 **Skipping the queue** Wed afternoons are as busy as weekends

👫 **Age range** All ages

🤸 **Activities** Playground; tennis courts (reserve on www.tennis.paris.fr); pony & donkey rides

⏱ **Allow** 1–2 hours

♿ **Wheelchair access** Yes, for museum and gardens

☕ **Café** Buvette des Marionnettes, in the garden; 01 43 26 33 04

🚻 **Toilets** Inside the park

Good family value?
The park itself may be free but the activities can add up. But there is nothing to beat it on a sunny day.

Palais du Luxembourg Marie de Médici built this palace in the style of the Pitti Palace in Florence to remind her of home. The palace also houses an art museum.

Nut breads, desserts and jars of jam on display in Bread & Roses

Take cover

The huge and slightly bizarre-looking **St-Sulpice** *(Pl St-Sulpice, 75006)*, just north of the Luxembourg Gardens on Place St-Sulpice, has murals by Delacroix and a fine organ. But it is its association with Dan Brown's novel *The Da Vinci Code* that has put it on the map. The novel claims that the church is associated with a secret society, the Priory of Sion, and built on the site of an ancient temple. However, according to the church authorities, the letters P and S in the small round windows at both ends of the transept refer to Peter and Sulpice, the patron saints of the church, and not the Priory of Sion.

Eat and drink

Picnic: under €25; Snacks: €25–45; Real meal: €45–90; Family treat: over €90 (based on a family of four)

PICNIC Eric Kayser *(87 Rue d'Assas, 75006; 01 43 54 92 31; www. maison-kayser.com; closed Sun)* is one of the best bakers in the city and has many branches. Picnic on the main lawns or on the benches under shady trees on the Jardin du Luxembourg's western side.
SNACKS Bonpoint Concept Store *(6 Rue Tournon; www.bonpoint. com; 10am–6pm Tue–Sat)* has a lovely tearoom with a leafy terrace.
REAL MEAL Bread and Roses *(62 Rue Madame, 75006; 01 42 22 06 06; www.breadandroses.fr; closed Sun)*, famous for its nut breads and desserts, is a good spot for brunch.
FAMILY TREAT La Closerie des Lilas *(171 Blvd du Montparnasse, 75006; 01 40 51 34 50; bar 11– 1:30am, brasserie noon–1am; www. closeriedeslilas.fr)* is one of the many Parisian cafés once frequented by

artists and writers. Author Ernest Hemingway preferred the Lilas to other cafés. It is quieter than most, and not at all a tourist trap. Eat in the brasserie or, on a sunny day, on the café's glassed-in terrace.

Shopping

Rue Vavin and Rue Brea, near the southwestern corner of the garden, are packed with toyshops and fashionable boutiques for children. There are branches of **Catimini**, **Petit Bateau** and an **Oxybul Junior** for books and games on Rue Vavin. **IKKS** *(13 Rue Vavin, 75006)* was the first shop to sell its own trendy children's range, including fabulous shirts. **Tikibou** *(33 Blvd Edgar Quinet, 75014)* is a treasure trove of scale models, trains and toys.

Find out more

DIGITAL Older children will enjoy playing *The Da Vinci Code*, a video game for PS2, Xbox and Windows.
FILM The gardens are featured in Victor Hugo's novel *Les Misérables*. This is the place where the lovers Marius Pontmercy and Cosette first meet. Watch the 1978 film based on the book.

Attractive window displays along Rue Vavin

Next stop...

CHILDREN'S SHOPS & A TOWER Combine a trip to the gardens with a visit to the **Panthéon** *(see pp188–9)* and browse through the shops around **Rue Vavin**, an enclave of children's stores. After an afternoon in the park it is a wonderful experience to watch the sun set over a cold drink from the top of the **Tour Montparnasse** *(see p192)*. As darkness falls Paris starts to twinkle.

③ Musée Zadkine

Sculptures and gardens

The former home of the Russian Jewish artist Ossip Zadkine is a pretty but rustic house with a leafy garden complete with a dovecote. Inside is a small museum dedicated to the work of the sculptor, who lived and worked here from 1928 till his death in 1967. The main draw for kids is the pretty garden, which is full of sculptures, including his most famous piece, *The Destroyed City*, a memorial to the destruction of the Dutch city of Rotterdam in 1940. Born in Belarus, at that time in the Russian Empire, Zadkine went to

The atmospheric Cimetière du Montparnasse

school with the painter Marc Chagall. Both moved to Paris, where they became part of the strong artistic community that flourished in Montparnasse in the early 20th century.

Letting off steam

Zadkine is buried in the sprawling **Cimetière du Montparnasse** *(3 Blvd Edgar Quinet, 75014)*, a tranquil place for a stroll among the tombs of famous writers, actors and artists, including writer Simone de Beauvoir, singer Serge Gainsbourg, author Guy de Maupassant and philosopher Jean-Paul Sartre. Turn right into Rue Joseph Bara and cut across the back streets to Boulevard Edgar Quinet, a 10-minute walk away. On the other side of the cemetery is the underground graveyard, the **Catacombes** *(see p214)*, open for public viewing since 1867. The caverns and tunnels add to a spooky afternoon out.

④ Tour Montparnasse

Up, up, up in the air

At 210 m (688 ft), the Tour Montparnasse is the tallest skyscraper in France. There was such a fuss when it was finished in 1972 that building

any more of them in the city centre was banned. As the solitary skyscraper in the city, it provides unparalleled views of the rest of Paris from its rooftop terrace – great for watching the spectacular Bastille Day fireworks each 14 July. Pack binoculars to see the planes taking off at Orly airport from the outdoor viewing deck. In the evening, watch the lights come on and the Eiffel Tower begin to sparkle. It is often overlooked, as most visitors rush to the Eiffel Tower instead. It has the added bonus of rarely being busy, as well as, some might say, the advantage of being the only place in the city from where you can't see Tour Montparnasse.

Letting off steam

In winter there is an ice-skating rink at the foot of the **Tour Montparnasse** by the Christmas Market and there is always an old-fashioned merry-go-round. Just behind the Monoprix supermarket on Rue Poinsot is **Square Gaston Baty**, a little playground.

The Lowdown

🌐 **Map reference** 14 E3
   Address 100 bis Rue d'Assas, 75006; 01 55 42 77 20; www.paris.fr

🚗 **Métro** Notre-Dame des Champs; Vavin, line 4. **RER** Port Royal, line B. **Bus** 38, 82, 83 & 91

🕐 **Open** 10am–6pm, closed Mon and public hols

💲 **Price** Free, but there is a charge for temporary exhibitions

🚩 **Guided tours** On some Wed & Sat; 01 55 42 77 20

👫 **Age range** All ages

⏱ **Allow** 30–45 minutes

♿ **Wheelchair access** Limited

🍴 **Eat and drink** *Picnic* Jean Charles Rochoux *(16 Rue d'Assas, 75006; closed Sun & Mon am)* sells chocolates. Try the strawberry bar. Picnic in the Jardin Atlantique. *Snacks* Bagels and Brownies *(12 Rue Notre-Dame des Champs, 75006; 01 42 22 44 15)* names its bagels after US cities.

👫 **Toilets** In the museum

The Lowdown

🌐 **Map reference** 13 C3
   Address Access from Rue de l'Arrivée, 75015; 01 45 38 53 16; www.tourmontparnasse56.com

🚗 **Métro** Montparnasse Bienvenüe, lines 4, 6, 12 & 13 or Edgar Quinet, line 6. **Bus** 58, 82, 88, 89, 91, 92, 94, 95 & 96

🕐 **Open** Apr–Sep: 9:30am–11:30pm; Oct–Mar: 9:30am–10:30pm Sun–Thu, till 11pm Fri & Sat

💲 **Price** €23–33; under 7s free

🚩 **Guided tours** Group tours available

👫 **Age range** All ages

🏃 **Activities** Children's treasure hunts during school hols

⏱ **Allow** 1 hour

♿ **Wheelchair access** Yes

🍴 **Eat and drink** *Picnic* Marché Edgar Quinet *(Rue Edgar Quinet, 75014; 9am–7:30pm Sat & Sun)* has stalls selling picnic supplies. Eat in the Jardin Atlantique on top of Gare Montparnasse. *Snacks* Le 360 Café is the highest panoramic bar in Europe and serves sandwiches and salads.

👫 **Toilets** In the visitors' centre

Paris from the 56th floor of Tour Montparnasse

Prices given are for a family of four

Larger-than-life sculpture of a horse, Musée Antoine Bourdelle

⑤ Musée Antoine Bourdelle

Minotaurs and Greek heroes

The studio of the sculptor and star pupil of Rodin, Antoine Bourdelle, is a quiet oasis in a little side street, well off the main tourist trail. He worked here from 1884 until his death in 1929, creating some enormous sculptures – their sheer size makes them appealing to children, especially those of a gigantic horse and statues of the Minotaur, Hercules and Apollo. The artist Marc Chagall also briefly worked here. There is a lovely garden full of Bourdelle's work, which makes it a fun visit with children.

Take cover

On the other side of the main road is the **Musée du Montparnasse** (*21 Ave du Maine, 75015; 01 42 22 91 96*), once home of the Russian painter Marie Vassilieff, who ran a canteen for needy artists during World War I, among them Picasso, Modigliani, Chagall and Zadkine. Stroll down Boulevard du Montparnasse to the **La Coupole** (*102 Blvd Montparnasse, 75014*), a huge, iconic Art Deco brasserie where bustling waiters serve classic dishes.

Seafood on display in La Coupole, a classic Parisian brasserie

The Lowdown

🌐 **Map reference** 13 B3
Address 18, Rue Antoine Bourdelle, 75015; 01 49 54 73 73; *www.bourdelle.paris.fr*

🚇 **Métro** Montparnasse Bienvenüe, lines 4, 6, 12 & 13 or Falguière, line 12. **Bus** 28, 48, 58, 88, 89, 91, 92, 94, 95 & 96

🕐 **Open** 10am–6pm, closed Mon & public hols

💶 **Price** Free, except for temporary exhibitions

👫 **Age range** 5 plus

👫 **Activities** Workshops for children in French; 01 49 54 73 91/92

⏱ **Allow** 45 minutes–1 hour

♿ **Wheelchair access** Limited. Call prior to visit and the museum will install ramps

🍽 **Eat and drink** *Picnic* Poilâne (*8 Rue du Cherche Midi, 75006; 01 45 48 42 59; closed Sun*) has been baking since 1933. Picnic in the Jardin d'Atlantique. *Family treat* Les Cedres du Liban (*5 Ave du Maine, 75015; 01 42 22 35 18; www.lescedresduliban.com; noon–2:30pm & 7–10:45pm*) is a good option for vegetarians. There are lots of little dishes for kids.

👫 **Toilets** In the museum

⑥ Musée de la Poste

Letters and a little prince

One of Paris's best offbeat museums, the Musée de la Poste has an engaging collection of old postboxes, telephone cubicles and interactive displays, which make for a fun outing. The museum chronicles the history of the postal and telecommunications service, beginning with a Mesopotamian clay tablet. The author of The Little Prince, Antoine de St-Exupéry, whose childhood classic was inspired by his aviation experiences for the postal service, is featured

Models of postmen and postal vans, Musée de la Poste

here among other heroes. The museum also charts the history of France in a unique and accessible way for children. There is a room devoted to the hot-air balloons and carrier pigeons that were used during the siege of Paris in 1871.

Letting off steam

The modern **Jardin Atlantique** (Blvd de Vaugirard) is located on top of the Gare Montparnasse station. Take a lift from Boulevard Vaugirard to the park. Kids like the location and it is also a great place to feed the birds or watch the locals playing tennis and ping pong.

⑦ Musée Jean Moulin

Secret messages, spies and war movies

The tiny Musée Jean Moulin and its accompanying museum, the Mémorial du Maréchal Leclerc de Hauteclocque, focus on life in the French Resistance during World War II and the dramatic days of the

The Lowdown

- 🌐 **Map reference** 13 B4
  Address 34 Blvd de Vaugirard, 75015; 01 42 79 24 24; www.ladressemuseedelaposte.fr
- 🚗 **Métro** Montparnasse Bienvenüe, lines 4, 6, 12 & 13, exit Pl Bienvenüe; or Pasteur, lines 6 & 12. **Bus** 28, 58, 88, 89, 91, 92, 94, 95 & 96
- 🕐 **Open** 10am–6pm (until 8pm Thu), closed Sun & public hols
- 💲 **Price** €17–27; under 13s & under 26s with EU passport free
- 🚶 **Skipping the queue** Paris Museum Pass accepted
- 🚩 **Guided tours** Audio guide in English and French: €6.50 per person including entry ticket
- 🚹 **Age range** 5 plus
- 🏃 **Activities** Activity leaflet and children's and family workshops in French
- 🕐 **Allow** 1–2 hours
- ♿ **Wheelchair access** No
- 🍴 **Eat and drink** Picnic Le Bon Marché (24 Rue des Sèvres, 75007; closed Sun), the oldest department store in the city, has an incredible food hall, La Grande Epicerie (www.lagrandeepicerie.fr). Picnic in the small garden in front of Le Bon Marché on Rue des Sèvres opposite the Hôtel Lutetia. Snacks Marino Pietro Pizza (65 Blvd de Vaugirard 75015; 01 43 22 61 46; www.pietroristorante.com; 11am–3pm, 7–11pm daily) is a friendly pizzeria with a small terrace, serving great pizzas and salads.
- 🚻 **Toilets** Near the reception desk

The Lowdown

- 🌐 **Map reference** 13 C4
  Address 23 Allée de la 2e Division Blindée, Jardin Atlantique, 75015. Take the lift on Blvd de Vaugirard or the stairs in the building opposite the elevator; 01 40 64 39 44; www.paris.fr
- 🚗 **Métro** Montparnasse Bienvenüe, lines 4, 6, 12 & 13, exit Pl Bienvenüe; Gaite, line 13; and Pasteur, lines 6 & 12. **Bus** 28, 58, 88, 89, 91, 92, 94, 95 & 96
- 🕐 **Open** 10am–6pm, closed Mon & public hols
- 💲 **Price** Free, charges for some exhibitions
- 🚩 **Guided tours** In English by appt
- 🚹 **Age range** 10 plus
- 🕐 **Allow** 30 minutes–1 hour
- ♿ **Wheelchair access** Yes
- 🍴 **Eat and drink** Picnic Mansard Vincent (6 Rue Falguière, 75015; closed Mon) is a good bakery. Real meal Crêperie du Manoir Breton (18 Rue d'Odessa; 01 43 35 40 73; noon–11pm) is the best place to eat crêpes.
- 🚻 **Toilets** Off the left-side gallery

liberation of Paris. Both museums document this period through the lives of the Resistance leader Jean Moulin, who is buried in the nearby Panthéon (see pp188–9), and the military leader, Marshal Leclerc. On 25 August 1944, Leclerc set up his command post in Gare Montparnasse station and it was here that the German General Von Choltitz signed the ceasefire.

There is a fascinating collection of coded messages, underground newspapers, photographs and films that bring the Occupation to life. Look out for a radio hidden in a suitcase.

Modernist façade of the Musée Jean Moulin, by the Jardin Atlantique

Visitors studying the scientific instruments at the Musée Pasteur

Letting off steam
The museum is located right by the **Jardin Atlantique**, so it is easy to combine a visit with a run around, away from the hustle and bustle of Montparnasse.

Letting off steam
Take a short walk from the Musée Pasteur to the lovely playground in picturesque **Place Adolphe Chérioux**, which is located close to the Métro station Vaugirard.

⑧ Musée Pasteur
Beastly bacteria, mad dogs and rotten wine

Always remember to raise a toast to the world-renowned scientist Louis Pasteur before drinking a glass of milk. He discovered the process of milk pasteurization, as well as a cure for rabies. The apartment in which he spent the last seven years of his life has been preserved as it was when he died in 1895. It is on the first floor of the scientific centre, Institut Pasteur, which is named after him. Look out for his personal belongings, a vast collection of microscopes and scientific instruments. The famous scientist is buried in the cellar surrounded by mosaics recalling his discoveries.

Tomb of Louis Pasteur, in a cellar lined with mosaics celebrating his work

The Lowdown

🌐 **Map reference** 13 A4
Address 25 Rue du Docteur Roux, 75015; 01 45 68 82 83; www.pasteur.fr
🚇 **Métro** Pasteur, lines 6 & 12. **Bus** 95
🕐 **Open** 2–5:30pm Mon–Fri, closed Aug. Visiting hours: 2pm, 3pm and 4pm
💶 **Price** €20–30
🎧 **Guided tours** Compulsory, book in advance for tours in English
👫 **Age range** 10 plus

⏱ **Allow** 45 minutes
♿ **Wheelchair access** Yes
🍴 **Eat and drink** Picnic Des Gâteaux et du Pain (63 Blvd Pasteur, 75015; www.desgateauxetdupain.com; closed Tue) sells cakes and other goodies inside a shop that looks more like a jewellery store with its chic black walls. Real meal Le Baribal (186 Rue de Vaugirard, 75015; 01 47 34 15 32; 11:45am–midnight) is a good neighbourhood bistro.
🚻 **Toilets** Yes

Picnic under €25; **Snacks** €25–45; **Real meal** €45–90; **Family treat** over €90 (based on a family of four)

Beyond
the City Centre

Outside Paris's bustling centre lie some of its greatest treasures, including colourful markets, the popular rides of the Jardin d'Acclimatation, an atmospheric hall-of-fame cemetery and the creepy Catacombes. There are several parks and Modernist spaces to explore, from the vast Bois de Vincennes to the Parc André Citroën. The high-tech Parc de la Villette is especially good for kids, with its playgrounds and science museum.

Jardin d'Acclimatation

Parc de la Villette

Central Paris

Highlights

Cité des Sciences et de l'Industrie
Step into the world of machines, rockets and aircraft at the biggest science museum in Europe (see p202).

Parc des Buttes-Chaumont
Enjoy a peaceful stroll through one of the most romantic parks in Paris (see p204).

Marché aux Puces de St-Ouen & Marché aux Puces de Vanves
Rifle for good bargains from the fascinating piles of junk in the flea markets at Porte de St-Ouen and Porte de Vanves (see p206 & p215).

Jardin d'Acclimatation
Look out for farm animals at the oldest funfair in the city, which has been entertaining children for over a century (see pp210–11).

Parc André Citroën
Scramble through jets of water on a hot day in this Modernist park on the banks of the Seine (see pp212–13).

Catacombes
Take a walk through the spooky underground passages and see the bones of six million people arranged in macabre patterns (see p214).

Above left Shops selling antiques, art and bric-a-brac in the Marche aux Puces de St-Ouen
Left Cooling off from the summer heat in Parc André Citroën

The Best of
Beyond the City Centre

If the children already know central Paris, or just want to do something different, take the Métro or RER a few stops further out to find some of the city's hidden treasures. Hunt for famous names in the cemeteries, visit Europe's biggest science museum, ride on a canal boat, or check out the beautiful Château de Malmaison, once home to Napoleon and Josephine. In summer, the scientific Parc de la Villette and the leafy Bois de Vincennes are great places to picnic.

A perfect day out

Start the day by having fun in the **Parc de la Villette** (see pp202–203), with its super child-friendly **Cité des Enfants** (see p202) and **Cité des Sciences et de l'Industrie**, where kids can press buttons and learn about science the easy way. Work up an appetite walking over to the **Parc des Buttes-Chaumont** (see p204), explore the grotto and then eat lunch in the lively restaurant **Rosa Bonheur** (see p204) in the park.

Spend the afternoon hunting for famous names in the **Cimetière du Père Lachaise** (see p204), then stroll along the **Canal St-Martin** (see p203) at Quai de Valmy, checking out the shops. Take a trip on a canal boat and finish the day off with dinner at the welcoming Asian restaurant **Ari Madame Shawn** (see p203). In some cases, the distance between one place and the next is quite large, especially from **Parc des Buttes-Chaumont** to **Cimetière du Père Lachaise** and from there to **Canal St-Martin**. The area is, however, easily accessible by bus and Métro.

Left Parc de la Villette's Cité des Sciences et de l'Industrie
Below Peacocks in the Jardin d'Acclimatation

Grand designs

Napoleon put his stamp on the city by building the sprawling **Cimetière du Père Lachaise** and diverting the River Ourcq into the **Canal de l'Ourcq** (see p203) to bring fresh drinking water to the capital. Baron Haussmann built a vast abattoir at **Parc de la Villette** in the mid-19th century, which is now home to the cutting-edge park designed by Bernard Tschumi.

The Modernist President Pompidou loved cars, and built the ring road that runs around the city, the Périphérique, to make it easier to get about. President Mitterrand left his mark too, building the giant arch in the business district of **La Défense** (see p211) and the spacious **Parc de Bercy** (see p205). Next to the park, by the river behind Gare de Lyon, is an important sports and music venue, the **Palais Omnisports** (see p205), another Mitterrand-era project. Stop for a drink in the lively **Bercy Village** (see p205) nearby, whose renovated wine warehouses are filled with shops and restaurants.

Pick a park

Paris has lots of parks, some of the best of which are outside the city centre. Baron Haussmann laid out the craggy gardens of the **Parc des Buttes-Chaumont** in the middle of the 19th century, and in the south created the lovely **Parc Montsouris** (see p214) with its vast lawns and duck pond. Napoleon III fell in love with Hyde Park while in exile in England, and when he returned to France he ordered up two English-style parks, the **Bois de Vincennes** (see pp204–5) and the **Jardin d'Acclimatation** (see pp210–11), where it is fun to row boats on the lake and let off steam at the oldest amusement park in town. The gardens at the 17th-century **Château de Malmaison** (see p212) are also beautiful on a sunny day. Paris parks have kept up with the times. The landscaped **Parc André Citroën**

Above Children riding bikes through caves in the craggy Parc des Buttes-Chaumont
Below Home of the French Open, the Stade Roland Garros

(see pp212–13), the strikingly modern **Parc de Bercy** and the scientific **Parc de la Villette** are very popular with families as they have great facilities for children.

Get sporty

Visit the **Stade de France** (see p207) where France won the football World Cup in 1998. Stop off to kick a ball about in the **Jardin d'Acclimatation**, then it is tennis time at the **Stade Roland Garros** (see p211) where the giants of world tennis battle it out to win the French Open. The **Palais Omnisports** is Paris's major indoor sports venue, and also has an ice-skating rink. Alternatively, hire bikes to ride and boats to row in the **Jardin d'Acclimatation** and the **Bois de Vincennes**. Rollerblade over the bridge, the **Passerelle Simone de Beauvoir** (see p205), next to the **Parc de Bercy,** or jog around the craggy hill in the **Parc des Buttes-Chaumont**.

Parc de la Villette and around

Eastern Paris has a good mix of indoor and outdoor activities off the main tourist track. The creatively designed Parc de la Villette houses a fantastic science museum, and for history buffs there is a fascinating cemetery, Cimetière du Père Lachaise. The Parc des Buttes-Chaumont is the most romantic park in the city, with a craggy cliff that offers splendid views, while the Bois de Vincennes has a castle with a giant keep, lakes and lots of space. For something different, try the modern Parc de Bercy. On a sunny day, explore the canals de l'Ourcq or St-Martin, and picnic on the towpath, or in the parks.

Picturesque Cimetière du Père Lachaise

The Lowdown

Métro Porte de la Villette, line 7 or Porte de Pantin, line 5; Père Lachaise, lines 2 & 3; Philippe Auguste, line 2; Gambetta, line 3; Alexandre Dumas, line 2; Porte Dorée, line 8; Château de Vincennes, line 1; Bercy, lines 6 & 14; Porte de Clignancourt, line 4 or Garibaldi, line 13; Basilique de St-Denis, line 13; St-Denis Porte de Paris, line 13. **RER** Vincennes, line A; La Plaine Stade de France, line B; Stade de France St-Denis, line D. **Bus** 26, 46, 56, 60, 69, 75, 85, 86, 87, 95, 137, 139, 150, 152, 153, 166, 173, 249, 253, 255, 302, PC1, PC2 & PC3. **Taxi** 01 45 30 30 30; Taxi G7: 01 47 39 47 39; Taxi Bleu: 08 91 70 10 10. **Canal boat** Canauxrama, 13 Quai de la Loire, 75019; 01 42 39 15 00; www.canauxrama.com. Paris Canal, 19–21 Quai de la Loire, 75019; 01 42 40 96 97; www.pariscanal.com
Getting around Lines 7, 7 bis & 5 link the area with central Paris. The PC2 runs to Vincennes from Porte de la Villette.

i **Visitor information** Kiosks: Gare du Nord, 18 Rue de Dunkerque, 75010; 8am–6pm daily, closed 1 May, 25 Dec & 1 Jan. Gare de l'Est, Pl du 11 Novembre 1918, 75010; 8am–7pm Mon–Sat, closed 1 Jan, 1 May & 25 Dec. Office de Tourisme de Vincennes, 28 Ave de Paris,

94300; 01 48 08 13 00; www.vincennes-tourisme.fr; daily Tue–Sat, closed public hols & Thu mornings (except Jul & Aug)

Supermarkets Franprix, 126 Rue de Picpus, 75012, 13 Rue des Vignerons, 94300. Monoprix, 119 Ave de la Flandre, 75019 & 7 Rue Louise Thuliez, 75019. **Markets** Marché St-Martin 31/33, Rue de Château d'Eau, 75010; 9am–8pm Tue–Sat, 9am–2pm Sun. Marché Père Lachaise, Blvd de Menilmontant, 75011; 7am–2:30pm Tue & Fri

Festivals Foire du Trône funfair, Bois de Vincennes (Apr–Jun). Children's concerts, Les Pestacles, Bois de Vincennes (Jun–Sep). Open-air film festival, Cinema en Plein Air, Parc de la Villette (Jul–Aug)

Pharmacies Grand Pharmacie Daumesnil, 6 Pl Félix Eboué, 75012; 01 43 43 19 03; 8:30am–9pm daily. Pharmacie Européenne, 6 Pl Clichy, 75009; 01 48 74 65 18; open 24 hours

Nearest playgrounds Parc de la Villette (see pp202–03). Parc des Buttes-Chaumont (see p204). Le Parc Floral de Paris, Bois de Vincennes (see pp204–5). Crue Crimée, Pl de Bitche, 75019; dawn–dusk

0 km 1

0 miles 1

Places of interest

SIGHTS
1. Parc de la Villette
2. Cimetière du Père Lachaise
3. Bois de Vincennes
4. Parc de Bercy
5. Marché aux Puces de St-Ouen
6. Basilique St-Denis
7. Stade de France

Beyond the City Centre

Parc de la Villette

Jardin
d'Acclimatation
p208

Central
Paris

Above Alouette III helicopter, Cité des Sciences
Below Children at the slides in Parc des Buttes-Chaumont

Statue of Louis XVI, Basilique St-Denis

① Parc de la Villette

Museums, themed gardens and canal boats

In the northeastern corner of Paris, the old slaughterhouses and livestock market have been transformed into a wonderfully wacky park that runs along Canal de l'Ourcq. Full of playgrounds for kids, the complex also houses a concert hall, music centre and exhibition pavilion. The main attraction for families is the Cité des Sciences, Europe's biggest science museum – it houses the interactive Cité des Enfants, a ground-breaking zone just for children.

Children playing in Parc de la Villette

Key Features

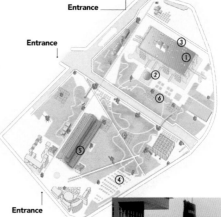

Entrance

Entrance

Entrance

① **Cité des Sciences et de l'Industrie** This futuristic science museum excites children with dazzling hands-on displays. Fly over the surface of Mars in the Planetarium, discover the wonders of the world, or travel through the human body in the Explora exhibit.

② **La Géode** The giant hemispherical screen makes 3D movie-watching a truly grand experience.

③ **La Cité des Enfants** This thematic museum is the place for children aged 2–12 to be TV presenters, weather forecasters, or robot designers.

④ **Philharmonie de Paris** Paris musical concert venue and exhibition space designed by Jean Nouvel.

⑤ **Grande Halle** Once a cattle market, when La Villette was a huge abattoir, it now hosts temporary exhibitions.

⑥ **L'Argonaut** Discover marine life through the radar screens and periscopes of this 1930s submarine.

The Lowdown

🌐 **Map reference** 6 F2
Address Parc de la Villette: 211 Ave Jean Javrès, 75019; 01 40 03 75 75; www.lavillette.com. Cité des Sciences: 01 40 05 80 00; www.cite-sciences.fr. La Géode: 08 92 68 45 40; www.lageode.fr. Philharmonie de Paris: 01 44 84 44 84; www.philharmoniedeparis.fr

🚗 **Métro** Porte de la Villette, line 7 for Cité des Sciences; Porte de Pantin, line 5 for Philharmonie de Paris. **Bus** PC2, PC3, 75, 139, 150, 152 & 249

🕐 **Open** Parc de la Villette: daily; restricted access: 1am–6am. Cité des Sciences: 10am–6pm, till 7pm Sun, closed Mon. La Géode: 10:30am–8:30pm, closed some public hols. Philharmonie de Paris: noon–6pm Tue–Fri, 10am–6pm Sat–Sun, closed Mon & 1 May. L'Argonaut: 10am–5:30pm Tue–Sat; 10am–6:30pm Sun

💶 **Price** Parc de la Villette: Free; Cité des Sciences: Explora: €28–38. Cité des Enfants: €12–22. La Géode: €24–31; Joint ticket: €63–73; €3 supplement for the Planetarium. Family ticket: €64–74. Philharmonie de Paris: €14–24, call or check website for concert rates

👫 **Skipping the queue** Paris Museum Pass accepted at the museums. Buy tickets online

🚩 **Guided tours** French guided tours in the park and museums. Shows in the Planetarium are in English & French; the 2pm show is usually in English

👫 **Age range** Parc de la Villette: all ages; Cité des Sciences: 2 plus; L'Argonaute: 6 plus; La Géode: 7 plus; other attractions: 5 plus

🎨 **Activities** Art & science workshops

⏱ **Allow** 1 day

♿ **Wheelchair access** Yes

Letting off steam

In front of the Cité des Sciences et de l'Industrie museum there are 10 different **themed gardens**, among them the gardens of mirrors, mists and acrobatics.

The park has follies, walkways and playgrounds, and children's activities at weekends. Watch a show on the canal boat *Antipode* (*55 Quai de la Seine, 75019; 01 42 03 39 07; www.penicheantipode.fr; Wed, Sun & school hols*).

Eat and drink

Picnic: under €25; Snacks: €25–45; Real meal: €45–90; Family treat: over €90 (based on a family of four)

PICNIC Canal Bio (*46 bis Quai de Loire, 75019; 01 42 06 44 44; 2:30–8pm Mon, 10am–8pm Tue–Fri*) is a small canalside shop selling organic produce. Picnic alongside the canal or anywhere in the park.
SNACKS Le Cafézoïde (*92 Quai de la Loire, 75019; 01 42 38 26 37; www.cafezoide.asso.fr*) is a café with a difference. Here kids can play games, watch concerts or join in a workshop, as well as refuel. It is 10 minutes away on foot along the canalside to the south.
REAL MEAL Ari Madame Shawn (*3 Rue des Récollets, 75010; 01 42 72 36 06*) serves delicious Thai food at big wooden tables near Canal St-Martin. It is a good place to round off the day.
FAMILY TREAT Les Grand Tables du 104 (*104 Rue d'Aubervilliers, 75019; 01 40 37 10 07; Tue–Sun*) has good international cuisine and a lively vibe. In the afternoon, there are workshops for children.

🛒 **Café** In the Cité des Sciences et de l'Industrie and the Philharmonie de Paris

🏷️ **Shops** La Boutique de la Cité des Sciences, Cité des Sciences et de l'Industrie

🚻 **Toilets** Baby-changing facility in Cité des Sciences et de l'Industrie

Good family value?
The park is pricey but kids love the science museum. On a summer night during the Cinema en Plein Air festival, families can watch films in the park late in the evening.

Garden of acrobatics, one of the themed playgrounds in Parc de la Villette

Find out more

DIGITAL Visit the interactive site *http://www.universcience.fr/fr/juniors/contenu/c/1239022828832/surprises/*. Watch an Ariane space rocket take off at *www.arianespace.com*. Get to grips with more science at *www.bbc.co.uk/schools/scienceclips/index_flash.shtml* and *www.kids-science-experiments.com*. Watch films by the Lumière brothers on *http://tinyurl.com/ybvdbuq*.

Shopping

Concept store **Antoine et Lili** (*95 Quai Valmy, 75010; www.antoineetlili.com*), on the Canal St-Martin near the park, has household items and clothes for women and little girls.

Next stop...
CANAL TOURS & BEACHES
Take a cruise on a canal boat (*see p29*) or stroll along the towpath of Canal de l'Ourcq, built by Napoleon. He knew that to gain the trust of the Parisians he needed plenty of fresh water, which was always in short supply in the city, so he diverted the River Ourcq into a 100-km (62-mile) long canal. It joins with the leafy Canal St-Martin, with its iron footbridges, which heads south to Bastille. In summer, the towpaths of the two canals are at their liveliest from mid-Jul to mid-Aug when the popular **Paris Plages** (*see p68*) turn them into a street party.

② Cimetière du Père Lachaise

Dead famous

Far from being grim and spooky, Paris's cemeteries are full of bizarre and fascinating monuments that make them well worth a visit.

The tombs here read like a roll call of famous people, among them singers Edith Piaf and Jim Morrison, and playwright Oscar Wilde, although the first person to be buried in Père Lachaise, in 1804, was Adélaïde Paillard-Villeneuve, who was just 5 years old. Many tombs have life-size sculptures of those who lie in them and are works of art in themselves.

The 19th-century Columbarium, or "dovecot", houses the funerary urns of more celebrities within its memorial-covered compartments. The Mur des Fédérés, in the southeastern corner of the cemetery, is the wall against which supporters of the Paris Commune, called

The Columbarium in the Cimetière du Père Lachaise

fédérés, were executed by government troops in 1871.

Letting off steam

By the southeastern corner of the cemetery there are some pretty cobbled streets running off Rue de Bagnolet and a small playground at the top of Rue des Balkans. The romantic landscape of **Parc des Buttes-Chaumont** (*Rue Manin, 75019*), with its craggy cliffs, grotto, colonnaded folly and waterfalls is a great place to feed the ducks, spend time in the playground and get a fine view of Paris.

The Lowdown

🌐 **Address** Rue des Repos 75020; 01 71 28 50 82; *www.pere-lachaise.com*

🚇 **Métro** Père Lachaise, lines 2 & 3; Philippe Auguste, line 2; Gambetta, line 3 or Alexandre Dumas, line 2. **Bus** 60, 69 & 102

🕐 **Open** 8am–5:30pm daily (from 8:30am Sat, 9am Sun & public hols); summer: till 6pm

Ⓖ **Price** Free

👫 **Age range** All ages

⏱ **Allow** 1–1.5 hours

🍵 **Eat and drink** *Picnic* La Boulangerie Véronique Mauclerc (*83 Rue de Crimée, 75019; closed Mon*), a picture-postcard bakery near the Parc des Buttes-Chaumont, is famous for its nut breads and also has a miniature tearoom with lilac tiled walls and 1930s frescoes. *Real meal* Rosa Bonheur (*2 Allée de la Cascade, 75019; 01 42 00 00 45; www.rosabonheur.fr; noon–midnight Thu–Fri, from 10am Sat & Sun*) is a hip place to eat in summer in the Parc des Buttes-Chaumont. This *guinguette*, an open-air café and dance floor, opened in 1867 and serves tapas-style food. It is a great place to watch the sunset over Paris.

👫 **Toilets** No

③ Bois de Vincennes

Butterflies, lions and fish

To the southeast of the city centre lies the vast parkland of the Bois de Vincennes. Its most dramatic feature is the Château de Vincennes, which was a royal residence until Versailles was built in the 17th century. On a sunny day, picnic in the park, once a royal hunting ground where St Louis used to administer justice under an oak tree. The château has a lovely flower garden, Le Parc Floral de Paris, where there is an excellent playground and lots of activities for the summer, such as electric cars, train rides and a mini-golf course.

There is also a tropical garden and a city farm, La Ferme de Paris, as well as puppet shows and pony rides. Amidst its greenery are four lakes, including a boating lake. The big attraction from Palm Sunday to the end of May is the largest funfair in France, the Fête du Trône.

Miniature train chugging through the Bois de Vincennes

Rowing on the lake in the Bois des Vincennes

Take cover

The **Cité Nationale de l'Histoire de l'Immigration** *(293 Ave Daumesnil, 75012; www.histoire-immigration.fr)* charts the story of immigration in France. Kids will love the aquarium *(www.aquarium-portedoree.fr)* in the basement. **Cirque Pinder** *(Pelouse de Reuilly, 75012; 01 45 90 21 25; www.cirquepinder.com)*, France's oldest travelling circus, puts on shows in the winter months. It is a traditional show with animal acts.

The Lowdown

- 🌐 **Address** Bois de Vincennes: Château de Vincennes: Ave de Paris, 94300; 01 48 08 31 20; www.chateau-vincennes.fr
- 🚗 **Métro** Porte Dorée, line 8; Château de Vincennes, line 1. **RER** Vincennes, line A. **Bus** 46, 56, 86, 87, 112, 115, 325, PC1 & PC2
- 🕐 **Open** Bois de Vincennes: dawn–dusk. Château: 10am–6pm; winter: till 5pm; closed public hols. La Ferme de Paris: weekends & public hols; 1:30–6:30pm; winter: till 5pm; closed Mon during school hols. Le Parc Floral: 9:30am–8pm; winter: till 5pm
- 💶 **Price** Château de Vincennes: €18–28; under 18s free; EU citizens under 26 free. La Ferme de Paris: free. Le Parc Floral: free but additional charge for concerts and some children's activities
- 🚻 **Age range** All ages
- 🤸 **Activities** Go rowing on the Lac Daumesnil or Lac des Minimes; €11.80 per hour (€10 deposit). Concerts for children in Le Parc Floral in summer and a wide range of activities at the city farm. Puppet shows near Lac de St-Mandé.
- ♿ **Wheelchair access** Château: limited access
- 🍴 **Eat and drink** *Snacks* Au Pur Beurre *(10 Ave de Paris, 94300; 01 43 28 13 61; closed Mon)* serves *brioche* and restorative cups of tea. Les Fées Papilles *(13 Rue Lejemptel, 94300; 01 43 28 49 71)* serves Sunday brunch and teatime treats. *Family treat* Le Chalet des îles Daumesnil *(Lac Daumesnil–Bois de Vincennes, 75012; 01 43 07 00 10; www.lechaletdesiles.com; closed Mon & Tue)* has a terrace, pretty lawns and traditional cuisine.
- 🚻 **Toilets** In the castle, Le Chalet des Iles and at Sanisette, on Ave de Nogent by the Château de Vincennes station

④ Parc de Bercy

A skater's heaven

This park was once the wine storehouse of Paris, and many of the pathways retain the rails of the trains that once brought barrels of wine from river boats to the warehouses. There are fountains and statues and plenty of ducks to feed, and the park has a small skating rink. The area of the park named for the late Israeli Prime Minister Yitzak Rabin is a lovely spot dedicated to peace. Rollerbladers should take a turn across the Seine on the Passerelle Simone de Beauvoir bridge near Bercy Village, a 20-minute walk away on the Quai de Bercy. Bercy Village is a good stop for a drink. Several wine warehouses have been converted into shops and cafés.

Take cover

The park houses the **Palais Omnisports** *(01 40 02 60 60; www.bercy.fr/patinoire)*, which is the place to enjoy ice-skating. It is also a major music and sports venue. On the northwestern edge of the park is **La Cinémathèque Française** *(51 Rue de Bercy; 01 71 19 33 33; www.cinematheque.fr)*, a museum of French cinema.

Lush green lawns of the Parc de Bercy on a sunny day

The Lowdown

- 🌐 **Map reference** 16 G5 **Address** Rue Paul-Belmondo 75012; 01 53 46 19 19; www.paris.fr
- 🚇 **Métro** Bercy, lines 6 & 14
- 🕐 **Open** 8am–5:30pm; summer: till 9:30pm
- 💶 **Price** Free
- 🚻 **Age range** All ages
- 🍴 **Eat and drink** *Picnic* Monop' *(60/62 Cour St-Emilion, 75012; 01 44 68 64 70)* sells salads and sandwiches. Picnic in Parc de Bercy. *Real meal* Partie de Campagne *(36 Cour St-Emillion, 75012)* has a varied menu.
- 🚻 **Toilets** No

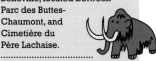

Shoppers in the busy Marché aux Puces de St-Ouen

⑤ Marché aux Puces de St-Ouen

Treasure hunting, mussels and bargains galore

The biggest flea market in Europe is at the top end of the 18th *arrondissement* under the Périphérique, the dual-carriageway ring road. The market began in the 1870s when the city's rag-and-bone men, who resettled outside the city limits to avoid paying taxes, began to spread their wares on the ground on a Sunday morning. Today, it is an Aladdin's cave of memorabilia with 3,000 stalls arranged in 15 different markets. On a sunny day, concentrate on the nicest and most retro flea markets – Serpette, Paul Bert and Vernaison – which sell silverware, antiques and second-hand toys.

Take cover

At the weekend there is plenty of good street theatre here to entertain the kids. If the weather turns nasty, the covered **Marché Serpette**, housed in an old garage, is a good option.

Shop selling antiques in Marché aux Puces de St-Ouen

Prices given are for a family of four

The Lowdown

- 🌐 **Address** Rue des Rosiers, 93400; 08 92 70 57 65; *www.marchesauxpuces.fr*
- 🚗 **Métro** Porte-de-Clignancourt, line 4. **Bus** 56, 60, 85, 95, 137, 166, 255 & PC3
- 🕐 **Open** 9am–6pm Sat, 10am–6pm Sun & 11am–5pm Mon
- Ⓖ **Price** Free
- 👫 **Skipping the queue** Go early in the morning or on Mon. Keep a close eye on pre-teens who could easily get lost, and watch out for pickpockets. Most trading is done in cash.
- 👫 **Age range** 5 plus
- 👜 **Eat and drink** *Snacks* Have lunch at one of the many cafés and stands in the market, though more for the atmosphere than the food. *Real meal* Le Picolo (58 Rue Jules Valles 93400, St-Ouen; 01 4011 11 19; www.lepicolo.com; Sat, Sun & Mon during market hours) is the oldest café in the market, and serves mussels, veal blanquette and sausages.
- 👫 **Toilets** Yes

⑥ Basilique St-Denis

Headless saints and royal bones

After St Denis, the first bishop of Paris, had his head chopped off by the Romans in AD 250, he picked it up and walked for about an hour before handing it to a woman and dropping down dead. Today, a basilica stands on the spot where he was buried. The abbey of St-Denis, the first in the world to be built in the Gothic style, was a political powerhouse in the Middle Ages and an important place of pilgrimage. In the 7th century King Dagobert who, according to the revolutionary ditty *Le Bon Roi Dagobert*, wore his trousers back to front, decided that he too would be buried here. It set a trend and nearly all the kings and queens of France followed him into the vaults. During the Revolution, the royal tombs were

Tombs of Louis XII and Anne of Brittany, Basilique St-Denis

The Lowdown

- 🌐 **Address** 1 Rue de la Légion d'Honneur, 93200; 01 48 09 83 54; http://saint-denis. monuments-nationaux.fr
- 🚗 **Métro** Basilique de St-Denis, line 13. **Bus** 153 & 253
- 🕐 **Open** Apr–Sep: 10am–6:15pm Mon–Sat; noon–6:15pm Sun; winter: till 5:15pm; closed 1 Jan, 1 May & 25 Dec. Closed to tourists during certain ceremonies and services; check website for timings
- Ⓖ **Price** Church: free; Crypt: €15–25; under 18s free; EU citizens under 26 free
- 👫 **Skipping the queue** Visit on a sunny day when the stained-glass windows are at their best
- ☞ **Guided tours** Audio guide in English; €4.50. Guided tours in English by reservation only
- 👫 **Age range** 8 plus
- 👫 **Activities** Children's activity leaflet, storytelling and workshops in French; 01 48 09 83 54
- 🕐 **Allow** 1 hour
- ♿ **Wheelchair access** Yes
- 👜 **Eat and drink** *Snacks* Le Mets du Roy opposite the cathedral is the best place for a quick drink. The area is not a good place to linger, so head back to the centre to eat.
- 👫 **Toilets** By the entrance to the crypt

Façade of Basilique St-Denis

opened and the bodies dumped in two large pits. Some of the corpses, particularly Henri IV's, were amazingly well preserved. The graves were reopened in 1817, but the bones were all mixed up and it was impossible to identify any of the royals individually. The remains were placed in an ossuary in the cathedral crypt behind two marble plates inscribed with the names of the kings and queens and their children.

Letting off steam
There is a small pedestrianized square in front of the cathedral. The area is not very nice though, so it is better to head back towards more central parks for a run around.

⑦ Stade de France
Home of Les Bleus

Built for the 1998 football World Cup, the French national stadium is the fifth-largest in Europe and is home to the French football and rugby teams. Stand on the edge of the pitch where the home team won the World Cup, visit the changing rooms and re-live some of the great moments in sporting history in the museum.

Nearly one billion seeds were sown to produce the first pitch, on which France defeated Brazil to win its first World Cup in 1998. The final of the Coupe de France is played here and the stadium is also used for other sporting events and music concerts. From December to January, the stadium is transformed into a winter paradise with activities such as snowboarding,

skating, ice climbing, snowman-building and sledging.

Letting off steam
Get back on the RER and whizz down to the **Jardin du Luxembourg** *(see pp190–91)*, which has a puppet theatre and tennis courts, among other attractions. There is nowhere near the stadium to have a proper run around.

The Lowdown

- 🌐 **Address** ZAC du Cornillon Nord, 93210; 08 92 70 09 00; www.stadefrance.com
- 🚗 **Métro** St-Denis Porte de Paris, line 13. **RER** La Plaine-Stade de France, line B or Stade de France St-Denis, line D. **Bus** 139, 302, 153, 255 & 173
- 🕐 **Open** Guided tours only. Summer & school hols: 10am–5pm; winter: 11am–1pm & 3–5pm weekends & public hols. In English: 10:30am & 2:30pm high season & school hols only; closed Mon in winter
- 💰 **Price** €30–40; under 18s €10; under 5s free; family ticket: €40; for tickets to sporting events and concerts check the website
- 👫 **Age range** 5 plus
- 🤸 **Activities** Sledging and skating
- ⏱ **Allow** 1 hour 15 minutes
- ♿ **Wheelchair access** Yes
- ☕ **Eat and drink** *Snacks* Le 98 is a simple self-service eaterie, which serves a buffet and daily specials. *Family treat* Le Panoramique (01 55 93 04 40; weekends & evenings: by reservation only) is open for lunch from Mon to Fri and has stunning views across the pitch.
- 🚻 **Toilets** Yes

The lost Dauphin
After the execution of his father, 10-year old Louis XVII was dragged off and locked up in Paris's Temple prison. Some stories say he died there in 1795, while others say an unknown boy replaced him. A watchmaker, a naturalist and even a Native American missionary all later claimed to be Louis XVII. However, when the boy believed to be the prince died in prison, a doctor cut out his heart and preserved it in alcohol. It is now in the crypt at St-Denis. DNA tests showed it was definitely that of a Habsburg family member, like his mother Marie Antoinette. So, far from escaping, Louis XVII did die alone in a prison cell.

Jardin d'Acclimatation and around

Amusement parks took off in Europe at the end of the 19th century. The Jardin d'Acclimatation, in the Bois de Boulogne, was inaugurated by Napoleon III in 1860 and is the main children's attraction on the western side of Paris, but there is an interesting mix of other things in the area, old and new. A good way to get around here is by using the Métro, unless you are heading to the Château de Malmaison, which is accessed via RER and bus.

Beyond the City Centre

Parc de la Villette
p200

Central Paris

Jardin d'Acclimatation

Places of interest

SIGHTS

1. Jardin d'Acclimatation
2. Château de Malmaison
3. Parc André Citroën
4. Statue of Liberty
5. Catacombes
6. Parc Montsouris
7. Marché aux Puces de Vanves

Kids on a temporary mini-beach during the summer holidays, Jardin d'Acclimatation

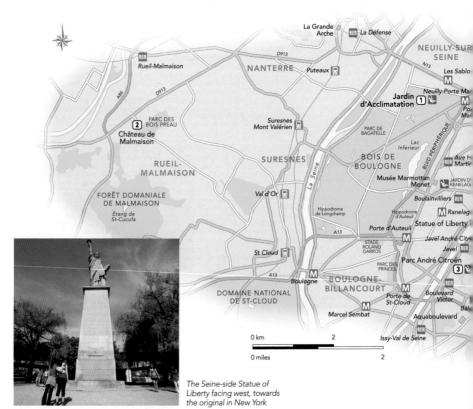

The Seine-side Statue of Liberty facing west, towards the original in New York

The Lowdown

Métro Les Sablons or Porte Maillot, line 1; Javel Andre Citroën, line 10; Lourmel, line 8 or Balard, line 8; Denfert-Rochereau, lines 4 & 6; Alesia, line 4; Porte de Vanves, line 13; Ranelagh, line 9; Porte d'Auteuil, line 10. **RER** Malmaison, lines A & C; Grande Arche La Défense, line A; Blvd Victor, line C; Denfert-Rochereau, line B; Cité-Universitaire, line B.
Bus 95 links southern Paris with the north. 73 runs from the Champs-Elysées to La Défense, passing near the Jardin d'Acclimatation at Les Sablons. 62 links Parc Montsouris with Parc André Citroën.
Tram Pont du Garigliano, T3

i **Visitor information** Paris-Expo, 1 Pl de la Porte de Versailles, 75015; 11am–7pm during trade shows (both professional and open to the public), held all year long

Supermarkets Monoprix Sablons, 72 Ave Charles de Gaulle, 92200 Neuilly. Monop', 113 Ave Charles de Gaulle, 92200 Neuilly. Franprix, 19 Rue Campagne Première, 75014; 6 Blvd Jourdan, 75014; 17 Rue de Javel, 75015 & 109 Ave Paul Doumer, 92500 Rueil-Malmaison. Carrefour, 43 Blvd Brune, 75014. Lidl, 102 Ave Gén Leclerc, 75014. Carrefour City, 154 Rue St-Charles, 75015. Bio C' Bon, 119 Ave Alésia, 75014.

Markets Marché Brune, Blvd Brune, 75014; 7am–2:30pm Thu & Sun. Marché aux Puces de Vanves, Ave Georges-Lafenestre & Ave Marc-Sangnier, 75014; 7am–5pm Sat & Sun. Marché du Livre Ancien et d'Occasion, Parc Georges Brassens, 75015; 9am–6pm Sat & Sun

Festivals French Tennis Open, Stade Roland Garros, 2 Ave Gordon Bennett, 75016; *www.rolandgarros.com* (May–Jun). Solidays, Hippodrome de Longchamp, Bois de Boulogne, 75016; *www.solidays.org*: three-day music festival for the benefit of AIDS charities (Jun). Open-air theatre, Jardin de Shakespeare, Bois de Boulogne, 75016 (May–Oct). Christmas market, La Défense (Nov–Dec).

Pharmacies Dhéry Pharmacy, 84 Champs-Elysées, 75008; 01 42 25 49 95. Pharmacie des Arts, 106 Blvd du Montparnasse, 75014; 9am–midnight Mon–Sat

Nearest playgrounds Jardin d'Acclimatation, Bois de Boulogne, 75016; summer: 10am–7pm; winter: till 6pm (*see pp210–11*). Jardin du Ranelagh, access Chaussée de la Muette/Ave du Ranelagh/Ave Ingres/Ave Prudhon/Ave Raphael, 75016; 10am–7pm; winter: till 6pm (*see p211*). Parc André Citroën, Rue Balard, 75015, 10am–7pm; winter: till 6pm (*see pp212–13*). Parc Montsouris, entrances at Blvd Jourdan and Ave Reille, 75014 (*see pp214–15*). Parc Georges Brassens, from 9am daily; closing time varies seasonally (*see p215*)

Above Parc André Citroën, with families soaking up the sun
Below Bric-a-brac for sale, Marché aux Puces de Vanves

① Jardin d'Acclimatation
Puppet shows, an enchanted river and farm animals

For generations of kids, the epicentre of the vast and leafy Bois de Boulogne has been the wonderfully retro Jardin d'Acclimatation, a *belle époque* amusement park opened by Napoleon III in 1860. There is a large selection of activities and rides for all ages, and plenty of water to splash about in on a hot day. If they tire of that, the surrounding parkland is great for cycling, running and exploring, although leave well before sunset as it gets unsavoury after dark.

A ride to enjoy in Jardin d'Acclimatation

Key Features

① **La Grande Volière** A huge aviary dating from the 1860s, this large enclosure is full of budgerigars, pheasants, partridges and parrots.

② **Gate to Heaven** This gate opens into Le Jardin de Séoul, a beautiful tranquil garden that was given to the people of Paris by the Korean capital.

③ **Rivière Enchantée** The "Enchanted River", which opened in 1927, offers one of the loveliest rides in the park and is perfect for little children.

④ **Le Théâtre du Jardin** This theatre hosts musical shows aimed at kids on Wednesdays, Saturdays and Sundays at 3:30pm, often based on fables or fairy stories. Timings may vary.

⑥ **La Maison de Kiso** This wooden Japanese farmhouse was brought from Japan and rebuilt here in 1860.

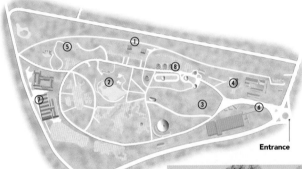

⑤ **La Petite Ferme** Full of turkeys, guinea fowl, rabbits, pigs, swans, sheep, goats, donkeys and even llamas, this little farm is a great place to be.

⑦ **Le Théâtre de Guignol** Located in Napoleon III's Great Stables, this puppet theatre hosts popular shows.

⑧ **Village des Manèges** The innumerable roundabouts and rides for all ages are a major attraction here. The vintage carousel is not to be missed.

Entrance

The Lowdown

🌐 **Map reference** 1 A3
Address Carrefour des Sablons, Bois de Boulogne, 75116; 01 40 67 90 85; www.jardindacclimatation.fr

🚇 **Métro** Les Sablons or Porte Maillot, line 1. **Bus** 43 from Opéra, 73 from the Champs-Elysées, 82 from Trocadéro
Getting around Buses PC1, 174 & 244 serve the Bois and the garden. For a bite to eat, take the PC1 bus two stops from Porte Maillot to Porte de Passy, or walk across the Bois to the 16th *arrondissement*, which has plenty of restaurants. Le Petit Train runs

through the garden from Porte Maillot to its entrance. Round-trip fare: €22.40 with entry ticket

🕐 **Open** Apr–Sep: 10am–7pm Mon–Sun, 10am–10pm Fri; Oct–Mar: 10am–6pm Mon–Sun (to 7pm Sat & Sun), 10am–10pm Fri

💰 **Price** €9–19

👫 **Skipping the queue** Avoid weekends & Wed afternoons, when primary schools are closed

👫 **Age range** All ages

👫 **Activities** Workshops in French: 10am–noon & 2–4pm Wed & Sat, Mon–Sat during school hols; 01

40 67 99 05; book in advance. Puppet shows: 3pm–4pm Wed, Sat & Sun; daily in school hols

🕐 **Allow** 2–3 hours
♿ **Wheelchair access** Yes
🛍 **Shop** By the front gate
🚻 **Toilets** Inside the park

Good family value?
The park's rides are pricey and can soon add up. Keep costs down by spending time in the children's farm and the two playgrounds, which are included in the admission price.

Prices given are for a family of four

Letting off steam

Rent bikes near the entrance of Jardin d'Acclimatation and cycle down to the Lac Inferieur. Avoid the southern part of the park, notorious for prostitution. The "Bois" is best avoided altogether after dark.

Eat and drink

Picnic: under €25; Snacks: €25–45; Real meal: €45–90; Family treat: over €90 (based on a family of four)

PICNIC Les Délices de Bagatelle *(1 Rue Ernest Deloison Neuilly-sur-Seine, 92200)* is a lovely bakery. Picnic in the garden or in the Bois de Boulogne.
SNACKS There are kiosks selling sweet and savoury snacks, three cafés and a crêperie in the Jardin d'Acclimatation.
REAL MEAL La Matta *(23 Rue de l'Annonciation, 75016; 01 40 50 04 66)* serves exceptional pizzas with friendly Italian flair. Try a sorbet to top off the meal.
FAMILY TREAT La Gare *(19 Chaussée de la Muette, 75016; 01 42 15 15 31; http://restaurantlagare. com; Sun brunch; book in advance)*, the old station of La Muette to the south of the Jardin d'Acclimatation, has a lovely terrace and is open all day for drinks and food. On Sundays, clowns and magicians entertain the customers.

Find out more

DIGITAL Watch a film of Jardin d'Acclimatation's marionette puppets in action on *http://tinyurl. com/3gvap5b*.

Magic show enthralling children at La Gare restaurant

Take cover

For a quick culture fix, visit the **Musée Marmottan-Claude Monet** *(2 Rue Louis Boilly, 75016; 01 44 96 50 33; closed Mon)* by the Jardin du Ranelagh, housing 165 of Claude Monet's paintings, his palette and sketchbook. On the other side of the huge Bois de Boulogne, sports fans can take a tour of the **Parc des Princes** (www.lesparcdesprinces.fr), home to Paris St-Germain, the city's top football team, or **Stade Roland Garros** (www.rolandgarros.com), where the French Open tennis tournament is held.

Next stop...

LA DÉFENSE Do not miss this French-style mini Manhattan. Paris's business district is home to a huge modern arch, La Grande Arche, built to mark the Revolution's 200th anniversary. From the front steps is a stunning view along a straight avenue through the **Arc de Triomphe** *(see pp134–5)* to the **Louvre** *(see pp104–5)*.

The popular, open-air La Gare restaurant, bustling with diners

Empress Joséphine's bed, Musée Château de Malmaison

② Château de Malmaison

An emperor's new house

Napoleon's first wife, the charming Joséphine de Beauharnais, bought Malmaison in 1799 when Napoleon was campaigning in Egypt. She spent a small fortune transforming the house and the gardens. There

was soon a heated orangerie with 300 pineapple plants, perhaps to evoke her native Caribbean island of Martinique, and an exotic garden full of kangaroos, llamas, ostriches and zebras.

Napoleon was at his happiest in this small and cosy house and, during the early part of his reign, he took many of his most important decisions here. After their separation, Joséphine continued to live here until her death in 1814. Napoleon came back to spend several days here after his defeat at Waterloo, before departing into exile on the island of St Helena.

There is a fascinating collection of swords in the house. Also on display is the famous painting of Napoleon's dramatic crossing of the Alps by French painter Jacques Louis David, and the cups from which he drank his coffee.

Letting off steam

Little ones might like to pretend to be a bee in this stunning rose garden, choosing a favourite scent and colour from among the hundreds of varieties growing here. Stroll beneath the old trees in the

Above *Tethered hot-air balloon, Parc André Citroën*
Below *Sparkling pool at Aquaboulevard*

romantic **Parc de Bois Preau** (*01 41 29 05 55*), just a few minutes' walk north of the château, to see the statue of Joséphine in her typical empire-line dress. South of the château, the extensive forested grounds include a 15-minute walk down to **Etang de St-Cucufa** (*www.mairie-rueilmalmaison.fr*), a small lake.

③ Parc André Citroën

Water, balloons and old cars

Built on the site once occupied by the Citroën car factory that manufactured the first mass-produced cars in Europe, this park is a wonderful place on a hot day, full of fountains and interesting water features. Kids can run through 120 jets of water that shoot up out of the ground. The big attraction in summer is the tethered hot-air balloon that sails up to 150 m (492 ft) over Paris, offering great views of the city.

There are gardens too: the Jardin Blanc with white flowers and the sunken Jardin Noir, full of dark, almost black foliage. Six other gardens and greenhouses are themed to each represent a different colour, metal, planet, day of the week, type of water and human sense – the Silver Garden, for example, has silvery plants and symbolizes the Moon, Monday, the river and sight. Let the kids try to work out the other five.

Take cover

Whizz down slides, jump in the waves and relax under the palm trees until late at night in Europe's biggest water park **Aquaboulevard** (*4 Rue Louis Armand, 75015; www. aquaboulevard.fr*). It is to the south of the park by the Périphérique.

The Lowdown

🌐 **Address** Ave du Château de Malmaison, 92500 Rueil-Malmaison, Yvelines; 01 41 29 05 55; *www.chateau-malmaison.fr* **Distance** 12 km (7 miles) northwest of Paris along RN13

🚗 **RER** A, La Défense, then bus 27 to stop Le Château

🕐 **Open** 10am–12:30pm & 1:30–5:15pm; weekends till 5:45pm; summer: till 5:45pm Mon–Fri, till 6:15pm Sat & Sun; closed Tue & public hols

💶 **Price** €12–22; under 18s and EU citizens under 26 free

🎧 **Guided tours** Children's audio guide and family tours in English; book in advance

👫 **Age range** 8 plus

🏃 **Activities** Children's activity leaflets and workshops in French

🕐 **Allow** 2 hours

🍽 **Eat and drink** Picnic Au Pain du Cardinal (*3 Pl Richelieu, 92500 Rueil-Malmaison; 01 47 51 22 45; closed Tue*) is good for bread and cakes. Picnic in the park. *Family treat* Les Ecuries de Richelieu (*21 Rue du Docteur Zamenhof, 92501 Rueil-Malmaison; 01 47 08 63 54; noon–2pm & 7–10:30pm, closed Mon; www.ecuries-richelieu.com*) serves classic French food that changes by the season.

🚻 **Toilets** Near the entrance

The Statue of Liberty looking out over the Seine

The Lowdown

- 🌐 **Address** Quai Andre Citroën, 75015; 01 56 56 11 56; www.jardins.paris.fr. Ballon Air de Paris: 01 44 26 20 00; www.ballondeparis.com

- 🚇 **Métro** Javel André Citroën, line 10; Lourmel or Balard, line 8. **RER** Blvd Victor Pont du Garigliano, line C. **Bus** 42, 62, 88 & PC1. **Tram** T3.

- 🕐 **Open** 9am–7:30pm; summer: till 8:30pm; Jul & Aug: till 9:30pm. Ballon Air de Paris: 9:30am–till 30 mins before the park closes

- Ⓒ **Price** Park: free. Ballon Air de Paris: €38–48; €46–56 on weekends, under 3s free

- 👫 **Age range** All ages

- 🤾 **Activities** Playground in the Jardin Blanc: bring table tennis racquets and a bucket and spade as there are sandpits

- ⏱ **Allow** 45 minutes

- 🍴 **Eat and drink** *Picnic* Le Quartier du Pain (74 Rue St-Charles, 75015; closed Sun) is an excellent bakery selling home-made sandwiches and tempting fruit tarts and cakes. Have a picnic in the park. *Family treat* Le Quinzième (14 Rue Cauchy, 70015; 01 45 54 43 43; www.restaurantlequinzieme.com; noon–2pm, 7:45–10pm Mon–Fri) has tables in a quiet pedestrianized sidestreet delighting everyone on a summer evening, and specializes in contemporary French cooking. Kids will enjoy watching the bustling kitchen through the bay window.

- 🚻 **Toilets** By the greenhouses

④ Statue of Liberty
Not in New York

Not only is the French model quite a bit shorter than her sister in New York at 11.5 m (37 ft), she is also a little younger. After creating the giant Statue of Liberty for New York in 1886, the French sculptor Frédéric Bartholdi was commissioned in 1889, by American residents in Paris, to make a copy. She stands on an island in the Seine, gazing westwards and holding a tablet in her left hand. It is engraved with two dates in gold, those of the American and French Revolutions, whereas the New York tablet has only the American date. The Ile aux Cygnes where she stands guard gets its name from an island that is now part of the Champ-de-Mars, where Louis XIV kept his *cygnes* (swans).

Letting off steam
Take a stroll on the island, along the bank of the Seine, or head south to **Parc André Citroën**, a fascinating park with landscaped architecture.

Topiary inside the atmospheric Parc André Citroën

The Lowdown

- 🌐 **Address** Pont de Grenelle, Ile aux Cygnes, 75015

- 🚇 **Métro** Javel André Citroën, line 10. **RER** Javel, line C. **Bus** 70, 72 & 88

- 🍴 **Eat and drink** *Picnic* Poilâne (49 Blvd de Grenelle, 75015; 01 45 79 11 49) is a branch of one of the best bakeries in town and sells quiches and cakes. Picnic beside the riverbank. *Snacks* Dalloyau (69 Rue de la Convention, 75015; 01 45 77 84 27), the Modernist tearoom in one of the city's oldest food shops, is great for tea and cakes.

- 🚻 **Toilets** No

Skulls and bones stacked up in the Catacombes

⑤ Catacombes

Bones, bones and yet more bones

Take a spooky walk past the bones of six million people stacked up from floor to ceiling. A spiral staircase leads down to a labyrinth of tunnels that run under the city, only 2 km (1.25 miles) of which are on view. Eerie and awesome, it is an unusual experience. Although there is often a queue, out of season the tour becomes a much less busy experience, and all the more atmospheric for that.

The city's cemeteries were such a health hazard by the end of the 18th century that they were emptied and the bodies reburied in an old quarry here. Among them are the remains of Jean de la Fontaine and Charles Perrault, authors of some of the most famous fairytales and fables, and the revolutionaries Danton and Robespierre. The Catacombes were opened to the public in 1810 and were originally lit only by flickering candles.

Letting off steam

Carry on the theme and stroll through the tranquil and expansive **Cimetière du Montparnasse** (see p192), which is the nicest in Paris. It is on Rue Froidevaux, about a 10-minute walk from the Catacombes. Among the famous names buried here are the writer Guy de Maupassant and the car manufacturer, André Citroën.

Walk down Avenue René Coty to the atmospheric **Parc Montsouris** where kids can run around.

The Lowdown

🌐 **Address** 1 Ave du Colonel Henri Roi-Tanguy, 75014; 01 43 22 47 63; www.catacombes-de-paris.fr

🚇 **Métro** Denfert-Rochereau, lines 4 & 6. **RER** Denfert-Rochereau, line B. **Bus** 38 & 68

🕐 **Open** 10am–5pm (last admission 4pm), closed Mon and pub hols and during bad weather

💶 **Price** €24–34; under 13s free

👪 **Skipping the queue** Only 200 people are allowed in at a time. Expect to queue 1–2 hours at the weekend and during school hols, especially in bad weather.

👫 **Age range** 10 plus

⏱ **Allow** 45 minutes

🍽 **Eat and drink** *Picnic* Rue Daguerre has a multitude of bakeries and eateries, so is a good stop for breads and pastries. On a sunny day, head to Parc Montsouris for a picnic. *Family treat* Justine (Hotel Pullman Paris Montparnasse, 9 Rue du Commandant Réné Mouchotte, 75014; 01 44 36 44 00; no brunch Jul–Aug) is a great place to relish a sumptuous buffet and offers a baby brunch of mini-hamburgers, candy floss and entertainers in the children's section.

👫 **Toilets** No

⑥ Parc Montsouris

Ducks, puppets and pony rides

Pretty Parc Montsouris is one of the city's most charming parks, with lots of quiet corners and beautiful waterfalls. Off the tourist beat, it is a good place to enjoy Paris like a Parisian. There is a lake with plenty of ducks to feed, as well as huge lawns to picnic on, puppet shows and pony rides. Near the Cité-Universitaire, the park has a lively atmosphere and pretty little cobbled streets run off the western side. There were once a lot of mills in this part of Paris, which attracted hordes of mice, hence the name, Mount Mice. Medieval legend says it was here that the giant Isoire was slain by Guillaume d'Aquitaines. Russian Revolutionaries Trotsky and Lenin used to stroll in the park when they lived in Montparnasse.

Take cover

Over 700 items a day are lost in Paris and end up at the **Lost and Found Office** (Service des Objets Trouvés, 36 Rue des Morillons,

The Lowdown

🌐 **Address** Blvd Jourdan and Ave Reille, 75014

🚇 **Métro** Alésia, line 4. **RER** Cité-Universitaire, line B. **Bus** 21, 67 & 88. **Tram** T3

🕐 **Open** 8am–sunset daily, from 9am Sat & Sun

💶 **Price** Free

👫 **Activities** Concerts at the bandstand in summer. For info on puppet shows visit equipement. paris.fr/theatre-de-guignol-du-parc-montsouris-3414

🍽 **Eat and drink** *Snacks* La Bonbonnière, next to the lake, has a very pretty terrace and serves delicious crêpes and salads. *Family treat* Pavillon Montsouris (20 Rue Gazan, 75014; 01 43 13 29 00; www. restaurant-gastronomique-paris-sud.com; noon–2pm & 7:30–10:30pm; closed Sun dinner, Oct–Apr & two weeks in Feb) is a classic French restaurant. It has a terrace overlooking the park and is particularly lovely on a summer evening.

👫 **Toilets** By the entrance on the corner of Ave Reille and Rue de la Gazan

Peaceful lawns by the lakeside, Parc Montsouris

75015; 08 21 00 25 25). Among the mountains of umbrellas, phones and bags that have been handed in was a false leg found on Bus No. 168 in 2003. Two skulls were left on the Métro in 2002 and a young man mislaid a funeral urn containing his granny's ashes at Père Lachaise Métro station. Also on display in the little museum here are a set of false teeth, a brand new wedding dress and top-secret documents.

⑦ Marché aux Puces de Vanves

Books, buttons and bric-a-brac

Vanves is more old-fashioned and chaotic than the larger flea market at Clignancourt, the Marché aux Puces de St-Ouen (see p206), and a better option with children as it is less expensive and more friendly. On a sunny summer morning, stroll under the acacia trees and find interesting souvenirs among the array of buttons, old teapots and every possible knick-knack. There is an interesting second-hand book market, Marché du Livre Ancien et d'Occasion, located in two

open-air pavilions that were once used as abattoirs. Also on sale are plenty of classic cartoon books.

Letting off steam/Take cover

Parc Georges Brassens, located to the north of Boulevard Lefébvre, is named after the famous singer Georges Brassens, who lived nearby, and has ponds, playgrounds, sculptures and a scented garden.

If it rains, go five Métro stops to the **Musée du Montparnasse** (21 Ave du Maine, 75015; 01 42 22 91 96; www.museedumontparnasse.net). A canteen for needy artists during World War I, it is now an art gallery.

The Lowdown

* 🌐 **Address** Ave Georges Lafenestre & Ave Marc-Sangnier, 75014. Marché du Livre Ancien et d'Occasion: Rue Brancion, 75015
* 🚗 **Métro** Porte de Vanves, line 13. **Bus** 58, 95, 19. **Tram** T3
* 🕐 **Open** Marché aux Puces de Vanves: 7am–5pm Sat & Sun. Marché du Livre Ancien et d'Occasion: 9am–6pm Sat & Sun
* 🎟 **Price** Free
* 🚻 **Skipping the queue** Arrive early for the best selection
* 👫 **Age range** 8 plus
* ⏱ **Allow** 2 hours
* 🍴 **Eat and drink** Picnic Au Délices du Palais (60 Blvd Brune, 75014; closed Wed) is the best bakery in the area. The Parc Georges Brassens is a good picnic spot. Family treat Le Grand Pan (20 Rue Rosenwald, 75015; 01 42 50 02 50; 12:30–2pm & 7:30–11pm Mon–Fri, closed Sat & Sun) is a trendy bistro and a meat-eater's delight.
* 👫 **Toilets** No

Second-hand furniture, old books and china on sale at the Marché aux Puces de Vanves

Picnic under €25; **Snacks** €25–45; **Real meal** €45–90; **Family treat** over €90 (based on a family of four)

Day Trips

Ile-de-France, the region that surrounds Paris, has areas that represent the very essence of provincial France, with castles, abbeys, villages and forests. Whether it is losing track of time like Little Red Riding Hood in the forests of Fontainebleau, pretending to be part of the Sun King's court at Versailles, or joining a French cartoon world at Parc Astérix or an American one at Disneyland, there is plenty to see and do.

Highlights

Château de Versailles
Discover farming royal-style at Marie Antoinette's rustic retreat, the Petit Hameau, and her private palace, the Petit Trianon. Then watch the fireworks on Saturday nights in summer (see pp220–23).

Parc Astérix
Zoom around the loops, dips and bends on Europe's best roller coasters in this Gallic theme park (see pp226–7).

Disneyland® Paris
Meet Mickey and Goofy, ride a runaway mountain train, be Pocahontas, or fly with Peter Pan in this magical park (see pp230–33).

Provins
Watch the eagles fly over the ramparts, or play damsels in distress in the Tour César. Then picnic on Brie de Melun cheese on the ramparts (see p234).

Fontainebleau
Run wild, climb, ride a bike, and relax over a leisurely picnic in the forest, then explore the Renaissance palace (see pp236–7).

Auvers-sur-Oise
Visit a museum designed for kids at Château d'Auvers – it tells of the times, events and places that inspired the Impressionists (see p228).

Left Sparkling blue lake with Marie Antoinette's Petit Hameau farm in the background, in the gardens of Versailles
Above left Characters from the world of Astérix the Gaul in Parc Astérix

Day Trips from Paris

The urban motorway ring road, the Périphérique, divides central Paris from its suburbs like a modern city wall. Beyond the suburbs and the outer, encircling A86, the Ile-de-France has many beautiful rural areas. Some of the best countryside runs in an arch from Provins in the east to Rambouillet in the west, and is dotted with great sights, be they cultural, educational, recreational or just plain fun. They are all perfect for day trips, whether visited on organized guided tours from Paris or independently by public transport or car.

Astérix and his arch-enemies, the Romans, at Parc Astérix

Places of interest

SIGHTS

1. Château de Versailles
2. Rambouillet
3. Le Parc Zoologique de Thoiry
4. France Miniature
5. Parc Astérix
6. Auvers-sur-Oise
7. Abbaye de Royaumont
8. Musée de l'Air et de l'Espace
9. Disneyland® Paris
10. Provins
11. Vaux-le-Vicomte
12. Château de Blandy-les-Tours
13. Fontainebleau

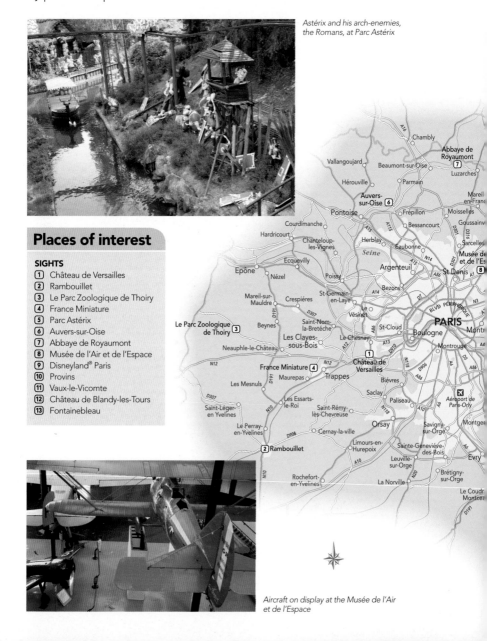

Aircraft on display at the Musée de l'Air et de l'Espace

Colonnaded façade of the Château de Versailles

The Lowdown

RER The RER services many places in the Ile-de-France and trains run right across central Paris, making it a good option to use for a day out. **Train** The suburban train network also connects the main towns and tourist sites with Paris's principal stations. **Car** Ile-de-France is easy to get around by car. The speediest way to reach sights in the west is to take the tunnel to Versailles from Nanterre, €6. Avoid Fri evening and Sun late afternoon when the roads are very busy

Visitor information 25 Rue des Pyramides, 75001; *www.nouveau-paris-ile-de-france.fr*; 10am–7pm daily, May–Oct: 9am–7pm daily; closed 1 May

Supermarkets Monoprix, 58 Rue Grande, 77300, Fontainebleau. Monoprix, 11 Pl Mar Leclerc, 77160, Provins. Monoprix, 5 Rue Clemenceau, 78000, Versailles. Auchan, Val d'Europe shopping centre, Chessy–Marne la Vallée **Markets** La Halle du Marché, 77300, Fontainebleau; Tue, Fri & Sun am. Pl de la Libération, Rambouillet; Sat am. Pl de la Louvière, Rambouillet; Sun am.

Marché Notre-Dame, Carrés Notre-Dame, Versailles; 7:30am–2pm Tue, Fri & Sun; Halles Notre-Dame; 7am–7:30pm Tue–Sat, 7am–2pm Sun. Marché St-Louis, Pl de la Cathédrale St-Louis, Versailles; 7:30am–1:30pm Sat

Festivals Château de Versailles: Les Grandes Eaux Musicales (Apr–Oct: Sat & Sun & some public hols). Les Grandes Eaux Nocturnes (mid-Jun–Sep: Sat). Provins: Les Médievals de Provins; *www.provins-medieval.com*. Son et Lumière (Jun, 1st Sat in Jul & Aug). Harvest festival (last Sun in Aug). Christmas market and living crib (Dec). Disneyland® Paris: St David's Welsh Festival (Mar). St Patrick's Day (17 Mar). Disney Halloween Festival (Oct). Mickey's Magical Fireworks & Bonfire (Nov). Disney Enchanted Christmas (Nov–Jan). There are also special events in the summer season

Pharmacies For details of a late-night chemist anywhere in France visit *www.pharmaciesdegarde.com* or consult the list posted in the window of the nearest pharmacy. Pharmacies can be identified by the green neon cross flashing outside

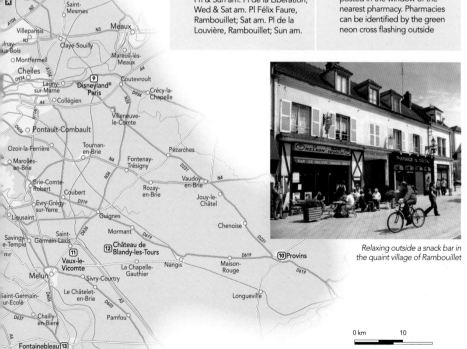

Relaxing outside a snack bar in the quaint village of Rambouillet

0 km 10

0 mile 10

① Château de Versailles
Playground of a Sun King and a shepherdess queen

A stunning palace with fabulous gardens, Versailles is a great place for a day trip, or even a weekend, as there is so much to see and do. All that stood here before 1661 was an old royal hunting lodge, but Louis XIV converted it into Europe's largest palace (see pp222–3). The gardens were just as important to him, and his gardener, André Le Nôtre, spent 40 years flattening hills and draining marshes to make them perfect. Truly special, they are full of fountains and home to two smaller palaces, the Grand and Petit Trianons.

Key Features of the Gardens

① **Orangerie** Louis XIV loved oranges, which were a delicacy, and built this huge garden so he could grow his own.

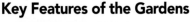

Main Entrance

④ **Potager du Roi**
1 km (0.6 miles)

Palace (see pp222–3)

Hameau de la Reine ⑥
1.5 km (1 mile)

② **Fountains** Ranging from bombastic multi-tiered creations to calm mirrors, fountains abound here. Find the one with a writhing dragon, or where the sun god Apollo is having a bath.

③ **Grand Canal** Louis XIV held extravagant boating parties here. He also kept gondolas, a gift from the Republic of Venice, at the head of the canal in a building known as "Little Venice".

The Lowdown

Address Pl d'Armes, Versailles, 78000 (21 km (13 miles) southwest of Paris); 01 30 83 78 00; www.chateauversailles.fr

RER Versailles Rive Gauche, line C; trains depart every 15 minutes. **Train** SNCF Montparnasse to Versailles Chantiers or St-Lazare to Versailles Rive Droite, both a 20-minute walk from the palace. **Car** A13, exit 2. **Taxi** By the train stations; 01 39 50 50 00 or 01 39 51 04 04

Getting around A mini-train runs from the Château to the Trianon palaces & Hameau de Marie Antoinette (20 minutes on foot);

family ticket €25–35; electric cars €30 per hour; the best option is to hire a bike, €6.50 per hour

Visitor information 2 bis Ave de Paris, 78000; 01 39 24 88 88; www.versailles-tourisme.com; Apr–Sep: 9am–7pm Tue–Sun, 10am–6pm Mon; Oct–Mar: 9am–6pm Tue–Sat, 11am–5pm Sun–Mon

Open Gardens: 7am–6:30pm daily; summer: till 8:30pm; closed Mon & public hols. Palace: 9am–5:30pm Tue–Sun; winter: till 6:30pm; summer: closed Mon & public hols. Potager du Roi: Mar–Oct: 10am–6pm Tue–Sun

Price €30–40; under 18s free; EU citizens under 26 free. Trianon palaces: €20–30; gardens: free. Passport to all sights: €36–46. Grandes Eaux Musicales & Jardins Musicaux; special sessions when all the fountains are turned on, with music and, at night, fireworks: €50–60

Skipping the queue Buy tickets online or at www.fnac.com. Paris Museum Pass accepted; entrance C with a passport ticket is for joint RER tickets sold at stations. The palace is busiest on Tue & Sun. For concerts and firework shows book in advance.

④ **Potager du Roi** Louis XIV loved food, especially melons, figs, peas and asparagus. The king's vegetable garden, Potager du Roi, outside the main gardens, in front and to the left of the entrance to the palace, is a fun place to explore with kids in the summer and autumn months.

⑤ **Petit Trianon** This small château was given to Marie Antoinette by her husband, Louis XVI, when she was 18 years old. It is a magical palace in miniature.

⑥ **Hameau de la Reine** About 1.5 km (1 mile) from the main palace is a thatched village, the Hameau de La Reine. This was Marie Antoinette's dream world, with a ballroom disguised as a barn and a large billiard room.

⑦ **Grand Trianon** On summer evenings, Louis XIV would hold parties at this small palace. Only the ladies of the court were invited.

KIDS' CORNER

Look out for...

1 Apollo. Why are statues and paintings of the Greek Sun God all over the palace?
2 Statues representing the rivers of France around the Water Parterre. Can you name three of them?
3 Golden babies are on the Children's Island on the north side of the garden. How many are there?

Answers at the bottom of the page.

Where's the Queen?

Marie Antoinette spent too much time hiding away at the Petit Trianon. It set tongues wagging, alienated the court and added to her reputation for being an airhead. She alone held the key to the palace, which was decorated with 531 diamonds.

A FRIVOLOUS QUEEN

While Marie Antoinette tied blue bows around the necks of her sheep, French peasants starved to death – the eruption of a volcano in Iceland led to poor harvests, which were followed by bitterly cold winters.

Flying sheep

Plenty of scientific discoveries were made at Versailles. Louis XIV brought the best scientific minds to the palance and founded an Académie des Sciences here in 1666. He also had a rhinoceros brought all the way from India to put in his personal zoo. There was an electricity demonstration in the Hall of Mirrors and in 1783 the first hot-air balloon took to the air. The passengers were a rooster, a duck and a sheep called *Mont au Ciel*, or "Up to the Sky."

Answers: 1 Louis XIV, who was known as the Sun King, identified with him. **2** The Marne, the Garonne and the Rhône. **3** Six.

Guided tours Audioguide for kids over 8 years old. The palace shop sells a useful children's guide *My Little Versailles*. Tours in English €46–56, under 10s free. Download podcasts from *www.chateauversailles.fr*

Age range 5 plus for château

Activities Children's workshops in French. Son et Lumière, History Galleries; 01 30 83 78 00; Oct–Jun: school hols & some weekends. Farm workshop at the Petit Trianon

Allow 2–3 hours

Wheelchair access Yes

Café Grand Café d'Orléans, just outside the palace, and several restaurants along the canal

Shop Children's books in English available at the Librairie des Princes, a delightful children's bookshop

Toilets Cour Royale, Hameau de Marie Antoinette, La Petit Venisse & the Buvette du Dauphin for baby changing facilities

Good family value?
Excellent value especially if visitors get around on foot. Although it can be tiring, the sheer diversity of things to see makes boredom impossible.

① Château de Versailles continued ▶

Château de Versailles continued
2,300 rooms, 67 staircases and 1,944 windows

After Louis XIV moved into his splendid new palace, he made most French aristocrats come and spend time at his court. Around 3,000 people lived in the palace at any one time, often in cold and dingy apartments, but near the centre of power and favours. It symbolized all that was wrong with the Ancien Régime and only just escaped being destroyed in the Revolution. Head for the Hall of Mirrors, passing through the first-floor rooms, and then head for the park.

Queen's bedroom

Key Features of the Palace

King's Bedroom This room was strategically located on the axis of the sun's journey across the sky, affirming that Louis XIV was at the centre of the world.

Chapelle Royale Louis XIV attended mass here every morning. The first floor was reserved for the royal family and the ground floor for the court.

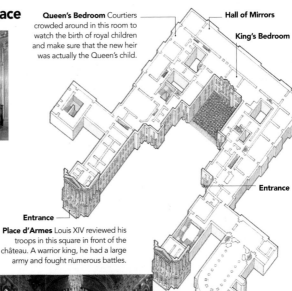

Queen's Bedroom Courtiers crowded around in this room to watch the birth of royal children and make sure that the new heir was actually the Queen's child.

Hall of Mirrors

King's Bedroom

Entrance

Chapelle Royale

Entrance

Place d'Armes Louis XIV reviewed his troops in this square in front of the château. A warrior king, he had a large army and fought numerous battles.

Hall of Mirrors The treaty that ended World War I was signed in this sparkling hall in June 1919.

Eat and drink

Picnic: under €25; Snacks: €25–45; Real meal: €45–90; Family treat: over €90 (based on a family of four)

PICNIC Guinon (*60 Rue de Paroisse, 78000; 01 39 50 01 84; closed Mon & Sun pm*) is the place to shop for a picnic in the town of Versailles. This bakery has been cooking up food since 1802. Picnic in the gardens.
SNACKS La Parmentier de Versailles is a refreshment stand, which in high season is at the Grand Trianon Square and Southern bank of the Grand Canal and in low season at Domes Grove Alley and Grand Trianon Square. It sells baked potatoes with different toppings.
REAL MEAL Angelina (*Pavillon d'Orleans, Château de Versailles 78000; closed Mon*), located in the château, is the place for a teatime treat. Eat macaroons and drink the famous hot chocolate. There are many cafés and ice cream stalls in and around the château and gardens.
FAMILY TREAT Trianon Palace (*1 Blvd de la Reine, 78000; 01 30 84 50 00; www.trianonpalace.fr*), located outside the gardens, is a

Angelina, a great teatime spot in the Château de Versailles

Prices given are for a family of four

Shopping at the vegetable and fruit shop in the Potager du Roi

hotel with a restaurant run by Gordon Ramsay. Try Sunday brunch, which is served here on the terrace overlooking the park in summer and, in winter, in the room where President Clemenceau once dictated the terms of the 1919 peace agreement. It is especially good at Christmas, when there is a Christmas market, a skating rink and cooking classes for children in the hotel.

Find out more

DIGITAL At *http://tinyurl.com /239gsg8* watch *Marie Antoinette, The Last Queen of France*, a drama-documentary that sheds a different light on the accepted story of a frivolous, self-indulgent queen who alienated France. Two historical video games, *Versailles Mysteries* and *Marie Antoinette* and the *War of Independence*, can be found at www.nemopolis.net.
FILM Older children will enjoy watching *Marie Antoinette* (2006), directed by Sofia Coppola, which gives a Hollywood view of life at Versailles, while *Versailles: Le Rêve d'un Roi* (2007) is a colourful French drama about Louis XIV.

Shopping

There are plenty of designer shops selling children's clothes in the town of Versailles but shopping is a bit stuffy and prim. Pick up some unusual vegetables at the **Potager du Roi** *(see p221)*, the former palace kitchen garden where, in the 18th century, they grew new and exotic fruits from the colonies.

Next stop...

FUN AND FROLICS Watch the sword-wielding riders at the **Bartabas Academy of Equestrian Arts** *(Grande Ecurie du Roi; www. bartabas.fr)*, which puts on shows in the former royal stables at weekends and on certain weekdays. Take a quick look at the **Salle du Jeu de Paume** *(Rue du Jeu de Paume; tours: Sat 3pm)*, the old tennis court, where a meeting was held in June 1789 that sparked the French Revolution. In summer head for **France Miniature** *(see p225)*, and feel like a giant in Europe's largest miniature model. The **Playmobil Funpark** *(www.playmobil-funpark. fr)*, 17 km (11 miles) east at Fresnes, is an ideal place for younger kids.

(see p221)

(see p225)

Kids playing in the colourful Playmobil Funpark

② Rambouillet
Lambs, trains and trees

Rambouillet is a lovely, classic French town, situated on the edge of the Forêt de Rambouillet, an enchanting forest full of birds of prey, deer and wild boar. It is dominated by the **Château de Rambouillet**, the official summer residence of the French president, which has fairytale towers and the Queen's Dairy, where Marie Antoinette used to play at being a milkmaid. Napoleon spent his last night in France here on 30 June 1815.

For kids, the highlight of the trip is bottle-feeding the lambs during lambing season at the **Bergerie Nationale**, the national sheep

Lions being fed at Le Parc Zoologique de Thoiry

Geese on the lush lawns of the Château de Rambouillet

farm, founded in 1784. Don't miss the **Musée Rambolitrain**, which has 4,000 miniature train models.

Letting off steam

Climb trees and get up close to the birds at Odyssée Verte, the forest park at **Espace Rambouillet** (*3 Rue de Groussay, Rambouillet, Yvelines, 78120; 01 34 83 05 00; www.onf.fr/espaceramb*), which features 19 bridges and 18 platforms. Take a walk and enjoy rock climbing by the Abbaye des Vaux-de-Cernay, a ruined abbey in the old stone quarries located on the edge of the Forêt de Rambouillet. In winter there is also an ice-skating rink in Place Félix Faure in the town centre.

③ Le Parc Zoologique de Thoiry
Animal magic

Kids will love the drive through this safari park, one of Europe's finest, full of elephants, giraffes, hippos and bears. There is also a zoo, which can be visited on foot. Here children can watch lions from glass tunnels and get face to face with a tiger. Among other inhabitants are red pandas, lemurs and even Komodo dragons. The park also features gardens of rare plants, laid out in 1708, and there is a great maze with a few raised bridges from which to plan a route to the middle, or spot lost kids. It makes for a great day out with a good mix of entertainment and culture.

Take cover

Visit the **Château de Thoiry** in the park, which includes the Salon Blanc, where everything, including the piano, is white. The château is uniquely positioned so that during the summer and winter solstices, the sun's rays form a "bridge of light" in the main hall that lights up the building like a lantern.

Getting close to the animals in the zoo at Le Parc Zoologique de Thoiry

The Lowdown

🌐 **Address** Rambouillet, Yvelines, 78120 (55 km (34 miles) southwest of Paris); www.rambouillet-tourisme. fr. Bergerie Nationale: Parc du Château, 78120; www.bergerie-nationale.educagri.fr. Musée Rambolitrain: 4 Pl Jeanne d'Arc, 78120; www.rambolitrain.com

🚆 **Train** Gare Montparnasse to Rambouillet. **Car** A13, then A12, then N10
Getting around Baladobus runs from the station to the main sights on Sun & public hols from Apr–Oct. Day pass: €11–21 for a family

ℹ️ **Visitor information** Pl de la Libération, 78120; 01 34 83 21 21; 9:30am–noon & 2:30–5:30pm; Jul–Aug: till 6pm; tourist office hires out pocket computers programmed with information in English, €5

🕐 **Open** Château de Rambouillet: 10am–noon & 2–5pm; summer: till 6pm; closed Tue, public hols and

when the president is in residence. Bergerie Nationale: Wed, Sat, Sun & public hols 2–5pm; daily in school hols; winter: Sat & Sun; closed three weeks Dec–Jan. Musée Rambolitrain: 10am–noon & 2–5:30pm Wed–Sun; closed two weeks in Jan

💰 **Price** Château de Rambouillet: €14–24, under 18s free; Bergerie Nationale: €20–30, under 3s free; Musée Rambolitrain: €12–22

🧒 **Activities** Children's workshops during the school hols at the château & the Musée Rambolitrain

⏱️ **Allow** At least half a day

🍴 **Eat and drink** *Picnic* La Vieille Boulange (*6 Rue Général de Gaulle, 78120*) sells sweet and savoury snacks. Picnic in the forest. *Real meal* Villabate (*15 Ave du Maréchal Leclerc, 78120; 01 30 88 67 35; closed Wed*) serves good pizza.

🚻 **Toilets** In the château and museum

The Lowdown

🌐 **Address** Rue du Pavillon de Montreuil, Thoiry, 78770 (40 km (25 miles) west of Paris); 01 34 87 40 67; www.thoiry.net

🚗 **Car** The only way to visit with a family is by car. Take the A13, followed by the N12, exit at Thoiry. The nearest train station is over 6 km (4 miles) away

🕐 **Open** 10am–5pm; summer: till 6pm; winter: till 4:30pm

💲 **Price** €130–140; under 3s free

🍴 **Guided tours** Tours are in English for the château by a guide in period costume. Trips to Thoiry from central Paris. The visit includes transport through the park, visit to the zoo, gardens and château; www.pariscityvision.com

👫 **Age range** All ages

⏱ **Allow** A full day

☕ **Eat and drink** *Picnic* Migros Hypermarket *(Centre Commercial Val Thoiry, Thoiry, 01710)* is best for buying supplies. There are also several places to picnic in the zoo. *Snacks* There are several kiosks selling drinks and sandwiches in the park.

🚻 **Toilets** At several locations in the park and in the château

④ France Miniature
Cut down to size

Laid out on a piece of land shaped like the map of France, this miniature landscape is crisscrossed by rivers, and train tracks with engines whizzing over bridges and into tunnels. An outdoor theme park, it features scale models of major French landmarks and monuments. Look out for the Alps; the Autoroute de Soleil, which runs next to the Mediterranean; the amphitheatre at Arles; and St-Tropez with film star yachts bobbing in the bay. Feel like a giant beside a mini version of the famous Eiffel Tower. The Parisian monuments offer a different perspective on some very well-known buildings. All in all there are 116 models of the most fascinating places in France.

Take cover
The park is almost entirely outdoors, but kids aged 4 to 10 will have great fun driving little electric cars around a cartoon town in **Ronde des Zotos** while the grown-ups watch.

Examining the small-scale wonders at France Miniature

The Lowdown

🌐 **Address** Blvd André Malraux, Elancourt, 78990 (40 km (25 miles) southwest of Paris); 01 30 16 16 30; www.franceminiature.com

🚆 **Train** Gare Montparnasse to Elancourt La Verrière, then bus 411. **Car** A13, then A12 and N12 direction Dreux

🕐 **Open** 10am–6pm; summer: till 7pm; autumn & spring opening times vary; closed winter

💲 **Price:** €70–80; under 4s free; tickets are cheaper if bought online seven days in advance

👫 **Age range** All ages

⏱ **Allow** Half a day

☕ **Eat and drink** *Picnic* Intermarché *(Rue du Fond des Roches, Les 4 Arbres, Elancourt, 78990)* is the closest supermarket. There is a large, partly covered picnic area in the park, with an Eiffel Tower view. *Real meal* Les Provinces, located in the park, has surprisingly good food for a theme park.

🚻 **Toilets** By the entrance, the picnic area and Ronde des Zotos

Picnic under €25; **Snacks** €25–45; **Real meal** €45–90; **Family treat** over €90 (based on a family of four)

⑤ Parc Astérix
Greedy Gauls, rotten Romans and roller coasters

By 50 BC, Julius Caesar had conquered most of Gaul, now France, except for a tiny unnamed village situated in the province of Armorica. Parc Astérix is centred on this legendary village, which Astérix the Gaul and his sidekick Obélix famously defended from the Roman invaders. The park, which has lots of charm and was approved by Astérix's creator, Albert Uderzo, has exhilarating rides and, of course, plenty of colourful characters to meet and greet.

Figure of a Roman in Parc Astérix

Key Features

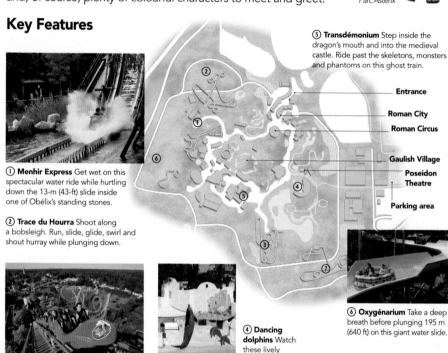

⑤ **Transdémonium** Step inside the dragon's mouth and into the medieval castle. Ride past the skeletons, monsters and phantoms on this ghost train.

Entrance

Roman City

Roman Circus

Gaulish Village

Poseidon Theatre

Parking area

① **Menhir Express** Get wet on this spectacular water ride while hurtling down the 13-m (43-ft) slide inside one of Obélix's standing stones.

② **Trace du Hourra** Shoot along a bobsleigh. Run, slide, glide, swirl and shout hurray while plunging down.

③ **Goudurix** Twirl upside-down seven times at a speed of 75 km (47 miles) per hour on this thrilling roller-coaster ride.

④ **Dancing dolphins** Watch these lively creatures in a superb magical show that will enchant kids.

⑥ **Oxygénarium** Take a deep breath before plunging 195 m (640 ft) on this giant water slide.

⑦ **Tonnerre de Zeus** Ride the biggest wooden roller coaster in Europe, which whizzes along at 80 km (50 miles) per hour to the summit of Mount Olympus.

Letting off steam

The park features a range of rides and attractions. There is a huge playground beside the Gaulish Village, the **Druids' Forest**. Walk in the footsteps of the wise old druid Getafix, through the menhirs and the shifting swamps. It is located next to the **Ronde des Rondins**, a mini roller coaster suitable for younger members of the family. When the park opens for the Christmas holidays there are plenty of shows and entertainment and also a lovely ice-skating rink.

Prices given are for a family of four

Eat and drink

Picnic: under €25; Snacks: €25–45; Real meal: €45–90; Family treat: over €90 (based on a family of four)

PICNIC Bring your own food to keep costs down, buying picnic provisions in Paris. Picnic by the lake.
SNACKS Food kiosks and cafés are scattered across the park.
REAL MEAL Aux Fastes de Rome is a fast-food outlet in the Roman City, with a pleasant terrace. **Le Cirque** is the best bet for a good hot meal. It also has an indoor play area for kids near the Oxygénarium.

Fun façade and entrance to the park's popular restaurant, Arcimboldo

FAMILY TREAT Arcimboldo, located near the exit of the Gaulish Village, is decorated with a mountain of plastic fruits and vegetables and has classic dishes on the menu.

The Lowdown

🌐 **Address** Plailly, Oise, 60128; 08 26 46 66 26; www.parcasterix.fr

🚗 **RER** Aéroport Charles de Gaulle, line B3. Shuttle bus leaves every 30 minutes, 9:30am–6:30pm. Joint train and entry tickets available.
Bus Direct shuttle-bus to Parc Astérix from Paris; departs from Carrousel du Louvre: 8:45am, return 6:30pm; €70–80 return
Car A1 in the direction of Lille, exit Parc Astérix; parking €8
Distance 35 km (22 miles) north of Paris

🛒 **Supermarket** Leclerc; off A1 at Fosses; exit 7, about a 20-minute drive from Parc Astérix

➕ **First-aid centre** Near the windmill on the main street up from the entrance

🕐 **Open** Apr–Aug: 10am–6pm Mon–Fri, 9:30am–6pm Sat, Sun; Sep–Oct: 10am–6pm Sat, Sun; late-night opening for Gaulish nights in Jul & Aug. Check website for timings

💲 **Price** €157–167; under 3s free. Check website for special offers

👫 **Skipping the queue** Avoid Sun. Buy tickets online.

👫 **Age range** 7 plus

👫 **Activities** Water-based rides

⏱ **Allow** A full day

👫 **Toilets** On the left by the entrance, on the left of the village and by the circus big top

Good family value?
Kids have to love the stories of Astérix to get the best out of the trip. Cut costs by bringing a picnic.

Water tours inside the Gaulish Village

Shopping
There is no end to the souvenirs here featuring Astérix, Obélix, Dogmatix and the rest – on towels, glasses, T-shirts, key rings and fridge magnets. The park also offers a good selection of the books and films in English. *Astérix and the Golden Sickle*, the second volume in the famous comic-book series, is set in Lutetia, now Paris.

Find out more
DIGITAL: A magical web potion can be taken at www.asterix.com
FILM: There are as many as 11 films based on this popular comic strip. *The Twelve Tasks of Astérix* (1976) is unique as it is not based on an existing book. The Romans almost win in *Astérix and the Big Fight* (1989). Gérard Depardieu is hilarious as Obélix in *Astérix and Obélix*

(1999), *Astérix and Obélix: Mission Cleopatra* (2002) and *Astérix and the Olympic Games* (2008).

Take cover
There are daily shows at the Poseidon Theatre and the Roman Circus, but usually only at weekends and in high season.

Next stop...
FORÊT D'ERMENONVILLE Be Getafix and gather leaves to make magic potions in the Forêt d'Ermenonville. To get there take the A1 to the city of Senlis, 10 km (6 miles) north of the theme park, then the D330A east for 4 km (2 miles) and south on the N330 through the forest. Head back to Lutetia to check the old Roman amphitheatre at Arènes de Lutèce (see p178).

Well-manicured garden at the Château d'Auvers

Exhibits on Impressionism in the multimedia museum, Château d'Auvers

⑥ Auvers-sur-Oise

An Impressionist day out

Some of the most famous painters of the late 19th and early 20th century were drawn to the beautiful views and river walks in and around the picturesque village of Auvers-sur-Oise. Kids will love the **Château d'Auvers**, an interesting multimedia museum specially designed to introduce children to the Impressionists and the city that inspired them. In 1890, famous Dutch painter Vincent van Gogh spent the last two months of his life at Auvers.

Penniless and exhausted, he worked day and night, frantically painting 70 paintings in 70 days, working outside in all kinds of weather. He died in room No. 5 at the **Auberge Ravoux** after shooting himself in the stomach. After his death, the room was never let out again.

Letting off steam

Stroll along the banks of the Oise to Pontoise, a favourite walk of the artist Camille Pissarro, or dig sandcastles in the huge sandy beach at **Isle d'Adam**, which was a favourite weekend spot of painter Marc Chagall and his family.

⑦ Abbaye de Royaumont

Monks, mills and forests

Surrounded by wetlands and beautiful forests, the medieval Abbaye de Royaumont is a tranquil place with avenues of chestnut trees and a garden of medicinal plants. Centred a magnificent cloister, it was built in 1228 by King Louis IX, and was one of his favourite places. Until the Revolution, it remained one of the most important Cistercian monasteries in France. In 1791 it was converted into a cotton mill and the church was destroyed. The giant bell in the middle of the courtyard is all that remains. The restored abbey is now a cultural centre.

Letting off steam

Take a walk from the car park across the fields. King Louis IX was inspired to build the Abbaye de Royaumont after a walk in the nearby fairytale **Forêt de Carnelle**, just south of the abbey. Park by the lake, La Lac Bleu, just off the D85 near St Martin du Tertre.

The Lowdown

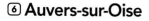

🌐 **Address** Oise, 95430; www.auvers-sur-oise.com. Château d'Auvers: www.chateau-auvers.fr. Auberge Ravoux: www.maisondevangogh.fr

🚗 **Train** From Paris, Gare St-Lazare, change at Pontoise. Direct train from Gare du Nord at 9:56am, Apr–1 Oct, Sat, Sun & pub hols. **Car** A86/A15, then A115 in the direction of Clergy-Pontoise. Exit Auvers-sur-Oise in the direction of the Château d'Auvers. **Distance** 35 km (22 miles) north of Paris. **Getting around** In summer, take the ferry from Auvers to Isle d'Adam. Rent bikes in front of the tourist office

ℹ️ **Visitor information** Rue de la Sansonne, 95430; 01 30 36 10 06; www.lavalleedeloise.com; 9:30am–12:30pm & 2–5pm; summer: till 6pm; closed Mon

🕐 **Open** Chateau d'Auvers: 10:30am–6pm; winter: till 4:30pm; closed Dec, Jan & Mon. Auberge Ravoux: 10am–6pm Wed–Sun; closed Nov–Mar

💶 **Price** Chateau d'Auvers: €46–56; under 6s free. Auberge Ravoux: €20–30; under 11s free

👫 **Skipping the queue** Pass Auvers offers reduced-price entry to the museum. Visit during the weekend and school hols to avoid sharing space with school trips

🎧 **Guided tours** Château d'Auvers has an audio guide

👫 **Age range** 5 plus

🤸 **Activities** Château d'Auvers has workshops on Wed & school hols

⏱️ **Allow** A full day

♿ **Wheelchair access** No

🍽️ **Eat and drink** *Snacks* Sous le Porche (35 Pl de la Marie, 95430; 01 30 36 16 50; www.sousleporche.com), in front of the town hall, is a great place to have ice cream. *Real meal* l'Impressionist Café (Château d'Auvers, 95430; 01 34 48 48 48) has a beautiful enclosed courtyard. The café serves traditional French food, from simple lunches to gastronomic meals.

🚻 **Toilets** In the Château d'Auvers and Auberge Ravoux

Beautiful cloister garden of the Abbaye de Royaumont

The Lowdown

🌐 **Address** Asnières-sur-Oise, Oise, 95270; 01 30 35 59 70; www.royaumont.com

🚗 **Car** A1 north, exit 5, then D922 east. **Distance** 35 km (22 miles) north of Paris

🕐 **Open** 10am–5:30pm

💶 **Price** €28–38; under 7s free; family ticket €20

👫 **Age range** 6 plus

🎭 **Activities** Concerts, workshops & family activity leaflet in French

⏱ **Allow** 1–2 hours

♿ **Wheelchair access** Yes

🍴 **Eat and drink** Picnic Carrefour (Route d'Asnières, 95270; closed Sun) is good for buying supplies. Picnic in the gardens. Snacks The abbey café serves tea at weekends and on public hols. They also serve savoury tartines, cakes and salads.

🚻 **Toilets** In the abbey

⑧ Musée de l'Air et de l'Espace

Up, up in the air

Air travel began in France when the Montgolfier brothers invented the hot-air balloon in 1783. The air and space museum is located in one corner of the terminal of the Le Bourget, which is the oldest airport in Paris. Begun in 1919, the museum collection is one of the oldest of its kind in the world, although it was only moved to its present site in 1975. Discover how Louis Bleriot won £15,000 flying across the Channel, climb aboard a World War II bomber and get up close to a Concorde. Look out for the only remaining piece of the Oiseau Blanc, the White Bird, which took off from Le Bourget in 1927 to attempt a Transatlantic crossing, but

Aircraft models outside the Musée de l'Air et de l'Espace

disappeared over the Atlantic. The museum shop has a wide selection of models.

Letting off steam

There is nowhere close by to run about in. Get back on the Métro and head into town: line 7 stops at the Palais Royal–Musée du Louvre station. Enjoy a peaceful stroll in the beautiful gardens of the **Jardin des Tuileries** (see p108).

An aircraft at the Musée de l'Air et de l'Espace

The Lowdown

🌐 **Address** Aéroport de Paris, Le Bourget, 93352; 01 49 92 70 00; www.museeairespace.fr

🚇 **Métro** La Courneuve, line 7, then bus 152. **RER** Le Bourget, line B. **Bus** 152 from Porte de la Villette or 350 from Gare l'Est and Gare du Nord. **Car** A1, exit 5. **Distance** 35 km (22 miles) north of Paris

🕐 **Open** 10am–6pm; winter: till 5pm; closed Mon, 1 Jan & 25 Dec

💶 **Price** Allow €65–75; permanent exhibitions are free but there are additional charges to visit some of the planes and to use the simulator

🎧 **Guided tours** Audio guide in English; €12 for four people

👫 **Age range** 5 plus

🎭 **Activities** Daily in English in the Planète Pilot; 10:30am, noon, 1:30pm & 3pm

⏱ **Allow** 1–2 hours

🍴 **Eat and drink** Real meal L'Hélice is ideal for lunch and snacks too. In summer, there are tables almost under the wings of a 747.

🚻 **Toilets** At the entrance

⑨ Disneyland® Paris
Mickey's kingdom

There is hardly a kid on the planet who would turn down a trip to Disneyland, so it is not surprising that Disneyland® Paris is the most visited theme park in Europe. In fact it comprises two theme parks – Disneyland® and Walt Disney Studios®. Here, children can meet their favourite cartoon characters and take a spin on some of the best rides on the continent. In addition, there is the Disney® Village, which has restaurants, shops and the Buffalo Bill Wild West Show. The main Disneyland® Park is divided into five different lands, linked by the 19th-century-style shopping street, Main Street, USA®.

Mickey in Buffalo Bill's Wild West show, Disney® Village

Key Features

① **Main Street, USA®** Based on Disney's home town of Marceline, Missouri, this fantasy land is full of shops and restaurants. The magical Disney parade takes place here every afternoon, making it a good place to finish the day.

② **Disneyland Railroad** Walt Disney was a great train enthusiast and had his own miniature steam train in his garden. The railroad runs along the perimeter of the park and stops in Main Street, USA®; Frontierland®; Fantasyland® and Discoveryland®.

③ **Adventureland®** Enjoy the wild rides and exciting animatronics, be Peter Pan and battle the pirates here. Take a perilous jungle ride with Indiana Jones, then play Swiss Family Robinson up in the trees.

Walt Disney Studios®

Entrance

Disney® Village

④ **Frontierland®** Visit the haunted house, ride on a paddle steamer and get the adrenalin going on the thrilling roller coaster, Big Thunder Mountain, in this homage to America's Wild West. Phantom Manor is a ghost ride with excellent special effects.

⑤ **Sleeping Beauty's Castle** Step into the pink fairytale castle, which features a dragon in its dungeon and stained-glass windows showing popular characters.

⑥ **Discoveryland®** With a futuristic theme, this is the place to set off on an intergalactic adventure. It includes Buzz Lightyear Laser Blast®, an interactive ride, and is the most interesting part of the park for older kids.

⑦ **Fantasyland®**
Make this the first stop – it's where the true Disney magic is found. All the classic characters are here to be greeted. It is the perfect part of the park for younger kids, with fairytales such as Snow White and the Seven Dwarfs being brought to life.

KIDS' CORNER

Look out for...
1 King Arthur's Sword in the Stone in Fantasyland®.
2 Captain Hook's pirate ship in Adventureland®.
3 Aladdin's lamp in Adventureland®.
4 Alice's amazing maze, the Curious Labyrinth, in Fantasyland®.

Top 10 Rides

1. PHANTOM MANOR
Ghoulish laughter and ghostly apparitions provide scary company on this classic ghost train ride in Frontierland®. The graveyard scenes are a little scary for very small children.

2. BIG THUNDER MOUNTAIN
Enjoy discovering an abandoned mine aboard a runaway train that cranks and creaks in the most ominous way before plunging at high speed into the darkness. One of the park's most popular attractions, it is in Frontierland®.

3. PINOCCHIO'S FANTASTIC JOURNEY
Set in Fantasyland®, this ride revisits the second full-length feature film made by Disney, as the little wooden puppet struggles to become a real boy.

4. IT'S A SMALL WORLD
In Fantasyland®, this is the best ride in the park for very small children. Take the kids on a musical tour of the world, watching out for the monkeys swinging overhead.

5. SNOW WHITE AND THE SEVEN DWARFS
Travel through the forest past the wicked witch and then watch Snow White being rescued by her prince in Fantasyland®. This ride is quite scary for very young children.

6. PETER PAN'S FLIGHT
Located in Fantasyland®, this is perhaps the most magical ride in the park. Jump aboard a pirate ship and fly across London at night, all the way to Neverland.

7. PIRATES OF THE CARIBBEAN
Watch pirates attack a Spanish fort from a river boat on this great boat ride in Adventureland®.

8. INDIANA JONES™ AND THE TEMPLE OF PERIL
Rattle on a roller coaster through a jungle full of exotic ruins on this perilous ride in Adventureland®.

9. SPACE MOUNTAIN: MISSION 2
Blast off into space and travel to the edge of the universe on the biggest thrill ride in Discoveryland®. Not for the faint-hearted, and only for those over 1.32 m (4 ft).

10. BUZZ LIGHTYEAR LASER BLAST®
Head to Discoveryland® for this exciting, interactive game – ride in laser-armed star cruisers and help Buzz save the universe.

HAPPY BIRTHDAY MICKEY!
Mickey Mouse's birthday is officially 18 November 1928, even though he first put in an appearance in May 1928. He was originally voiced by Walt Disney himself.

How well do you know your cartoons?
1 Which was Disney's first full-length feature film?
2 What is the name of Disney's flying elephant?
3 What poisoned fruit does the Queen give Snow White?
4 What animal does Pinocchio turn into?
5 What is the Little Mermaid's real name?
6 Which movie features Captain Jack Sparrow?

Answers at the bottom of the page.

Monsieur Disney
Walter Disney was descended from a Norman knight, Robert d'Isigny, who invaded England with William the Conqueror in 1066. In 1918, during World War I, Disney came to France to drive an ambulance.

Answers: 1 *Snow White and the Seven Dwarfs* (1937) **2** Dumbo. **3** An apple. **4** A donkey **5** Ariel. **6** Pirates of the Caribbean.

⑨ Disneyland® Paris continued ▶

Disneyland® Paris continued

Letting off steam

There are two playgrounds: the Pocahontas Indian Village in Frontierland® and the Plage des Pirates in Adventureland®.

Eat and drink

Picnic: under €25; Snacks: €25–45; Real meal: €45–90; Family treat: over €90 (based on a family of four)

PICNIC Even though picnics are not allowed in the park, no one is going to stop kids from eating so carry snacks and water. The money-saving

option is to buy biscuits from the souvenir shops. There is a designated picnic area outside the entrance too.

SNACKS Casey's Corner *(Main Street, USA®)* serves hot dogs. Eat a waffle from one of the stands that are scattered all over the park.

REAL MEAL Rainforest Café® *(Disney® Village; 01 60 43 65 65)* is where visitors can experience eating in a jungle, complete with a tropical rainstorm every 30 minutes.

FAMILY TREAT Auberge de Cendrillon *(Fantasyland®; 01 60 30 40 50)* is the best – and the most

expensive – restaurant in the park. Classic French dishes are on offer, but the main draw for kids is the chance to spend time with Cinderella and her mice, and other Disney characters. Reserve in advance.

Find out more

DIGITAL Go to www.disney.fr, www.disney.co.uk/playhouse-disney or www.hiddenmickeys.org for fun and games.

FILM Watch DVDs of the cartoons with a French feel such as *Aristocats* (1970), *Beauty and the Beast* (1991), *Sleeping Beauty* (1959), *Cinderella* (1950), *The Hunchback of Notre-Dame* (1996) and *Ratatouille* (2007).

Shopping

The **Disney® Village**, just outside the park, is full of shops and restaurants, which stay open after the park has closed so there is no need to rush to shop in the park itself. Purchases made in the park before 3pm can be delivered to hotels or to the Disney® Village for collection at the end of the day. Souvenirs are expensive, so choose the bigger shops where there is more choice among the cheaper

Guests enjoy a meal in the tropical-themed Rainforest Café®

The Lowdown

🌐 **Address** Marne la Vallée, 77705 (32 km (20 miles) east of Paris); www.disneylandparis.com

🚗 **Train** RER A to Marne la Vallée, just outside the park, takes 45 minutes from Paris; trains run every 15 minutes; joint RER & entry ticket available. Direct Eurostar from London St Pancras; www.eurostar. com. **Bus** Airport buses from Charles-de-Gaulle & Orly airports every 30 minutes; www.vea.fr. **Car** A4, exit 14; parking €15

ℹ️ **Visitor information** City Hall, Main Street, USA®. Studio Services, Walt Disney Studios®, Pl des Frères Lumière. Lost & found: Kids who get lost in the park are taken to Coin Bébé by the Plaza Gardens Restaurant, Main Street, USA®. Lost property is taken to City Hall, Main Street, USA®

➕ **First-aid centre** In the park by the Plaza Gardens Restaurant, Main Street, USA®

🕐 **Open** 10am–9:30pm Mon–Fri, 10am–10pm Sat & Sun; check the website before visiting as there are different hours for the main park and Walt Disney Studios®. Times may also vary according to season. Disney® Village is open all day until very late at night.

💲 **Price** One-day one-park pass for main park only: €168–248; under 3s free; day pass, for both parks: €228–308; under 3s free. Tickets are cheaper if bought online; 2–3-, 4- and 5-day passes available. Look out for promotions, especially in Jan–Mar when ticket price covers admission to all parks. See the website for promotions on hotel packages; there are often good deals for families but they change seasonally. Disney® Village: free

👥 **Skipping the queue** There can be long queues both to get into the parks and for individual rides – up

to an hour in high season. To avoid entrance queues, arrive at least 30 minutes before the park opens, or book in advance online, by phone, through a travel agent, on Channel ferries, at Eurostar terminals, at Disney Stores or at RATP Métro stations. Avoid Sundays and, if possible, peak holiday seasons. Once inside, the **Fastpass®** system allows visitors to pre-book for some rides without queueing: insert the park ticket into the Fastpass machine at a ride entrance to get a Fastpass ticket with a time slot, and return at the allotted time. However, each person can only hold one Fastpass ticket at a time and many rides are fully booked by noon. The **VIP Fastpass®** offered by some Disney hotels gives instant access to some rides, and the **Disneyland® Hotel Fastpass®** gives timed entry to a choice of attractions for guests. Disney hotel guests can enter the park at 8am in high season.

Prices given are for a family of four

Colourful entrance to the Disney Store in the Disney® Village

The fantasy-castle architecture of the Disneyland® Hotel

options. The **Liberty Arcade** *(Main Street, USA®)* shop is a good option. Buy books, stationery, videos, posters and CDs at the cosy **Storybook Store** *(Main Street, USA®)*. **La Boutique du Château** *(Fantasyland®)* is a year-round Christmas-themed shop. Shop here for Christmas cards and holiday decorations. Kids will enjoy spending hours in the big **Disney Store** *(Disney® Village)* and browsing through the collection of merchandise, including clothes and toys. **World of Disney**, located at the entrance of Disney® Village, offers a vast and exciting range of Disney merchandise.

Staying over

The best way to relax is to stay overnight at one of the on-site hotels, which are also in Disney®

Village. For children the bonus is that at the end of the day, when the park is empty, it is possible to have several goes on some of the rides. The hotels closest to the park are the most expensive. The most luxurious hotel is the **Disneyland® Hotel** *(see p247)*. The main attraction here is a view of the fairytale castle down Main Street, USA®, and the copious breakfast with Disney characters. Kids will love **Hotel Cheyenne®** *(see p247)*, which looks like a Wild West movie set. Some hotels also have indoor and outdoor pools. Watch out for seasonal package deals available for families on the official website.

Next stop...

WALT DISNEY STUDIOS® Under-10s will be exhausted by a day out at Disneyland® Park, so do not plan anything for the first evening. On day two head over to **Walt Disney Studios®**, the smaller theme park, next to the Disneyland® Park. This is the place to discover the world of the movies and find out how films are made, especially animated cartoons in the Toon Studio. The central feature of Front Lot, just inside the giant studio gates, is a fountain in the shape of Mickey. The big attraction is Toy Story Playland with rides such as the Toy Soldiers Parachute Drop and the Slinky Dog Zigzag. Do not miss the Studio Tram tour, which travels through an earthquake in an oilfield and on to the destroyed city of London. The Twilight Zone Tower of Terror™ is a white-knuckle ride, good for older children.

Baby Switch allows parents to take turns holding the baby while the other one rides, without going to the back of the queue. **Queue fatigue busters** An information board in the Central Plaza lists queueing times. Some attractions in Adventureland® rarely get busy: Les Cabanes des Robinson, Adventure Isle, Le Passage Enchanté d'Aladdin and Sleeping Beauty's Castle in Fantasyland®. In bad weather rides may be closed, so take cover in the Liberty and Discovery arcades.

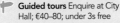 **Guided tours** Enquire at City Hall; €40–80; under 3s free

Age range All ages

Activities Disney Parade, 5pm daily; check website or central notice board by the Plaza Gardens Restaurant, Main Street, USA®. Get an entertainment programme from City Hall.

Allow A full day, or 2 days for both parks. If staying in a Disneyland® hotel, arrive the night before to meet the Disney characters at breakfast.

Café There are food kiosks and cafés across the park and a baby change with microwaves by the Plaza Gardens Restaurant, Main Street, USA®.

Toilets Across the park. Baby facilities by the Plaza Gardens Restaurant in the Central Plaza, Main Street, USA®

Good family value?
Disneyland® Paris is very expensive, and it is not everybody's cup of tea – some visitors feel it has not stood the test of time well and is getting a little shabby – but most kids love it. It is well worth seeking out special promotions and planning your visit carefully to make the most of it.

Entrance to the all-action Walt Disney Studios® park

Picnic under €25; **Snacks** €25–45; **Real meal** €45–90; **Family treat** over €90 (based on a family of four)

Children riding bikes in the delightful town of Provins

The Lowdown

🌐 **Address** Seine-et-Marne, 77160 (75 km (47 miles) southeast of Paris); www.provins.net

🚗 **Train** From Paris, SNCF Gare de l'Est. **Car** A5 direction Troyes, exit 16 then D408 and D619

ℹ **Visitor information** Office de Tourisme de Provins, Chemin de Villecran, 77482; 01 64 60 26 26; 10am–5:30pm daily; Apr–Sep: till 6:30pm

💲 **Price** €27–37 for all sights; €30 for a family pass to see four monuments; budget €12–22 to visit one sight

🍴 **Guided tours** Weekends & public hols; GPS video guide available from the tourist office is good for families

👫 **Age range** All ages

👫 **Activities** Horse and warfare shows: 01 60 67 39 95; www. equestrio.fr. Birds of prey: 01 60 58 80 32; www.vollibre.fr. Easter egg hunt. In summer the tourist train drawn by a tractor cuts down walking; €19

⏱ **Allow** At least 3 hours

♿ **Wheelchair access** Limited

🍽 **Eat and drink** *Picnic* Intermarché (15 Ave du Maréchal de Lattre de Tassigny, 77160) is the best place to buy supplies. Picnic on the ramparts. *Family treat* La Taverne des Oubliées (14 Rue St-Thibault, 77160; 06 70 50 08 58; www. provins-banquet-medieval.com) is perfect for kids to enjoy a medieval banquet.

👫 **Toilets** In the tourist office

Prices given are for a family of four

⑩ Provins

Ramparts, eagles and medieval warfare

High on a plateau, the medieval capital of the Counts of Champagne dominates the pretty surrounding countryside and is often used as a film set for medieval Paris. Plunge into a world of knights and princesses, exploring the ramparts that still surround the old town and the mysterious underground tunnels. Be Rapunzel in the Tour César, a huge keep that was occupied by the English during the Hundred Years' War. In summer there are spectacular horse shows and displays of medieval warfare. Do not miss the fascinating birds of prey in action on the city walls.

Letting off steam

Run along the ramparts, which are especially lovely at sunset. With vast, fortified gates, they were built between the 11th and 14th centuries and are uniquely well preserved.

⑪ Vaux-le-Vicomte

A château fit for Puss in Boots

Vaux-le-Vicomte is so beautiful that when Louis XIV saw it in 1661, he had a fit of jealousy. Nicolas Fouquet, the king's Lord High Treasurer, had hired the most talented artists of his time to create this storybook château, and it was so opulent that Louis was convinced Fouquet had stolen the money from his treasury to build it. Louis condemned Fouquet to life imprisonment and stole his architect, Le Vau, to design his own new home at Versailles *(see pp220–23)*. Vaux-le-Vicomte is a great place to visit with children. There are plenty of things to do in addition to special events organized for kids. It is at its most enchanting on summer evenings, when it is lit by candlelight, and at Christmas.

Letting off steam

Children can choose from several puzzle books, available in English as well as French, in which they have to solve riddles and find clues to help them make their way around the castle and its beautiful gardens, laid out by Louis XIV's landscape gardener, André Le Nôtre.

Souvenirs and fancy dress on display in a shop at Vaux-le-Vicomte

Old and young enjoy Vaux-le-Vicomte, seen across the André Le Nôtre gardens

The Lowdown

🌐 **Address** Seine-et-Marne, 77950 (55 km (34 miles) southeast of Paris); 01 64 14 41 90; www.vaux-le-vicomte.com

🚗 **Train** From Paris, SNCF & RER D Gare de Lyon to Melun, then a 20-minute ride in a taxi, or château bus from the station on weekends in summer; return ticket €7. **Car** A6, A4 then join A5 in the direction of Troyes, exit St-Germain Laxis

🕐 **Open** Mar–Nov: 10am–6pm daily. Check website for details

💶 **Price** Family ticket €47; under 6s free

👫 **Skipping the queue** Avoid busy summer weekends

🚩 **Guided tours** Audio guide & children's guide in English €2; fancy dress tours; costume hire €4 weekends, public & school hols

👫 **Age range** All ages

👫 **Activities** Easter weekend egg hunt. Candlelight tours & fireworks some Sats in summer. Chocolate Fair, Nov. Christmas events for children, Dec. Fountain show in the gardens, Mar–Nov

⏱ **Allow** At least half a day

♿ **Wheelchair access** Limited

☕ **Eat and drink** Picnic Carrefour (Rond-Point de la Main Verte, Lieusaint, 77127) is best for buying supplies if coming by car. Picnic in the gardens. Family Treat L'Écureil (01 60 66 95 66), an upmarket café and restaurant in the stables at the château is ideal for Sun lunch. There are drawing activity sheets for kids. The restaurant also serves snacks in the self-service area.

👫 **Toilets** By the restaurant

⑫ Château de Blandy-les-Tours

Tantalizing towers and commanding views

The imposing Château de Blandy-les-Tours, located in the heart of the peaceful medieval village of the same name, looks as if it has jumped out of a storybook. This fortified castle was built by one of the knights who fought with Philippe Auguste at the Battle of Bouvines in 1214, when the English were badly defeated.

Most sections of the castle were rebuilt during the Hundred Years' War, when it was on the front line.

Climb up onto the ramparts and admire the views from the towers.

Letting off steam

The village is in the heart of pretty countryside famous for its tasty Brie cheese. From the castle there is a lovely walk across the fields to the old windmill at **Chaunoy** (follow yellow arrows from church).

Towers of the Château de Blandy-les-Tours

The Lowdown

🌐 **Address** Seine-et-Marne, 77115 (70 km (44 miles) southeast of Paris); 01 60 59 17 80

🚗 **Car** The only way to visit Blandy-les-Tours with a family is by car. A5 direction Troyes, exit 16, then follow D47

🕐 **Open** 10am–12:30pm & 1:30–6pm (until 5pm in winter), closed Tue & public hols

💶 **Price** €12–24; under 25s free

👫 **Skipping the queue** Visit on weekdays, when there are few visitors

🚩 **Guided tours** Children's guides in French for kids aged 6–8 and 9–12

👫 **Age range** 3 plus

⏱ **Allow** 1 hour

♿ **Wheelchair access** Limited

☕ **Eat and drink** Picnic Proxi (20 Pl des Tours, 77115) is the place to buy supplies. Picnic by the river. Real meal Le Donjon (19 Pl Tours, 77115; 01 60 66 90 66; closed Tue), the local village café-restaurant, has outside tables. Try the omelette made with local Brie cheese.

👫 **Toilets** In the main courtyard

Picnic under €25; **Snacks** €25–45; **Real meal** €45–90; **Family treat** over €90 (based on a family of four)

⑬ Fontainebleau

Tranquil forests and formal gardens

The royal château at Fontainebleau was little more than a hunting lodge when, in the early 16th century, it was transformed into a Renaissance palace by François I, who discovered this new style while campaigning in Italy. Later kings, queens and mistresses have left their mark too and it was one of Napoleon's favourite residences. Much quieter and more intimate than Versailles, it is surrounded by beautiful gardens and a fairytale forest with pretty villages and winding paths.

Colouring book in the château shop

Key Features

Jardin de Diane This garden features a bronze fountain of goddess Diana as huntress.

The Grand Parterre The largest formal garden in Europe, it was created between 1660 and 1664 by André Le Nôtre and Louis Le Vau.

Throne room Napoleon's grandiose throne room is decorated with golden eagles and bees, both of which were the symbols of his power.

Chapel Louis XV was married to the Polish princess Marie Leczinska here.

Main Apartments

Escalier du Fer-à-Cheval

Galerie François I

Cour de la Fontaine

Entrance–Cour d'Honneur

Escalier du Fer-à-Cheval The famous horseshoe-shaped staircase, designed by Jean Androuet du Cerceau, dates from the reign of Louis XIII and was based on a Renaissance model.

The Grand Parterre

Grand Canal Henri IV commissioned a 1,200-m (3,937-ft) long canal to run through the wooded park.

Galerie François I François I was so proud of this gilded gallery that he was the only person allowed to carry the key.

The Lowdown

🌐 **Address** Seine-et-Marne, 77300; 01 30 71 50 70; www.musee-chateau-fontainebleau.fr

🚗 **RER** Gare de Lyon, SNCF Grandes Lignes. Bus 1 runs from the bus station to the château. **Train** Gare de Lyon; combined train & entrance ticket available. **Car** A6 direction Lyon, exit Fontainebleau. **Distance** 69 km (43 miles) south of Paris **Getting around** Bike hire from the tourist office costs €5 per hour, but a car is necessary to explore the whole area. Baby carriers are available

ℹ **Visitor information** 4 Rue Royale, 77300; 01 60 74 99 99; www.fontainebleau-tourisme.com

🕐 **Open** Château: 9:30am–5pm, till 6pm in summer, closed Tue; gardens: 9am–5pm, till 7pm in summer

🎫 **Price** Château: €22–32; under 18s free for main apartments; Gardens: free. Check website for extra charges for tours and some areas of the château

🎫 **Guided tours** Audio guide €3; children's audio guide in French

👫 **Age range** All ages

🏃 **Activities** Activity leaflets and workshops for children in French. Canoeing trips and sporting activities: Ikopa Adventure, 19 Rue Paul Séramy, Fontainebleau, 77300; 06 21 09 37 50; www.ikopa.com. Top Loisirs, Moret sur Loing; 01 60 74 08 50;

www.toploisirs.fr. Walks and bike routes: Champagne sur Seine; 01 60 39 07 04

♿ **Wheelchair access** Yes for the château

🕐 **Allow** 1.5 hours

☕ **Café** In the Cour de la Fontaine in spring and summer

🛍 **Shop** At the exit of the château, stocking a good selection of colouring books for kids

🚻 **Toilets** At the entrance & the exit from the château

Good family value?
Fontainebleau is not pricey and offers both indoor and outdoor sightseeing, which makes it ideal for a family day out. Entry prices are halved an hour before it closes.

View of the château at Fontainebleau from across the garden

Letting off steam

Kids will enjoy running along the paths around the Grand Canal and playing at the playground in the château gardens. Row across the castle lake in a boat or ride in a horse-drawn carriage in the grounds. Another option is to go horse riding at **Horse Dreams** (www.horse-dreams.com), near Ury, which takes around 15 minutes by car. There are also workshops, visits and events available for families to discover the château together. See website for details (www.musee-chateau-fontainebleau.fr).

Eat and drink

Picnic: under €25; Snacks: €25–45; Real meal: €45–90; Family treat: over €90 (based on a family of four)

PICNIC Monoprix (58 Rue Grande, 77300) is the best place to shop for supplies. Rue des Sablons has shops selling excellent bread, tasty cheese, fruit and vegetables. Picnics are prohibited in the palace gardens but not in the park.
SNACKS Le Grand Café (33 Pl Napoleon Bonaparte, 77300), one of the cafés by the old-fashioned merry-go-round, is a good place to stop for a drink and to observe the bustle of the town.

Walking paths in the lush, green forest of Fontainebleau

REAL MEAL Pizza Pazza (1 Rue Bouchers, 77300; 01 60 72 05 61), a popular and friendly pizzeria, serves small versions of any pizza on their menu for children.
FAMILY TREAT La Table des Maréchaux (9 Rue Grande, 77300; 01 60 39 55 50; noon–11pm), located in the luxurious Hôtel Napoleon, has a beautiful terrace overlooking the garden and an excellent buffet diner.

A window display featuring books for kids at Reel Books

Shopping

Reel Books (9 Rue de Ferrare, 77300) sells children's books in English and French. Look out for farm shops along the side of the road. The area east of Fontainebleau is famous for its Brie and Coulommiers cheese.

Find out more

FILM Louis XIII, one of the characters in The Three Musketeers (1993), was born at Fontainebleau.

Next stop...

FORESTS OF FONTAINEBLEAU
South of the château, via the Carrefour de Matignon on the N6, Fontainebleau's forests have walking trails with beautiful views. There is a lovely walk from the village of Barbizon, 10 minutes northwest by car along the D64. Barbizon was the home of the landscape painter Jean-François Millet, who inspired Van Gogh. Also a short drive away is the medieval town of Moret-sur-Loing, which inspired Impressionist painter Alfred Sisley. Hire a canoe here for a trip on the River Loing.

Where to Stay in Paris

Hotels tend to cluster by type in Paris. Most of the deluxe hotels, among them some of the most family-friendly in Europe, are to be found around the Champs-Elysées and the Tuileries, while boutique hotels, which have fewer family facilities, are more numerous on the Left Bank and in Montmartre.

AGENCIES

RentApart
http://france-appartements.com
The most upmarket of the rental agencies. Rates begin at around €100 per night for a studio apartment.

Haven in Paris
www.haveninparis.com
A boutique vacation rental agency, which offers luxury apartments and villa rentals across Paris.

Ile de la Cité, Ile St-Louis and around

HOTELS

Relais du Louvre
Map 10 G4
19 Rue des Prêtres–St-Germain-l'Auxerrois, 75001; 01 40 41 96 42; http://relais-du-louvre-paris.com; Métro: Pont Neuf
This historic hotel is situated just by the church of St-Germain l'Auxerrois, next door to the Louvre. The highlight for families is the huge top-floor apartment, which can accommodate five people and has adjoining rooms that can easily make a family suite. Breakfast is served in the room only.
P
€€

Hôtel Britannique
Map 10 H4
20 Ave Victoria, 75001; 01 42 33 74 59; www.hotel-britannique.fr; Métro: Châtelet
Located just moments from the main sights on Ile de la Cité, this three-star hotel shows considerable attention to detail and oozes Grand Tour charm. The suite for four is good value and the hotel is air-conditioned. There is a hearty breakfast and a warm welcome for children.
€€€

Hôtel du Jeu de Paume
Map 11 C6
54 Rue St-Louis en l'Ile, 75004; 01 43 26 14 18; www.jeudepaumehotel.com; Métro: Pont Marie
A discreet courtyard entrance leads to a unique 17th-century timbered building that was once a tennis court. A golden Labrador greets guests at the door and sets the tone for this homely yet ultra-chic hotel. For the upper price band it is good value, and has room service. The relaxing atmosphere in the heart of the Ile St-Louis makes this one of the loveliest hotels in the city. There are also two apartments for long stays (five nights minimum) with a kitchen, living room and several bedrooms.
€€€

SELF-CATERING

Résidence Le Petit Châtelet
Map 10 H4
9 Rue St-Denis, 75001; 01 42 33 32 31; www.lepetitchatelet.com; Métro: Châtelet
Housed in a charming old-fashioned house in the heart of historic Paris, the Résidence Petit Châtelet offers air-conditioned apartments for four to six people. The apartments on the top floors have small balconies but the downside is that there is no lift, and it can be a bit noisy at night.
€

Citadines St-Germain-des-Prés
Map 10 G5
53 Quai des Grands Augustines, 75006; 01 44 07 70 00; www.citadines.com; Métro: St-Michel
Located opposite the Ile de la Cité, these self-catering apartments are within walking distance of many of the main sights. All apartments have a kitchenette and air conditioning. There is a laundry room, which is great for families. The hotel offers a babysitting service and breakfast is optional.
P
€€€

Beaubourg & the Marais

HOTELS

Hôtel du Nord – Le Pari Vélo
Map 11 D1
47 Rue Albert Thomas, 75010; 01 42 01 66 00; www.hoteldunord-leparivelo.com; Métro: République or Jacques Bonsergent
The excellent-value family room in this small, cosy hotel just north of the Marais is one of the best budget options in Paris. The breakfast, served in the cellar room, is tasty and there are adult bikes – free for guests. *Vélo* is French for bikes, hence the name.
€

Hotel Ibis Bastille Opéra
Map 12 F5
15 Rue Breguet, 75011; 01 49 29 20 20; www.ibishotel.com; Métro: Bastille or Breguet-Sabin
This no-frills chain hotel has air-conditioned rooms that are cheaper at weekends and if booked online. The rooms are basic but modern. The bonus for families is a

Contemporary decor at the Hôtel du Jeu de Paume

great price for the location, even if you have to book two rooms.
🔲 P €€

Hôtel Jeanne d'Arc Map 11 D5
3 Rue de Jarente, 75004; 01 48 87 62 11; www.hoteljeannedarc.com; Métro: St-Paul
This two-star hotel is located just moments from Place Ste-Catherine, where there are lovely bars and restaurants. The family room for four people is a bargain. The mosaic mirror in the breakfast room might give kids some creative ideas. Breakfast is competitively priced. €€

Novotel Les Halles Map 11 A4
8 Pl Marguerite de Navarre, 75001; 01 42 21 31 31; www.novotelparis.com; Métro: Les Halles
This branch of the family-friendly Novotel chain is a good choice for those planning to spend a day at Disneyland, because of its proximity to the RER train station. Two children can stay free in their parents' room, making this one of the best bargains for families in central Paris. There is also a 50 per cent discount on a second room. The hotel has a kids' play area.
🔲 €€

Le Pavillon de la Reine Map 11 D5
28 Pl des Vosges, 75003; 01 40 29 19 19; www.pavillon-de-la-reine.com; Métro: Bastille or St-Paul
This has suites for families of four and, although there is no restaurant, the café Carette, on the doorstep, more than compensates for this. Place des Vosges has a sandpit for kids. The hotel is air-conditioned and has a spa. Babysitting is provided.
🔲 P €€€

BED & BREAKFAST
Appartement d'Hôtes de la Folie Mericourt Map 12 F3
20 Rue de la Folie Mericourt, 75011; 01 77 15 69 54; www.appartement-hotes-folie-mericourt.com; Métro: St-Ambroise
This B&B, in a self-contained apartment for four to six people, offers breakfast and the option of dinner. Cots are available. There are two other locations, near Oberkampf and République, if this apartment is already booked.
🔲 €

Entrance to the charmingly old-fashioned Hôtel Chopin

Bonne Nuit Paris Map 11 D3
63 Rue Charlot, 75003; 01 42 71 83 56; www.bonne-nuit-paris.com; Métro: République or Temple
Built in 1609, this tastefully restored house is full of old beams and plenty of modern comforts. The owners serve home-made jams and their own honey for breakfast. A baby cot and child's folding bed are available. €€

SELF-CATERING
Citadines Marais Bastille Map 12 E4
37 Blvd Richard Lenoir, 75011; 01 53 36 90 00; www.citadines.com; Métro: Bastille, Breguet-Sabin or Chemin Vert
This branch of the Citadines aparthotel chain is in a great location close to the cafés of the Marais, and is ideal for a long stay with children. Air-conditioned apartments for up to four people each have a kitchenette, and a babysitting service is offered.
🔲 €€

See also Hôtel Britannique, p238

Tuileries, Opéra & Montmartre
HOTELS
Hôtel de la Cité Rougemont Map 4 H6
4 Cité Rougemont, 75009; 01 47 70 25 95; www.hotel-paris-rougemont.com; Métro: Grands Boulevards
This basic but friendly two-star hotel, close to the Musée Grevin and the main shopping area, offers good-sized family rooms for four people. Ideal as a short stay option, it has cable Internet connection. €

Hôtel Alba Opéra Map 4 G4
34 Rue de la Tour d'Auvergne, 75009; 01 48 78 80 22; http://albaoperahotel.com; Métro: Notre-Dame de Lorette
A boutique hotel offering rooms for four people, with basic kitchenettes including a microwave. The hotel has plenty of history – Louis Armstrong and Toulouse-Lautrec stayed here – and it is within walking distance of the Musée Grevin.
🔲 €€

Hôtel Chopin Map 4 G6
10 Blvd Montmartre (46 Passage Jouffroy), 75009; 01 47 70 58 10; www.hotelchopin.fr; Métro: Richelieu Drouot
This old-fashioned two-star hotel opened in 1846. The tiny rooms are basic but there is a romantic view across rooftops from the top floor. It is a good location for families, in the Passage Jouffroy next to the Musée Grevin and the staff are friendly. €€

Hôtel des Trois Poussins Map 4 F4
15 Rue Clauzel, 75009; 01 53 32 81 81; www.les3poussins.com; Métro: St-Georges
This modern, air-conditioned hotel has good-sized rooms with bathrooms, including one triple room. Cots and a kitchenette are available on request. The hotel does not have a restaurant but there are plenty located close by.
🔲 €€

Cosy interiors of Le Pavillon de la Reine

Price Guide
The following price ranges are based on one night's accommodation in high season for a family of four, inclusive of service charges and any additional taxes.
€ Under €200; €€ €200–350; €€€ over €350

Key to symbols see back cover flap

Ibis Berthier Porte De Clichy
Map 3 C1

163 bis Ave de Clichy, 75017; 01 40 25 20 20; www.ibishotel.com; Métro: Porte de Clichy

An excellent-value chain hotel with family and interconnecting rooms. The draw for families, besides the price, is the location opposite a modern park on the edge of the Batignolles district, which has another more traditional park. There is also an indoor swimming pool in the hotel.

|O| P €€

Tim Hotel
Map 4 F2

11 Rue Ravignan, 75018; 01 42 55 74 79; www.timhotel.com; Métro: Abbesses

A picturesque hotel located in a pedestrianized square not far from Sacré-Coeur. The rooms are tiny and basic, but are outstanding value given the location. For families there are rooms for three with great views.

€€

Hôtel du Louvre
Map 10 F3

Pl André Malraux, 75001; 01 44 58 38 38; http://louvre.concorde-hotels.fr; Métro: Palais Royal–Musée du Louvre

Built in 1887, this lovely hotel is located just across the road from the Louvre. The large double rooms, which are misleadingly called suites, can accommodate an extra bed and cot. There are six actual suites, one of which hosted famous actress Angelina Jolie's sizeable family.

|O| P €€€

Beautiful belle époque exterior of The Westin Paris–Vendôme

Le Burgundy
Map 9 D2

6–8 Rue Duphot, 75001; 01 42 60 34 12; www.leburgundy.com; Métro: Madeleine

Le Burgundy offers family-friendly luxury all round. A light and airy hotel with a welcome pack and teddy bears for children, its duplex rooms are excellent for families. The location is great, being within walking distance of many of the top sights. There is a swimming pool. A babysitting service is offered.

|O| €€€

Park Hyatt Vendôme
Map 10 E1

5 Rue de la Paix, 75002; 01 58 71 12 34; www.paris.vendome.hyatt.com; Métro: Opéra

This is the chic place to stay for film stars and celebrities. The rooms are state of the art, and there are four restaurants, a spa and a baby-sitting service. The big draws are the quiet rooms overlooking the patio, and the spectacular suites.

|O| P €€€

Terrass Hôtel
Map 4 E2

12 Rue Joseph de Maistre, 75018; 01 46 06 72 85; www.terrass-hotel.com; Métro: Blanche

This renovated four-star hotel is in a lovely building with a stunning seventh-floor terrace. It has big, airy suites and junior suites that are ideal for families. Many have balconies with amazing views and one of the suites has an interactive touch-screen table and floating bed that will delight older kids.

|O| €€€

The Westin Paris–Vendôme
Map 9 D2

3 Rue Castiglione, 75001; 01 44 77 11 11; www.starwoodhotels.com; Métro: Tuileries

This rather grand, family-friendly four-star hotel is right opposite the Jardin des Tuileries. The rooms are large but the smaller attic rooms have the most charm. Cots and high chairs are provided.

|O| €€€

BED & BREAKFAST
Loft Paris
Map 4 E2

7 Cité Véron, 75018; 06 14 48 47 48; www.loft-paris.fr; Métro: Pl du Clichy

These four quirky fully equipped apartments are in a little cobbled road just behind the Moulin Rouge,

Entrance to the fully equipped apartments of Résidhome Paris-Opéra

with plenty of restaurants close by. The atmosphere is cosy, but it is not a good option for those with small children as there is no lift.

€€

Paris Oasis
Map 4 H2

14 Rue André del Sarte, 75018; 01 42 55 95 16; www.paris-oasis.com; Métro: Anvers

These family-sized top-floor apartments are well maintained. Kids will love the indoor pool and the garden. There is a minimum stay of three nights but it is excellent value for the location. Guests can use the washing machine but there is no breakfast.

€€

SELF-CATERING
Adagio Apartments Montmartre
Map 4 G3

10 Pl Charles Dullin, 75018; 01 42 57 14 55; www.adagio-city.com/montmartre; Métro: Pigalle

The big draw for families is the good location, just moments from Sacré-Coeur in an area packed with restaurants and delis. There are fully modern air-conditioned apartments for up to seven people, each with a kitchenette and microwave. It also features a small, pretty garden, which is a welcome bonus for the children. Cots are available and there is a laundry room.

P €

Résidhome Paris-Opéra
Map 3 D5

30 Rue Joubert, 75009; 01 56 35 00 35; www.residhome.com; Métro: Havre Caumartin

This hotel offers modern, air-conditioned apartments, some of which are duplexes for up to six people. There are wooden floors and all amenities for babies. The apartments are cleaned weekly but additional cleaning is available. There is also a babysitting service.

🗁 P   €€

See also Relais du Louvre, p238, Adagio Haussmann, p242, Hotel Apollon, p244 & Pullman Montparnasse, p245

Champs-Elysées & Trocadero

HOTELS

Hôtel Residence Foch   Map 1 B4
10 Rue Marbeau, 75116; 01 45 00 46 50; www.foch-paris-hotel.com; Métro: Porte Maillot
These spacious, air-conditioned apartments for up to five people are excellent value. The hotel has a breakfast lounge and there are several good restaurants nearby.

🍶   €€

Four Seasons Hotel George V   Map 2 F5
31 Ave George V, 75008; 01 49 52 70 00; www.fourseasons.com/paris; Métro: Georges V
This lovely traditional deluxe hotel has a fantastic array of children's activities, which include whizzing up some sumptuous madeleines in the kitchen with the pastry chef and special kids' tours of Paris. Kids have their own animal soap set and are greeted by a toy and a welcome pack. There is an indoor swimming pool. Babysitting is provided.

🍶 🍽️ P   €€€

Hôtel Baltimore   Map 1 D6
88 Ave Kléber, 75016; 01 44 34 54 54; www.accorhotels.com; Métro: Boisière
The Hôtel Baltimore is part of the MGallery boutique chain, within the Accor hotels group. It is in a peaceful area, and some of the rooms have a view of the Eiffel Tower. Only one child under 11 is permitted to share a room with their parents but interconnecting rooms are available. The hotel has a fitness centre and a babysitting service is available.

🍽️ P   €€€

Hotel de la Trémoille   Map 2 G6
14 Rue de la Trémoille, 75008; 01 56 52 14 00; www.tremoille.com; Métro: Alma Marceau
Located on a quiet street in the heart of Paris's 8th *arrondissement* close to the Champs-Elysées and Avenue Montaigne, this hotel opened in 1923. Although the exterior has maintained its original Haussmann façade, with original features including wrought-iron balconies, the interiors are ultra-modern. The big draw for families is the exquisite service and the 13 suites. Some of the guestrooms have their own private balconies. There is also a fitness centre.

🍽️ P   €€€

Hôtel du Collectionneur   Map 2 G3
51–57 Rue de Courcelles, 75008; 01 58 36 67 00; www.hoteldu collectionneur.com; Métro: Courcelles
This luxury hotel, decorated in Art Deco style, has good-sized rooms. The location is excellent, just a stone's throw from the Champs-Elysées and by the golden gates of the Parc Monceau. The 59 suites are the best option for families and the executive lounge has all-day refreshments, which is a bonus for children. There is an outdoor terrace restaurant in summer. A baby-sitting service is provided.

🍶 🍽️ P   €€€

Hôtel Elysées Regencia   Map 2 F5
41 Ave Marceau, 75016; 01 47 20 42 65; www.regencia.com; Métro: Kléber
This modern, chic hotel has a cosy atmosphere and is just a short walk from the Champs-Elysées. The rooms are good value for a four-star hotel

and most have a small sitting room. There are interconnecting family rooms but there is no restaurant.

       €€€

Hôtel Keppler   Map 2 E5
10 Rue Kepler, 75016; 01 47 20 65 05; www.keppler.fr; Métro: Kléber
This boutique hotel is a good base for exploring the area around Trocadéro. The hotel has facilities for families and provides impeccable service. The big draw is the five suites with balconies and views of the Eiffel Tower. Babysitting is provided.

P   €€€

Le Bristol   Map 3 B6
112 Rue du Faubourg St-Honoré, 75008; 01 53 43 43 25; www. lebristolparis.com; Métro: Miromesnil
One of the best palace hotels in the city for families, this is a place where kids can relax. The rooms are big and there are many interconnecting suites, including two with roof terraces. There is an excellent, child-friendly gourmet restaurant, the 114, and a special Japanese breakfast. Babysitting services are provided. Children will love the indoor penthouse swimming pool.

🍶 🍽️ P   €€€

Plaza Athénée   Map 2 G6
25 Ave Montaigne, 75008; 01 53 67 66 65; www.plaza-athenee-paris.fr; Métro: Franklin D Roosevelt
This world-famous hotel bends over backwards to welcome families. There is free bike hire, with picnics supplied, a private river boat and in winter, an ice rink. The hotel has an incredible range of huge suites, as well as a spa. Babysitting services are provided.

🍶 🍽️ P   €€€

Pretty garden of one of Paris's finest hotels, Le Bristol

Key to symbols *see back cover flap*

Warm, cosy interior of the Hôtel du Palais Bourbon

Hôtel Shangri-La
Map 8 E1
10 Ave d'Iéna, 75016; 01 53 67 19
98; www.shangri-la.com; Métro: Iéna
This beautiful building was once
the home of Napoleon's grand
nephew and has been tastefully
restored. There are good spacious
rooms and suites, some with
stunning views of the Eiffel Tower
and along the Seine. There are
three restaurants and a swimming
pool. Babysitting is also provided.
🐾 🍴 P €€€

SELF-CATERING
Adagio Haussmann
Map 2 H4
129–131 Blvd Haussmann, 75008;
01 56 88 61 00; www.adagio-city.
com; Métro: Miromesnil
One-bedroom, air-conditioned
apartments for four people, each
have a kitchenette and a microwave;
the bedroom has twin beds and
there is a double sofa bed. Cots are
available, and there is a launderette.
🏠 P €€

Citadines Trocadéro
Map 1 C6
29 bis Rue St-Didier, 75116; 01 56
90 70 00; www.citadines.com;
Métro: Victor Hugo
A short walk from the museums and
gardens of Trocadéro, the location
of these apartments is perfect for
families. The air-conditioned apartments can accommodate up to six
people, and each has a kitchenette
with a grill and microwave. Babysitting and breakfast are provided.
🏠 P €€

Jays
Map 1 D5
6 Rue Copernic, 75016; 01 47
04 16 16; www.jays-paris.com;
Métro: Victor Hugo
The draw for families here is the
beautiful, spacious suites, in

a great location close to Trocadéro
and the Arc de Triomphe. There
is a warm welcome for children.
Daily cleaning and breakfast
are provided.
🏠 P €€€

Eiffel Tower &
Les Invalides
HOTELS
Hôtel du Palais
Bourbon
Map 9 B5
49 Rue de Bourgogne, 75007; 01 44
11 30 70; www.hotel-palais-bourbon.
com; Métro: Varenne
Close to the Musée d'Orsay and a
short walk from the Tuileries gardens,
this is a good hotel for families. There
is an air-conditioned quadruple family
room, which is larger than normal.
There is also a lift.
€€

Hôtel Mayet
Map 13 C2
3 Rue Mayet, 75006; 01 47 83 21
35; www.mayet.com; Métro: Duroc
On a quiet street south of the
Invalides, this colourful little hotel
with minimalist designer bedrooms
is in a lively area within walking
distance of the main sights on the
Left Bank. There are no connecting
rooms but guests can opt for two
rooms on the same floor. There is
also an apartment that sleeps four.
Breakfast is included and a
babysitting service is offered.
€€

Novotel Eiffel Tower
Map 7 C5
61 Quai de Grenelle, 75015; 01 40
58 20 00; www.novotel.com;
Métro: Dupleix
This family-friendly Novotel chain
hotel has a good location, in a
modern high-rise just a 10-minute
walk from the Eiffel Tower. There is
a kids' playroom, swimming pool
and a Japanese restaurant. There
is a 50 per cent reduction on a
second room.
🍴 P €€

Hôtel Ares Eiffel
Map 8 F5
7 Rue du General de Larminat,
75015; 01 47 34 74 04; www.
ares-paris-hotel.com; Métro: La
Motte Piquet Grenelle
This four-star hotel, close to
the Champ-de-Mars, offers
excellent deals online. The decor
is a chic combination of Baroque

and contemporary, and the
deluxe rooms have two single
sofa beds for kids.
P €€€

SELF-CATERING
Adagio Paris Tour Eiffel
Map 7 C5
14 Rue du Théâtre, 75015; 01 45
71 88 88; www.adagio-city.com;
Métro: Dupleix
This hotel offers unbeatable value
apartments for up to six people,
each kitted out with a kitchenette
and microwave, in a high-rise that
offers stunning views across the
city. There is a laundry room and a
small swimming pool. It is just a
10-minute walk to the Eiffel Tower.
🏠 P €€

St-Germain &
the Latin Quarter
HOTELS
Hôtel des Grandes
Ecoles
Map 15 A3
75 Rue du Cardinal Lemoine, 75005;
01 43 26 79 23; www.hotel-grandes-
ecoles.com; Métro: Cardinal Lemoine
or Place Monge
Situated in the heart of the Latin
Quarter, this hotel has some rooms
that open onto a leafy courtyard
and garden. The traditional rooms
are very good value, and the family
room can put up four people. There
is room service but no outside food
is allowed in the rooms. The hotel
is, however, close to the restaurants
on Rue Mouffetard. A babysitting
service is provided.
🐾 P €

Hôtel Marignan
Map 14 H1
13 Rue du Sommerard, 75005; 01 43
54 63 81; www.hotel-marignan.com;
Métro: Maubert Mutualité
This basic hotel is located in a quiet
street and room prices include
breakfast, free laundry and use
of a microwave and fridge. Some
rooms can accommodate up to
five people.
🏠 €

Grand Hôtel des
Balcons
Map 14 F1
3 Rue Casimir Delavigne, 75006;
01 46 34 78 50; www.balcons.com;
Métro: Odéon
This two-star hotel is good value for

the location, just 10 minutes from both Notre-Dame and the Jardin du Luxembourg. It has five simple but spacious family rooms for four people, with good-sized bathrooms, and the rates are very competitive. Some rooms have balconies, as the name would suggest. Parking is available nearby.

€€

Hôtel de Collège de France   Map 14 H1
7 Rue Thénard, 75005; 01 43 26 78 36; www.hotel-collegedefrance.com; Métro: Maubert Mutualité
In this two-star hotel in the heart of the Latin Quarter, an extra bed for under 14s is supplied free of charge. Rooms are small, but the central location makes it a good option.

€

Hôtel de Fleurie   Map 10 F6
32–34 Rue Grégoire de Tours, 75006; 01 53 73 70 00; www.hoteldefleurieparis.com; Métro: Odéon
This three-star hotel is a good place to stay for exploring the Left Bank. The family suite is better for those travelling with older children, as rooms are connected by a corridor. Under-12s can stay free in their parents' room. Cots are available.

€€

Hotel Design Sorbonne   Map 14 G2
6 Rue Victor Cousin, 75005; 01 43 54 58 08; www.hotelsorbonne.com; Métro: Cluny La Sorbonne
This Baroque-style hotel is close to the Jardin du Luxembourg. Older kids will love the iMac computer in each room with free Wi-Fi and films. However, the bathrooms are small.

€€

Seven Hôtel   Map 14 H4
20 Rue Berthollet, 75005; 01 43 31 47 52; www.sevenhotelparis.com; Métro: Censier Daubenton
This ultramodern designer hotel with floating beds has the wow factor to impress older kids, and comes with a reasonable price tag. The hotel has a patio garden.

🟤   €€

Hôtel de Buci   Map 10 F6
22 Rue de Buci, 75006; 01 55 42 74 74; www.buci-hotel.com; Métro: Mabillon
Situated in the little shopping street behind the church of St-Germain, this four-star hotel offers suites for families but the regular rooms are small. The location pushes the price up, but it is possible to walk to many of the main sights from here. A babysitting service is provided.

€€€

Hôtel de l'Université   Map 10 E5
22 Rue de l'Université, 75007; 01 42 61 09 39; www.universitehotel.com; Métro: Rue de Bac
This three-star hotel in a 17th-century mansion is said to be haunted, so it is perhaps a good thing there is a discount for children sharing a room. There is also plenty of old-world charm, with fireplaces and friendly staff. The air-conditioned rooms are a good size and have refrigerators. Some rooms also have a terrace and there is a small lift.

€€€

Hôtel Résidence Henri IV   Map 14 H2
50 Rue des Bernadins, 75005; 01 44 41 31 81; www.residencehenri4.com; Métro: St-Michel
This hotel is located in the heart of the Latin Quarter, opposite a pretty playground and close to the Panthéon. All rooms have a

Entrance to the delightfully luxurious boutique hotel, Relais Christine

kitchenette, and some interconnect, so that a family can take over an entire floor. The hotel attracts a lot of guests with very small children.

🍴   €€€

Hôtel St-Jacques   Map 14 H2
35 Rue des Ecoles, 75005; 01 44 07 45 45; www.paris-hotel-stjacques.com; Métro: Maubert Mutualité
A great place to stay on a first trip to Paris, this three-star hotel has lots of charm. Ask for a room with a balcony with a view across to the Panthéon. The air-conditioned rooms are small, so it is not ideal for families with young children.

€€€

Relais Christine   Map 10 G6
3 Rue Christine, 75006; 01 40 51 60 80; www.relais-christine.com; Métro: Odéon
The highlight of this luxurious boutique hotel, right in the centre of St-Germain-des-Prés area is the rooms that open out directly onto the little garden. There are suites for families, but there is no restaurant. Cots are available.

🟤 P   €€€

The Five   Map 14 H5
3 Rue Flatters, 75005; 01 43 31 74 21; www.thefivehotel.com; Métro: Gobelins
With floating mattresses and a Jacuzzi on the terrace of the suite, this hotel is all about statement – from the red leather lift interior to the customized room fragrance and the twinkling, star-studded ceilings. The designer family room for up to four people is excellent value, though quite small.

€€€

Comfortably spacious and modern room at the Seven Hôtel

Key to symbols *see back cover flap*

SELF-CATERING

Résidence des Arts   Map10 G6
14 Rue Gît le Couer, 75006;
01 55 42 71 11; www.
hotelresidencedesartsparis.com;
Metro: St-Michel or Odéon
Located just 5 minutes' walk from
Notre-Dame, this hotel has an
air-conditioned family suite
accommodating up to six people
with a kitchenette and microwave.
The price is not very competitive
for the locality but the kitchenette
keeps costs down. There is a lift
and breakfast is provided.

€€€

Résidence Le Prince
Regent   Map 14 G1
28 Rue Monsieur le Prince,
75006; 01 56 24 19 21; www.
leprinceregent.com; Métro: Odéon
A great option for families staying
for more than just a few nights,
these modern, air-conditioned
apartments for up to six people
have fully fitted kitchens. There is
one duplex, and a spa with a pool.
It is spectacular value for this area.

€€€

See also Citadines St-Germain-des-
Prés, p238, Hôtel des Grands Hommes,
below & Hôtel du Panthéon, p245

Luxembourg &
Montparnasse

HOTELS

Hotel Apollon   Map 13 B5
91 Rue de l'Ouest, 75014; 01 43 95
62 00; www.paris-hotel-paris.net;
Métro: Pernety
South of Montparnasse centre, this
basic, modern hotel has air-
conditioned family rooms for four.

The beautifully-lit dining area of
Hôtel des Grands

Key to Price Guide see p239

There are excellent deals if
booked online in advance. The
hotel has a lift and and is located
in a lively area with theatres
and cafés.

P   €€

Hôtel du Parc   Map 13 D4
6 Rue Jolivet, 75014; 01 43 20 95
54; www.hotelduparcparis.com;
Métro: Edgar Quinet
A good-value hotel, especially
if booked online. There are air-
conditioned rooms for three
people. Cots are available. It is
a good location to get the feel
of family life in Paris, and for
eating out.

€€

Luxembourg Novotel
Montparnasse   Map 13 B4
17 Rue du Cotentin, 75015; 01 53 91
23 75; www.novotel.com;
Métro: Montparnasse Bienvenüe
This hotel, located just behind
Montparnasse station, is excellent
value. There is one suite, numerous
family rooms, cots, a playroom and
even a computer terminal for kids.

|O| P   €€

Novotel Vaugirard   Map 13 A3
257 Rue de Vaugirard, 75015; 01
40 45 10 00; www.novotel.com;
Métro: Vaugirard
A reliable member of the family-
friendly chain, with outside space
for the kids to run around in. The
bar has a splendid view of the
Eiffel Tower, but is open in high
season only. Seven rooms and two
suites have Eiffel Tower views as
well, but they get booked up very
quickly. There is a kids' play area,
computers in the main hall and a
50 per cent reduction on a second
room, plus two children under 16
can share their parent's room for no
extra charge.

|O| P   €€

Hôtel Aviatic   Map 13 C2
105 Rue de Vaugirard, 75006;
01 53 63 25 50; www.aviatic.fr;
Métro: Montparnasse Bienvenüe or
Saint-Placide
This friendly, intimate boutique
hotel is keen to welcome families
and is close to the Invalides and
the Jardin du Luxembourg. Staff
are happy to pack guests a picnic
for a day in the park.

P   €€€

Pretty, elegant interiors of the chic
boutique hotel La Belle Juliette

Hôtel des Académies
et des Arts   Map 14 E3
15 Rue de la Grande Chaumière,
75006; 01 43 26 66 44; www.hotel-
des-academies.com; Métro: Vavin
Located in the street where the
painter Modigliani had his studio,
this boutique hotel has a tearoom
that serves delicious macaroons.
The rooms are small but
air-conditioned, and the draw for
families is the hotel's proximity
to the Jardin du Luxembourg.

€€€

Hôtel des Grands
Hommes   Map 14 H2
17 Pl du Panthéon, 75005; 01 46 34
19 60; www.hoteldesgrandshommes.
com; Métro: Cardinal Lemoine
The pretty Hôtel des Grands
Hommes has a brilliant location
right opposite the Panthéon and
close to the Jardin du Luxembourg.
There are five family rooms for
three people and three suites,
while some rooms have balconies
overlooking the Panthéon. Cots
are available. Guests get a friendly
welcome and the staff are
exceptionally helpful. Parking
is available nearby.

€€€

Hôtel Louis II   Map 14 F1
2 Rue St-Sulpice, 75006; 01 46
33 13 80; www.hotel-louis2.com;
Métro: St-Sulpice
An excellent location near the
Jardin du Luxembourg as well as
charming, characterful suites in the
roof are the highlight here for
families. There are good deals
online that cut the cost of extras
such as breakfast. The hotel is close
to plenty of restaurants and shops.

€€€

Hôtel du Panthéon   Map 14 H3
19 Pl du Panthéon, 75005; 01 43 54 32 95; www.hoteldupantheon.com; Métro: Cardinal Lemoine
The hotel has great views across to the Panthéon, and the feel of an 18th-century town house – some rooms have four-poster beds and big bathrooms. It also has two triple air-conditioned rooms for families.
€€€

Hôtel Petit Belloy St Germain   Map 14 G1
1 Rue Racine, 75006; 01 43 26 87 13; http://en.hotel-petit-belloy-saint-germain.com; Métro: Odéon
This chic boutique hotel on the Left Bank features Ligne Rosset designed rooms in neutral tones. It includes family rooms for four people, some of which have balconies and views over the Saint Germain neighbourhood. Cots are also available, upon request.
P   €€€

Hotel Victoria Palace   Map 13 D2
6 Rue Blaise Desgoffe, 75006; 01 45 49 70 00; www.victoriapalace.com; Métro: St-Placide
Children staying two nights or more are greeted with a welcome gift at this four-star Left Bank hotel. There are family suites and connecting rooms, and one child under 13 can stay free in an extra bed. Cots and babysitting are available. A copious buffet breakfast is included in the room price. There is no restaurant, but light meals can be ordered.
P   €€€

La Belle Juliette   Map 13 D1
92 Rue de Cherche Midi, 75006; 01 42 22 97 40; www.hotel-belle-juliette-paris.com; Métro: Duroc
Situated just a short walk from both St-Germain and Montparnasse, this hotel is as delightful as its name suggests, although rooms are quite small and the two-room suite is expensive. Every room has an iMac computer, and there is a spa.
|O| €€€

Pullmann Montparnasse
Map 13 C4
19 Rue du Commandant René Mouchotte, 75014; 01 44 36 44 36; www.pullmanhotels.com; Métro: Gaîté
This hotel has good-sized modern family rooms with two double beds

for three or four people. There are excellent deals to be had online. There is children's entertainment at Sunday brunch, and a babysitting service is provided.
P   €€€

Villa des Artistes   Map 14 E3
9 Rue de la Grande Chaumière, 75006; 01 43 26 60 86; www.villa-artistes.com; Métro: Vavin
Families will like the patio garden and the pretty fountain here. There are good-size, modern, simple family rooms for five people. Cots are available and babysitting is also provided. The location is great as it is close to an area of kids' shops and the Jardin du Luxembourg.
🐾   €€€

Villa Madame   Map 14 E2
44 Rue Madame, 75006; 01 45 48 02 81; www.hotelvillamadameparis.com; Métro: St-Sulplice
This four-star, elegant hotel is good for families with older children and is close to the Jardin du Luxembourg and the church of St-Sulpice. There is a small garden and room service. Kids will enjoy the board games and a treat in the tearoom.
🐾   €€€

SELF-CATERING
Hôtel Résidence Quintinie Square   Map 13 A4
5 Rue La Quintinie, 75015; 01 47 83 94 34; www.paris-hotel-quintinie.com; Métro: Volontaires
Located in a residential area close to the Institut Pasteur and the head-quarters of UNESCO, the rooms in this residence all have kitchenettes and can accommodate up to three people. There is a laundry room.
🍴P   €

Beyond the City Centre
HOTELS
Hôtel du Parc Montsouris
4 Rue du Parc Montsouris, 75014; 01 45 89 09 72; www.hotel-parc-montsouris.com; Métro: Porte d'Orléans
Close to Parc Montsouris, this hotel offers a family room that is one of the best budget options in the city, though there is no restaurant. There are, however, cafés and restaurants close at hand.
€

Ibis Styles
77 Rue de Bercy, 75012; 01 53 46 50 50; http://ibisstyleshotel.ibis.com; Métro: Bercy
This is probably the best budget option in the city. The small rooms are divided into two for a family of four. For kids there is a welcome box, Disney Channel, games room, high chairs and changing mats. The breakfast is good. The restaurant is closed at weekends but the hotel is near to Bercy Village, with its many restaurants, and Bercy Park.
|O| €

Hôtel de la Porte Dorée
273 Ave Daumesnil, 75012; 01 43 07 56 97; www.hotelportedoree.com; Métro: Porte Dorée
This charming hotel is run by a young mother who goes out of her way to make families welcome. There are family rooms for three and four people and excellent deals online that take the hotel down into the lower price band. Cots are provided. This is a good location, close to parks and Bercy Village.
P   €€

Cot and toys for kids at Hôtel de la Porte Dorée

Key to symbols *see back cover flap*

Hôtel Le Vert Galant
*43 Rue Croulebarbe, 75013; 01
44 08 83 50; www.vertgalant.com;
Métro: Pl d'Italie*
A French provincial atmosphere
prevails in this calm haven with
rooms that look on to a garden.
The larger rooms all have kitchenettes (€10 charge per night).
It is good for families as it is close
to a park and an example of the
excellent value to be had just away
from the centre.

🍽 🦟 👕 P   €€

Mama Shelter
*109 Rue Bagnolet, 75020; 01 43 48
48 48; www.mamashelter.com;
Métro: Gambetta*
This trendy hotel near Cimetière du
Père Lachaise has spacious rooms
kitted out with Wi-Fi and an iMac
computer, and free on-demand
movies. There is also a microwave.
Babysitting is offered.

🍽 P   €€

Le Citizen Hôtel
*96 Quai de Jemmapes, 75010; 01 83
62 55 50; www.lecitizenhotel.com;
Métro: Gare du Nord*
This bright and modern hotel is just
a 10-minute walk from Gare du
Nord. The double rooms are
spacious and can sleep up to five
people. There is also a suite and an
apartment, without a kitchen.

€€€

BED & BREAKFAST
A Room in Paris
*130 Rue Lafayette, 75010; 06 33
10 25 78; www.aroominparis.com;
Métro: Gare du Nord*
This is good-value accommodation,
close to the Gare du Nord, with a
friendly host who offers breakfast
and the option of dinner, as well as
a laundry service. The rooms are
spacious. A separate flat is available.

P   €

La Villa Paris
*33 Rue de la Fontaine à Mulard,
75013; 01 43 47 15 66; www.
la-villa-paris.com; Métro: Tolbiac*
Marie, the owner of this charming
red-brick 1920s mansion, greets
visitors like family. Situated between
the Butte aux Cailles and Parc
Montsouris quarter, this B&B offers
air-conditioned accommodation
and a truly Parisian experience.

€€

Spacious deluxe room at the Hôtel Trianon Palace

Manoir de Beauregard
*43, Rue des Lilas, 75019; 0142 03
10 20; www.manoir-de-beauregard-
paris.com; Métro: Pré St-Gervais*
Breakfast, with home-made jam, is
served in the garden of this B&B in
summer. The decor is traditional
French and there is a family room
for four people. A minimum
booking for two nights is required.

🦟 P   €€

Hôtel Paradis
*41 Rue des Petites-Écuries, 75010;
01 45 23 08 22; www.hotelparadis
paris.com; Métro: Bonne Nouvelle/
Chateau d'Eau*
This boutique hotel in Paris's up-
and-coming 10th *arrondissement*
has a trendy decor and attracts a
cool clientele. The 6th-floor suite
sleeps four people and features its
own coffee machine.

€€€

SELF-CATERING
Hôtel Home
*36 Rue George Sand, 75016; 01
45 20 61 38; www.hotelhome.fr;
Métro: Jasmin*
The spacious apartments at the
top of this hotel have two to three
bedrooms and can sleep six
people. There are cots and a
shopping service is available. The
daily cleaning is also a bonus. It is
close to a kosher deli and
restaurant. Babysitting is available.

🦟 P 👕   €€

Day Trips – Versailles

HOTELS
Novotel Château de Versailles
*4 Blvd St-Antoine, 78150 Le
Chesnay; 01 39 54 96 96;
www.novotel.com/1022*
The hotel offers classic Novotel
family-friendly facilities just
5 minutes' walk from the palace.

Children under 16 can stay free in
their parents' room and there is a
late checkout on Sundays. There is a
50 per cent reduction on a second
room, and a children's play area.

🍽 P   €

Hôtel Trianon Palace Versailles
*1 Blvd de la Reine, Versailles,
78000; 01 30 84 50 50;
www.trianonpalace.com*
This is one of the most serene
hotels in the region. The rooms are
very spacious and some have park
views. The Gordon Ramsay bistro,
La Veranda, has a children's menu
and serves a Sunday brunch. The
hotel also has an indoor swimming
pool and spa, and sometimes at
Christmas there is a skating rink.

🍽 P   €€€

BED & BREAKFAST
L'Orangeraie
*7 Rue Hardy, 78000, Versailles;
01 39 53 26 78; www.versailles-
orangeraie.com*
Located 5 minutes from the RER
and the château in an attractive part
of Versailles town, this house has an
enclosed garden and a family room
with a kitchenette and garden access.
There is a charge for use of a folding
bed and the kitchenette.

🦟 👕 P   €

CAMPING
Huttopia Versailles
*31 Rue Berthelot; 01 39 51 23 61;
www.huttopia.com*
This campsite is just a short walk
from the Palace of Versailles, and a
30-minute train ride from Paris to the
nearby Porchefontaine RER station.
It has cabins for up to six people and
gypsy caravans for five, a games
room, swimming pool, bike hire,
a children's club and Wi-Fi. The
minimum stay is two nights.

🍽 P   €

Rambouillet

HOTEL
Relay du Château Mercure Rambouillet
1 Pl de la Libération, 78120 Rambouillet; 01 34 57 30 00; www.mercure-rambouillet.com
This excellent-value four-star hotel, now part of the Accor group, is located opposite the château in Rambouillet. There is room for one extra bed in a double room, and a 50 per cent discount on a second room, making it a bargain at the price and a great place for a weekend break. Cots are available.

🍽 P €

Parc Astérix

HOTELS
Hôtel les Trois Hiboux
Parc Astérix, Plailly, 60128; 03 44 62 68 00; www.parcasterix.com
Tucked away in the woods, the rustic "three owls" hotel is full of charm and comes with the chance to meet the Gaulish characters at breakfast. Kids will like the games room and the entertainers in the bar. The buffet dinner is pricey and basic, so it is better to bring a picnic, especially in the summer. The rooms can accommodate up to seven people, with bunk beds in an alcove separate from the main room. All rooms have balconies. Cots and a babysitting service are available.

🎱 🍽 P €€

Disneyland® Paris

HOTELS
Disneyland® Hotel
Disneyland® Paris BP 112, Marne-la-Vallée Chessy, Seine-et-Marne 77777; http://hotels.disneylandparis.co.uk
The rooms here can accommodate up to five people and the big draw is an excellent buffet breakfast with the Disney characters – start the day with a cuddle from Minnie Mouse! The Snow White and Seven Dwarfs mirror in the bathroom is a nice touch, and kids will enjoy the playroom and the swimming pool. There are suites with a view of the fairytale castle, plus a VIP Fast Pass®

for rides. Book online for the best deals, as it is very expensive.

🍽 P €€€

Hotel Cheyenne®
Disneyland® Paris BP 112, Marne-la-Vallée Chessy, Seine-et-Marne; 084 48 008 898; http://hotels.disneylandparis.co.uk
Take a trip to the Wild West in this clapboard hotel that will delight the kids. The spacious rooms can put up four people, with bunk beds for kids. Look out for the horseshoe on the door, and a cowboy-boot-shaped lamp. There is a restaurant, playroom and outdoor play area. Book online for the best deals.

🎱 🍽 €€€

Provins

BED & BREAKFAST
Le Logis de La Voulzie
16 Rue Aristide Briand, 77160 Provins; 06 14 02 25 10; www.en.logisdelavoulzie.com
This B&B enjoys a lovely location in the historic town of Provins, which is classified as a UNESCO World Heritage Site. It is an ideal stop for a weekend in the countryside. There are four spacious bedrooms, with additional beds to convert into family rooms. Guests are welcome to use the kitchen and the charming, leafy garden. A typically French breakfast is served every morning. It is a 30-minute drive to Disneyland® Paris.

🚫 🎱 🏠 P €

Woodland setting of the Hôtel les Trois Hiboux in Parc Astérix

Beautiful façade of the Hôtel de Londres

Fontainebleau

HOTELS
Novotel Fontainebleau Ury
Route Nationale 152, 77760, Ury; 01 60 71 24 24; www.novotel.com
This hotel is on the edge of a pretty village, a 15-minute drive from Fontainebleau and in a great location from which to enjoy the forest. Kids can stay free in their parents' room and there is a 50 per cent reduction on a second room. The outdoor heated pool is a hit with kids and there is also bike hire, a spa, a tennis court and table tennis.

🎱 🍽 P €

Hôtel de Londres
1 Pl Général de Gaulle, 77300 Fontainebleau; 01 64 22 20 21; www.hoteldelondres.com
This family-run hotel offers spacious rooms for four, as well as suites. Some rooms have a fabulous view of the château. There is also a lovely secluded patio. The hotel is located in a peaceful setting close to the town centre, and makes a good weekend base for exploring this area. It is closed over Christmas and for two weeks in August.

🎱 P €€

BED & BREAKFAST
Le Clos de Tertre
6 Chemin des Vallées, 77760, La Chapelle la Reine, near Fontainebleau; 01 64 24 37 80; www.leclosdutertre.com
This friendly B&B has a home away from home atmosphere. There are toys for kids and a kitchen corner at the disposal of guests. It is a good option for those who plan to stay overnight to see Vaux-le-Vicomte by candlelight. Disneyland® Paris is also just a short drive away.

🚫 🎱 🏠 P €

Key to symbols *see back cover flap*

Panoramic view of Paris from the
Eiffel Tower, with the Eglise du
Dôme in the foreground

Paris
MAPS

Paris City Maps

Inner Paris is delineated by the ring road, the Périphérique. Within it, the city is divided into 20 numbered districts, or *arrondissements*, which also form the last two numbers of Parisian postcodes. The map below shows the division of the 16 pages of maps in this section, the *arrondissements* and the main areas covered in the sightseeing section of this book. The smaller inset map shows Central Paris and the area covered in Beyond the City Centre.

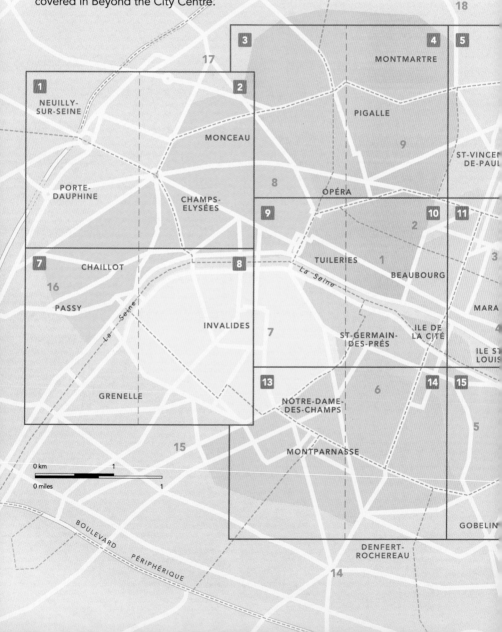

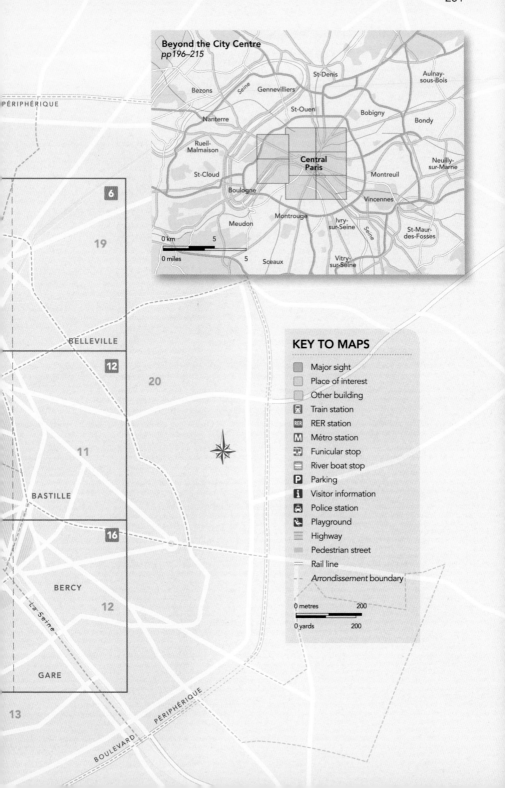

Beyond the City Centre
pp196–215

St-Denis
Aulnay-sous-Bois
Bezons
Gennevilliers
Seine
St-Ouen
Bobigny
Bondy
Nanterre
Rueil-Malmaison
Neuilly-sur-Marne
St-Cloud
Central Paris
Montreuil
Boulogne
Vincennes
Montrouge
Meudon
Ivry-sur-Seine
St-Maur-des-Fosses
Seine
Sceaux
Vitry-sur-Seine

0 km 5
0 miles 5

PÉRIPHÉRIQUE

6
19
BELLEVILLE
12
20
11
BASTILLE
16
BERCY
12
La Seine
GARE
13
PÉRIPHÉRIQUE
BOULEVARD

KEY TO MAPS

Major sight
Place of interest
Other building
Train station
RER station
Métro station
Funicular stop
River boat stop
Parking
Visitor information
Police station
Playground
Highway
Pedestrian street
Rail line
Arrondissement boundary

0 metres 200
0 yards 200

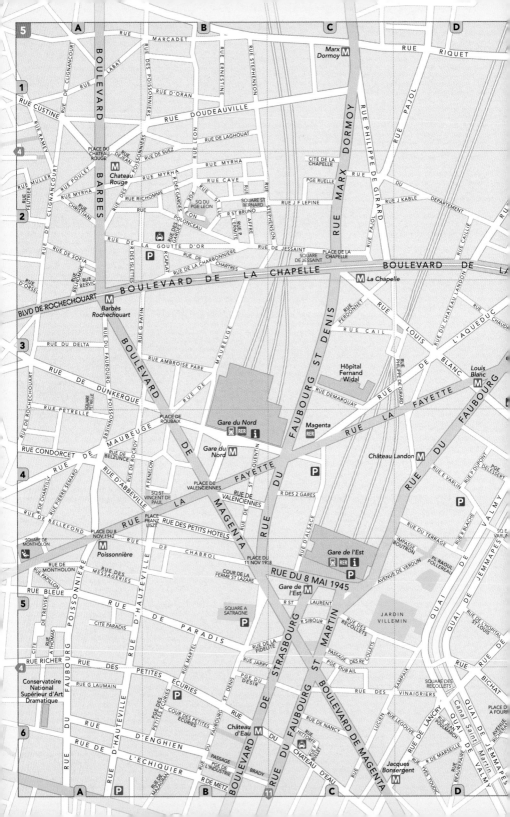

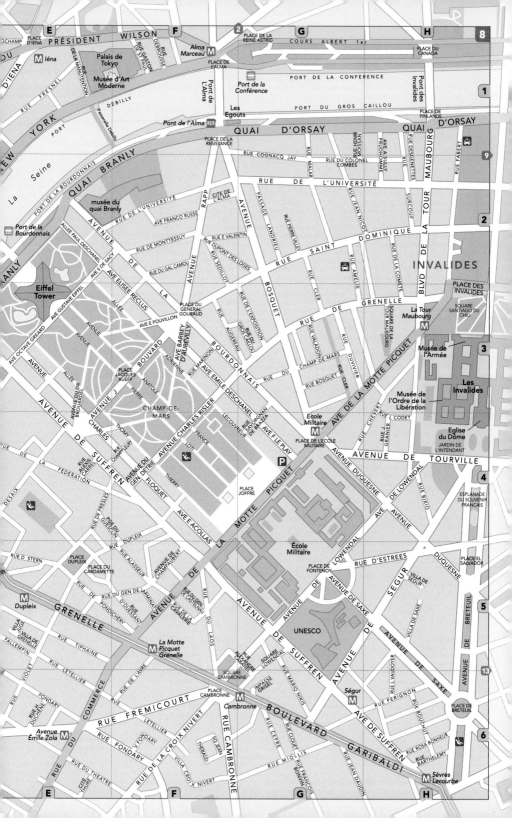

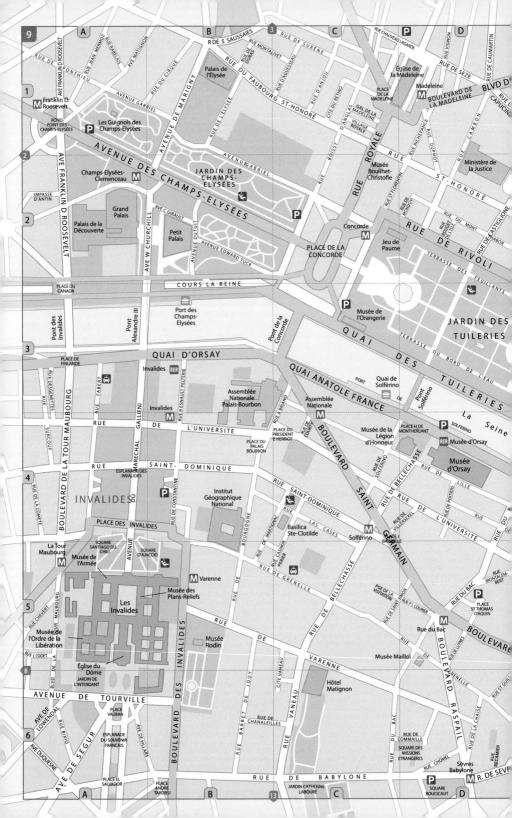

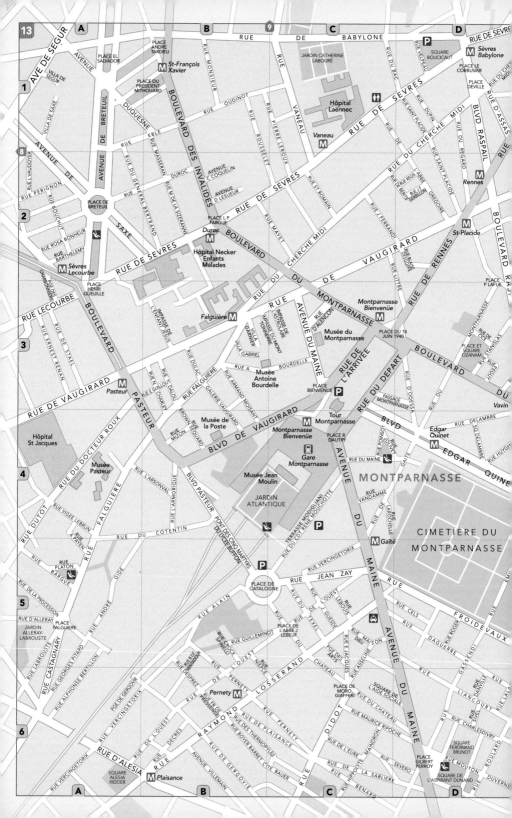

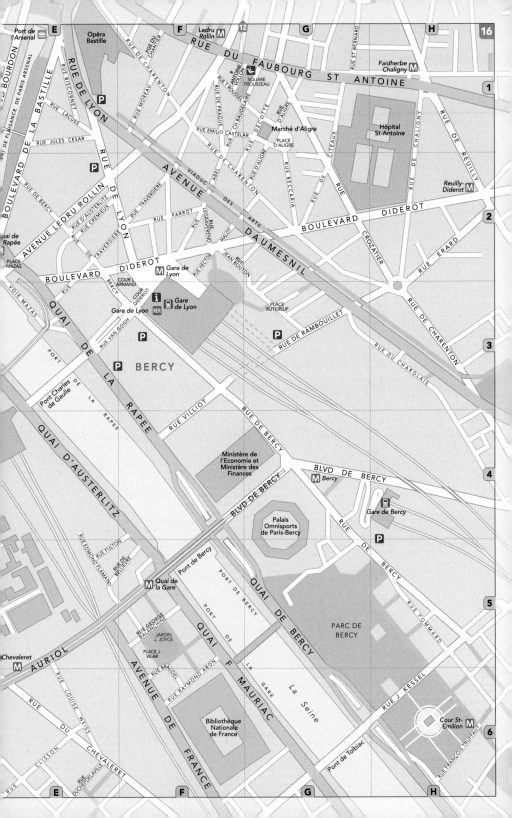

Paris Maps Index

Index

Acknowledgments

Dorling Kindersley would like to thank the following people whose help and assistance contributed to the preparation of this book.

Main Contributor
Journalist Rosie Whitehouse has spent over 20 years travelling with her five children. She has interrailed to the Arctic Circle and crisscrossed Europe by car numerous times with her kids bundled in the back seat. Her travels began in the south of France, and took her to revolutionary Romania and the war-torn Balkans, where she lived for five years. Rosie's reporter husband is both French and English, as are her children. With family in Paris, Rosie has explored every nook and cranny of the French capital, and has spent most of her adult live deciphering what makes the French tick.

Editorial Consultant
Nick Rider

Additional Photography
Max Alexander; Neil Lukas; Eric Meacher; John Parker; Rough Guides/James McConnachie; Peter Wilson.

Design and Editorial
PUBLISHER Vivien Antwi
LIST MANAGER Christine Stroyan
SENIOR MANAGING ART EDITOR Mabel Chan
SENIOR CARTOGRAPHIC EDITOR Casper Morris
SENIOR EDITOR Michelle Crane
EDITOR Fay Franklin
ASSISTANT EDITOR Claire Bush
JACKET DESIGN Tessa Bindloss, Louise Dick
ICON DESIGN Claire-Louise Armitt
SENIOR DTP DESIGNER Jason Little
PICTURE RESEARCH Chloe Roberts, Ellen Root
PRODUCTION CONTROLLER Rebecca Short
READERS Anna Streiffert, Debra Wolter
FACT CHECKER Anna Brooke, Lyn Parry
PROOFREADER Vincent Crump
INDEXER Hilary Bird

With thanks to Douglas Amrine for his help in developing this series.

Revisions Team
Vicki Allen, Emma Anacootee, Chris Barstow, Louise Cleghorn, Vidushi Duggal, Karen Fitzpatrick, Lydia Halliday, Kaberi Hazarika, Susanne Hillen, Cincy Jose, Bharti Karakoti, Sumita Khatwani, Kim Laidlaw, Beverly Smart, Ajay Verma

Photography Permissions
Dorling Kindersley would like to thank all the museums, galleries, churches and other sights that allowed us to photograph at their establishments.

Auvers-Sur-Oise, Café de Flore, The Café Maure de la Mosquée, Centre Pompidou, Cupcakes Berko, De l'Assemblée Nationale, Laura Farrow at Disneyland® Paris, Dragon Elysées, Florian Payen at Espace Dalí, Hotel Britannique, Le Musée de la Poupée-Paris, Le Musée en Herbe, Maison de Victor Hugo, Marionnettes du Champ-de-Mars, Musée Bourdelle, Musée Curie, Musée d'Art et d'Histoire du Judaïsme, Musée de l'Air et de l'Espace, Musée de La Poste, Audrey Gouimenou & Frédérique Desvergnes at Musée des Arts et Métiers, Frédéric Lenoir at Le musée du quai Branly, Musée Grévin, Claire Bourrasset at Muséum National d'Histoire Naturelle, Florence Choloux at Musée Rodin, Parc de la Villette, Residence & Spa Le Prince Regent, Restaurant Chartier, La Sainte-Chapelle, Shakespeare and Company.

Works of art have been reproduced with the permission of the following copyright holders:

L'Ecoute by Henri de Miller © ADAGP, Paris and DACS, London 2012 79br; *The Profile of Time* © Espace Dalí 101t; Keith Haring artwork © Keith Haring Foundation 113tl.

Picture Credits
a = above; b = below/bottom; c = centre; f = far; l = left; r = right; t = top.

The publisher would like to thank the following individuals, companies and picture libraries for their kind permission to reproduce their photographs:

ALAMY IMAGES: AA World Travel Library 70cr, 70clb; age fotostock 94tl; The Art Archive 160crb, 221tc, 222cla; Martin Bache 105ca; Peter Barritt 106cl; 126bc; GM Photo Images 70c; Hemis 1c, 17bl, 82br, 130b, 181bl, 185br; John Kellerman 188cb; Keystone Pictures USA 53tc; Hideo Kurihara 164–165; Look Die Bildagentur der Fotografen GmbH 77bl; Frank Javier Medrano 248–249; Antony Nettle 160cr; Pawel Libera Images 68br; Chuck Pefley 162cl; PjrTravel 165cl; Kumar Sriskandan 232cl; Jack Sullivan 64crb.

CORBIS: Hemis/Bertrand Gardel 1–2.

DISNEYLAND® PARIS: 230tr, 230crb, 230bl, 230br, 231tl, 231cla, 231clb, 231bc, 233tl, 233tr, 233br.

DREAMSTIME.COM: Ivanbastien 26bl, Nikonaft 73cl.

DK IMAGES: Courtesy of CNHMS, Paris, 59c; courtesy of Musée Carnavalet 94bl; courtesy of the Musée du Louvre, Paris, Philippe Sebert 104br; courtesy of Sacré-Coeur, 122tl, 122cl; Designer garden, courtesy of Isabelle Devin & Catherine Rannou 202tr; courtesy of Architect: Adrien Fainsilber 202cr; courtesy of Musée du Petit Palais 136tl; Gilt bronze bust of Gustave Eiffel at the base of the Eiffel Tower by Emile-Antoine Bourdelle 154c, courtesy of Musée

National du Moyen-Age Thermes de Cluny 167br, 176cr; courtesy of Musée National du Moyen-Age Thermes de Cluny 176tl; courtesy of CNHMS, Paris 183cl, 188cr, 188crb; courtesy of Château de Malmaison 212tl; courtesy of l'Etablissement public du musée et du domaine national de Versailles 222tr, 222clb,/220clb; Reunion des Musees Nationaux/Art Resource, NY, 222cb.

FÉDÉRATION FRANÇAISE DE TENNIS: 199br.

FESTIVAL COULÉE DOUCE: MOGAN DANIEL 45br.

FÊTE DES VENDANGES: Droits Réservés 16bl.

GETTY IMAGES: Bloomberg 145tc.

HÔTEL DE LA PORTE DORÉE: 245br.

HOTEL LE BRISTOL: 241br.

INSTITUTE PASTEUR: François Gardy 195t, 195c.

JARDIN D'ACCLIMATATION: Frédéric Grimaud 198b, 210cl.

LADURÉE PARIS: 37bl, 135bl.

LE MUSÉE DU QUAI BRANLY: 151t, 156cr.

MASTERFILE: Axiom Photographic 18bl; Kathleen Finlay 31br; R Ian Lloyd, 107cl.

MON PREMIER FESTIVAL: 16br.

THE MUSÉE DE LA MAGIE: 96tl.

MUSÉE DES ARTS ET MÉTIERS: JC Wetzel - Images et sons 86cla, 86cr, 86cb; M Favareille 86tr, 86br; Studio cnam 86bl.

MUSÉE GREVIN: 116cl, 116cr, 116tr, 116br.

MUSEUM NATIONAL D'HISTOIRE NATURELLE: 181tl; Bernard Faye 166cr, 180tl, 180c.

MUSÉE NATIONAL PICASSO-PARIS: Béatrice Hatala 95tl.

PARC ASTÉRIX: 226cl, 226c, 226cr.

PHOTOLIBRARY: Age fotostock/David Barnes 58–59,/ Kordcom 128–129,/Sylvain Grandadam 12br; Alamy/ Andrzej Gorzkowski Photography 225cl,/The Art Gallery Collection 52cr, 54bl,/Business 223tl,/ Directphoto.org 17br, 41br,/Peter Horree 43bl,/ John Kellerman 221clb,/National Geographic Image Collection 15bl,/Shopping Mall 41bl,/Jordan Weeks 15br; Arco Images /Pfeiffer Juergen 196–197; Tibor Bognár 190crb; Bridgeman Art Library 50cr, 51tl, 54cr, 107c,/Giraudon 105tc, 170c, 171cl; De Agostini Editore /G Dagli Orti 52clb; Design Pics RM/Michael

Interisano 150b; Chad Ehlers 11bl; Eye Ubiquitous 8–9; Michiel Fokkema 47bl; Garden Picture Library/ Erika Craddock 11t; Hemis/Chicurel Arnaud 100cr,/ Gardel Bertrand 61t,/Maisant Ludovic 198cl,/Sonnet Sylvain 13t, 131br, 182–183; Iconotec/Pepeira Tom 24cl; Index Stock Imagery/Thomas Craig 19bc; JTB Photo 20bl; Lonely Planet Images/Olivier Cirendini 126cl; Photononstop/Brigitte Merle 71tl,/Rosine Mazin 44bl,/Christophe Lehenaff 70cl, 106tr,/Daniel Thierry 150cr,/Godong 61bl; Pixtal Images 105tl; The Print Collector 106cr; Radius Images 220cla; Christian Reister 76b; Robert Harding Travel/Stuart Dee 47t; Ticket/Chris L Jones 77t, 166b; Universal History Archive 50cla, 55tc, 107tl, 171c; Steve Vidler 56–57.

PLAYMOBIL: Sylvain Cambon 223bl.

SALON ANGELINA: Emmanuel Valentin 222br.

TRIANON PALACE VERSAILLES, A WALDORF ASTORIA HOTEL: 246tr.

JACKET IMAGES: Front: ALAMY IMAGES: eye35.px cb; DREAMSTIME.COM: Anastasiia Vorontsova tc; GETTY IMAGES: Doug Armand tl, RYUICHI SATO tr. BACK: 4CORNERS: SIME/Massimo Ripani tc; PHOTOLIBRARY: Robert Harding Travel tl; SUPERSTOCK: Nomad tr. SPINE: TIPS IMAGES: Riccardo Sala t.

All other images © Dorling Kindersley
For further information see www.DKimages.com

SPECIAL EDITIONS OF DK TRAVEL GUIDES
DK Travel Guides can be purchased in bulk quantities at discounted prices for use in promotions or as premiums.

We are also able to offer special editions and personalized jackets, corporate imprints, and excerpts from all of our books, tailored specifically to meet your own needs.

To find out more, please contact:
(in the US) **specialsales@dk.com**
(in the UK) **travelguides@uk.dk.com**
(in Canada) **specialmarkets@dk.com**
(in Australia) **penguincorporatesales@ penguinrandomhouse.com.au**

Phrase Book

Making Friends

Hello	Bonjour	boñzhoor
How are you?	Comment vas-tu?	kom-moñ vah too
Very well, thank you	Très bien, merci	treh byañ, mer-see
What is your name?	Comment t'appelles tu?	kom-moñ ta-pel too
My name is...	Je m'appelle...	zhuh ma-pel...
How old are you?	Quel âge as-tu?	kel ahzh a too
I am ... years old	J'ai ... ans	zhay ..° . ons
Do you speak English?	Parlez-vous anglais?	par-lay voo oñg-lay
boy	garçon	gar-sonh
girl	fille	fi

Communication Essentials

Yes	Oui	wee
No	Non	noñ
Please	S'il vous plaît	seel voo play
Thank you	Merci	mer-see
Excuse me	Excusez-moi	exkoo-zay mwah
Goodbye	Au revoir	oh ruh-vwar
Good evening	Bonsoir	boñ-swar
morning	le matin	matañ
afternoon	l'après-midi	l'apreh-meedee
evening	le soir	swar
yesterday	hier	eeyehr
today	aujourd'hui	oh-zhoor-dwee
tomorrow	demain	duhmañ
here	ici	ee-see
there	là	lah
What?	Quel, quelle?	kel, kel
When?	Quand?	koñ
Why?	Pourquoi?	poor-kwah
Where?	Où?	oo

In an Emergency

Help!	Au secours!	oh sekoor
Stop!	Arrêtez!	aret-ay
Call...	Appelez	apuh-lay
a doctor!	un médecin!	uñ medsañ
an ambulance!	une ambulance!	oon oñboo-loñs
the police!	la police!	lah poh-lees
the fire brigade!	les pompiers!	lay poñ-peeyay
Where is the nearest hospital?	Où est l'hôpital le plus proche?	oo ay l'opeetal luh ploo prosh
Where is the nearest telephone?	Où est le téléphone le plus proche?	oo ay luh taylayfon luh ploo prosh

Health

My child needs to see a doctor	Mon fils/ma fille a besoin de voir un médecin	mon fis/ma fi a beysoyn d vwah uñ medsañ
asthma	l'asthme	las-zh-ma
allergy	allergie	al-er-gee
bandage	pansement	pan-zay-men
cough	toux	tooh
diarrhoea	la diarrhée	dee-ya-rey
fever	fièvre	fi-ev-ra
vomit	vomi	vom-mi

Useful Phrases

Where is/are...?	Où est/sont...?	oo ay/soñ
Which way to...?	Quelle est la direction pour...?	kel ay lah deer-ek-syoñ poo
I don't understand	Je ne comprends pas	zhuh nuh kom-proñ pah
Do you speak English?	Parlez-vous anglais?	par-lay voo oñg-lay
I'm sorry	Excusez-moi	exkoo-zay mwah
How are you?	Comment allez-vous?	kom-moñ talay vous

Useful Words

big	grand	groñ
small	petit	puh-tee
hot	chaud	show
cold	froid	frwah
good	bon	boñ
bad	mauvais	moh-veh
open	ouvert	oo-ver
closed	fermé	fer-meh
left	gauche	gohsh
right	droit	drwah
straight ahead	tout droit	too drwah
near	près	preh
far	loin	lwañ
early	de bonne heure	duh bon urr
late	en retard	oñ ruh-tar
entrance	l'entrée	l'on-tray
exit	la sortie	sor-tee
toilet	les toilettes, les WC	twah-let, vay-see
beach	la plage	pla-zhuh
playground	l'aire de jeux	ayer d zhuh
roundabout	le carrousel	ka-roo-sel
sandpit	le bac à sable	bak a saar-blu
slide	le toboggan	toh-bog-an
swimming pool	la piscine	pisin
swing	balançoire	bal-an-swah
car	la voiture	vwahtoor
garage	la garage	garraj
motorway	l'autoroute	ohto-root
road	la route	root
traffic lights	les feux	fuh
van	la camionnette	kamionet
vehicle registration documents	la carte grise	kart greez
car park	le parking	par-keeng

Making a Telephone Call

I'd like to place a long-distance call	Je voudrais faire un interurbain	zhuh voo-dreh fehr uñ añter-oorbañ
I'd like to make a collect call	Je voudrais faire une communication PCV	zhuh voo-dreh fehr oon komoonikah-syon peh-say-veh
I'll try again later	Je rappelerai plus tard	zhuh rapel-erayploo tar
Can I leave a message?	Est-ce que je peux laisser un message?	es-keh zhuh puh leh-say un mehsazh
Hold on	Ne quittez pas, s'il vous plait	nuh kee-tay pah seel voo play
Could you speak up a little please?	Pouvez-vous parler un peu plus fort?	poo-vay voo parlay puh ploo for

Shopping

How much does this cost?	C'est combien, s'il vous plaît?	say kom-**byañ** seel voo play
I would like …	je voudrais…	zhuh voo-**dray**
Do you have?	Est-ce que vous avez?	es-**kuh** voo zavay
I'm just looking	Je regarde seulement	zhuh ruh**gar** suhl**moñ**
Do you take credit cards?	Est-ce que vous acceptez les cartes de crédit?	es-**kuh** voo zaksept-**ay** leh kart duh kreh-**dee**
Do you take travellers' cheques?	Est-ce que vous acceptez les chèques de voyage?	es-**kuh** voo zaksept-**ay** leh shek duh vway**azh**
What time do you open?	A quelle heure vous êtes ouvert?	ah kel urr voo zet oo-**ver**
What time do you close?	A quelle heure vous êtes fermé?	ah kel urr voo zet oo-**ver**
This one	Celui-ci	suhl-wee-**see**
That one	Celui-là	suhl-wee-**lah**
expensive	cher	shehr
cheap	pas cher, bon marché	pah shehr, boñ mar-shay
size, clothes	la taille	tye
size, shoes	la pointure	pwañ-**tur**
crayon	crayon de couleur	cray-on de koo-ler
games	les jeux	zhuh
pencil	crayon	crey-onh
toys	les jouets	zooh-eh

Colours

white	blanc	bloñ
black	noir	nwahr
red	rouge	roozh
yellow	jaune	zhohwn
green	vert	vehr
blue	bleu	bluh
orange	orange	oh-ran-zhuh
purple	violet	vee-oh-lay
pink	rose	roze

Types of Shops

antiques shop	le magasin d'antiquités	maga-**zañ** d'onteekee-tay
bakery	la boulangerie	booloñ-**zhuree**
bank	la banque	boñk
bookstore	la librairie	lee-**brehree**
cake shop	la pâtisserie	patee-**sree**
cheese shop	la fromagerie	fromazh-**ree**
chemist	la pharmacie	farmah-**see**
department store	le grand magasin	groñ maga-**zañ**
delicatessen	la charcuterie	sharkoot-**ree**
gift shop	le magasin de cadeaux	maga-**zañ** duh ka**doh**
grocery	l'épicerie	epee-ser-ree
greengrocer	le marchand de légumes	mar-**shoñ** duh lay-**goom**
hairdresser	le coiffeur	kwafuhr
market	le marché	marsh-**ay**
newsstand	le magasin de journaux	maga-**zañ** duh zhoor-**no**
post office	le bureau de poste	boo**roh** duh pohst
supermarket	le supermarché	soo pehr-**marshay**
tobacconist	le tabac	tabah
travel agent	l'agence de voyages	l'azhoñs duh vwayazh

Sightseeing

abbey	l'abbaye	l'abay-**ee**
art gallery	la galerie d'art	galer-**ree** dart
bus station	la gare routière	gahr roo-tee-**yehr**
cathedral	la cathédrale	katay-**dral**
church	l'église	l'ay**gleez**
garden	le jardin	zhar-**dañ**
library	la bibliothèque	beebleeo-tek
museum	le musée	moo-**zay**
railway station	la gare (SNCF)	gahr (es-en-say-ef)
tourist information office	les renseignements touristiques, le syndicat d'initiative	rohnsayn-**moñ** too-rees-**teek**, sandeeka d'eenee-syateev
town hall	l'hôtel de ville	l'oh**tel** duh veel
closed for public holiday	fermeture jour férié	fehrmeh-tur zhoor fehree-**ay**

Staying in a Hotel

Do you have a vacant room	Est-ce que vous avez une chambre?	es-kuh voo-zavay oon shambr
double room with double bed	la chambre a deux personnes, avec un grand lit	shambr ah duh pehr-**son** avek un gronn lee
twin room	la chambre a deux lits	shambr a duh lee
single room	la chambre a une personne	shambr ah oon pehr-**son**
room with a bath, shower	salle de bains, une douche	sal duh bañ, oon doosh
porter	le garçon	gar-**soñ**
key	la clef	klay
I have a reservation	J'ai fait une reservation	zhay fay oon rayzherva-**syoñ**

Eating Out

Have you got a table?	Avez-vous une table libre?	avay-**voo** oon tahbl leebr
the bill please	L'addition s'il vous plait	l'adee-**syoñ** seel voo play
menu	le menu, la carte	men-**oo**, kart
fixed-price menu	le menu à prix fixe	men-**oo** ah pree feeks
cover charge	le couvert	koo-**vehr**
wine list	la carte des vins	**kart**-deh vañ
high chair	chaise haute de bébé	shay-zee ohte d bey-bey
glass	le verre	vehr
bottle	la bouteille	boo-**tay**
knife	le couteau	koo-**toh**
fork	la fourchette	for-**shet**
spoon	la cuillère	kwee-**yehr**
breakfast	le petit déjeuner	puh-**tee** deh-**zhuh-nay**
lunch	le déjeuner	deh-**zhuh-nay**
dinner	le dîner	dee-nay
dish of the day	le plat du jour	plah doo zhoor
main course	le plat principal	plah prañsee-**pal**
rare	saignant	**say**-noñ
medium	à point	ah pwañ
well-done	bien cuit	byañ **kwee**

Menu Decoder

apple	la pomme	pom
baked	cuit au four	kweet oh foor
banana	la banane	banan
beef	le boeuf	buhf
beer, draught	la bière	bee-yehr
boiled	bouilli	boo-yee
bread	le pain	pan
butter	le beurre	burr
cake	le gâteau	gah-toh
cheese	le fromage	from-azh
chicken	le poulet	poo-lay
chips	les frites	freet
chocolate	le chocolat	shoko-lah
coffee	le café	kah-fay
cordial/squash	le sirop	see-rop
dessert	le dessert	deh-ser
drink	un boisson	uñ bwah-ssoñ
dry	sec	sek
duck	le canard	kanar
egg	l'oeuf	l'uf
fish	le poisson	pwah-ssoñ
fizzy drink	boisson gazeuse	bwah-ssoñ gaz-erz
fresh fruit	le fruit frais	frwee freh
fruit juice	le jus de fruit	zhuh duh frwee
garlic	l'ail	l'eye
grilled	grillé	gree-yay
ham	le jambon	zhoñ-boñ
ice, ice cream	la glace	glas
jam	la confiture	con-fee-tyor
lamb	l'agneau	l'anyoh
lemon	le citron	see-troñ
lobster	le homard	omahr
meat	la viande	vee-yand
milk	le lait	leh
mineral water	l'eau minerale	l'oh meeney-ral
mustard	la moutarde	moo-tard
oil	l'huile	l'weel
olives	les olives	leh zoleev
onions	les oignons	leh zonyoñ
orange	l'orange	l'oroñzh
fresh orange juice	l'orange pressée	l'oroñzh press-eh
fresh lemon juice	le citron pressé	see-troñ press-eh
pepper	le poivre	pwavr
poached	poché	posh-ay
pork	le porc	por
potatoes	les pommes de terre	pom-duh tehr
prawns	les crevettes	kruh-vet
rice	le riz	ree
roast	rôti	row-tee
roll	le petit pain	puh-tee pañ
salt	le sel	sel
sauce	la sauce	sohs
sausage, fresh	la saucisse	sohsees
seafood	les fruits de mer	frwee duh mer
shellfish	les crustacés	kroos-ta-say
snails	les escargots	leh zes-kar-goh

soup	le potage	poh-tazh
soup	la soupe	soop
steak	le bifteck, le steack	beef-tek
strawberry	une fraise	frayz
sugar	le sucre	sookr
tea	le thé	tay
toast	le toast	toast
vegetables	les légumes	lay-goom
vinegar	le vinaigre	veenaygr
red wine	le vin rouge	vañ roozh
white wine	le vin blanc	vañ bloñ

Numbers

0	zéro	zeh-roh
1	un, une	uñ, oon
2	deux	duh
3	trois	trwah
4	quatre	katr
5	cinq	sañk
6	six	sees
7	sept	set
8	huit	weet
9	neuf	nerf
10	dix	dees
11	onze	oñz
12	douze	dooz
13	treize	trehz
14	quatorze	katorz
15	quinze	kañz
16	seize	sehz
17	dix-sept	dees-set
18	dix-huit	dees-weet
19	dix-neuf	dees-nerf
20	vingt	vañ
30	trente	tront
40	quarante	karoñt
50	cinquante	sankoñt
60	soixante	swasoñt
70	soixante-dix	swasoñt-dees
80	quatre-vingt	katr-vañ
90	quatre-vingt-dix	katr-vañ-dees
100	cent	soñ
1,000	mille	meel

Time and Days of the Week

one	une minute	oon mee-noot
one hour	une heure	oon urr
half an hour	une demi-heure	oon duh-mee urr
Monday	lundi	luñ-dee
Tuesday	mardi	mar-dee
Wednesday	mercredi	mehrkruh-dee
Thursday	jeudi	zhuh-dee
Friday	vendredi	voñdruh-dee
Saturday	samedi	sam-dee
Sunday	dimanche	dee-moñsh
the weekend	le week-end	luh weeh-end